GILBERT

Labor Law

MICHAEL Z. GREEN
Professor and Director, Workplace Law Program,
Texas A&M University School of Law

Thirteenth Edition

GILBERT

444 Cedar Street, Suite 700
St. Paul, MN 55101
1-877-888-1330

Printed in the United States of America

ISBN: 978-1-63659-878-9

In memory of Margaret E. Green *and for* Patricia A. Jefferson *and* Marcia Reed Woodard.

In memory of Margaret E. Green *and for* Patricia A. Jefferson *and* Marcia Reed Woodard.

Preface

It has been two decades since the last edition of this summary in 2002. In many ways, key judicial opinions previously decided, especially at the Supreme Court level, continue to provide consistency as to established labor law principles. As a result, many aspects of the summary have not changed in those two decades. The Supreme Court has rarely issued decisions specifically addressing labor law issues since the last edition.

A few exceptions include some decisions driven most recently by constitutional analysis related to applying First Amendment limits on collecting union dues from public sector employees culminating with Janus v. AFSCME Council (2017). Also, the Court decided recently another public sector case asking whether a California law requiring union access to migrant workers involved an illegal constitutional taking of the employer's property. Cedar Point Nursery et al. v. Hassid et al. (2021). There was also a Supreme Court decision addressing federal preemption of labor issues. Chamber of Commerce v. Brown (2008). There was another decision finding that undocumented immigrant workers are not entitled to back pay or reinstatement. Hoffman Plastic Compounds, Inc. (2002).

The Supreme Court also decided a couple of issues related to appointments by the President to positions at the National Labor Relations Board (Board or NLRB). This includes deciding the minimum number of NLRB member appointments necessary to constitute an operational quorum, New Process Steel, L.P. v. NLRB (2010), when the President can make NLRB member recess appointments, NLRB v. Noel Canning (2014), and how an acting NLRB General Counsel's actions may no longer be valid when the President appoints the person to also serve as the permanent NLRB General Counsel. NLRB v. SW General, Inc. (2017).

The Supreme Court decided several cases over the last decade regarding arbitration including how a union may agree to a clear and unmistakable waiver of an employee's right to pursue statutory discrimination claims by requiring resolution according to the terms of an arbitration clause in the collective bargaining agreement. 14 Penn Plaza v. Pyett (2009). Also, there was a decision finding that a dispute about whether a collective bargaining agreement including an arbitration clause had been ratified was to be decided by a court and not an arbitrator. Granite Rock Co. v. International Brotherhood of Teamsters (2010). Finally, the Court decided that employee attempts to pursue class litigation claims did not involve protected concerted activity prohibiting an employer from compelling resolution instead in arbitration. Epic Systems v. Lewis (2018).

The most significant changes since the last edition, however, have mostly arisen in key decisions by the NLRB. Board decisions have become increasingly cyclical by reversing precedents decided by a prior Board until being changed again by a subsequent Board. Many who follow labor law may believe the only reason for the differing decisions is the political majority of the Board at the time of the decision. Whether that represents a correct assessment, staying up to date on many of the issues covered in this Summary from transitions to one Board versus another Board when the political party of the President appointing those Board members has also changed will continue to create many challenges. One should check the Board's rules to stay up to date.

Also, as a result of the political changes in the make-up of its members, the Board has pursued an increasing number of policy decisions through rulemaking including establishing certain election procedures, establishing criteria to determine when multiple businesses may be deemed joint employers, and providing for a 45-day window for election petitions after voluntary recognition, to name a few. At the time of the last edition of this book, the Board had rarely used rulemaking to decide key matters being considered by the Board. In eschewing its longstanding practice of primarily using adjudication to resolve major questions, the Board will now have to face further rulemaking actions when a new political make-up of Board members decide to reverse any rules made by a prior Board's rulemaking efforts.

In attempting to stay up to date on the Board's changes either through adjudication or rulemaking, the NLRB has developed a vibrant and up-to-date website providing a tremendous amount of information about its functions, rules, and decision at http://www.nlrb.gov. I invite those seeking updates on any of the key subjects covered herein to visit the website as new issues arise or just to make sure no recent changes have been made. By August 2021, President Joseph Biden had appointed a full five-member Board consisting of three Democrats and two Republicans.

Also in 2021, President Biden appointed Jennifer Abruzzo as General Counsel for the Board. In an August 12, 2021 General Counsel Memorandum, GC 21-04. Abruzzo identified several issues that should be of ongoing interest beyond what is provided in this book. Changes related to these issues may at least continue to develop at least through 2025 when another Presidential election could lead to changes in the political make-up of the Board and a new General Counsel. The issues Abruzzo identified include: 1) Employer handbook rules; 2) Confidentiality provisions/Separation agreements and instructions; 3) What constitutes protected concerted activity; 4) Wright Line/ General Counsel's burden; 5) Remedial issues; 6) Union access; 7) Union dues; 8) Independent contractor determinations; 9) Board jurisdiction over religious institutions; 10) Employer duty to recognize and/or bargain; 11) Deferral; 12) Employee status and misclassification; 13) Weingarten; 14) National Mediation Board vs. NLRB jurisdiction; 15) Employer duty to recognize and/or bargain; 16) Employees' Section 7 right to strike and/or picket; 17) Make-whole remedies and compliance; 18) Employer interference with employees' Section 7 rights; and 19) Casehandling matters traditionally submitted to the General Counsel for advice.

Prior editions of this Summary were authored by Robert J. Gelhaus and James Oldham. There is no doubt that much of this work has stood the test of time. I am extremely thankful to have such an established platform to contribute to in this 13th edition. With all due respect, I am extremely appreciative of the tremendous work developed by Gelhaus and Oldham and exceptionally honored to take on the mantle in continuing from the legacy they created. I have been inspired by several excellent labor law professors who mentored, taught and guided me in understanding the complexities of this important area of law. As I continue to be a fellow labor law student, I hope this book supplements the important aspects that you will learn from your labor law teachers, the required textbooks and materials they assign, and any treatises or other supplements covering the subject. You should review the materials herein for what they are intended to provide: a summary and comprehensive overview of private sector labor law within the United States and suggestions on how to study and learn about this important legal topic. You should still confirm any matters identified herein with your labor law teachers. THESE SUMMARY MATERIALS SHOULD NOT BE CONSIDERED AS LEGAL ADVICE. READERS SHOULD CONSULT COMPETENT LEGAL COUNSEL TO UNDERSTAND THEIR RIGHTS AND ACTIONS RATHER THAN RELYING ON THESE MATERIALS IN CONSIDERING OR PURSUING LEGAL CLAIMS.

MICHAEL Z. GREEN
Fort Worth, Texas

March 31, 2022

Summary of Contents

Capsule Summary

I. BACKGROUND AND FOUNDATIONS OF LABOR LAW

A. HISTORICAL BACKGROUND OF PRESENT LABOR LAW

1. Rise of the Labor Movement After the Civil War

Isolated local groups started organizing workers in the early 1800s, but the first serious efforts were national unions (1850s) and the Knights of Labor (1880s). The Knights grew quickly but declined rapidly (due to conflicts with national unions).

a. American Federation of Labor ("AFL")

The AFL, formed in 1886 as a federation of national craft unions, had major goals of ***economic unionism*** (achieved through ***collective bargaining***) and ***exclusive union jurisdiction.*** By 1914, the AFL had more than two million members concentrated in skilled trades and a few industries.

2. Early Policies Toward Unions

The criminal conspiracy doctrine was used to attack early union organizing, but by the 1880s it was replaced by the use of ***civil injunctions***.

a. "Objectives" Test

The legality of union activity depended on the court's views of the union's ***objectives*** ("objectives" test). Most ensuing court decisions were very restrictive of union conduct.

b. Sherman Antitrust Act of 1890

This legislation was enacted to curtail business monopolies and restraints of trade. However, courts first used it against organized labor. The federal government obtained a Sherman Act injunction against leaders of the violent ***Pullman Strike*** in 1893.

c. Aftermath of Pullman Strike

(1) U.S. Strike Commission

Public concern after the Pullman Strike led to the appointment of a Strike Commission, which was generally sympathetic to unions.

(2) Erdman Act of 1898

This Act (recognizing unions in the railroad industry) marked a change in federal policy toward unions. However, employers ignored the Act and the Supreme Court held it ***unconstitutional*** in 1908.

3. Reaction to Labor Activity—1914–1932

Despite hostility from employers and the courts, support for union organizing continued to grow.

a. **Clayton Act (1914)**

The Clayton Act exempted legitimate union activity from antitrust laws and barred the use of injunctions in employer-employee disputes involving the terms and conditions of employment. Union membership grew to five million by 1920.

b. **"Backlash" of the 1920s**

Employers attempted to stem union growth with ***scientific management*** theories and ***company unions.*** At the same time, the Supreme Court emasculated the Clayton Act by applying an ***effects test,*** which resulted in a double standard: Courts applied a broad antitrust standard to business and a much more restrictive standard to unions.

c. **Union Advances**

Under the ***National War Labor Board,*** unions finally received government protection. Enactment of the ***Railway Labor Act*** of 1926 ("RLA") established compulsory arbitration and mediation in disputes and was found to be constitutional by the Supreme Court.

4. **Establishment of Labor Policy and Union Organization**

The New Deal led to federal legislation that established collective bargaining as a national policy. Current patterns of union organization also evolved after 1932.

a. **"Industrial Unionism"**

John L. Lewis and his followers challenged the AFL by seeking industry-wide unions (regardless of skills). The resulting conflict led to the formation of the ***Congress of Industrial Organizations ("CIO")*** in 1937.

(1) **Competition for Members**

Until the 1950s, the CIO and AFL competed aggressively for members and were involved in many jurisdictional disputes.

b. **Reconciliation and Merger**

Reconciliation attempts led to an ***AFL-CIO merger*** in 1955. National union autonomy was preserved (with qualifications), but exclusive jurisdiction issues still remain.

5. **Concurrent Theories of Employer-Employee Relationship**

Besides federal statutory rules (*infra*), courts have used other doctrines in adjudicating employer-employee relations. With the growing issues posed by the gig economy and technology platforms and their influence on work, debates about what is an employee and an employer are likely to continue.

a. ***"Employment at will"*** was the traditional rule, but it has been criticized and generated several exceptions to this rule in many states.

b. ***Tort, contract, and property theories*** are used increasingly by courts to protect employee job rights. And collective bargaining concepts (*e.g.*, grievance and arbitration procedures) influence employer-employee relationships.

B. STATUTORY FOUNDATIONS OF PRESENT LABOR LAW

1. **Introduction**

Current federal labor law is based primarily on four basic pieces of legislation:

2. Norris-LaGuardia Act ("Norris-LaGuardia") (1932)

Various procedures used to prevent effective union organizing (*e.g.*, yellow-dog contracts, objectives test, etc.) resulted in passage of Norris-LaGuardia. Norris-LaGuardia ***removed the power of federal courts to enjoin union activity*** absent fraud or violence.

3. National Labor Relations Act ("NLRA") of 1935 (Wagner Act)

This legislation expressed a national policy to encourage collective bargaining in labor relations. The NLRA was primarily concerned with the ***organizing phase*** of unions (section 7—rights of employees) and dealt almost exclusively with limiting ***employers' unfair labor practices*** (section 8).

4. Labor Management Relations Act ("LMRA") of 1947 (Taft-Hartley Act)

This Act attempted to ***"balance" obligations*** between employers and unions by restraining ***union*** as well as employer ***unfair labor practices*** and by providing ***alternatives to collective bargaining*** where public health or safety is seriously affected (mediation, emergency disputes, etc.).

a. Other Provisions

Taft-Hartley also prohibited ***closed shops*** and provided for the ***enforcement of labor agreements***.

5. Labor Management Reporting and Disclosure Act ("LMRDA") of 1959 (Landrum-Griffin Act)

Passed in reaction to union corruption uncovered in the 1950s, the Landrum-Griffin Act imposed some regulations on ***internal*** union affairs and established a "bill of rights" for union members.

C. SUMMARY OF NATIONAL LABOR POLICY

The basic ***goal of industrial peace*** is encouraged through ***collective bargaining*** and ***employee self-organization.*** Restraints on certain labor practices (*e.g.*, secondary strikes or boycotts) are permitted where the consequences outweigh the value to organizing. Where strikes imperil national health or safety, conciliation, cooling-off periods and/or government intervention may be used.

D. ROLE OF STATE LAW IN LABOR-MANAGEMENT RELATIONS—THE PREEMPTION DOCTRINE

1. Federal Preemption

State statutes are preempted by federal labor law wherever the two areas overlap (with certain exceptions, below).

2. Scope of Federal Power

The NLRA is interpreted very ***broadly*** so that an activity need only be ***arguably*** covered by federal law in order to preempt state jurisdiction. The party advocating such preemption must at least put forth an interpretation that has not been "authoritatively rejected" by the NLRB or the courts.

a. Wrongful Discharge Cases

These cases are important, and the area is somewhat challenging. If the wrongful discharge claim is ***independent*** of the collective bargaining agreement, it is ***not preempted.*** The reverse is also true—if the claim is ***dependent*** on the collective bargaining agreement, it ***is preempted.*** Finally, some courts had held that claims that are ***"conceptionally allied"*** with the collective bargaining agreement ***are***

preempted—a concept that has become difficult to apply and requires careful pleading to preserve state court jurisdiction. More recent cases indicate that the focus should be on determining whether the claim will require ***interpreting*** the collective bargaining agreement or whether the claim is ***inextricably intertwined*** with the labor contract terms. Preemption results if either one of those findings arises.

3. Exceptions to Federal Preemption

a. Judicial Exceptions

States may regulate matters of ***overriding local concern*** (violence, defamation, etc.), matters of ***"peripheral" federal concern*** (*i.e.*, some internal union matters), matters where state regulation ***promotes federal policy*** and the ***union duty of fair representation.*** However, state courts may have to apply ***federal law*** in some cases.

b. Statutory Exceptions

These include damages for unlawful strikes or boycotts, suits for breach of collective bargaining agreements, areas where the NLRB declines jurisdiction, and state limitations on union security agreements ("right to work" laws).

4. Preemption May Be Raised at Any Time

Federal preemption may be raised at any time, even on a motion for judgment notwithstanding the verdict.

II. ESTABLISHMENT OF THE COLLECTIVE BARGAINING RELATIONSHIP

A. SCOPE OF STATUTES GOVERNING SELF-ORGANIZATION

1. Railway Labor Act

The RLA created a National Mediation Board to mediate disputes in the railroad and airline industries. Some employees not directly engaged in transportation may be covered, but employees outside the United States usually are ***not*** covered. The Interstate Commerce Commission determines which employees are covered under the Act.

2. National Labor Relations Act

NLRA coverage depends on the existence of a ***labor dispute in or affecting interstate commerce.*** "Labor dispute" and "commerce" are interpreted broadly, but the NLRB may ***decline*** jurisdiction when interstate activities are minimal.

a. Jurisdiction over Employers

(1) Employers Not Covered by the NLRA

Government or union employers, private companies with municipal functions, and religious schools (in nonsecular operations) are ***excluded*** as employers under the NLRA.

(2) Health Care Employers

An amendment to the NLRA now ***extends coverage*** to health care employers (including religious institutions).

b. Jurisdiction over Employees

"Employee" is ***broadly interpreted*** to cover most workers. Additionally, workers on strike because of an unfair labor practice are still considered employees.

(1) Employees Not Covered by the NLRA

Supervisors, other managerial workers, and employees who act in a confidential capacity to managers (*e.g.*, secretaries), retired persons, most agricultural workers, domestics, and **independent contractors** are excluded from coverage under the NLRA.

(a) **Exceptions**

However, undocumented immigrants, hospital house staffs (*e.g.*, interns), and job applicants (including union organizers) are covered by the NLRA.

(2) **Independent Contractor Test**

Whether a person is an employee or an independent contractor depends on whether the employer has ***sufficient management and control*** over the worker's job performance and duties. There is some debate about the extent or limits on **entrepreneurial opportunity** that should be considered in determining whether the worker is an independent contractor. This issue is an ongoing debate that extends beyond labor law due to technological transformations in a gig-based economy.

3. National Labor Relations Board—Organization and Procedure

The National Labor Relations Board ("NLRB") administers the NLRA and consists of two independent divisions: (i) the ***Board itself adjudicates*** and (ii) the ***General Counsel*** handles ***election cases*** and ***litigates*** unfair labor practices cases.

a. Primary Functions of the Board

The NLRB's basic responsibilities are (i) to ***determine employee representatives as "R" representation cases*** and (ii) to decide whether a challenged activity is an ***unfair labor practice as "C" complaint cases***.

b. Decisionmaking Division

The NLRB has five members who may sit as a full panel or (for expediency) as a panel of three. The Board must always continue to have three members as a sufficient **quorum** to operate. The President can only make recess appointments to fill openings if the Senate has recessed for at least **three** days. Any Senate recess of less than **ten** days is **presumptively** too short for a Board member recess appointment.

(1) **Representation ("R") Cases**

The Board has ***complete and final authority*** in representation cases, although it may delegate its powers to the Regional Directors.

(2) **Unfair Labor Practices ("C") Cases**

After the General Counsel issues a complaint, the Board determines whether to act on it. If it does, an administrative law judge holds a hearing and issues an intermediate report, which is determinative if no exceptions are filed. If exceptions are filed, the Board reviews the record, basing its findings on a preponderance of the evidence.

(a) **Appellate Review**

Board decisions may be appealed to a federal court of appeals, which will uphold the decision if supported by "***substantial evidence*** contained in the record as a whole." The Board's findings of law are reviewable *de novo,* but an appellate court will give the Board's findings great weight.

(3) **Effect of Changing Composition of NLRB**

The Board is politically appointed. As a result, shifts in NLRB doctrine may occur when one president appoints several Board members.

c. General Counsel's Function and Procedure for Issuance of Complaints

If an acting General Counsel is then nominated by the President to become General Counsel upon approval by the Senate, the President must **appoint** someone else as acting General Counsel. Failure to do so will lead to any actions taken by the acting General Counsel being reversed as unauthorized once the nomination for General Counsel was made. The General Counsel issues most complaints through the appropriate Regional Director's office. The General Counsel's decision whether to issue a complaint is ***final*** except that the Board may ***dismiss*** a complaint once it has been issued.

B. PROTECTING THE RIGHT TO SELF-ORGANIZATION

1. Protection Against Employer Interference, Restraint, and Coercion—in General

Section 7 of the NLRA recognizes employees' basic rights to organize and to bargain collectively.

a. Unfair Labor Practice

Sections 8(a) and 8(e) protect employees' section 7 organizing rights. It is an unfair labor practice for an employer ***to interfere with, restrain, or coerce employees*** in the exercise of these rights.

b. Conduct Upsetting Election Conditions

Acts that fall short of being an unfair labor practice may still cause an election to be set aside if such acts destroy the required ***laboratory conditions***.

c. Not All Employer Activity Prohibited

An employer retains certain rights such as freedom of speech on matters affecting the business operation. Also, an employer may enforce certain policies and work rules as long as the rules would be enforced regardless of section 7 activity at issue.

2. Employer Actions Affecting Right to Self-Organization

a. Interrogation of Employees

Interrogation of employees about union activities or membership is closely scrutinized and will be judged on the "totality of the circumstances."

(1) Polling of Employees

It is ***unlawful*** for an employer to poll employees unless certain safeguards are met (the *Struksnes* test). Under certain conditions, however, a proper poll may be a ***substitute*** for an election.

b. Surveillance of Employees

Spies or informers may ***not*** be used in connection with any phase of employee rights to self-organization; and videotaping or photographing of employees is strictly scrutinized.

c. Solicitation and Distribution Rules

An employer may place certain ***nondiscriminatory*** restrictions on union solicitation or distribution by employees on ***company property or via use of company technology*** (*e.g.*, limiting solicitation to worker's free time, nonworking areas).

(1) Nonemployee Solicitation and Distribution

This may be prohibited anywhere on company property, provided the union has ***alternative means*** of communicating with employees and there are no state-law considerations to the contrary.

(2) "Shopping Center" Limitations

Constitutional free speech issues may be raised by prohibitions against solicitation or distribution in "quasi-public" areas. Generally, the "alternative means" test applies (absent a "company town" situation); but a "no solicitation" policy cannot be used only against union members.

d. Employer Free Speech

An employer has free speech rights under section 8(c), but these rights have limits because of the employer's economic power over employees.

(1) Coercive Statements

Threats of reprisal or ***promises of benefits*** are coercive, and thus are ***not*** protected. However, predictions of adverse consequences from unionization that are based on objective facts ***not under the employer's control*** are not coercive.

(a) "Coerciveness"

Statements that are noncoercive on their face may still be found coercive because of the ***context*** in which they were made.

(b) Rights Regarding Noncoercive Speech

Speech that is noncoercive cannot be used as evidence of other employer violations or be subject to state defamation laws.

(c) "Captive Audiences"

Antiunion speeches to employees ***on company time and property*** are permissible if not coercive. However, the union must have reasonable access to communicate with the employees.

(2) Ban on Speeches Within Twenty-Four Hours of Election

Free speech privileges of ***both*** the employer and the union are curtailed during the 24 hours preceding an election. However, employer speeches on ***employees' own time*** with ***voluntary attendance*** are permissible, and dissemination of campaign literature and messages is allowed. Presently, the Board will ***not*** set aside elections because of misrepresentations in last-minute campaign statements.

(3) Other Propaganda

When any other employer or union propaganda ***upsets the "laboratory conditions"*** necessary for union elections, the Board will set aside the election.

e. Changing Employee Benefits to Influence Election

An employer cannot confer unusual economic benefits (or withhold usual benefits) during an organizing campaign. However, an employer may announce future benefits as long as they were planned ***before*** the union campaign began.

3. Protection Against Union Restraint or Coercion

Section 8(b) prohibits ***union*** coercion of employees regarding section 7 rights. However, a union probably has greater leeway than an employer regarding organizing tactics (subject to the "laboratory conditions" test for elections).

a. Union Coercion and Free Speech

Employer free speech guarantees and restrictions also apply to unions.

b. **Physical Restraint or Coercion**

Union threats or violence against employees is prohibited, and acts of violence against an employer violate the NLRA. Moreover, union threats may be grounds to set aside an election.

c. **Economic Coercion**

Similarly, economic coercion by unions is prohibited.

d. **Picketing**

Peaceful picketing is allowed, but ***mass picketing*** or ***blocking plant entrances*** is unlawful.

e. **Coercion by Union Subordinates**

Under the NLRA, common law agency principles govern the liability of a union for the acts of an agent; ***apparent authority*** is sufficient to hold a union responsible. Union liability is more restricted in the few cases brought under the Norris-LaGuardia Act.

4. **Employer Domination or Assistance**

Domination, interference, and/or the ***contribution of financial or other support*** by an employer to a labor union is prohibited by section 8(a)(2).

a. **Test**

The test is whether a ***union is truly representing the employees*** in employer-employee disputes.

b. **Actions by Subordinates**

The NLRB also applies agency rules in determining whether acts of subordinates can reasonably be attributed to the employer. An employer must ***disavow*** the acts of supervisors to avoid liability.

c. **Illegal Conduct**

The following activities usually violate section 8(a)(2):

(1) ***Solicitation of membership*** by an employer for a favored union;

(2) ***Undue assistance*** in the establishment or operation of a union (although an employer ***may*** recognize an incumbent or one of two rival unions if it represents a clear majority);

(3) ***Supplying company facilities or support*** to one of several unions (but distinguish ***"support"*** (illegal) from ***mere cooperation*** (legal));

(4) ***Employer control*** through union constitution or bylaws; and

(5) ***Experimental workplace methods*** where they create improper "labor organizations."

5. **Employer Discrimination on Basis of Union Membership**

Section 8(a)(3) prohibits an employer from discouraging or encouraging union membership by discrimination in hiring and firing practices, or with respect to any term or condition of employment. Such discrimination requires a showing of ***improper motive***.

a. **Burden of Proof**

The General Counsel has the burden of showing an adverse effect on employees, whereupon the burden shifts to the employer to show a ***legitimate and substantial business purpose*** and no improper motive.

(1) **Inherently Destructive Conduct**

Where an employer's conduct is inherently destructive of union membership, the Board may ***assume*** improper motive. However, any lesser harm requires the Board to present ***independent*** evidence of an antiunion motive.

(2) **Circumstantial Evidence**

Improper motive can be established by circumstantial evidence (*e.g.*, percentage of union members affected, timing of employee dismissals, employer's antiunion background, etc.).

(3) **Proof in "Mixed Motive" Cases**

In "dual motivation" cases, the General Counsel must establish a prima facie case that the protected conduct was a ***motivating factor*** for the employer's acts, whereupon the employer must prove that the action would have been taken even absent the protected conduct.

b. **Examples of Employer Discrimination**

(1) **Discrimination in Hiring and Firing**

Discrimination based on union membership (or lack thereof) is prohibited—except under union security agreements.

(2) **Discrimination in Tenure, Terms, or Conditions of Employment**

Such discrimination or disparity in the treatment of union personnel or members (*e.g.*, super-seniority clauses) is an unfair labor practice. Employer decisions must not be based on, or have the ***effect*** of, encouraging or discouraging union membership.

(a) **Movement of Plant Operations**

An employer may move a plant if the change is dictated by ***sound economic considerations***— even when the effect is to thwart unionization.

(b) **Discontinuance of Business Operations**

An employer may terminate its ***entire*** business ***for any reason,*** including antiunion motives. However, a ***partial discontinuance*** is illegal if done with the ***purpose and foreseeable effect of discouraging unionization***.

c. **Exceptions for Building and Trades Industry**

The construction industry is allowed more restrictive union security agreements, provided the employer does not have reasonable cause to believe that union membership was unavailable to the employee. This exception is also subject to state laws and federal antitrust law.

6. **Discrimination by Unions**

Union practices that discriminate between members and nonmembers are prohibited by sections 8(b)(2), 8(b)(5), and 8(a)(3). (Landrum-Griffin and Civil Rights Act restraints are discussed *infra.*)

a. **Authority of NLRB**

The NLRB may not insist that a union admit all employees to membership. However, the union has a ***duty to represent fairly all employees in the bargaining unit***.

b. Union Discrimination Through Coercion of Employer

A union may not cause, or attempt to cause, employer discrimination against an employee (*e.g.*, make threats to strike), except for failure to pay normal union dues or fees. However, union hiring halls are not per se unlawful.

7. Judicial Remedies for Violation of the Right to Organize

Judicial relief usually involves a ***cease and desist order*** and/or an ***affirmative action*** order (*e.g.*, reinstatement with back pay). ***Temporary injunctions*** to restrain unfair labor practices may be available in emergency situations.

C. SELECTION OF THE BARGAINING REPRESENTATIVE—ELECTIONS AND BARGAINING UNITS

1. Introduction

Prior to bargaining, there must be a selection of the bargaining representative and designation of the appropriate bargaining unit. The NLRB administers representation elections and determines the proper unit, with most of its powers delegated to the Regional Directors.

2. Representation Elections

a. Types of Elections

Several types of elections may be conducted by the Board:

(1) Consent Elections

No NLRB hearing is required when the employer and proposed representative agree on the bargaining unit, the employees eligible to vote, and where and when to hold the election.

(2) Contested Elections

When the parties cannot agree, a contested election will be held if the necessary criteria (*infra*) exist.

(3) "Globe" Elections

When a specific group of employees could either bargain as a separate unit or be merged into an existing unit, they may choose either of these alternatives unless there is a ***pattern or history*** indicating the proper unit.

(4) Certification Elections

Employers frequently bargain with unions that prove they are authorized by a majority of employees (*e.g.*, by authorization cards). However, the union may still seek a certification election in order to guarantee a one-year period (free from rival union interference) to execute an agreement with the employer. Certification elections may also be used as a ***remedy*** for unfair labor practices.

(5) Decertification Elections

When employees claim that a union does not represent (or is no longer desired) by a majority, they may request a decertification election. Decertification elections are also subject to the one-year bar on interference by rival unions.

(6) Other Elections

The Board also conducts ***deauthorization*** and ***run-off*** elections.

b. Eligibility of Voters

Voters must be ***"employees"*** within the meaning of the NLRA, ***properly within the bargaining unit***, and ***sufficiently affected*** by employment conditions within that unit.

(1) Eligibility of Strikers to Vote

Economic strikers ***may*** vote (within 12 months of the strike's commencement) unless objective evidence shows the striker "abandoned interest" in the job. Employees hired as ***permanent*** replacements for economic strikers also may vote, but temporary replacements are ***not*** eligible to vote.

3. Election Procedure

Certain steps must be taken before the NLRB will recognize a bargaining representative.

a. Petitions

The procedure begins when a petition for certification is filed by ***employees*** or an ***employer***. (However, employers may ***not*** file to test the certification of an incumbent union, unless they have reasonable grounds for believing the union no longer has majority support; nor may an employer file a decertification petition.)

(1) Withdrawing Petitions

Petitions can be withdrawn if a union clearly disclaims interest. If withdrawal is approved, that union may not file another petition for at least ***six months***.

(a) Tactic

Unions can use withdrawal as an effective organizing device. Once an election is ordered, the employer must, within seven days, give the union a list of all eligible voters (*Excelsior* list). The union then withdraws and uses the list to campaign for six months.

b. Requirements for NLRB Action on Petitions

(1) Jurisdiction

The employer's business must meet the requirements for NLRB jurisdiction set forth in the NLRA.

(2) Appropriate Bargaining Unit

The union must claim (or hold) recognition as agent for employees in a unit appropriate for bargaining. In determining "appropriateness," the Board considers mutuality of interest (*i.e.*, similar wages, skills, conditions, etc.), any history of collective bargaining, employee desires, and other relevant factors.

(a) Limitations on NLRB Discretion

The NLRA restricts the Board's discretion in determining an appropriate bargaining unit. "Professional" employees may not be included (unless a majority vote for inclusion), prior Board decisions are not binding, and plant guards may not be included with other employees. Special rules also apply to health care employees. Courts will generally defer to a Board determination, unless it departs from traditional criteria used in an industry or incorrectly applies the criteria.

(b) Multiemployer Bargaining Units

Multiemployer bargaining units must have the consent of the union and the employers involved. The NLRB still must determine if the proposed unit is "appropriate," and it will look to the parties' desires and previous bargaining history when making this determination.

(3) Evidence of Employee Support

There must be evidence that at least ***30%*** of the employees in the unit support the petition. Employee support may be demonstrated by signed authorization cards, union membership cards, dues receipts, etc. (No such support need be shown when an employer petitions for elections.)

(4) No Charge of Unfair Labor Practice

There must be no unremedied unfair labor practice unless it is ***waived*** or ***unrelated*** to organizing or choice of representative.

(5) No Prior Certification

There can be no election (involving the same unit) ***within 12 months of a prior valid election,*** whether or not a union was certified in that election. Where the employer voluntarily recognizes a union and no employee files a petition within 45 days to challenge the recognition per Board rule, then a "recognition bar" may apply.

(6) No Existing Collective Bargaining Agreement—"Contract Bar" Rule

An existing valid contract will bar elections. This bar continues for the ***term of the contract,*** subject to a ***three-year maximum***.

(a) Removing the Bar

A rival petition must be ***timely filed*** (not more than 90 days nor less than 61 days before the contract terminates) in order to remove the bar.

(b) When Existing Contract Is Not a Bar

1) The contract has ***no fixed term;***

2) The contract is within ***an uncertified union*** that seeks certification;

3) The union becomes ***defunct;***

4) ***A schism develops*** within the bargaining unit;

5) There are ***"changes in circumstances";***

6) The contract expresses ***racial discrimination;***

7) The contract has an illegal ***closed-shop provision;***

8) The contract was ***prematurely extended.***

c. Judicial Review of Representation Proceedings

Judicial review of NLRB certification or decertification rulings is permissible only when review is ***incidental to restraining an unfair labor practice*** (*e.g.*, refusal to bargain) ***and*** when the NLRB has issued a final order.

(1) Relief in Equity

However, federal courts may compel or restrain an election upon a showing that the Board's decision was ***contrary to the NLRA***.

III. COLLECTIVE BARGAINING

A. NEGOTIATING THE COLLECTIVE BARGAINING AGREEMENT

1. Duration of Representative's Authority to Bargain

An employer must recognize the certified representative for at least ***one year,*** even if a majority of the employees subsequently disavow the union. This is designed to promote industrial peace and stability.

a. Extension Due to Employer Delay

If an employer fails to bargain in good faith, this period will be extended.

2. Scope of Union Negotiating Authority

The representative union has ***exclusive authority to represent all employees*** in the unit.

a. Individual Contracts

Individual contracts with employees are ***superseded*** by the collective bargaining agreement (except regarding matters not covered by and/ or not inconsistent with the agreement).

b. Section 9(a) Supersedes Section 7 Rights

When a union has exclusive authority under section 9(a), individual employees who engage in concerted activities without union approval are ***not*** protected by section 7 from discipline (*e.g.*, discharge). (However, relief may be available under Title VII of the Civil Rights Act.)

c. Limitations on Union Authority

The union's duty to bargain fairly extends to ***all employees,*** including nonmembers. Also, section 9(a) allows employees to adjust grievances ***directly with the employer,*** provided the adjustment is consistent with the agreement and that the union has an opportunity to be present. Note that an employer has no duty to bargain with the union as to the terms and conditions of employment of replacement workers.

3. Duty to Bargain in Good Faith

Both the employer and the union must make a ***sincere effort*** to reach an agreement through negotiations. However, section 8(d) does not ***compel*** either party to accept any proposal or make any concession.

a. Test

Good or bad faith is determined by considering the ***total course of conduct,*** rather than isolated actions.

b. Inferences of Bad Faith

(1) Content of Proposals

The Board looks to the ***reasonableness*** of a proposal in determining sincerity in negotiations (*e.g.*, offer to pay less than employees received even before certification).

(2) Negotiation Conduct

It is sometimes difficult to distinguish between permissible "hard bargaining" and impermissible "surface bargaining." Conduct that may imply bad faith includes ***dilatory tactics,*** demands that union ***drop pending charges, "take it or leave it"*** proposals, refusal to bargain about ***racial discrimination,*** and a ***refusal to provide certain information***.

(a) **Information That Must Be Disclosed**

Information that substantiates bargaining claims (*e.g.*, employer's financial information when the employer claims that it cannot meet union demands) and information about mandatory bargaining subjects generally must be disclosed.

c. **Duty During Bankruptcy Proceedings**

An employer in chapter 11 proceedings may ***not*** unilaterally alter an existing agreement. Any proposed change must first be presented to the union and can be approved by the court only after a "balance of the equities" are considered.

d. **Duty of New Employer to Bargain—"Contractual Successorship"**

After corporate mergers or acquisitions, whether the new employer is bound by an existing collective bargaining agreement depends on the method of acquisition and the nature of the new business.

(1) **If Successor Assumes Existing Contract**

The new employer is bound by the contract and must bargain with the designated representative.

(2) **If Successor Is the Survivor Corporation in a Statutory Merger**

The new employer may be bound under state corporation law to assume certain duties of the disappearing entity. A successor must also bargain with the representative and honor the grievance and arbitration procedure for matters arising out of the merger.

(3) **If Successor Acquires Business Other than by Merger or Purchase of Assets**

Here, the successor (such as a successful bidder for contracted services) is ***not*** bound by the existing contract of the predecessor. However, if a majority of the employees are retained, the new employer ***must recognize and bargain with the existing union representative.*** Also, there is a duty to ***correct unfair labor practices*** and ***Title VII violations*** committed by the former employer.

(a) **Note**

The successor employer may also be required to ***arbitrate*** under the existing contract if there is "substantial continuity of the work force." (But note the possible trend to the contrary.)

e. **Duty of Employer to Bargain with "Noncertified" Majority Representative**

(1) **When Employer Unfair Labor Practices Have Impaired Electoral Process**

If a fair election seems improbable (under *Gissel Packing* guidelines), the Board will order the employer to bargain based on union authorization cards signed by a majority of employees. The cards must ***clearly state their purpose on their face.*** The order can be made ***retroactive*** to the date of refusal to bargain.

(a) **NLRB Guidelines: From *Gissel* to *Joy Silk*?**

In response to criticism by the courts that the NLRB mechanically applied *Gissel Packing,* the NLRB General Counsel issued new guidelines in 1999 (listing eight factors to be considered) for when remedial action is required to correct "less outrageous and pervasive" employer conduct that nonetheless undermines majority strength and impedes the election process. In 2021, the NLRB General Counsel issued two memoranda suggesting that the Board may return to its process before *Gissel* and pursuant to its earlier *Joy Silk* case. Under that rationale, the Board may pursue a bargaining order when an employer has refused to recognize the union if the employer has committed unfair labor practices ***or*** is ***unable to explain*** its reasoning for doubting the union's majority status.

(2) When Electoral Process Not Impaired

If there are no unfair labor practices regarding an election, the employer ***need not recognize or bargain with the union*** on the basis of authorization cards or other nonelection evidence.

f. Remedies

If either side fails to bargain in good faith, the NLRB can issue a ***cease and desist order*** or take ***affirmative*** steps. In flagrant cases, the Board may order ***compensatory*** relief. However, the NLRB cannot force acceptance of a particular agreement.

4. Subjects of Collective Bargaining

a. Mandatory, Permissive, and Illegal Subjects of Bargaining

(1) Mandatory Subjects

Bargaining is ***compelled by statute*** over ***"wages, hours, and other terms and conditions of employment."*** This includes retirement benefits, work assignments, grievances, safety rules, and monitoring of employees in the workplace.

(a) Note

The parties need ***not*** bargain about modification of existing contract or about policy objectives.

(2) Permissive Subjects

If bargaining on an issue is ***neither foreclosed nor mandatory,*** collective bargaining may occur if both parties ***elect*** to do so.

(3) Illegal Subjects

Illegal subjects include those that cannot be bargained over because they ***must*** be included in the contract (*e.g.*, recognition of union), and those that ***cannot*** lawfully be included (*e.g.*, closed-shop provision).

b. Management Prerogatives and Union Participation

Most managerial prerogatives (*e.g.*, production decisions) are ***permissive*** topics, but under certain circumstances, they can become ***mandatory*** subjects.

(1) General Approach—"Balancing Test"

In this area, the Supreme Court requires a ***case-by-case balancing*** of an employer's need for "unencumbered decisionmaking" against the benefits to labor-management relations from bargaining over the matter. Note the statutory 60-day notice requirement for plant closing or layoffs (certain situations).

(2) Impact of Managerial Decisions

Even if the decision is a permissive bargaining matter (*e.g.*, sale or transfer of business), the employer must bargain over the ***effects*** of the decision on employees (*i.e.*, severance pay, pensions).

c. **Union Waiver of Bargaining Rights**

Any such waiver must be ***explicit*** and cannot involve ***fundamental*** employee rights.

5. **Employer Economic Weapons—"Lockout"**

A "lockout" occurs when an employer closes the plant to workers ***in anticipation of a strike***.

a. **Permissible Lockouts**

Lockouts are allowed where bargaining has reached an ***impasse*** or where ***special circumstances*** (*e.g.*, threat of economic loss) exist.

(1) **Replacements**

An employer may hire ***temporary*** replacements without consulting the union, to exert further pressure on the striking employees. (Note that one court would consider this an unfair labor practice.)

b. **Unlawful Lockouts**

Conversely, lockouts used to avoid good faith bargaining or ***to injure a union*** are unfair labor practices.

6. **Effect of a Strike on the Bargaining Process**

a. **Employer's Duty**

An employer must bargain until there is an agreement, an impasse, or a breach in negotiations that is not the employer's fault. Thus, the ***duty to bargain continues*** during a strike (or lockout) unless the strike violates the contract.

b. **Employer-Employee Relations During Impasse**

When a strike is not the result of employer unfair labor practices, the employer may hire replacements, poll striking employees, implement its final offer package (if ***all*** negotiation has ceased), and unilaterally increase wages (but ***not*** above the level offered in negotiations).

7. **Modifying or Terminating the Agreement—Union-Employer Bargaining Duties**

Either party wishing to modify or terminate an existing agreement must follow the ***notification and conference*** procedures in section 8(d).

B. **ADMINISTERING THE COLLECTIVE BARGAINING AGREEMENT**

1. **Introduction**

The duty to bargain in good faith applies to the interpretation as well as establishment of the agreement. Disputes can be settled ***informally,*** by ***arbitration,*** or ***in court*** (if there is an alleged breach of the contract).

2. **Arbitration Process**

An arbitration-of-grievances procedure is included in most agreements, and is usually mandatory if requested by either party. The arbitration process typically involves a series of steps and results in a ***decision*** on the issues (as opposed to mediation or conciliation). If the agreement calls for arbitration, resort to ***other pressures*** (*e.g.*, strike) to resolve the dispute is ***illegal***.

a. **Authority of Arbitrator**

The arbitrator's authority is provided in the arbitration clause of the contract. This authority is ***broadly construed*** to cover all disputes except those ***explicitly*** withdrawn by the terms of the contract or where ***public safety*** is at issue. However, whether an issue is arbitrable is ultimately a ***question of law***.

(1) Effect of Precedent

Note that arbitrators are ***not*** bound to follow prior awards. They may consider prior decisions involving the same parties and the same contract terms very persuasive.

b. Deferral by NLRB to Arbitration Process

Prior to an award, the NLRB generally defers to arbitration of grievances, which may also involve unfair labor practices (***Collyer*** doctrine). Deferral ***after*** an arbitration award is subject to greater constraints (***Spielberg/United Parcel Services*** doctrine).

c. Deferral by the Courts to Arbitration

Courts usually require an ***exhaustion of the arbitration process*** before hearing the issue. However, if a ***union refuses or fails adequately to represent*** an employee, the court will hear a suit filed under section 301. If there are internal union procedures open to the employee, courts exercise discretion in deciding whether to take the case.

(1) Statutory Claims

Suits under Title VII, the Fair Labor Standards Act, Sections 1981 and 1983, the ADEA and other workplace statutes are ***not*** foreclosed by a decision to arbitrate unless ***a clear and unmistakable waiver*** of those suits has been agreed to by the parties. Nor do such statutes ***prohibit parties from agreeing to arbitrate*** their statutory claims unless the statute clearly prohibits resolution through arbitration.

3. Judicial Enforcement of Collective Bargaining Agreements

Section 301 permits suits by a union or employer (or by an individual employee in certain cases) for breach of collective bargaining or other labor related contracts. Federal jurisdiction exists regardless of diversity or jurisdictional amount. ***State courts have concurrent jurisdiction*** under section 301.

a. Judicial Enforcement of Agreements to Arbitrate

Where one of the parties has refused to arbitrate under an agreement, and the other party has ***exhausted all remedies,*** a court may order specific performance of the agreement to arbitrate. If the claim appears arbitrable ***on its face,*** the court ***must*** order arbitration.

b. Judicial Review of Arbitration Awards—*"Steelworker Trilogy"*

Judicial review traditionally has been limited to whether the award was ***within the arbitrator's authority.*** If so, the award would be final and binding, and the merits of the grievance or award irrelevant.

(1) Court Determines Arbitrability

The court decides whether a grievance on its face falls within the agreement to arbitrate ("substantive arbitrability")—although "procedural arbitrability" may be an issue for the arbitrator, and the parties can ***waive*** judicial review of arbitrability.

(2) Expansion of Judicial Review

Despite the "finality" doctrine, some courts have scrutinized the merits of arbitration awards under the Federal Arbitration Act, pursuant to "public policy" grounds (*e.g.*, future public safety), and where the arbitrator clearly exceeds his or her authority.

c. **Judicial Enforcement of No-Strike Agreements**

A no-strike agreement is so necessary to an arbitration commitment that it will be ***implied*** if not expressly stated in the contract.

(1) **Injunctive Relief**

Strikes in violation of a no-strike clause may be enjoined as a ***Boys Market*** injunction if the ***dispute is arbitrable*** under the contract, there is a ***likelihood of irreparable harm to the employer,*** and the ***employer's injury exceeds harm to the union*** from the injunction. Unfair labor practices also may be enjoined.

(2) **Employer's Right to Terminate Agreement**

If a union breaches a no-strike clause, the employer may be able to terminate the entire agreement (under contract principles).

(3) **Right to Damages**

An employer may be entitled to damages for breach of the no-strike obligations (but not if the employer terminates the agreement).

IV. STRIKES, BOYCOTTS, AND PICKETING

A. CONSTITUTIONAL RIGHTS AND LIMITATIONS ON CONCERTED ACTIVITY

Federal policy is to balance employee rights to concerted activity against the public right to protection from potentially destructive conduct.

1. **Right to Strike**

The Supreme Court has never determined whether there exists an absolute constitutional right to strike, although it has determined that some strikes are ***not*** constitutionally protected.

2. **Picketing**

Picketing is constitutionally protected if conducted ***in a peaceful manner and for a lawful objective.*** Courts consider the entire setting in determining whether picketing is peaceful.

a. **Forms of Picketing**

(1) **Primary Picketing**

This occurs when employees picket their own employer. It enjoys the ***greatest protection.***

(2) **Stranger Picketing**

This involves nonemployee pickets (*e.g.*, an organizing attempt). It is protected subject to the "means" and "objective" requirements.

(3) **Secondary Picketing**

This occurs at the business of someone ***other than the employer with whom the union has its dispute.*** It is generally ***prohibited*** by statute.

B. STATUTORY REGULATION OF STRIKES, BOYCOTTS, AND PICKETING

1. **Statutory Sources of Right to Strike and Picket**

Federal regulation is based primarily on the NLRA, although the Norris-LaGuardia Act and the Sherman Antitrust Act also have some impact in this area.

a. **NLRA Provisions**

Sections 7 and 13 grant employees the ***right to strike and picket.*** Section 2(3) provides that strikers ***retain their employee status***.

b. **Waiver**

These rights may be waived, and such waivers are broadly construed.

c. **Unsafe Conditions**

Leaving work in good faith due to unsafe working conditions is ***not*** considered a strike.

d. **Health Care Institutions**

Section 8(g) requires a 10-day notice before ***any*** strike or picketing of these facilities may begin.

2. **Regulation of Concerted Activity—in General**

The ***means and objectives test*** is used to determine the lawfulness of activities regulated by the NLRA. Generally, primary activity is lawful while secondary activity is not.

3. **Regulation of Strikes**

a. **Illegal Strikes**

(1) **Primary Activity**

Violent strikes, strikes during the 60-day cooling-off period, partial or intermittent strikes, and strikes to compel discrimination or "featherbedding" receive no protection under the NLRA.

(2) **Secondary or Primary Activity**

Secondary ***or*** primary strikes to compel ***"hot cargo"*** provisions, to coerce a primary employer to recognize the union by striking at a secondary party, or to compel the ***recognition of an uncertified union despite the certification of a rival union*** arc ***illegal*** under section 8(b)(4).

(a) **Exempt Conduct**

However, ***employees may refuse to cross a picket line conducted against an employer other than their own, and the union may publicize a dispute*** in certain circumstances that might otherwise violate section 8(b)(4)(C).

(3) **Coercion Regarding Work Assignment Disputes**

A union cannot engage in primary or secondary strikes over work assignment disputes. (This usually occurs when several rival unions seek the same job.) In such cases, an ***NLRB hearing is required*** unless there is a voluntary settlement of the dispute (*e.g.*, by arbitration).

b. **Rights of Strikers and Discrimination Against Strikers**

The NLRB and the courts have read certain rights for striking employees into section 8(a)(1). Strikers are ***still considered employees*** and cannot be discriminated against by an employer.

(1) **Discharge and Reinstatement of Strikers**

Rights to reinstatement depend on the ***category*** of the strike.

(a) **"Economic Strikers"**

Those who strike for increased benefits or over other non-unfair-labor-practice issues are economic strikers and are ***not entitled to reinstatement.*** However, they may not be discriminated against in rehiring.

(b) **"Unfair-Labor-Practice Strikers"**

Employees who strike because of an employer unfair labor practice ***are*** entitled to reinstatement, unless the strike itself is unlawful (*e.g.*, violent, partial, or "wildcat").

1) **Back Pay**

If discharged during an unfair practices strike, employees are automatically entitled to ***back pay*** from the date of discharge.

2) **Discharge Before Replacement**

An economic striker may be converted into an unfair-labor-practice striker if the employer discharges the economic striker before hiring a replacement.

3) **Restriction on Reinstatement Rights**

Both economic and unfair-labor-practice strikers lose their protections if the strike is conducted in an unlawful manner or for any illegal, additional purpose.

(c) **Impact of No-Strike Clause in Contract**

Here, the right to discharge strikers is a matter of contract interpretation (*i.e.*, an arbitration issue), whatever type of strike is involved.

4. **Regulation of Picketing**

"Picketing" usually requires a ***confrontation*** between employees of the picketed employer and the picketing individuals.

a. **Regulating the Means of Picketing**

The NLRA prohibits ***mass picketing*** or picketing accompanied by ***threats or violence***.

b. **Regulating the Objectives of Picketing**

(1) **Picketing to Force Recognition of an Uncertified Union**

Such activity is illegal under section 8(b)(7) if (i) there is a ***currently recognized union,*** (ii) there has been a ***valid election within the preceding 12 months,*** and (iii) the object of picketing is to ***force the employer to recognize or bargain with*** the uncertified union.

(a) **Objective**

Picketing that does not have recognition or organization as one of its ***immediate*** objectives may be lawful. Likewise, picketing to induce an employer to pay ***"area standard"*** wages and truthful ***informational picketing*** (even if it has a recognitional or organizational objective) may be permitted.

(b) **Remedies**

Unlawful organizational picketing may be remedied by a ***speedy election*** or by an ***injunction***.

(2) **Picketing in Defiance of Prior Certification of Rival Union**

Such picketing is unlawful under section 8(b)(4)(C) if another union is ***validly certified,*** the picketing has a ***prohibited objective,*** and ***coercive tactics*** are used.

(3) **Secondary Picketing for Recognition of an Uncertified Union**

This is also ***unlawful*** (under section 8(b)(4)(B), which generally bans secondary boycotts). Lawful primary activity, refusal to cross picket lines, and some construction and garment industry picketing are ***exempted*** from this provision.

5. **Secondary Pressure—Regulation of Boycotts**

A secondary boycott involves union pressure on someone ***other than the employer*** with whom the union has a dispute, for the ultimate purpose of pressuring the primary employer to meet union demands. Section 8(b)(4) ***protects innocent secondary employers*** in this situation.

a. **Activities Proscribed**

A union cannot strike, refuse to handle goods (or induce another to do so), coerce an employer to enter a "hot cargo" agreement, force a third party to cease handling the goods or business of an employer, or compel an employer to assign work to one union rather than another.

b. **Specific Problems**

(1) **"Political Protest" Cases**

"Political protest" may be illegal secondary activity if a burden on neutral employers is one object of the activity.

(2) **Common Situs Situations**

Where more than one employer occupies the same physical location and the union and secondary employer have ***conflicting interests,*** these competing interests must be resolved pursuant to the ***"Moore Drydock" rules*** limiting picketing.

(3) **"Separate Gate" Cases**

Picketing of separate gates maintained for employees other than those of the primary employer is permitted only under limited circumstances (*i.e.*, work related to the ***primary employer***).

(4) **Contractor-Subcontractor Relationships in Construction Industry**

Construction sites pose problems in separating legal from illegal secondary activity. In disputes with a subcontractor, ***picketing the entire site is illegal. "Moore Drydock" rules apply*** in separate gate situations.

(5) **"Employer Allies"**

If the secondary employer is an "ally" of the primary employer (or if their business operations are ***closely related***), section 8(b)(4) affords ***no protection*** to the secondary employer.

(6) **Individual Coercion as "Boycott Activity"**

Union coercion of ***individual employees*** of a secondary employer can be illegal activity. The ***test*** is whether the union merely ***"asked"*** or whether it ***"induced" or "coerced."***

c. **Exceptions to Section 8(b)(4)—"Legal Boycotts"**

(1) **Requests Not to Cross Picket Lines**

Requests to employees of a neutral employer ***not to cross picket lines*** where an ***authorized*** strike is in progress are expressly ***permitted.***

(2) **"Publicity" Proviso**

Similarly, a union may ***advise the public by means other than picketing*** that products are being produced by an employer with whom the union has a dispute and are being distributed by a secondary employer.

(a) **Who Is a "Producer?"**

Courts generally find that a producer is anyone who enhances the economic value of the product (*i.e.*, ***anyone in the marketing chain***).

(b) **"Means Other than Picketing"**

Noncoercive picketing (*i.e.*, a "product" boycott) is permissible if it does not impose a total boycott on all products of the secondary employer. Problems arise in "one-product" businesses or where the product of the primary employer is ***merged*** into the total product sold by the secondary employer.

C. REMEDIES FOR ILLEGAL STRIKES, BOYCOTTS, AND PICKETING

1. Unfair Labor Practice Proceeding

This is the most expedient remedy. The employer files a charge against the union with the NLRB, which then must seek an ***immediate injunction*** if there is reasonable cause to believe the charge is true. Note that the Board must also seek an immediate injunction where it reasonably believes that the union is trying to ***compel a "hot cargo" provision*** or that there has been ***unlawful organizational*** picketing.

2. Injunctive Relief Against Acts of Violence

An employer (or other party) may also seek an injunction in ***either*** state or federal court to restrain acts of violence or coercion.

3. Injunctive Relief Under Collective Bargaining Agreement

Even if there is no violence, an employer may seek to enjoin activity barred by the collective bargaining agreement (*e.g.*, breach of a ***no-strike provision***).

4. Private Damages Action Against Union

Under section 303, an employer (or other injured party) may sue in state or federal court for damages due to economic loss resulting from the illegal union activity.

5. Right to Terminate Contract

An employer may also elect to terminate the collective bargaining agreement, but thereby forfeits any right to damages.

D. IMPACT OF THE ANTITRUST LAWS ON UNION CONCERTED ACTIVITIES

1. Legitimate Union Activities Exempt from Antitrust Laws

A union acting in its own self-interest and using only lawful means is exempt from antitrust attack.

2. Present Judicial Interpretation of Exemption

Generally, antitrust laws apply to a union only where it combines with a ***nonlabor group*** (*e.g.*, employers) and the combination results in a ***restraint of interstate trade or commerce***.

V. PROTECTION OF INDIVIDUAL RIGHTS

A. CONCERTED ACTIVITY PROTECTED UNDER THE NLRA

1. Statutory Source

Section 7 protects employees' right to concerted activity ***whether or not*** there is a union representative.

2. Requirements for Protection Under Section 7

For an activity to be protected, however, there must be a ***concert of action*** (pertaining to more than one employee) toward a ***specific purpose*** that is ***work related*** (broadly construed).

a. Propriety and Loyalty

The means used by employees must be appropriate (particularly with regard to economic actions), and employees owe some degree of loyalty to the employer. Activities that breach these duties (*e.g.*, public disparagement of employer's product) are ***not*** protected by section 7.

B. UNION OR EMPLOYER DISCRIMINATION—NLRA STANDARDS

1. Union Duty of Fair Representation

A union must fairly represent ***all*** employees in the bargaining unit. Suits for breach of this duty may be brought in either state or federal court.

a. Breach of Duty as Unfair Labor Practice

A breach of the duty may also be an unfair labor practice under section 8(b)(1)(A) if the union conduct is ***"arbitrary, discriminatory or in bad faith"*** (*e.g.*, race or sex discrimination, discrimination against nonunion employees).

b. Negligence

Ordinary negligence by the union in handling grievances or other duties does not constitute a breach of the duty of fair representation.

(1) Hiring Halls

Because of the employer-like setup, mere negligence in operating a hiring hall by the union ***could*** constitute a breach of the duty of fair representation.

(2) Gross Negligence or Indifference

Likewise, gross negligence or "reckless disregard" of an employee's rights ***can*** be a breach.

2. Employer Discrimination

Only one court has suggested that employer racial discrimination could be an unfair labor practice. The NLRB ***rejects*** this view.

C. UNION OR EMPLOYER DISCRIMINATION—CIVIL RIGHTS LEGISLATION

1. Introduction

Union or employer discrimination may be a violation of the Civil Rights Acts as well as an unfair labor practice. Note that an employee's rights under the Civil Rights Acts are ***independent*** of her claims under the NLRA or the collective bargaining agreement.

2. Civil Rights Act of 1866 ("Section 1981")

This legislation may apply to ***employer or union*** racial discrimination.

3. Title VII, Civil Rights Act of 1964

Title VII prohibits discrimination by unions, employers, or employment agencies on the basis of ***race, color, religion, sex, or national origin*** and is ***very broad in scope***.

4. Impact of Collective Bargaining Contract on Rights Under 1866, 1871 or 1964 Acts

If the contract contains nondiscrimination clauses, an employee may first pursue contract remedies (*e.g.*, arbitration) and then commence Title VII or Section 1981 or possibly Section 1983 (Civil Right Act of 1871 proceedings. However, time limits under Title VII are ***not tolled*** by contract proceedings.

5. Other Civil Rights Legislation

The Equal Pay Act, Age Discrimination in Employment Act, Title IX, Educational Amendments of 1972, and the Americans with Disabilities Act ("ADA") of 1990 also have generated considerable litigation. Note that where ADA requirements conflict with provisions in the collective bargaining contract, the ***contract*** has been held to prevail ***ordinarily*** unless the employee proves that special circumstances exist that would warrant an exception to applying the contract in a particular case.

D. THE INDIVIDUAL AND THE GRIEVANCE

1. Right to Adjust Grievances Directly with Employer

An employee can adjust grievances directly with the employer as long as the adjustment is ***consistent with the collective bargaining agreement*** and the union has an ***opportunity to be present***.

2. Right to Union Representation at Investigatory Interviews

An employee has the right to union representation at investigatory interviews that might result in disciplinary action. This right may be ***waived*** by the union.

3. Rights of Nonunion Employees

After reversing its position a couple of times, the NLRB now holds that a nonunion employee does not have the right to consult with and have a co-worker present at disciplinary interviews.

4. Right to Judicial Relief Against Employer

An employee cannot compel an employer to arbitrate directly with her or compel the union to act on her behalf. However, if the union arbitrarily refuses or fails to act on her behalf, the employee can sue the employer to enforce the agreement (as a ***third-party beneficiary***) as a hybrid duty of fair representation claim.

5. Right to Judicial Relief Against Union

If a union's failure to act breached its duty of fair representation, an employee can file an ***unfair labor practice*** charge with the Board, sue for ***damages*** under section 301, or initiate ***Title VII*** procedures where appropriate.

6. Independent Remedies Under Civil Rights Acts

An employee's Title VII rights are ***independent*** of any rights under the NLRA.

E. DEVICES INSURING UNION SECURITY

1. Introduction

Unions have long sought agreements from employers that would effectively make all employees union members.

2. Federal Regulation of Compulsory Union Membership Arrangements

Section 8(a)(3) allows certain union security devices to be negotiated.

a. Types and Legality of Compulsory Union Membership Agreements

(1) Closed Shop

Arrangements that require union membership ***before*** hiring are ***illegal***.

(2) Preferential Hiring

A system of union job referrals (*e.g.*, hiring hall) is ***legal*** providing the ***union does not discriminate*** against nonmembers in its referrals.

(3) Union Shop

An open shop situation in which membership is required only ***after hiring*** is legal if the union is the majority representative. There is a ***30 day grace period*** after hiring before membership is mandatory. However, ***only dues and initiation fees*** (not full membership) can be required—*i.e.*, ***agency shop*** status or membership whittled down to its financial core. There is also an ***exemption*** for religious objectors. Note also that employees may ***prevent*** use of their dues and fees by the union for noncollective bargaining purposes (*e.g.*, political activity).

b. Enforcement of Union-Security Agreement

Lawful compulsory membership agreements can be enforced by ***discharge*** of the employee if the employer has no reasonable grounds to believe that membership was unavailable to the employee on the same terms as to others or if the employee failed to pay the required dues.

c. Deauthorization

Employees may rescind union authority to negotiate security agreements in a special deauthorization election.

3. State Regulation of Compulsory Membership Agreements—"Right to Work" Laws

States may prohibit union security agreements otherwise lawful under the NLRA. However, state laws cannot impinge on the area of exclusive NLRB jurisdiction (*i.e.*, activity that is also unlawful under NLRA).

F. DISCIPLINE OF UNION MEMBERS

1. Limitations Imposed by State Law

States have tried to balance the union's need for authority over its members against the rights of individual workers. A union is usually permitted to punish conduct that has an ***adverse economic impact*** on the union (*e.g.*, working for below-scale wages), but the union generally may ***not*** punish the ***exercise of an individual's civic duty*** (*e.g.*, reporting violations of the law). ***Political activities*** are judged on a case-by-case basis.

2. Effect of the LMRA

Taft-Hartley limited union disciplinary power and made certain actions unfair labor practices.

a. Union Unfair Labor Practices

(1) Union Coercion of Employer

A union cannot coerce an employer to discriminate against an employee ***except for*** nonpayment of union dues under a valid union security agreement. If it does, the NLRB can order the ***union alone*** to pay damages (*e.g.*, back pay).

(2) Unfair Financial Practices

A union cannot charge "excessive or discriminatory initiation fees" (*e.g.*, to discourage new members).

(3) Union Restraint and Coercion of Employee Rights

A union cannot restrain or coerce employees in the exercise of their section 7 rights, but it may adopt and enforce internal union rules that are in the ***legitimate interests*** of the union. However, these rules can be enforced ***only against members,*** and employees must be free to ***resign*** from membership at any time.

(4) Enforcement

Even valid union rules must be enforced by legitimate means (*e.g.*, no violence or employer coercion). ***Expulsion*** and ***fines*** are the usual enforcement tools.

3. Limitations on Enforcement of Union Discipline

The Landrum-Griffin Act ("LMRDA") gives union members certain basic rights to insure democracy within unions. Freedom of speech and assembly (subject to ***reasonable*** regulation), and control over dues, fees, and assessments to protect the members are guaranteed. Members also have a right to sue and to testify against a union or its officers, ***subject to exhaustion of internal remedies***.

a. Due Process and Judicial Review

Members have ***due process safeguards*** in union disciplinary hearings, except for nonpayment of dues. Courts will review the fullness and fairness of a union hearing and require ***some*** basis in the evidence for the union finding.

(1) Distinction Between Members and Officers

The courts have distinguished between union members and officers by allowing unions to ***summarily discipline*** officers for malfeasance (*i.e.*, no procedural requirements).

(2) Civil Enforcement

Members whose rights are violated may sue in federal court for ***all appropriate relief*** (*e.g.*, damages, reinstatement, and attorney fees).

b. Retention of Existing Rights from Other Sources

Landrum-Griffin also provides inspection rights and ***preserves*** all other common law or statutory rights that members may have.

G. ELECTION OF UNION OFFICERS

1. Common Law Background

Courts at common law generally refused to hear complaints about an election of union officers, or, at most, granted ***limited*** relief.

2. Landrum-Griffin, Title IV

Today, Landrum-Griffin sets certain minimum requirements for free and democratic elections (*e.g.*, secret ballot, candidacy requirements, poll observers, etc.).

a. Enforcement Provisions

The Secretary of Labor and the courts have the power to protect a union member's rights in connection with union elections.

(1) No Preelection Remedy

No preelection remedies exist under Landrum-Griffin, except in connection with a candidate's right of equal distribution of literature. However, members may have some preelection remedies under ***state law***.

(2) Authority of Secretary of Labor

After an election, Title IV preempts state authority. Once the complainant has exhausted internal remedies, the Secretary can investigate complaints, sue to have the election set aside, and supervise a new election. Complaints usually come from a union member and must show ***probable cause*** for suit by the Secretary.

(3) Judicial Power to Invalidate Elections—"Nexus" Requirement

The court will set aside an election and order a new one only if, by a preponderance of the evidence, a violation is found that has a ***proximate relationship to the outcome*** of the election. A ***mootness*** objection due to subsequent elections is ***not*** recognized.

H. CORRUPTION IN UNIONS—LANDRUM-GRIFFIN TITLES II, III, AND V

1. Title II—Reporting and Disclosure Provisions

Title II requires reporting and disclosure of certain basic information (names of officers, procedures, financial transactions). ***Criminal penalties and civil remedies*** are available for violations.

2. Title V—Limitations on Union Officials

Intended to aid members in ridding their organizations of corrupt union officials, Title V puts union officers, stewards, etc., in a ***trustee relationship*** vis-a-vis the union and its members, and imposes fiduciary duties on its officers. ***Criminal and civil remedies*** likewise are provided for violations.

3. Title III—"Trusteeships"

Title III permits a trusteeship as a means of allowing an ***international union*** to govern a local union in which serious misconduct has occurred. However, trusteeships may be established and administered ***only*** as provided in the governing union's constitution and bylaws, and ***only*** to correct corruption, prevent misappropriation of assets, restore democratic procedures, and the like. Restrictions and reporting provisions are set out in the LMRDA.

Approach to Exams

Problems in labor law may be approached by focusing on the ***stage*** in the bargaining process at which they occur: ***pre-collective bargaining*** (the organization or recognition stage), or ***after bargaining has commenced*** (the negotiation or post-agreement stage). Certain factors—such as the use of concerted activity or demands for recognition by rival unions—may be present in either stage, but the applicable law still may depend on the stage of the bargaining relationship.

1. **Considerations Relevant to Either Stage**

   Several initial questions apply to either stage of the bargaining relationship:

   a. **Coverage**

      Is the employer covered by federal law? (Certain areas are governed by state law, or by federal and state law operating concurrently; *see* pp. 23–30.) Will the NLRB assume jurisdiction (pp. 35–41)? Do any provisions exempt the ***activity*** in question for this particular industry (*e.g.*, secondary activity in the garment industry; p. 175)?

   b. **Employee vs. Employer Rights**

      Does the activity interfere with the rights of individual employees? Of employees collectively, or of the union? Of the employer? Of the general public?

   c. **Constitutional Limitations**

      If concerted activity by employees or the union is involved, are there constitutional rights at issue (*e.g.*, free speech for both employees and employer)? Have both the primary and secondary effects of such activity been considered? Has the applicability of state law to the legality of the activity been examined?

   d. **Statutory Interpretation**

      Have all statutory provisions bearing on the problem been considered? If an activity appears to be barred by a general prohibition, is it permissible under another specific provision (or vice versa)?

   e. **Effect of Violation**

      Does the problem involve more than one violation (such as conduct that results in both union and employer unfair labor practices; pp. 70–77)? If so, does this affect the remedies or procedures available to the parties?

   f. **Remedies**

      If the rights of any party have been infringed, what are the available remedies and procedures, and what are the relative advantages or disadvantages of each? (Considering alternative remedies is very important in analyzing labor law problems since it may lead to the discovery of other violations that were overlooked at first.)

2. **Pre-Bargaining Stage (Organizing and Recognition)**

   The major problems at this stage involve union organizing campaigns and the selection of a bargaining representative by employees. The consideration is whether the requirements for a proper election ***and*** for an appropriate bargaining unit have been satisfied: Has there been an unfair labor practice or have laboratory conditions been upset? Who may participate in the election? When and how can the election campaign be started?

3. **Bargaining Stage (Negotiation and Administration)**

   a. **Collective Bargaining Issues**

      Are the parties under a duty to bargain over the particular subject of bargaining involved, and have they done so in good faith? If the rights of any party appear to have been infringed, have such rights been ***waived*** in the agreement (and is the waiver ***effective***)? Where enforcing the agreement is in issue, is it capable of enforcement (*i.e.,* do any terms violate applicable law)? Is the dispute amenable to arbitration? If so, will the parties be required to arbitrate? What is the ***effect*** of an arbitration award?

   b. **Strikes, Boycotts, and Picketing**

      When and where is picketing allowed? Are the strikers economic or unfair labor practice strikers? Can the employer hire permanent replacements?

   c. **Individual Rights**

      Have individual rights been protected? Has the union breached its duty of fairly representing ***all*** employees in the bargaining unit (nonmembers as well as members)?

Note: In addition to these general considerations, the chapter approach sections found at the beginning of each chapter offer additional exam-taking guidelines.

Introduction

Labor law governs the process by which workers and management resolve the terms and conditions of employment. It has at least two unique characteristics: It is based almost entirely on ***federal statutes*** enacted during the past 85 years, and it is uniquely American—developing in response to changing social and economic conditions in the United States. (For this reason, the historical background discussed in chapter I of the Summary should help in understanding current statutes and case law.)

BASIC GOALS

Traditional American labor law has certain recognized objectives:

(1) ***The principal goal is industrial peace and stability***, and this is thought to be best achieved through ***collective bargaining***—the settlement of industrial disputes through peaceful negotiation between employers and employee representatives. The collective bargaining process is viewed as a favored objective in itself, and as a means of achieving industrial peace.

(2) ***Self-organization of employees and equal bargaining power between workers and management*** are vital to collective bargaining and thus are important policy goals of labor law. Achieving these goals has meant placing limitations on employer interference and upon certain union activities as well.

SCOPE

Labor law traditionally has been thought to stem from three principal federal statutes: the Wagner Act ("NLRA"), the Taft-Hartley Act ("LMRA"), and the Landrum-Griffin Act ("LMRDA"), all of which are treated in this Summary. Labor lawyers and the courts have been increasingly engaged by the area of equal employment opportunity law and, most recently, by wrongful discharge cases brought under state law as exceptions to the "employment at will" doctrine. In this Summary:

(1) The basic civil rights statutes are mentioned, since they are additional and important federal statutes protecting workers from unjustifiable discrimination. However, no discussion of equal employment opportunity law is attempted.

(2) Wrongful discharge cases are ***not*** treated. This area of law continues to grow, but it is not unified by any federal statute, and there are such variations among the different states that it is not useful to try to summarize them here. Nonetheless, such cases represent an important source of rights for workers, of which labor lawyers should be aware.

(3) There are other federal statutes that bear upon the workplace but are only touched upon in a cursory fashion or are not addressed at all in this summary. These include the Railway Labor Act ("RLA"), the Fair Labor Standards Act ("FLSA"), the Occupational Safety and Health Act ("OSHA"), and the Employment Retirement Income Security Act ("ERISA").

Labor Law

Thirteenth Edition

Chapter One

Background and Foundations of Labor Law

CONTENTS	PAGE

Chapter Approach

You probably will not be tested on the historical details of American labor law (although some instructors do touch on this area). Keep in mind, however, that this is a ***statutory*** course, which means that you must know the basic provisions of the ***National Labor Relations Act*** ("NLRA"), including the 1947 ***Taft-Hartley amendments***, like the back of your hand. You should also understand the basic thrust and philosophy of the ***Norris-LaGuardia Act.*** Where the ***Landrum-Griffin Act*** ("LMRDA") is concerned, you must be guided by your instructor—some labor law courses cover this area, while others do not.

A. Historical Background of Present Labor Law

1. Rise of the Labor Movement After the Civil War

a. Industrialization of the American Economy

The period from 1865 to 1914 marked the industrialization of the American economy. During that time, there were more corporations, and the average corporation was larger than ever before. "Industrial empires" emerged under the control of a few powerful individuals. Personal relationships between employer and employee were rarely possible, and the individual worker had little or no bargaining power. The western frontier disappeared and was replaced by migration to the cities. In cities, workers came to depend on wages for survival and developed greater solidarity with others in the same situation. This solidarity increased after 1880, when unskilled immigrants began to flood the labor market.

b. Organizing Prior to the 1880s

(1) Organizing on a Local Level

The first organizing efforts among employees involved isolated local groups or associations of workers, beginning in Philadelphia around 1827. These craft societies advocated unilateral negotiations between employee and employer, rather than joint bargaining. Such tactics were often dictated by the refusal of employers to deal with unions. These initial organizing efforts were crushed by the depression of the late 1830s.

(2) Formation of National Unions

A second upsurge of organizing occurred in the 1850s. The first national groups were formed (notably the Printers Union), and for the first time, negotiation and arbitration were stressed. Although employer opposition and economic depression caused these groups to wane, they did not disappear.

c. The 1880s—Knights of Labor

The Knights of Labor developed a third level of union organizing—**a *confederation*** of local and national bodies into one large unit.

(1) **Origin**

Initially a secret society, the Knights were moralists and reformers. Their chief aim was to attack the perceived evils of the new industrial society through mass organization. As a result, local bodies included virtually every type of occupation—businessmen and farmers as well as workingmen.

(2) **Growth**

From 1880 to 1886, membership in the Knights grew to 700,000—largely because the Knights advocated popular political measures (such as tax reform) aimed at "equality for all."

(3) **Decline**

However, the Knights declined almost as fast as it had grown. Membership had shrunk to 100,000 by 1890, and the Knights had virtually disappeared by 1900, primarily because the alliance between workers and farmers broke under the pull of conflicting goals.

(a) **Comment**

The dissatisfaction of the larger national craft unions stemmed from the Knights' generous membership policy. The Knights promoted "dualism"—in which a local body could belong to ***both*** the national union and the Knights. As a result, the national unions and the Knights often conflicted over issues such as jurisdiction to call a strike.

d. 1880–1914—American Federation of Labor ("AFL")

In 1886, with a combined membership of 250,000, the national craft unions formed the American Federation of Labor. Samuel Gompers became the first AFL president, and his leadership during the next 40 years had a significant impact on the course of American unionism.

(1) **Basic Philosophy**

The AFL philosophy had two major tenets:

(a) **Economic Unionism**

First, the AFL accepted capitalism and dedicated itself to increasing worker bargaining power in dealing with management.

1) **Political Action**

Although political action such as lobbying was undertaken, it was nonpartisan and aimed solely at economic advancement for union members. Radical political reforms, and the notion of trade unions as a political party, were ***rejected.***

2) **Collective Bargaining**

Collective bargaining became the primary method for achieving economic gains. Reliance was placed on ***negotiation*** to settle disputes and obtain advances. Thus, during the 1890s and early 1900s, agreements reached through collective bargaining with employers—some on a national scale—became more and more common.

(b) **Exclusive Union Jurisdiction**

Second, to use collective strength effectively, the AFL sought to have all workers in a single occupation (or range of jobs) united, and competition for jobs curtailed. The AFL thus adopted the principle of exclusive jurisdiction: Each national (or international) union would have its own ***sphere of jurisdiction*** into which no other union could trespass.

1) **Note**

Exclusive jurisdiction has not been easy to apply, and it contributed to the labor split in the 1930s (*infra,* pp. 11 *et seq.*). But like economic unionism, it remains a basic tenet of organized labor today.

(2) **Growth of AFL**

By 1914, AFL unions had more than 2,000,000 members, concentrated in the skilled trades and a few industries. The AFL did ***not*** try to organize semiskilled or unskilled workers.

(a) **AFL Organizing Methods**

This membership growth was achieved mainly through social pressure to convert workers; through strikes, boycotts or picketing where organizing efforts failed; and to a lesser extent, through public support for organizing campaigns.

(b) **Employer Response**

At the same time, most employers opposed union organizing as a threat to profits and their own power. Many resorted to "self-help," using threats of reprisal, labor spies, blacklists, and professional strikebreakers to thwart organization. Employers also turned to the courts for judicial relief, as discussed below.

2. Early Policies Toward Unions

a. Early Use of Criminal Sanctions Against Unions

A conspiracy charge against employees striking for higher wages was first reported in the 1806 **Philadelphia Cordwainer's Case,** 3 Doc. Hist. of Am. Ind. Soc. 59 (2d ed. Commons 1910). There, the court ruled that ***the combination (the union) itself,*** quite apart from its actions, was ***illegal.***

(1) **But Note**

Although criminal indictments continued into the mid-1800s, many later cases attacked union ***tactics*** (especially pressure on nonunion members) rather than union organization per se.

b. Elimination of the Criminal Conspiracy Doctrine

A Massachusetts case, **Commonwealth v. Hunt,** 45 Mass. (4 Met.) Ill (1842), was a turning point in the use of criminal indictments. The court found that ***justifiable objectives*** validated the union's attempt to impose a closed shop. "Abuse"—actual or intended—had to be shown in order to find any union activity unlawful. This ended the era of criminal sanctions against union organizing activities.

c. Civil Actions—Injunctions

During the 1880s, opponents of labor turned to civil actions against unions—primarily suits to enjoin certain union activities. The courts recognized a general right to advance the interests of workers, but this right was narrowly circumscribed. The activity could not be "inimical to the public welfare" and could not involve the use of force to compel union membership or prevent "scabs" from taking the jobs of striking members.

(1) "Objectives" Test

The legality of union activity depended upon how any particular court chose to construe union objectives. Most decisions were very ***restrictive*** of union conduct.

e.g. **Example:** In **Vegelahn v. Guntner,** 44 N.E. 1077 (Mass. 1896), the court enjoined picketing or other "interference" with persons on the employer's premises, holding that "no one can lawfully prevent employers or persons wishing to be employed from the exercise of their rights." (***In dissent,*** Holmes, J., argued that the needs of workers to organize could justify even intentional infliction of temporary damage to an employer's business—that, short of force or threat of force, organized action such as picketing should be permitted.)

e.g. **Example:** In **Plant v. Woods,** 57 N.E. 1011 (Mass. 1900), the court enjoined strikes and picketing to enforce a union demand that the employers hire only its members, rather than members of a rival union. The court held that the need for protection of the organization was ***not*** sufficient to justify interference with the employer's right to be "free of molestation." (***Again dissenting,*** Holmes contended that the members' purpose—strengthening union power before bargaining over wages and working conditions—justified the strike: "Unity of organization is necessary to make the contest of labor effectual, and [unions] lawfully may employ in their preparation the means which they might use in the final contest.")

d. Sherman Antitrust Act of 1890

During this same period, certain corporations came to achieve great economic power. Under strong public pressure to curtail business abuses, Congress passed the Sherman Antitrust Act in 1890. The Sherman Antitrust Act purported to outlaw certain types of conduct (chiefly monopolization and restraints of trade) that were considered harmful to the public interest.

(1) But Note

These antitrust provisions were first employed against ***organized labor*** rather than business entities. Most courts viewed corporations as single "persons" confronted by "groups of persons" (*i.e.*, workers organized into unions), and found that the union posed a greater threat to society.

e. Pullman Strike

In 1893, Eugene Debs and others founded the American Railway Union ("ARU") and began to organize employees throughout that industry. Management reacted by forming a powerful employer association to coordinate wages and oppose union organization. When the Pullman Palace Car Company refused to negotiate with the ARU, many Pullman workers walked off the job. Substantial violence and property damage followed.

(1) **Effect**

At this point, the Attorney General (rather than the employer) obtained a Sherman Act injunction restraining all persons from interfering with the railroads or encouraging others to do so "by threats, persuasion, force, or violence." Debs and his associates were jailed for violating the injunction.

(2) **Denial of Habeas Corpus—Rationale**

In **United States v. Debs,** 64 F. 724 (N.D. Ill. 1894), the court of appeals denied Debs' petition for habeas corpus on the following grounds:

(a) ***Prohibition of "combinations or conspiracies in restraint of trade"*** in section 1 of the Sherman Act applied to labor union as well as business activities, and an injunction could properly issue on that basis.

(b) *The injunction was not intended to deny "the right to strike peaceably or to advise a peaceful strike"* (**although the language of the** injunction could certainly be construed in that manner), but was intended to prevent violence. In the opinion of the court, Debs must have known that "violence and wrongdoing" would be necessary to prevent the handling of Pullman cars, and he had therefore conspired to commit an unlawful act.

(3) **Supreme Court View**

On appeal, the Supreme Court held that federal intervention in the railroad strike was ***constitutional*** under both the Commerce Clause and the power to establish post offices. Moreover, the Court ruled that the government could use "all force at its command" (*e.g.,* armed troops) to see that its constitutional prerogatives were not threatened. The Court admonished strikers to redress wrongs in the courts or through the ballot box rather than through "mob violence." [***In re* Debs,** 158 U.S. 564 (1895)]

f. **Aftermath of the Pullman Strike**

(1) **Appointment of U.S. Strike Commission**

Public concern over the Pullman Strike resulted in the appointment of a Strike Commission to conduct hearings and file a report.

(a) **Commission Report Sympathetic to Unions**

The Commission Report recognized that ***inequality of bargaining power*** between the employer and individual employees was the primary cause of unrest and strike. Urging employers to recognize labor unions, the Report recommended that:

1) ***A permanent Strike Commission*** be established;

2) ***Federal courts be empowered to compel employers*** to obey rulings of the Commission; and

3) ***Compulsory arbitration and a cooling-off period* before** strikes must be required.

(2) **Erdman Act of 1898**

Congress responded to the Commission Report by passing the Erdman Act in 1898. [30 Stat. 424 (1898)] The Act applied only to employees engaged in the operation of interstate trains, but it marked a significant advance in federal policy toward organized labor.

(a) Recognition of Unions

The Erdman Act recognized unions as a voice for employees, and forbade discharge or threat of discharge because of union membership.

(b) Federal Intervention and Mediation

The Erdman Act provided that, on the request of either party, the Chairman of the Interstate Commerce Commission or the Commissioner of Labor could intervene in disputes and use his best efforts to reach a settlement by mediation.

(c) Arbitration

If these efforts failed, the Chairman or Commissioner was instructed to "induce" the parties to submit the dispute to arbitration.

(3) Failure of the Erdman Act

The Erdman Act was successful only when management chose to recognize the union. Most carriers refused to do so and violated the Erdman Act with impunity.

(a) Invalidity of the Erdman Act

Ultimately, the Supreme Court held the Erdman Act ***unconstitutional,*** on the ground that it deprived the employer of "property" without due process of law. The Court ruled that the Commerce Clause did not empower Congress to regulate employer-employee relationships because such relationships were purely "local" in nature and did not affect interstate commerce. [**Adair v. United States,** 208 U.S. 161 (1908)]

3. Reaction to Labor Activity—1914–1932

a. Union Movement Through 1920

Despite the use of injunctions and the failure of the Erdman Act, considerable support developed for recognition of unions by employers.

(1) Unions as a "Restraint upon Commerce"—"*Danbury Hatters* Case"

The Sherman Act, used at first as a strike-breaking weapon, was subsequently interpreted to cast doubt on the ***legality of unions per se.*** In **Loewe v. Lawlor,** 208 U.S. 274 (1908) (the "*Danbury Hatters* Case"), an employer complained of secondary boycotts by the union against his hats. Although the precise question before the Court was procedural (the employer merely sought to have his complaint sustained against a general demurrer), the opinion broadly declared that the Sherman Act prohibited "***any combination whatever*** to secure action which essentially obstructs the free flow of commerce between the States."

(a) Rationale

The Supreme Court noted that various legislative attempts to exempt farm and labor groups from the Sherman Act had been unsuccessful. Hence, it concluded that ***all*** restraints were unlawful, and following *Loewe*, many lower courts employed the Sherman Act against ***any*** labor activity.

(2) Passage of the Clayton Act (1914)

Pressure from the AFL in the wake of the *Danbury Hatters* Case led Congress to pass the Clayton Act. [38 Stat. 730 (1914)] Hailed as "labor's Magna Carta," two sections of the Clayton Act applied specifically to unions:

(a) ***Section 6*** provided that antitrust laws should ***not*** be construed to prohibit the existence of labor organizations or to prevent labor unions from "lawfully carrying out the legitimate objects thereof."

(b) ***Section 20*** barred the use of federal injunctions in disputes between an employer and employees, or between employers of employees, involving the terms and conditions of employment.

(3) Union Growth Following Clayton Act

Union membership rose significantly between 1914 and 1920—from 2,500,000 to 5,000,000. During 1918 and 1919, the AFL waged a vigorous organizing drive in the steel industry, and in September 1919, 350,000 steelworkers went on strike. Employers mounted a widespread and violent resistance, and within three months the strike was broken and the union obliterated. These developments in the steel industry reinforced hostile attitudes toward unions and foreshadowed battles to come.

b. "Backlash" of the 1920s

(1) Resistance to Unions by Employers

During the 1920s, management relied on several new weapons to combat union growth.

(a) Scientific Management

Through job standards and time-and-motion studies, "scientific management" purported to settle all disputes concerning a "fair day's work." When tied to incentive or piecework wages, there would (in theory) be no need for collective bargaining—since impartial experts would arrive at equitable, "scientific" settlements. In practice, such studies were rarely scientific or impartial, and their net effect was to stimulate union organizing efforts.

(b) Welfare Capitalism—the Employee-Representation Movement and Company Unions

Employers also formed "constitutional" systems in which employees selected representatives to a "legislature" in which the employer was also represented. Since representatives had to be company employees and ultimate decisions still rested with management, employees actually had little bargaining power. "Company unions" operated under similar constraints. Employers sometimes sweetened this approach with bonuses, profit sharing, and other benevolent personnel policies.

(c) AFL Membership Decline

From 1919 to 1928, membership in company-dominated organizations grew from 403,000 to 1,500,000 while AFL unions lost 400,000 members.

(2) Emasculation of Clayton Act by the Supreme Court

Throughout the same period, the Supreme Court all but destroyed sections 6 and 20 of the Clayton Act, above. The Court chose to apply one antitrust standard to business and another, far more restrictive standard to organized labor.

(a) *Duplex Printing* Case

In **Duplex Printing Press Co. v. Deering,** 254 U.S. 443 (1921), the Court upheld an injunction issued to break a secondary boycott imposed by the Machinists Union (whose members refused to work on printing presses manufactured by Duplex because Duplex had refused to recognize the union).

1) The Court held that ***section 6*** of the Clayton Act (exempting unions from the Sherman Act) was ***not*** available to shelter the union, since it protected only the "lawful" carrying out of "legitimate" objectives. The Court declared that secondary interference with a property right was neither lawful nor legitimate.
2) The Court found that ***section 20*** (barring injunctions in labor disputes) "by the natural meaning of the words used" applied ***only*** to the workers involved in an actual dispute—and not to union members boycotting activities in the plants of other employers.

(b) *Bedford Cut Stone* Case

In **Bedford Cut Stone Co. v. Journeymen Stone Cutters Association of North America,** 274 U.S. 37 (1927), the Supreme Court ruled that quarry owners were entitled to an injunction against union boycotts ordering members not to work on stone cut at nonunion quarries.

1) "Effects" Argument

The Supreme Court admitted that organizing the quarries was a legitimate union goal. Nevertheless, the Court found a restraint of plaintiffs' "interstate trade" and hence a violation of the Sherman Act. Even though the "restraint" occurred ***after*** physical transportation of the stone had ended, the ***goal*** of the union was not local in nature (*i.e.*, not confined to stone work after shipment) and it was ***"the result, not the means devised to secure it"*** that brought the defendant's actions into "interstate commerce" and under the antitrust laws.

2) Criticism

The Supreme Court had ***rejected*** this same "effects" test as applied to business conduct in **United States v. E.C. Knight Co.,** 156 U.S. 1 (1895), holding that manufacturing was not "commerce," and hence not within the scope of the Sherman Act. Thus, the Court seemed to have adopted a ***double standard:*** The Sherman Act would be read broadly to cover union activities, but narrowly to exempt business practices.

(c) Effect

Duplex Printing Press Co. and *Bedford Cut Stone Co.* exemplify the obstacles to union organizing in the 1920s. The treatment accorded unions in this period left a permanent residue of labor distrust and suspicion toward the courts.

c. Union Advances—1914–1932

Despite judicial setbacks, there were certain gains for organized labor during this period.

(1) Labor During World War I—National War Labor Board

The Wilson administration tried to prevent labor disputes that might disrupt war production, and to this end established a National War Labor Board. The National War Labor Board adopted and vigorously enforced "the right of workers to organize in trade unions and to bargain collectively." Such rights were not to be "denied, abridged or interfered with by employers in any manner whatsoever."

(a) Effect

For the first time, the right to organize and bargain collectively received effective government protection. Several plants were seized as a result of antiunion activities. However, with one exception (*see* below), this wartime attitude was ***abandoned*** during the 1920s "Era of Big Business."

(2) Railway Labor Act of 1926

The exception referred to above involved the passage of the Railway Labor Act of 1926 ("RLA"), the first peacetime measure to sanction and codify union-management bargaining. [44 Stat. 577 (1926); *and see infra,* p. 35] Of course, railway workers (and their unions) enjoyed a strategic economic position and clearly were engaged in interstate commerce.

(a) Major Provisions of the RLA

The following provisions of the RLA were (and still are) of major importance to unions:

1) Compulsory Arbitration

The ***National Railroad Adjustment Board*** was established to settle minor disputes over working conditions and contract interpretation. Arbitration of such disputes is ***compulsory***—an unusual feature in American labor legislation and practices.

2) Duty to Negotiate

The RLA imposed a ***duty*** on both sides to use "every reasonable effort to make and maintain agreements." [RLA § 2]

3) Mediation Board

In the event that negotiations broke down, a ***National Mediation Board*** was created to offer services to the parties, including inducements to arbitrate if a voluntary settlement could not be reached.

4) Investigative Board

Failing all else, the President could appoint an ***investigative board*** when any dispute threatened to disrupt essential rail service.

(b) Constitutionality Upheld

The RLA was upheld by the Supreme Court in **Texas & New Orleans Railroad v. Brotherhood of Railway & Steamship Clerks,** 281 U.S. 548 (1930). Amended in 1934 and extended to airlines in 1936, the RLA is the basis for collective bargaining in rail and air transportation today.

4. Establishment of Labor Policy and Union Organization

During the period of the New Deal, federal legislation established collective bargaining as a national policy (*see infra,* pp. 14 *et seq.*). After 1930, patterns of labor organization also evolved.

a. Rise of "Industrial Unionism"

(1) Formation of Congress of Industrial Organizations ("CIO")

Shifts in national policy toward unions during the New Deal were accompanied by significant changes within the union movement itself. The AFL (consisting of 80 to 100 affiliated unions) entered into this period with two unchallenged principles: ***national union autonomy*** and ***exclusive jurisdiction*** for each national union (even if the "chartered" union did not actually organize all workers in the assigned area). Both assumptions were challenged in the early 1930s by John L. Lewis and other labor leaders in the mass-production industries (coal, steel, etc.).

(a) Factors Leading to Break with AFL

Lewis and his followers considered craft organizations inappropriate where work skills were easily acquired and produced no group solidarity. They believed strong organizing efforts were necessary in these areas, in which antiunion sentiment ran highest. This approach conflicted with AFL notions of craft autonomy and spontaneous organization, and Lewis's personality further increased tensions.

(b) Origin of CIO

During the 1935 AFL convention, the Lewis group lost a battle over industrial unionism and immediately formed the "Committee for Industrial Organization," consisting of eight AFL unions. In 1936, the Committee was charged with violating the AFL constitution (by setting up a rival union and invading the territory of the International Brotherhood of Electrical Workers) and was ordered to disband. When the Committee refused to do so, the eight unions were suspended from the AFL, and the Congress of Industrial Organizations was formally organized in 1937.

(2) Rivalry Between AFL and CIO

The existence of two hostile federations presented new issues for union organizing.

(a) Communist Influence Within CIO Unions

Older unions in both the AFL and CIO retained the anti-Communist philosophy of the 1920s, but Communist Party members were able to reach high leadership posts in several CIO unions.

(b) Competition for Members

At the outset, most CIO unions were former AFL bodies. As the movement grew, however, new unions with overlapping jurisdiction were chartered by ***both*** the AFL and CIO (*e.g.,* in meatpacking and government service). This became a major problem for both federations during the 1940s.

(c) Jurisdictional Disputes

Rivalry between the federations also created problems for the newly formed National Labor Relations Board. The Board was responsible for determining the appropriate unit in which to conduct representation elections (*infra*), and each federation vigorously campaigned for its own policy of organization (craft or industrial).

b. Reconciliation and Merger of AFL and CIO

Despite an impressive start, the CIO by 1950 had far fewer members than the AFL. This was due partly to the expulsion of Communist-dominated unions, but more importantly to renewed organizing efforts by the AFL. During the 1950s, the two federations resolved their differences and merged into the present AFL-CIO Federation.

(1) Factors Contributing to a Merger

The older leaders in both federations passed from the scene, and their replacements—men like Walter Reuther of the CIO and George Meany of the AFL—were less dogmatic and anxious for merger. During World War II and the Korean War, members of the two bodies worked together and came to appreciate the position of each other, and in the early 1950s, both found common ground in facing a "hostile" Republican administration.

(2) History of Merger

The first step toward reconciliation was taken in 1953, when the two federations signed a "no-raiding" agreement. Sixty-five AFL and 29 CIO affiliates agreed not to attempt to displace or disrupt any other union that had an established bargaining relationship. The success of this agreement led in 1955 to unification and a constitution for the new AFL-CIO confederation.

(3) Resolution of Differences

As discussed above, the two fundamental issues dividing the AFL and CIO in the 1930s were ***autonomy*** and ***exclusive jurisdiction.***

(a) Autonomy

Under the present constitution, national union autonomy is preserved, ***with two major qualifications***:

1) ***The Executive Council of the AFL-CIO can suspend unions when it finds corruption or Communist influence***; and
2) ***The constitution prohibits racial discrimination*** in member unions (without suspension sanctions, however).

(b) Exclusive Jurisdiction

The present status of exclusive jurisdiction is ambiguous, since both craft and industrial unions were approved and a "no-raiding agreement" became mandatory. Bargaining rights have become a central issue among affiliated unions, compounded by the difficulty of ascertaining what the prior "organizing jurisdiction" of a union (under the no-raid pact) may have been.

5. Concurrent Theories of Employer-Employee Relationship

While collective bargaining under federal statutes became the basis for national labor policy after 1930, courts have used other theories as well to define the relationship between employers and employees.

a. Doctrine of "Employment at Will"

Historically, courts held that—unless otherwise specifically contracted for—employment was presumed to be for an indefinite period and was terminable at the will of either party. [*See, e.g.*, **Skagerberg v. Blandin Paper Co.,** 266 N.W. 872 (Minn. 1936)]

(1) Impact on Employees

Rigid application of the traditional "at will" doctrine led to what many considered harsh and inequitable results for employees. In *Skagerberg*, for example, the plaintiff accepted a job with the defendant paper manufacturer on a promise that the job would be permanent in nature. Relying on that promise, the plaintiff turned down another job offer and purchased a home near the plant where he was to begin work. After being fired, plaintiff sued for breach of contract. The court held that, without more, the promise of permanent employment meant only that the term was indefinite and that the hiring was at will.

(2) Criticism of Doctrine

Commentators argued that the employment-at-will doctrine assumed an employment "contract" negotiated by parties with equal bargaining power, when often that was not the case. ***Unionization*** was seen as a means of equalizing this bargaining power, because unions—if certified as the employees' representative—could demand that employers bargain in good faith and could achieve benefits (including job protection) for employees. (The attributes—and costs—of the collective bargaining process are the subject of this Summary.)

(3) "Public Policy" Exception

In some states, the employment-at-will doctrine will not be enforced if its application offends public policy. For example, in **Shick v. Shirey,** 716 A.2d 1231 (Pa. 1998), the Pennsylvania court held that, despite the employment-at-will doctrine, an employee who filed a workers' compensation claim and was then fired could sue for wrongful discharge. However, the Pennsylvania court in *Shick* cautioned that a ***state*** public policy must be at issue—because if all federal regulations constituted public policy, the exception could swallow the rule.

b. Other Bases for Employee Rights—Further Exceptions to the "at Will" Doctrine

The second half of the 20th century saw an increasing abandonment of the employment-at-will doctrine, and a "sea change" in state law toward protecting employee job rights under a variety of other theories. In some states, arbitrary or unreasonable dismissal may give rise to a cause of action in ***tort***; in others, courts have found ***contract*** rights in sources such as employee handbooks; and in still other states, employees have been held to have a ***property*** interest in their jobs, entitling them to certain protections.

(1) Note

Such common law doctrines are beyond the scope of this Summary, but it is interesting to note that their expansion in state law has coincided with a steady drop in the percentage of unionized workers in the private sector nationwide.

(2) And Note

The concepts embodied in the National Labor Relations Act (and its amendments) will govern many workplaces, and they exert an influence on the way in which employer-employee relationships are perceived. This is especially true of the ***grievance and arbitration process,*** a central feature of collective bargaining contracts and one that has been extraordinarily successful in resolving disputes between employers and employees. Many nonunion employers have adopted such procedures, and this trend is likely to accelerate in the future.

B. Statutory Foundations of Present Labor Law

1. Introduction

Federal labor law is based primarily on four major pieces of legislation: (i) the ***Norris-LaGuardia Act,*** which was as passed in 1932; (ii) the ***National Labor Relations Act ("NLRA")*** (or Wagner Act), passed in 1935; (iii) the ***Labor Management Relations (Taft-Hartley) Act,*** passed in 1947 (amended the NLRA); and finally, (iv) the ***Labor-Management Reporting and Disclosure (Landrum-Griffin) Act,*** passed in 1959 (further amendment of the NLRA).

2. Norris-LaGuardia Act (1932)

a. Background

By 1930, the courts had become a major frustration to union goals. Various doctrines and procedures, such as those below, were invoked to prevent union organizing or collective bargaining.

(1) "Yellow-Dog Contracts"

"Yellow-dog contracts" were contractual agreements that employers required employees to sign, and in which the employees promised not to join labor unions on penalty of losing their jobs. Such contracts were upheld by the courts [*see* **Hitchman Coal & Coke Co. v. Mitchell,** 245 U.S. 229 (1917)], and as a result were widely used to thwart organizing activity.

(2) "Objectives" Test

As demonstrated by the *Duplex Printing Press Co.* and *Bedford Cut Stone Co.* Cases (*supra,* p. 9), union organizing activity was judged according to the courts' own views of social and economic policy. The approach itself was suspect, but the greatest objection was to the "double standard" by which corporations and labor organizations received different treatment under the antitrust laws (*supra,* p. 5).

(3) Vicarious Responsibility

Under the rule laid down in **United States v. Debs** (*supra,* p. 6), a union that called a strike could be held responsible for any violence that resulted, even if the violence was not caused by union members and the union had exerted every effort to prevent it. Thus, a strike could be broken because of acts not authorized by the union and for which it would not be responsible under normal rules of agency.

(4) Injunctions

Certain procedural problems with injunctions also worked against organizing or bargaining efforts.

(a) ***Temporary injunctions halting a strike were customarily issued ex parte*** by a court of equity (after hearing only the ***employer's*** case).

(b) ***Although the union was entitled to a subsequent "show cause" hearing,*** the ***psychological effect*** of halting the strike was generally disastrous (particularly for new or weak organizations).

(c) ***Employers often could drag out court proceedings*** until union efforts were effectively quashed, whatever the final decision might be.

(d) ***The obscure language and brutal enforcement*** of most injunctions added a final note to demands for legislative reform.

b. Enactment of Norris-LaGuardia

Congress passed the Norris-LaGuardia Act in 1932. [47 Stat. 70 (1932)] Basically, the Norris-LaGuardia Act (which remains in effect today) ***removed the power of federal courts to enjoin*** coercive activity by unions that did not involve fraud or violence, except under very limited circumstances (*see infra,* pp. 186–187).

(1) Policy Statement

Congress declared that the worker, "though he should be free to decline to associate with his fellows, [must] have full freedom of association, self-organization, and designation of representatives of his own choosing to negotiate the terms and conditions of his employment; and [must] be free from the interference, restraint, or coercion of employers . . . in [these activities]."

(2) Effect

The Norris-LaGuardia Act placed ***no affirmative obligations on employers to negotiate*** with unions. Rather, it sought to aid union organizing and collective bargaining by changing common law precedents on the union's role in society. Together with subsequent ***state*** enactments, Norris-LaGuardia permitted unions to exert effective economic pressure against employers.

c. Judicial Response—Legitimate Union Activities Exempt from Antitrust Laws

With the more explicit language of Norris-LaGuardia, the Supreme Court (whose composition also changed during the 1930s) had little difficulty finding that legitimate labor activities were ***exempt*** from the federal antitrust laws.

(1) *Hutcheson* Decision

In **United States v. Hutcheson,** 312 U.S. 219 (1941), the Court held that union picketing and boycott activities against an employer, as part of a jurisdictional dispute with another union, did ***not*** violate the Sherman Act.

(a) Rationale

The Court read Norris-LaGuardia as establishing a public policy in favor of legitimate union activities, and in light of such policy, the Court refused to follow its previous narrow interpretation of section 20 of the Clayton Act (as in *Duplex Printing Press Co.* and *Bedford Cut Stone Co.*). Rather, the Court held that the clear purpose of section 20 was to ***protect*** labor's traditional weapons.

(b) Note

The Court emphasized that under the Clayton Act, judicial discretion was narrowly circumscribed. So long as a union was acting ***in its own interests*** (as opposed to combining with nonlabor groups) and used only ***lawful means*** (*i.e.*, no violence or threats thereof), the courts had no right to examine the "objectives" of the union's activities.

(2) Effect

Since *Hutcheson,* the antitrust laws rarely have been asserted against union activity—and then only where ***collusion between labor and management*** is shown to have caused a ***restraint in interstate trade.*** [**Allen Bradley Co. v. Local 3, International Brotherhood of Electrical Workers,** 325 U.S. 797 (1945); *and see* discussion *infra,* p. 188]

3. National Labor Relations Act (1935)

a. Background

The economic collapse of the 1930s helped complete the transition to a national policy of collective bargaining. "Welfare capitalism" disappeared after 1929, while political power shifted toward farm and labor groups. Under the New Deal, the Norris-LaGuardia Act was followed by the National Industrial Recovery Act ("NIRA") [48 Stat. 198 (1933)], which set "codes of fair competition" for business and encouraged voluntary collective bargaining by employers. Although the NIRA was declared unconstitutional (*see* Constitutional Law Summary) and government returned to a policy of competition, the impetus toward collective bargaining continued, culminating in the National Labor Relations Act (Wagner Act) of 1935 ("NLRA"). [49 Stat. 449 (1935)]

b. Basic Provisions of the National Labor Relations Act

(1) Section 7—Rights of the Employees

Section 7 is the heart of the NLRA. It guarantees employees:

(a) ***Freedom to form, join, or assist labor organizations;***

(b) ***Freedom to bargain collectively with the employer;*** and

(c) ***The right to engage in concerted activity*** for the purpose of collective bargaining or mutual aid and protection.

(2) Section 8—Duty of Employer to Bargain Collectively

Section 8 of the NLRA also imposes ***affirmative duties on employers*** to deal in good faith with unions.

(a) Note

Management was now ***obligated*** to bargain with the union designated as the exclusive representative for employees in a given bargaining unit.

(b) And Note

The bargaining unit was to be designated by a ***National Labor Relations Board*** ("NLRB" or "the Board")—the administrative body set up to administer the NLRA—and the bargaining representative was to be selected by a majority of employees in the unit.

c. Constitutionality

The NLRA immediately came under constitutional attack in test cases by major industries.

(1) Criticism of the NLRA

Opponents argued that the NLRA, as applied to manufacturing, went beyond the Commerce Clause and invaded the Tenth Amendment rights of the states. A second argument was that the NLRA denied employers due process of law by imposing restrictions upon freedom of contract.

(2) Constitutionality Upheld

However, these arguments were rejected, and the constitutionality of the NLRA was upheld by the Supreme Court in **NLRB v. Jones & Laughlin Steel Corp.,** 301 U.S. 1 (1937), and three companion cases.

d. Limitations of the National Labor Relations Act

Despite its great significance, the NLRA was ***not*** a complete labor code. Three limitations influenced later changes and extensions in federal law:

(1) ***The NLRA was primarily concerned with the organizing phase*** of labor relations.

(2) ***The NLRA dealt exclusively with employer tactics*** (referred to as "unfair labor practices").

(3) ***The NLRA left the substantive terms of employment entirely to private negotiation,*** with agreement to be induced by the costs to either side from disagreement.

4. Labor Management Relations Act of 1947 (Taft-Hartley or LMRA)

a. Background

Between 1935 and 1947, union membership increased from 3,000,000 to 15,000,000 employees. As national unions (particularly in the mass-production industries) became increasingly powerful, the public became apprehensive, especially due to the following:

(1) Strike During Periods of High Demand

From 1945 to 1947, the country experienced industrywide strikes in coal, oil, lumber, textiles, and maritime and rail transportation, multifirm strikes in the automobile and other industries, and even ***community*** strikes in certain areas. Such strikes were designed to force employer concessions at a time of peak consumer demand (following World War II). However, they exasperated the general public and alarmed many people when they threatened to cut off essential services.

(2) "Labor Bosses"

"Labor bosses" such as John L. Lewis also became a focal point for dissatisfaction. Like the "robber baron" corporate leaders at the turn of the century, these men seemed to wield an inordinate amount of economic power.

(3) Unfair Union Practices

Finally, there was widespread belief that certain union tactics (such as those listed below) should be curbed.

(a) ***Some unions imposed severe restrictions on membership*** ("labor protectionism").

(b) ***Others***—particularly the Teamsters—***used secondary boycotts*** to exert pressure on employers far removed from actual labor disputes with the union (*see infra,* pp. 175 *et seq.*).

(c) ***Jurisdictional disputes*** in the construction industry led to walkouts and long delays in key projects.

(d) ***Union abuses of "closed-shop" contracts*** led to proposals for an "open-shop" policy.

b. Passage of LMRA

The congressional response to these criticisms—the Labor Management Relations Act ("LMRA" or the Taft-Hartley Act)—was the product of diverse forces: opponents of ***all*** collective bargaining on the one hand, and critics of ***specific*** union abuses (who were still sympathetic to the labor movement) on the other. [61 Stat. 136 (1947)]

(1) Effect

Taft-Hartley was a highly controversial piece of legislation, and the controversy persists to this day. Organized labor bitterly opposed the measure, regarding it as a "sellout" to antilabor forces.

(2) Basic Provisions

The provisions of the LMRA (which ***amended*** the NLRA) illustrate the conflicting motives behind its passage:

(a) Legislative Role in Labor Disputes

First of all, Taft-Hartley ended the notion that the law had no role to play in handling labor disputes—although the points of intervention are still few in comparison with the areas left untouched.

(b) Prohibition of Union Unfair Labor Practices

The Taft-Hartley Amendments provide greater power to combat ***union*** "unfair labor practices" and to intervene in strikes that threaten the national welfare. A "balance of obligations" was sought by putting constraints upon the union similar to those originally placed on employers by the NLRA.

(c) Alternatives to Bargaining

While the LMRA upholds collective bargaining as the most desirable (and preferred) process for settling a labor dispute, it also recognizes that bargaining does not always resolve the issues, and that failure to reach agreement in certain situations might seriously damage the economy and the general public. Hence, several ***alternative processes*** were established:

1) Federal Mediation and Conciliation Service ("FMCS")

Congress created the FMCS to assist in any dispute affecting interstate commerce, and ***requires*** that labor or management notify the FMCS when any change in the terms or conditions of employment previously fixed by a collective bargaining agreement is desired.

2) National Emergency Disputes

Taft-Hartley also provides that the President may intervene when an industrywide dispute, in his opinion, would "***imperil the national health or safety***." The President can then appoint a Board of Inquiry to investigate and report on the facts of the dispute and on the parties' positions. The Board of Inquiry is precluded from making recommendations, but if the President concludes that the ***national health or safely*** is in jeopardy, he can seek an 80-day federal injunction against the strike or work stoppage. During the injunction, bargaining continues with the assistance of FMCS. After the first 60 days, a report on the status of the dispute is given to the President including the employer's, and within the next 15 days, a poll is taken by employees on management's final offer. The injunction, however, must expire within 80 days, and the strike may then continue, unless halted by special emergency legislation.

(d) Prohibition of Closed Shop

Taft-Hartley likewise undertakes to regulate certain provisions in the collective bargaining agreement itself: It ***outlaws the closed shop*** and ***limits the terms of pension funds and similar items***.

(e) Enforcement of Labor Agreements

Finally, the LMRA provides legal remedies for the enforcement of labor agreements. Lawsuits for violating the terms of an agreement are recognized, and the number of such lawsuits has increased significantly since 1950.

STATUTORY BASES FOR FEDERAL LABOR LAW

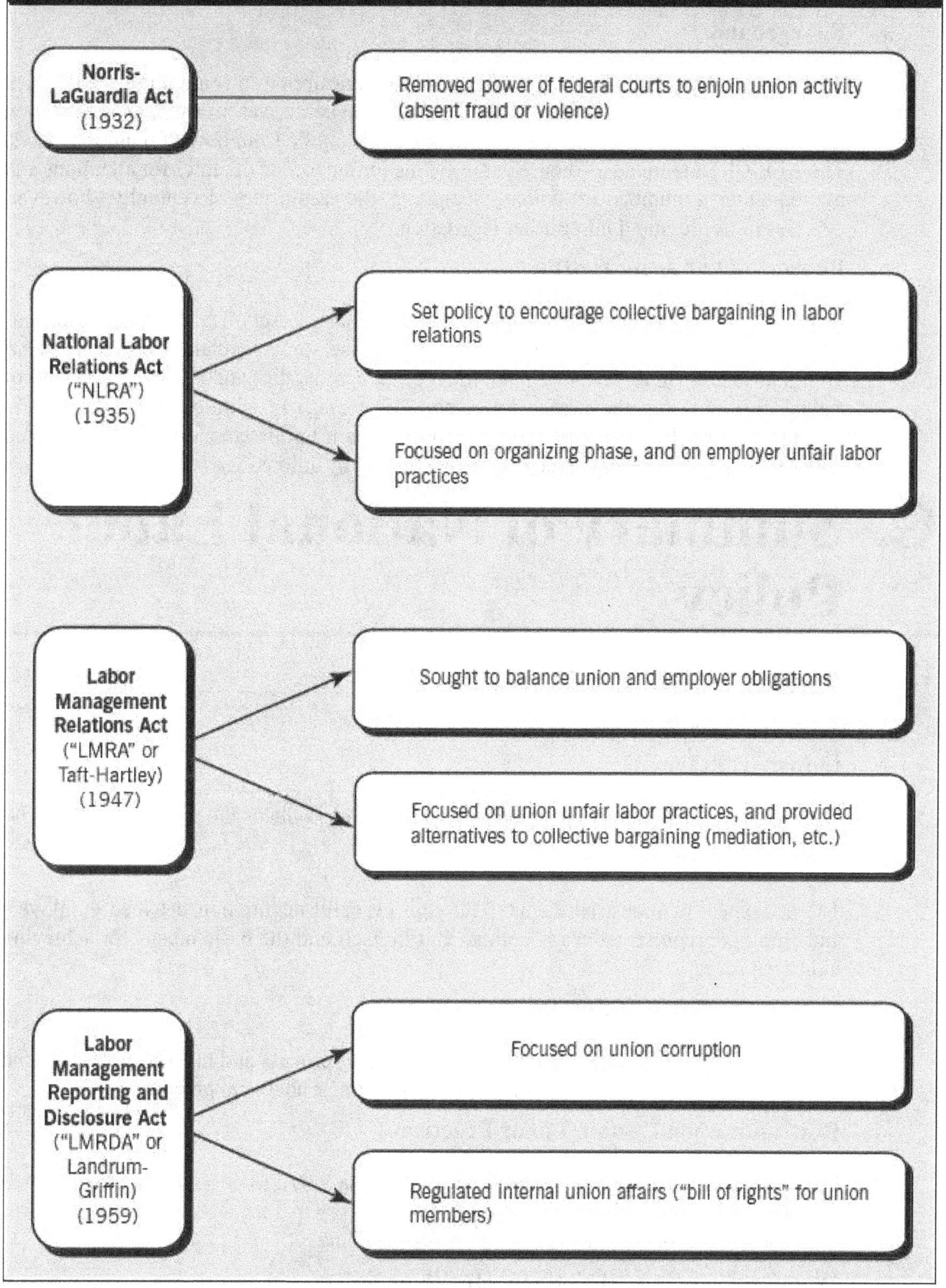

5. Labor Management Reporting and Disclosure Act of 1959 (Landrum-Griffin Act)

a. Background

Senate investigations during the 1950s uncovered corruption in some unions and a lack of democratic procedures in others. Public sentiment again was aroused, and legislation was demanded to protect individual workers and the public from powerful union leaders. The AFL-CIO attempted to "houseclean" by instituting a code of ethics for all unions and by expelling a number of unions, including the Teamsters. Eventually, however, Congress was pressured into further legislation.

b. Passage of Landrum-Griffin

Briefly, the Labor Management Reporting and Disclosure Act ("LMRDA" or Landrum-Griffin Act [73 Stat. 519 (1959)]) sought to impose some regulation on the ***internal*** affairs of unions (in an effort to make them more democratic) and to establish a "bill of rights" for union members. (*See infra,* pp. 219 *et seq.*) In addition, Landrum-Griffin amended the LMRA to define more carefully certain unfair labor practices connected with secondary pressure and recognitional picketing by unions (*see infra,* pp. 169 *et seq.*).

C. Summary of National Labor Policy

1. In General

Today, national labor policy can be summarized as follows:

a. Industrial Peace

Continued production, uninterrupted by strikes and lockouts, is the principal goal.

b. Collective Bargaining

The settlement of industrial disputes through peaceful negotiation between employers and employee representatives is both an end in itself and the basic means for achieving industrial peace.

c. Self-Organization of Employees

Self-organization is vital to the collective bargaining process and must be accomplished without employer interference, union coercion, or other unethical practices.

d. Restraints upon Certain Labor Practices

Restraints on certain labor practices (such as secondary strikes or boycotts, jurisdictional disputes, and featherbedding) are justified on the theory that the adverse consequences of such activities ***outweigh*** their value to labor organizing.

e. When Strikes Imperil National Health or Safety

When strikes that imperil national health or safety occur, every effort short of compulsory arbitration must be used to settle the dispute. (Some ***states*** require compulsory arbitration of certain disputes, but this procedure has been attacked as defeating the policy of free, private negotiation and settlement between the parties.)

(1) Conciliation and Mediation

The FMCS offers its services in any labor dispute affecting interstate commerce. (Similar machinery is provided by many states as well.)

(2) Waiting or Cooling-Off Periods

Under the Taft-Hartley Act, the President may empanel a commission to investigate and report on any labor dispute that threatens the national health and welfare. Also, if the President concludes from the report that national security is threatened, the President may petition a federal district court for an injunction against a strike for a limited period of time of no more than 80 days.

(3) Affirmative Intervention

When all else fails, the federal government has the power to intervene directly—*e.g.,* by seizure or by using the Army or National Guard to run affected industries. Such intervention would be justified only in extreme emergencies, however, since it tends to defeat the basic policy of allowing employees to strike over grievances and economic demands.

D. Role of State Law in Labor-Management Relations—the Preemption Doctrine

1. Federal Preemption

State labor relations laws cover a wide variety of subjects. Some statutes expressly ban picketing and boycotting (*infra,* p. 187). Others (notably antitrust provisions) have been read to limit union activities. Still other states have comprehensive statutes similar to the NLRA. However, the interest in a uniform national labor policy clearly outweighs any recognized interest in state regulation. Hence, ***subject to certain exceptions*** discussed below, ***state statutes are preempted by federal labor law wherever the two areas overlap.*** [**Garner v. Teamsters Local 776,** 345 U.S. 991 (1953)] There are two types of preemptions "necessary to implement federal labor policy." [**Chamber of Commerce v. Brown,** 554 U.S. 60, 65 (2008)] There is a preemption that forbids state interference with the NLRB's interpretation and enforcement of the NLRA. [**Brown**, *supra*] There is also a preemption that forbids the NLRB and states from regulating areas intended to be "left 'to . . . free play of economic forces.' " [**Brown**, *supra*]

2. Scope of Federal Power

The NLRA is interpreted very broadly. If an activity is even ***arguably*** regulated or protected by federal law, the states have ***no jurisdiction*** to regulate that activity. [**San Diego Building Trades Council v. Garmon,** 359 U.S. 236 (1959)] Also, when Congress expressly chose to leave certain aspects of labor law unregulated, in particular uncoerced speech advocating for or against unions as allowed pursuant to Section 8(c) of the NLRA, then state efforts to regulate that speech are preempted. [**Brown**, *supra*, [p. 23]]

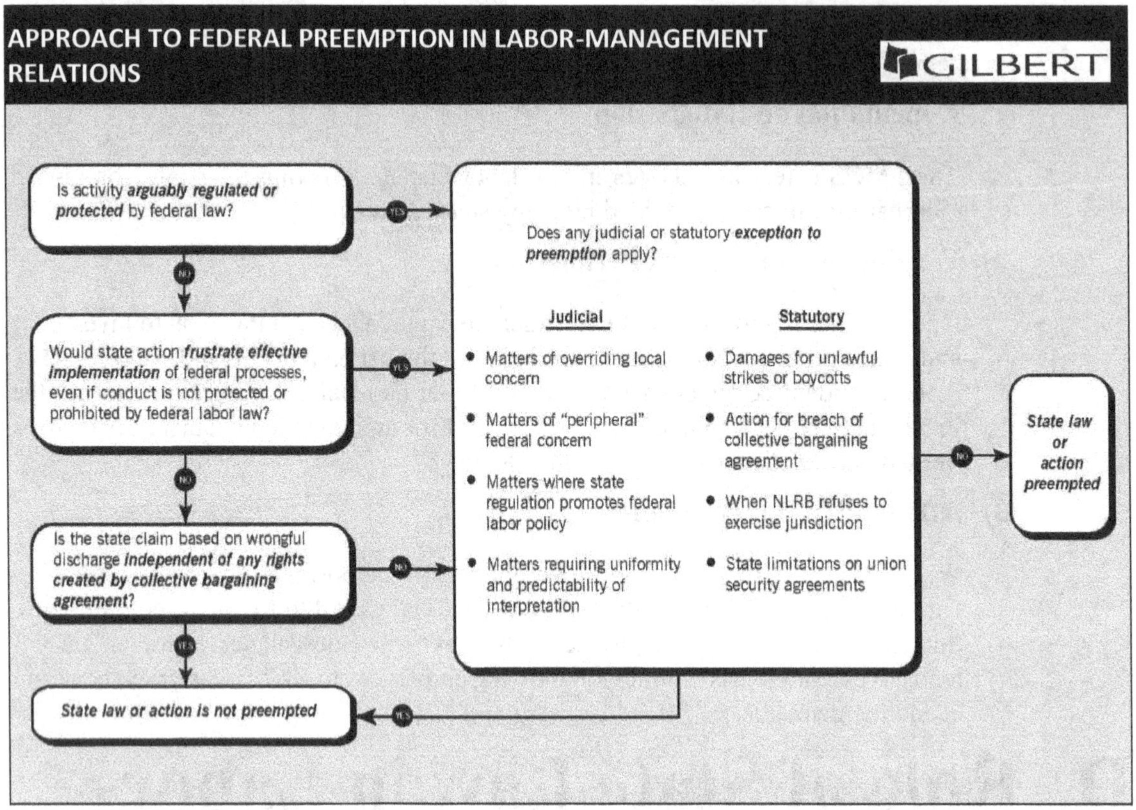

e.g. **Example:** Union members were barred from bringing breach of contract suits in state court for wrongful suspension from union membership, where the sanction imposed was discharge from employment, because this sanction was *arguably* subject to section 7 or 8 of the NLRA. [**Amalgamated Association of Street, Electric Railway & Motor Coach Employees v. Lockridge,** 403 U.S. 274 (1971)]

a. Minimum Showing Required

The party contending that an activity is "arguably protected" by the NLRA must at least put forward an interpretation that has not been "authoritatively rejected by the NLRB or by the courts." [**International Longshoremen's Association v. Davis,** 476 U.S. 380 (1986)]

(1) Note

This requirement was not met by a union that had been held liable under state law for misrepresentations to a supervisor and claimed preemption, since supervisors ordinarily are not "employees" under the NLRA. [**International Longshoremen's Association v. Davis,** *supra*]

(2) But Note

The requisite showing was made where a party contended that a state statute that ***characterized*** supervisors as "employees" conflicted with national labor policy as embodied in the NLRA. [**Beasley v. Food Fair of North Carolina, Inc.,** 416 U.S. 653 (1974)]

b. Preemption to Insure "Effective Implementation of Federal Processes"

Moreover, there is a preemption of state action that would frustrate effective implementation of federal processes—even if the conduct in question is neither protected nor prohibited by federal labor law. [**Lodge 76, International Association of Machinists & Aerospace Workers v. Wisconsin Employment Relations Commission,** 427 U.S. 132 (1976) ("*Machinists*")] In *Machinists,* the Wisconsin Board had enjoined a concerted refusal by employees to work overtime—conduct not specifically covered by federal statutes. However, the Supreme Court held that such conduct was among the activities left unregulated by Congress "so as to be controlled by the free play of economic forces," and any state interference was thus precluded because of its impact on the implementation of federal processes.

(1) Reversal of Prior Case Law

The Court in *Machinists* expressly overruled **Local 232 v. Wisconsin Employment Relations Board,** 336 U.S. 245 (1949) which had held that states were not preempted from regulating conduct that was neither protected nor prohibited by federal labor law.

(2) Application

The Court later disapproved a city's conditioning of the renewal of a taxicab franchise on the settlement of a labor dispute, since this would restrict the economic "self-help" weapons that Congress had intended to be allowed to operate freely. [**Golden State Transit Corp. v. City of Los Angeles,** 475 U.S. 608 (1986)]

c. Wrongful Discharge Cases

Another area of law is the extent to which wrongful discharge cases brought under state common law theories are preempted by federal labor law. Typically, these cases arise when an employee has been unsuccessful in gaining reinstatement under the grievance and arbitration procedures of the collective bargaining agreement, or when the employee simply bypasses the grievance procedure for a state court action in hopes of achieving a better remedy (such as punitive damages). Assessing preemption in these cases requires a determination of whether the claims are *inextricably intertwined* with the collective bargaining agreement or they operate separately *without the need to interpret the agreement.*

(1) Claim Independent of Interpreting the Collective Bargaining Agreement

When the state law claim is independent of interpreting any rights created by the collective bargaining agreement, the Supreme Court has held that it is ***not preempted*** by federal law and may properly be brought in state court because there is *no need to interpret the contract.* [**Lingle v. Norge Division of Magic Chef, Inc.,** 486 U.S. 399 (1988)—state court action for alleged retaliatory discharge permitted; *and see* **Paige v. Henry J. Kaiser Co.,** 826 F.2d 857 (9th Cir. 1987)]

(a) And Note

When the state law claim is clearly independent, a state agency ***cannot decline to enforce*** the state law in the case of unionized employees. [**Livadas v. Bradshaw,** 512 U.S. 107 (1994)—state must enforce penalty clause of state wage-payment statute, even though employees were union members covered by a collective bargaining agreement with grievance and arbitration procedures that might determine wages at issue because just looking to that labor contract's provisions without needing to interpret it in resolving state wage payment violations did not warrant preemption]

(2) Claim Dependent upon Interpreting the Collective Bargaining Agreement

If the discharge claim *requires interpretation of the collective bargaining contract,* or is otherwise *intertwined* with or substantially dependent upon that contract, it ***will be preempted.*** [**Newberry v. Pacific Racing Association,** 854 F.2d 1142 (9th Cir. 1988)—employee's tort claim involved determination of whether discharge was proper under terms of the collective bargaining agreement; *and see* discussion *infra,* p. 29]

(3) Claims Based on Contract or Tort Theory Inextricably Intertwined with the Bargaining Agreement

If a state tort claim is "inextricably intertwined with the terms of the collective bargaining contract," federal interests in uniformity and predictability are paramount and the state law claim will be preempted. [**Allis-Chalmers Corp. v. Lueck,** 471 U.S. 202 (1985)] The Ninth Circuit has also held that wrongful discharge actions in state court are preempted if they are based on a breach of contract or tort theory that is "conceptually allied" with the collective bargaining agreement, but this may be difficult to discern in practice. [*Compare* **Olguin v. Inspiration Consolidated Copper Co.,** 740 F.2d 1468 (9th Cir. 1984), *with* **Garibaldi v. Lucky Food Stores,** 726 F.2d 1367 (9th Cir. 1984)] Also, these Ninth Circuit cases have been questioned as they were decided before *Lueck* which requires preemption only when the state law claim requires interpretation of a collective bargaining agreement to prevail and *Lueck* did not appear to follow a conceptually allied approach. [**Miller v. AT&T Network Sys.,** 850 F.2d 543 (9th Cir. 1988) and **Hyles v. Mensing,** 849 F.2d 1213 (9th Cir. 1988)] "[N]ot every dispute . . . tangentially involving a provision of a collective-bargaining agreement is pre-empted by [Taft-Hartley] § 301." [**Lueck,** *supra*]

(a) Pleading May Be Determinative

Careful pleading in this area may preserve state jurisdiction. For example, when an employee covered by a collective bargaining agreement was discharged for alleged shoplifting and brought a tort claim in state court for conspiracy and outrageous conduct creating emotional distress, the state claim was allowed to stand even though parallel arbitration proceedings were being pursued by the union under the bargaining agreement. [**Albertson's, Inc. v. Carrigan,** 982 F.2d 1478 (10th Cir. 1993)]

3. Exceptions

Despite the broad scope of federal preemption, there are certain exceptions where state law may apply.

a. Judicial Exceptions to Federal Preemption

(1) Matters of Overriding Local Concern

The Supreme Court has carved out an exception to the preemption doctrine to permit state regulation of conduct that "touches interests deeply rooted in local feeling and responsibility." [*See* **Amalgamated Association of Street, Electric Railway & Motor Coach Employees v. Lockridge,** *supra,* p. 24]

(a) Violence in Labor Disputes

This exception has been applied primarily to allow state courts to remedy ***acts of violence or threats thereof*** in labor disputes. State courts may grant injunctions to restrain violence or may award damages against those engaging in such conduct, even though the activities in question would also constitute an unfair labor practice under the NLRA. *Rationale:* The states are the natural guardians of the public against violence, and prevention of violence is a matter of genuine local concern. [**UAW-CIO v. Russell,** 356 U.S. 634 (1958); **UAW v. Wisconsin Employment Relations Board,** 351 U.S. 266 (1956)]

(b) Malicious Defamations in Labor Disputes

Similarly, there is an overriding state interest in preventing "malicious" defamations in labor disputes, thereby permitting local courts to award damages in tort actions based thereon. [**Linn v. United Plant Guard Workers Local 114,** 383 U.S. 53 (1966)]

1) Note

To fall outside the preemption doctrine, however, the defamation must be "malicious" within the standard established in **New York Times Co. v. Sullivan,** 376 U.S. 254 (1964), *i.e.,* uttered with ***deliberate or reckless disregard for the truth***. (*See* Torts Summary.) State courts cannot award damages based on any ***lesser*** showing of malice because federal law sets the limit on free speech in labor disputes, and federal law requires a showing of deliberate or reckless falsity. [**Old Dominion Branch No. 496, National Association of Letter Carriers v. Austin,** 418 U.S. 264 (1974)]

(c) Intentional Infliction of Mental Distress

A state court action by an employee against his union for intentional infliction of mental distress is not preempted by the NLRA—provided that the conduct in question is unrelated to alleged employment discrimination, or particularly abusive tactics of discrimination are involved. [**Farmer v. United Brotherhood of Carpenters & Joiners Local 25,** 430 U.S. 290 (1977)]

1) But Note

A claim of intentionally inflicted emotional distress arising in the context of an ***alleged unfair labor practice*** and the events surrounding the employee's discharge has been held preempted by federal law. [**Viestenz v. Fleming Companies, Inc.,** 681 F.2d 699 (10th Cir. 1982)]

2) And Note

If an employee's claims of emotional distress require ***interpretation of a collective bargaining contract***, such claims are preempted. [**DeCoe v. General Motors Corp.,** 32 F.3d 212 (6th Cir. 1994); **Baker v. Farmers Electric Cooperative,** 34 F.3d 274 (5th Cir. 1994)]

(d) **Unemployment Benefits**

State statutes regulating the availability of unemployment benefits to strikers have also been upheld. [**Ohio Bureau of Employment Services v. Hodory,** 431 U.S. 471 (1977)—state statute disallowing benefits; **New York Telephone Co. v. New York State Department of Labor,** 440 U.S. 519 (1979)—state statute allowing benefits; **Fort Halifax Packing Co. v. Coyne,** 482 U.S. 1 (1987)—state statute providing for severance pay in case of plant closing]

(e) **Arguably Protected Activity Violating State Law**

The NLRA has been held not to preempt state court jurisdiction over an employer's action to enforce state trespass laws against picketing that is both arguably protected and arguably prohibited under federal law. [**Sears, Roebuck & Co. v. San Diego County District Council of Carpenters,** 436 U.S. 180 (1978)]

(f) **Breach of Contract and Misrepresentation Suits by Strike Replacements**

An employer who hires replacements for striking employees and promises them permanent positions can be sued in state court for breach of contract and misrepresentation when the replacements are discharged to allow strikers to return to work. [**Belknap, Inc. v. Hale,** 463 U.S. 491 (1983)] Such employees otherwise would be innocent victims without a remedy, and allowing them to proceed in state court supports a strong state interest without unduly impinging on federal labor policy.

(g) **Distinguish—Tortious Interference with Employment Contract**

However, the Supreme Court has ***refused*** to extend either the "overriding local concern" exception or the "peripheral federal concern" exception (below) to permit the state court claim of a low-level supervisor that the union tortiously interfered with his employment relationship by obtaining his discharge after he refused to join the union. [**Local 926, International Union of Operating Engineers v. Jones,** 460 U.S. 669 (1983); *and see* **Viestenz v. Fleming Companies, Inc.,** *supra,* p. 27]

(2) **Matters of "Peripheral Federal Concern"**

The Supreme Court has also stated that the preemption doctrine does not apply when the matter is of only "peripheral" concern to federal labor policy. [**San Diego Building Trades Council v. Garmon,** *supra,* p. 23]

(a) **"Purely Internal Union Matters"**

Normally, union disputes with its members are regulated by NLRA sections 7 and 8, thus preempting state regulation. However, the Court has recognized that some cases may involve purely internal union affairs, which are of only peripheral concern to national labor policy, in which case, state regulation and adjudication may be proper. [*See* **International Association of Machinists v. Gonzales,** 356 U.S. 617 (1958)—member sued for reinstatement and damages following expulsion from union that allegedly violated union constitution and bylaws; Court upheld state's power to award damages, viewing it as basically a "breach of contract" dispute rather than a matter of employment or labor policy]

1) Caution

The *Gonzales* case has been ***narrowly*** construed in subsequent decisions. [*See* discussion in **Amalgamated Association of Street, Electric Railway & Motor Coach Employees v. Lockridge,** *supra,* p. 24] A recent example of this narrow construction includes a member's state law claim of a breach of contract against a union for breaching the terms of a union constitution. [**Garcia v. Service Emps. Int'l Union,** 993 F.3d 757, 763 (9th Cir. 2021) (finding "§ 301 preempts state law claims based on a union constitution to the extent the constitution is a contract" and "[e]very court of appeals to have addressed the question agrees"). The court in *Garcia* summarily rejected the argument that the later passage of the LMRDA and its saving clauses seeking to preserve state claims and remedies brought by union members seeking to enforce a union constitution had acted to repeal the preemptive force of § 301 by finding; "The LMRDA contains no words repealing § 301 or its preemptive effect." *Garcia*, 993 F.3d at 764]

(3) Matters Where State Regulation Will Promote, Rather than Impede, Federal Labor Policy

The Supreme Court also has disregarded the preemption doctrine where the particular rule of law invoked in state court is so structured that state regulation would promote, rather than interfere with, federal labor policy.

(4) Matters Requiring Uniformity and Predictability of Interpretation—Concurrent Jurisdiction Under Federal Law

As noted previously, where a state tort claim is "inextricably intertwined with the terms of the collective bargaining contract," federal interests in uniformity and predictability are paramount and the state law claim will be preempted. [**Allis-Chalmers Corp. v. Lueck,** *supra,* p. 26] State courts have ***concurrent jurisdiction*** to hear such cases (under Taft-Hartley section 301), but they must apply ***federal law*** in doing so (*see infra,* p. 139).

e.g. **Example—union duty of fair representation:** The failure of a union to represent all of its members fairly is an unfair labor practice under the NLRA (*see infra,* p. 197). However, state courts may hear duty-of-fair-representation suits by union members, applying ***federal substantive law augmented by state remedial law.*** [**Vaca v. Sipes,** 386 U.S. 171 (1967)] (*Note:* The ***federal courts and the NLRB*** share jurisdiction over fair representation suits, regardless of whether they are accompanied by claims against employers or whether they involve issues as to which the Board may have special knowledge. [**Breininger v. Sheet Metal Workers Local 6,** 493 U.S. 67 (1989)])

e.g. **Example—duty to provide safe workplace:** A state law tort claim alleging that the union was negligent and breached its duty to provide an employee with a safe workplace is preempted by federal law when the collective bargaining agreement requires no undue risks for employees. The employee's state claim is not sufficiently independent of the collective bargaining agreement to avoid federal preemption. [**International Brotherhood of Electrical Workers v. Hechler,** 481 U.S. 851 (1987)]

cf. **Compare—individual employment contracts:** When a state court suit involves ***individual*** employment contracts and does not substantially depend upon an interpretation of a collective bargaining agreement, preemption may not occur since such contracts are not inevitably superseded by a subsequent collective agreement. [**Caterpillar, Inc. v. Williams,** 482 U.S. 386 (1987); *and see infra,* p. 100]

b. **Statutory Exceptions**

In addition to the foregoing judicial limitations on preemption, certain exceptions have been ***explicitly*** provided by Congress.

(1) **Damages for Unlawful Strikes or Boycotts**

Under Taft-Hartley section 303, suits to recover damages for certain types of unlawful strikes or boycotts (*infra,* p. 187) may be brought in state court even though the activity is also an unfair labor practice under federal law.

(2) **Action for Breach of Collective Bargaining Contract**

Likewise, Taft-Hartley section 301 permits suit for breach of a collective bargaining agreement in either federal or state court, whether or not the breach of contract claim also constitutes a federal unfair labor practice (*infra,* p. 139).

(3) **If the NLRB Refuses to Exercise Jurisdiction**

Section 14(c) of the 1959 Landrum-Griffin Amendments provides that state courts or state agencies may exercise jurisdiction over activities as to which the NLRB has declined jurisdiction because of an insubstantial effect on commerce.

(4) **State Limitations on Union Security Agreements**

Finally, NLRA section 14(b) provides that the states may prohibit (through "right to work" laws) union security agreements otherwise valid under federal law. These agreements are commonly referred to as "***union shops***" (where employees must join the union within 30 days after securing employment) or "*agency shops*" (where employees must pay dues and initiation fees to the union, but need not join). (*See* discussion *infra,* pp. 209–210.)

(a) **Distinguish—Closed Shop**

The "closed shop," where employees must be union members before they are hired, is *outlawed* under both federal and state law.

4. Preemption May Be Raised at Any Time

Since federal preemption goes to the *power* of a state court to act, it can be raised at any time, even on a renewed motion for judgment as a matter of law (JNOV). [*See* **International Longshoremen's Association v. Davis,** *supra,* p. 24—state law rule requiring claim of federal preemption be pleaded as an affirmative defense or be deemed waived was ***itself*** preempted by federal law]

EXAM TIP GILBERT

Remember that labor law is a ***statutory*** subject—"common sense" reasoning ordinarily will not suffice. ***Always*** try to connect your answers to ***specific*** statutory provisions.

Chapter Two

Establishment of the Collective Bargaining Relationship

CONTENTS	PAGE

Chapter Approach

The establishment of a collective bargaining relationship is an important topic on labor law exams. After describing the structure and procedural framework of the NLRB, this chapter covers the two major steps in a collective bargaining relationship (and the likely subjects of exam questions):

(i) Union organizing, and

(ii) Selecting a bargaining representative through the election process.

In this and all subsequent areas of labor law, it is important to note the Board's decisions and whether or not its reasoning has been accepted by the federal courts on appeal.

1. **Organizing Campaigns**

   The NLRB has changed its mind frequently on some of the basic rules for union organizing campaigns. For your exam, be sure to have current Board rulings in mind, and remember an important distinction: The Board regulates organizing campaigns on both the unfair-labor-practice level ***and*** the elections' "laboratory conditions" level. Thus, you should analyze employer or union behavior ***on each level.*** If the behavior is not serious enough to constitute an unfair labor practice, does it nevertheless "upset laboratory conditions" and thus require a new election? And in any question about an organizing campaign, look closely for the following activities and the special factors noted for each:

   a. ***Attempts to win employee votes through "captive audience" speeches, polling, written propaganda, or conferring economic benefits.***

      Special factors:

      — ***When and where*** any such speech or polling took place.

      — Whether the written propaganda contains ***inflammatory racial or ethnic statements.***

      — Whether the economic benefits in question had been ***regularly scheduled*** prior to the organizing campaign.

   b. ***Union attempts to gain access to the employer's premises for campaigning.***

      Special factors:

      — Whether the premises are ***private or open to the public.***

      — What ***alternative means of communication*** are available to the union.

   c. ***Employer enforcement of "no solicitation" or "no distribution" rules.***

      Special factors:

      — How ***consistently*** such rules have been applied in the past.

      — Whether the employer's business has ***special characteristics*** that would justify more stringent restrictions on solicitation or distribution activities.

      Finally, remember that discrimination against employees because of their union activity rarely is overt, but must be shown by ***circumstantial evidence.***

2. **Election of a Representative**

   In addition to the rules and regulations under which the NLRB conducts an election (which may or may not be raised on the exam), be sure you understand two important matters in this area:

a. How it is decided what group of employees will be allowed to participate in the election (*i.e.*, determination of the ***bargaining unit***); and

b. ***When*** and ***how*** election campaigns can be started.

A. Scope of Statutes Governing Self-Organization

1. Railway Labor Act

As noted previously, the RLA created a National Mediation Board to mediate disputes in the railroad and airline industries. The National Mediation Board is responsible for determining which ***air carriers*** are subject to the RLA. [N.M.B. Case No. R-1706]

a. Distinguish—Rail Carriers

The Interstate Commerce Commission ("I.C.C.") determines whether a particular railroad is subject to the RLA. Findings of the I.C.C. are binding on the National Mediation Board unless overruled by the courts. [N.M.B. Case No. R-276]

b. Distinguish—Employees

Similarly, the I.C.C. rather than the National Mediation Board has jurisdiction to determine whether particular groups of employees are subject to the RLA. [**National Council of Railway Patrolmen's Unions v. Sealy,** 152 F.2d 500 (5th Cir. 1945)]

(1) Nontransportation Employees

Employees may be covered by the RLA even though they are not directly engaged in transportation. [**Virginian Railway v. System Federation No. 40 Railway Employees Department,** 300 U.S. 515 (1937)—shop mechanics]

(2) Employees Outside United States

Employees based in foreign countries usually are ***not*** covered by the Act. [N.M.B. Case No. R-2139]

2. National Labor Relations Act

a. Jurisdiction—in General

The following factors determine whether an employer or employee is covered by the National Labor Relations Act ("NLRA"):

(i) ***Is there a "labor dispute"*** within the meaning of NLRA section 2(9)?

(ii) ***Does the employer's business activity*** fall within the meaning of ***"commerce"*** in NLRA section 2(6)?

(iii) ***Or, does the employer's business activity*** fall within the meaning of ***"affecting commerce"*** in section 2(7)?

(1) "Labor Dispute"

A labor dispute is any controversy concerning the terms, tenure, or conditions of employment, or concerning the association or representation of persons in negotiating, fixing, maintaining, changing, or seeking to arrange terms or conditions of employment. The disputants need ***not*** stand in the relationship of employer and employee. [NLRA § 2(9)]

(a) Note

Generally, a very broad interpretation has been given to what constitutes a labor dispute within the meaning of the NLRA. [**Liner v. Jafco, Inc.,** 375 U.S. 301 (1964)—single picket at job site can be a labor dispute]

(2) "Commerce"

This requirement is met if the employer engages in trade, transportation, or communication among the several states, or between the District of Columbia or any territory of the United States, or between points in the same state but through any other state, territory, etc. [NLRA § 2(6)]

(3) "Affecting Commerce"

The term "affecting commerce" means in commerce, or burdening or obstructing commerce or the free flow of commerce, or leading or tending to lead to a labor dispute burdening or obstructing commerce or the free flow of commerce. [NLRA § 2(7)] In short, the standard for "affecting commerce" is the broad Commerce Clause test. (*See* Constitutional Law Summary.)

APPROACH TO NLRB JURISDICTION

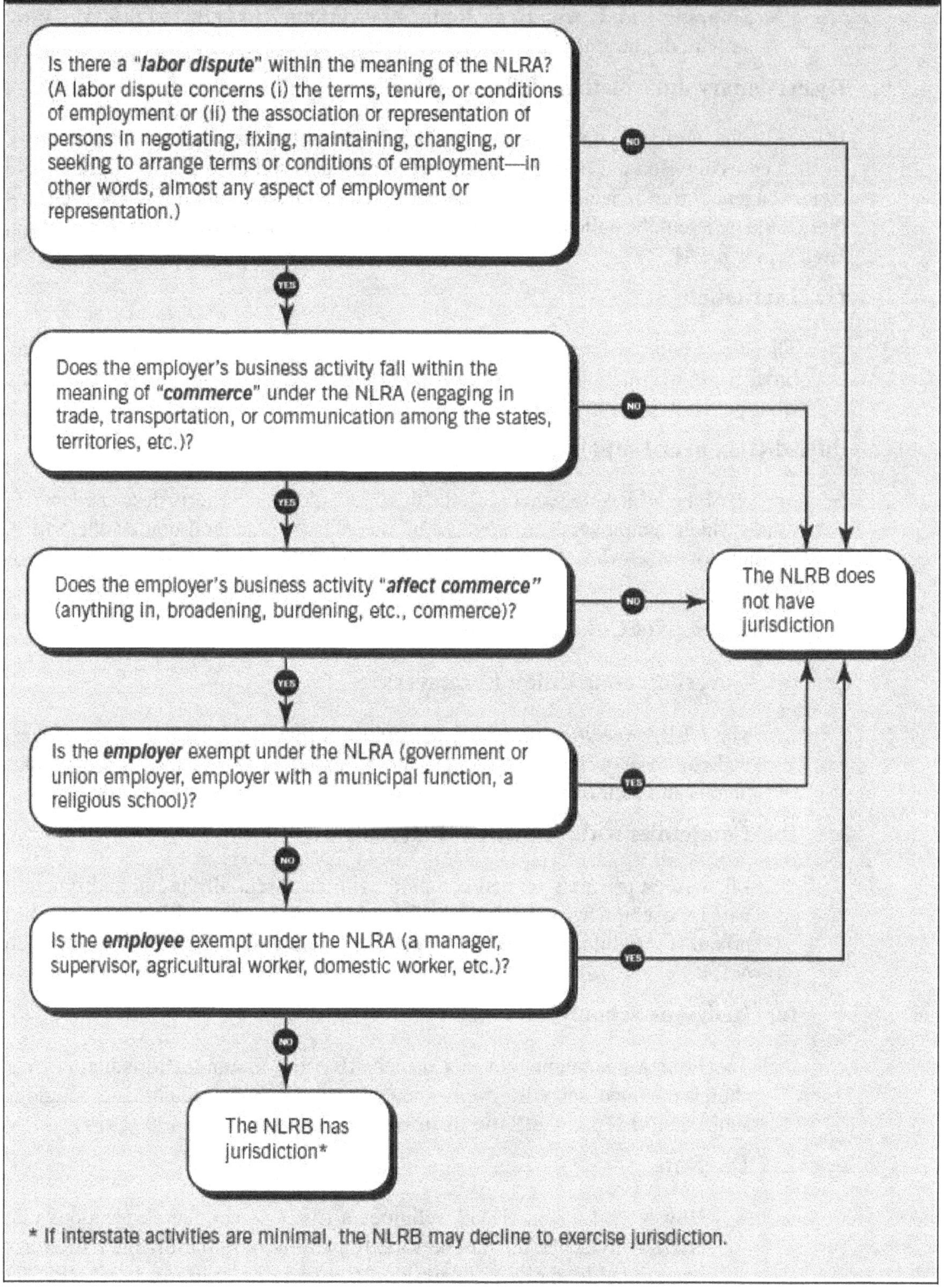

(a) But Note

Picketing a ***foreign*** vessel in an American port has been held ***not*** to be an "activity affecting commerce." Even though the picketing was for the avowed purpose of increasing American wage rates, there was not a sufficient showing that the picketing would in any way ***affect*** interstate commerce. [**Windward Shipping Ltd. v. American Radio Association,** 415 U.S. 104 (1974)—since activity did not "affect" commerce, state injunctive relief was permissible]

b. Discretionary Jurisdiction of the NLRB

If interstate activities are only ***minimal,*** the NLRB may ***decline*** to exercise jurisdiction. In such cases, the Board usually leaves the settlement of disputes to the appropriate state or local agency. But in deciding these cases, the state authority may not reach decisions that would undercut the policies of the NLRA. [**Beasley v. Food Fair of North Carolina, Inc.,** *supra,* p. 24]

(1) Limitation

The 1959 Landrum-Griffin Amendments to the NLRA provide that the NLRB may broaden its jurisdiction ***but may not narrow it*** from the position adopted by the Board in cases prior to 1959.

c. Jurisdiction over Employers

Section 2(2) of the NLRA, together with the three jurisdictional criteria described above, determines which "employers" are covered by the Act. As a general matter, the NLRA applies only to those who act as employers or (directly or indirectly) as agents of employers.

(1) Employers Not Covered by the Act

(a) Government or Union Employers

The NLRA ***specifically excludes*** employers that are federal or state offices, Federal Reserve Banks, employers subject to the Railway Labor Act, and labor unions and their officers and agents (other than when acting as employers).

(b) Companies with Municipal Function

Likewise, a privately owned company with an essentially municipal function will be exempt from the NLRA. Examples include school bus services and private firefighting companies. [*See, e.g.,* **Camptown Bus Lines, Inc.,** 226 N.L.R.B. 4 (1976)]

(c) Religious Schools

The First Amendment prevents the NLRB from assuming jurisdiction over church-operated schools, even when they teach both secular and religious subjects. [**NLRB v. Catholic Bishop of Chicago,** 440 U.S. 490 (1979)]

1) Note

However, if a school with religious affiliations conducts operations that are largely secular and not pervaded by a religious mission, the NLRA has been found to apply. [**Universidad Central de Bayamon v. NLRB,** 793 F.2d 383 (1st Cir. 1985)]

(2) Statutory Inclusion of Health Care Employers

Although health care institutions were ***formerly excluded*** as "employers," this exemption was eliminated by the 1974 Health Care Amendments to the NLRA.

(a) Note

The NLRB (or the "Board") also has asserted jurisdiction over health care institutions operated by religious bodies, based on the legislative history of the 1974 Federal Health Care Amendments. [**MidAmerican Health Services, Inc.,** 247 N.L.R.B. 752 (1980); **Volunteers of America v. NLRB,** 752 F.2d 345 (7th Cir.), *cert. denied,* 472 U.S. 1028 (1985)]

d. Jurisdiction over Employees

The term "employee" [NLRA § 2(3)] is read broadly to include almost everyone within the common meaning of the term. In addition, the NLRA specifically provides that workers do not lose their status as employees when they go on strike or stop working because of an unfair labor practice.

(1) Employees Not Covered by the NLRA

(a) Managers

Persons performing ***managerial functions*** are not considered employees, and thus are ***excluded*** from protection under the NLRA. [**NLRB v. Bell Aerospace Co.,** 416 U.S. 267 (1974)—*all* managerial employees are excluded, not merely those susceptible to conflicts of interest in labor-management relations]

e.g. **Example:** Full-time faculty members of a private university who are shown to have substantial, independent decisionmaking authority on policy and operations issues are excluded from protection. [**NLRB v. Yeshiva University,** 444 U.S. 672 (1980)]

e.g. **Example:** Likewise, employees (*e.g.,* secretaries) who act in a confidential capacity for persons who determine and effectuate management policies in the labor relations field are excluded. [**NLRB v. Hendricks County Rural Electric Corp.,** 454 U.S. 170 (1981)—approving NLRB "labor nexus" test]

(b) Supervisors

Employees who are "supervisors" within the terms of NLRA section 2(11) are not covered by the NLRA. However, the Board and the circuit courts of appeal frequently disagree as to who is an "employee" (covered) and who is a "supervisor" (not covered). Generally, the Board has construed "employees" expansively, while the courts have been more restrictive.

e.g. **Example:** Captains and mates on riverboat casinos have been held to be employees by the NLRB, but supervisors by the Seventh Circuit. [**Empress Casino Joliet Corp. v. NLRB,** 204 F.3d 719 (7th Cir. 2000)]

(c) Nurses Under the NLRA

Whether nurses are employees or supervisors continues to be a subject of controversy.

1) The Supreme Court has held that nurses are supervisors (and excluded from coverage) if they direct other employees—even if their primary duties involve patient care. [**NLRB v. Health Care & Retirement Corp. of America,** 511 U.S. 571 (1994)—a closely divided court reversed NLRB ruling that such nurses were protected "employees"]

2) Although the Board had initially taken the position that the use of "independent judgment" resulting purely from the exercise of "professional or technical" expertise would indicate that a nurse was not a supervisor, the Supreme Court later ruled that the NLRB had no authority to categorically exclude "professional" judgments from those "independent judgments" that would indicate a nurse's supervisory status. [**NLRB v. Kentucky River Community Care, Inc.,** 532 U.S. 706 (2001)]

(d) Specifically Excluded Employees

Certain other workers are specifically excluded by NLRA section 2(3), *i.e.,* agricultural workers, domestics, employees covered by the Railway Labor Act, and independent contractors.

(e) Retired Persons

Similarly, the term "employee" has been limited to "working" persons and does not cover those who have retired. [**Allied Chemical & Alkali Workers, Local No. 1 v. Pittsburgh Plate Glass Co.,** 404 U.S. 157 (1971); *and see infra,* p. 119]

(2) Employees Not Categorically Excluded

(a) Undocumented Immigrant Workers

Immigrants unlawfully working and residing in the United States are "employees" entitled to the protections of the NLRA. [**Sure-Tan, Inc. v. NLRB,** 467 U.S. 883 (1984)] But the Board may not award back pay or reinstate these unauthorized workers even if they are considered employees. [**Hoffman Plastic Compounds, Inc. v. NLRB,** 535 U.S. 137, 151 (2002)]

(b) Hospital House Staff and Some Student Workers

Traditionally, hospital house staff—interns, residents, and clinical fellows—were considered students, rather than employees covered by the NLRA, despite the fact that they received compensation and benefits. [**Physicians House Staff Association v. Fanning,** 642 F.2d 492 (D.C. Cir. 1980), *cert. denied,* 450 U.S. 917 (1981); **Cedars-Sinai Medical Center,** 223 N.L.R.B. 251 (1976)] However, in an important policy change, the NLRB ruled that interns, residents, and fellows at a teaching hospital *are "employees"* under the NLR. [**Boston Medical Center Corp.,** 330 N.L.R.B. 152 (1999)] In *Boston Medical Center,* the NLRB considered such staff personnel to be more like apprentices (who are covered employees) than mere students. Graduate students who act as teaching and research assistants were not employees in 2004. [**Brown University,** 342 N.L.R.B. 483 (2004)] The Board reversed that decision in 2016, [**Columbia University,** 364 N.L.R.B. No. 90 (2016)], and continues to find they are employees. [**Yale University,** 365 N.L.R.B. No. 40 (2017) (approving unit of student assistants)] In March 2021, the Board withdrew its 2019 proposed rule to make students non-employees. The student debate has extended to whether student athletes may be considered employees. [*Compare* **Northwestern University,** 362 N.L.R.B. 1350 (2015) (declining to exercise jurisdiction over a representation petition seeking to represent Northwestern University's college football players as employees) with Statutory Rights of Players at Academic Institutions (Student-Athletes) Under the National Labor Relations

Act, NLRB General Counsel Memorandum 21-08 (Sep. 29, 2021), https://www.nlrb.gov/guidance/memos-research/general-counsel-memos (asserting intention to pursue employee status of student athletes at private universities)]

(c) Job Applicants/Union Organizers

Job applicants, including union organizers who apply for jobs to help organize a nonunion business from the inside (a tactic commonly referred to as "salting"), are considered employees covered by the NLRA. [**NLRB v. Town & Country Electric, Inc.,** 516 U.S. 85 (1995)]

(3) "Employee" vs. "Independent Contractor"

Occasionally it is necessary to distinguish between an employee and an independent contractor, because only "employees" are subject to the NLRA. The distinction usually turns on whether the employer has enough ***management and control*** over the performance of work done by the workers in question that they may be considered "employees."

(a) Comment

The above test grew out of litigation involving newsboys in the Hearst newspaper chain. The NLRB (and the Supreme Court) held that the newsboys were "employees" under the NLRA. [**NLRB v. Hearst Publications, Inc.,** 322 U.S. 111 (1944)] However, Congress legislatively overruled *Hearst* on the ground that the newspaper had no supervision or control over the newsboys once they received their allotments of newspapers and thus they were independent contractors. [*See* **NLRB v. Amber Delivery Services,** 651 F.2d 57 (1st Cir. 1981)] The NLRB has oscillated about the test it will use for independent contractor determinations and will likely continue to wrestle with the best analysis to adopt. [*See* **Supershuttle DFW, Inc.,** 367 N.L.R.B. No. 75 (2019) (criticizing the Board for having previously shifted from a right to control test to overemphasizing ***entrepreneurial opportunity*** for gain or loss) overruling **FedEx Home Delivery,** 361 N.L.R.B. 610 (2014) (considering economic realities and giving weight to actual, not merely theoretical, ***entrepreneurial opportunity*** and any constraints placed on a worker to pursue such opportunities before finding independent contractor status).] On December 27, 2021, the Board invited briefs from the parties and amici to consider whether to continue with the *Supershuttle* standard or return to the *FedEx Home Delivery* standard or adopt some new standard to assess independent contractor status. [**Atlanta Opera, Inc.,** 371 N.L.R.B. No. 45 (2021)] The question of independent contractor status will likely become an increasing issue of importance with the rising "gig economy" where technology platforms use apps to connect certain worker with customers to perform specific tasks. Uber and Lyft drivers represent a key and increasingly debated example of this ongoing issue.

SUMMARY OF "EMPLOYEES" UNDER THE NLRA	
COVERED	NOT COVERED
• Workers on strike • Hospital house staff and graduate students • Job applicants (including union organizers) • Undocumented immigrants	• Supervisors/managerial workers • Workers in confidential portions (*e.g.*, secretaries) • Retirees • Domestics • Independent contractors

3. National Labor Relations Board—Organization and Procedure

The NLRA is administered by the NLRB, the NLRB General Counsel, and numerous field agents of the NLRB and General Counsel. The NLRB is split into separate and independent divisions: The Board itself is the adjudicatory body, while the General Counsel's office handles election cases and litigates unfair labor practice cases.

a. Primary Functions of the Board

The two major functions of the NLRB are (i) ***to determine employee representatives*** within industries under the jurisdiction of the NLRA as "R" or representation petition cases, and (ii) ***to decide*** whether a particular challenged activity constitutes an ***unfair labor practice*** as "C" or complaint cases.

b. Decisionmaking Division

The NLRB is composed of five members, each of whom is appointed by the President (with Senate approval) for a term of five years. Only the President may remove a Board member from office. Removal is permitted only for "malfeasance in office or neglect of duty" and must be preceded by a formal hearing.

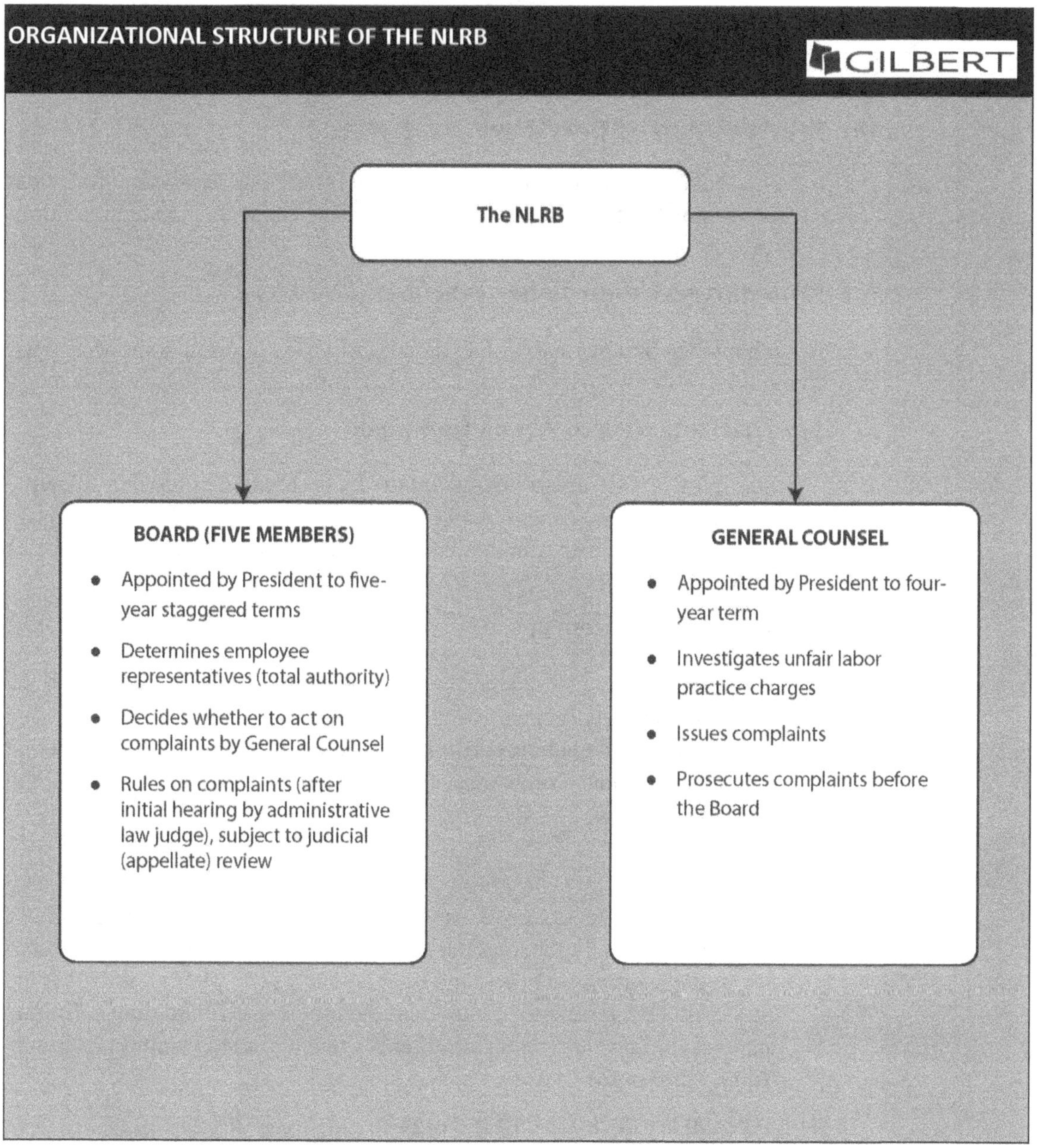

(1) Organization

The Board may sit as a full panel of five, or, in the interest of expediting cases, it may delegate its powers to a panel of three—any two members of which will constitute a majority for decisionmaking purposes. The Board must maintain a three-member Board to have a quorum to operate. [**New Process Steel, L.P. v. NLRB,** 560 U.S. 674 (2010)] The President may not make a recess-appointment to the Board unless the Senate has agreed it is in recess of at least three days. Any Senate recess of at least three days and less than ten days is presumptively too short to allow the President to make a recess appointment to keep the Board at a minimum quorum of three. [**NLRB v. Noel Canning,** 573 U.S. 513 (2014)]

(a) Delegation of Powers Under Landrum-Griffin Act

The Landrum-Griffin Act authorizes the Board to delegate its powers to the ***Regional Directors*** for cases involving union representation and deauthorization elections by the Board (*see* below). In such cases, there may be limited review of the Regional Director's decisions.

(b) Procedures—Representation "R" Cases

In representation cases (*infra,* p. 81), the Board has ***complete and final authority***, much of which is delegated to field personnel under Landrum-Griffin.

(c) Procedures—Unfair Labor Practice "C" Cases

In unfair labor practice cases, NLRB authority is exercised somewhat more formally.

1) Determination to Act on Complaint

The NLRB first determines ***whether*** to proceed to a hearing after the General Counsel has issued a complaint (*see infra*, p. 46). This decision will turn on whether continued prosecution would "effectuate the policies of the [NLRA]."

2) Hearing and Report

An administrative law judge ("ALJ") then holds a hearing—at which the complaining party (generally the employer or union) may intervene—and issues an intermediate report with recommended findings and remedial measures. Ordinary rules of evidence generally apply in conducting the hearing.

3) Effect of Report

If neither party files exceptions to the intermediate report within 20 days, the report typically receives the ***same weight as a decision*** by the Board itself. If ***exceptions are filed***, the Board assumes complete control over the case. After reviewing the record and the report, the Board may substitute its own findings and remedial order for those of the examiner, or it may adopt those of the trial examiner.

4) Appeal from Board's Findings

If either party takes exception to the ***Board's*** findings, that party may take the case to the appropriate federal court of appeals.

(2) Appellate Review and Degree of Proof

Prior to 1947, the NLRB was not required to base its findings on a preponderance of the evidence. In other words, a Board decision would be upheld by the court of appeals if the decision was merely "supported by the evidence." [**NLRB v. Tex-O-Can Flour Mills Co.,** 122 F.2d 433 (5th Cir. 1941)]

(a) Current Standard

The Taft-Hartley Act established more stringent standards for both NLRB findings of fact ***and*** judicial review of Board decisions. Section 10(c) now specifically provides that ***the Board's findings must be based on a "preponderance of the evidence"*** and sections 10(e) and 10(f) provide that appellate courts must uphold decisions by the Board if the decisions are supported by "substantial evidence contained in the record as a whole." [**Universal Camera Corp. v. NLRB,** 340 U.S. 474 (1951); *and see* Administrative Law Summary]

(b) Review of Findings of Law

Findings of law by the NLRB always are reviewable *de novo* on appeal. Despite this rigid standard of review, however, the courts still give Board determinations "great weight." [*See, e.g.,* **Crane Sheet Metal v. NLRB,** 675 F.2d 256 (10th Cir. 1982)]

EXAM TIP GILBERT

On your exam, be sure to remember the different levels of review for findings of fact and findings of law. The Board's ***findings of fact*** must be based on a ***preponderance of the evidence***, and an appellate court must uphold the Board's decision if it is supported by ***substantial evidence*** contained in the record as a whole. ***Findings of law***, however, are reviewable ***de novo*** by the appellate courts (although the courts generally give Board determinations great weight).

(3) Effect of Changing Composition of NLRB

The decisionmaking history of the NLRB is a good one, with the agency administering a complex statute through judgments based on accumulated expertise. During the 85-year history of the Board, many members have had great longevity, serving across several presidential administrations. Nevertheless, Board members ***are*** political appointees, and when enough new appointments fall to a single president, the Board tends to become identified with that particular administration.

c. The General Counsel

The General Counsel is appointed by the President and confirmed by the Senate for a four-year term. If an acting or interim General Counsel is appointed to serve in the position of General Counsel pending Senate approval, any further actions while in the position of interim General Counsel before completing the appointment to the permanent position with the advice and consent of Senate, are prohibited by the Federal Vacancies Reform Act of 1998, [**NLRB v. SW General, Inc.,** 137 S. Ct. 929, 944 (2017)] As a result, once an acting General Counsel is nominated to become the General Counsel, the President must appoint someone else as acting General Counsel or face having any actions taken by the acting General Counsel being reversed as unauthorized.

(1) Scope of Duties

Under NLRA section 3(d), the General Counsel has "final authority, on behalf of the Board, in respect to the investigation of charges and issuance of complaints (regarding unfair labor practices), and in respect to the prosecution of such complaints before the Board . . . and such other duties as the Board may prescribe or as may be provided by law."

(2) Regional Offices

To discharge these duties effectively, the General Counsel's division has several regional offices throughout the country. The General Counsel has engaged in some restructuring of the regional offices over the last ten years. In a December 2012 restructuring, the number of regional offices was reduced from thirty-two to twenty-eight. In July 2013, further restructuring continued and the current listing at the end of fiscal year 2020 included twenty-six regional offices, nine sub-regional offices, and thirteen resident offices. Each regional office is headed by a Regional Director appointed by and responsible to the General Counsel in Washington, D.C.

d. Procedure for Issuing Complaints

A formal complaint is generally issued by the appropriate Regional Director based on charges filed by a party located within that particular region. The General Counsel may issue complaints, but generally does so only in unusual cases.

(1) Appeal to General Counsel

If the Regional Director refuses to issue a complaint, the complainant may appeal to the General Counsel. The General Counsel's decision on such matters ***is final***, and there is ***no further appeal unless the General Counsel acts in excess of statutory authority***. [**Associated Builders, Inc. v. Irving,** 610 F.2d 1221 (4th Cir. 1979), *cert. denied*, 446 U.S. 965 (1980)] Instances of such excess are rare (*e.g.,* clear mistake of law). [*See* **Leedom v. Kyne,** *infra,* p. 96]

(2) NLRB Review

Although the NLRB cannot order the General Counsel to issue a complaint, it may dismiss complaints if it believes that the policies of the NLRA would not be served by prosecution.

(a) Attorneys' Fees Possible

If a respondent in an unfair labor practice proceeding shows that the General Counsel was not substantially justified in filing and pursuing the complaint, a court may award attorneys' fees against the NLRB under the Equal Access to Justice Act. [**Inter-Neighborhood Housing Corp. v. NLRB,** 124 F.3d 115 (2d Cir. 1997); *and see* **Blayblock Electric v. NLRB,** 121 F.3d 1230 (9th Cir. 1997)]

(3) Settlements by General Counsel

The informal settlement of an unfair labor practice charge by the General Counsel after issuance of a complaint but prior to a hearing is considered a prosecutorial, rather than a judicial, determination; therefore, it is not subject to judicial review. [**NLRB v. United Food & Commercial Workers Union, Local 23,** 484 U.S. 112 (1987)]

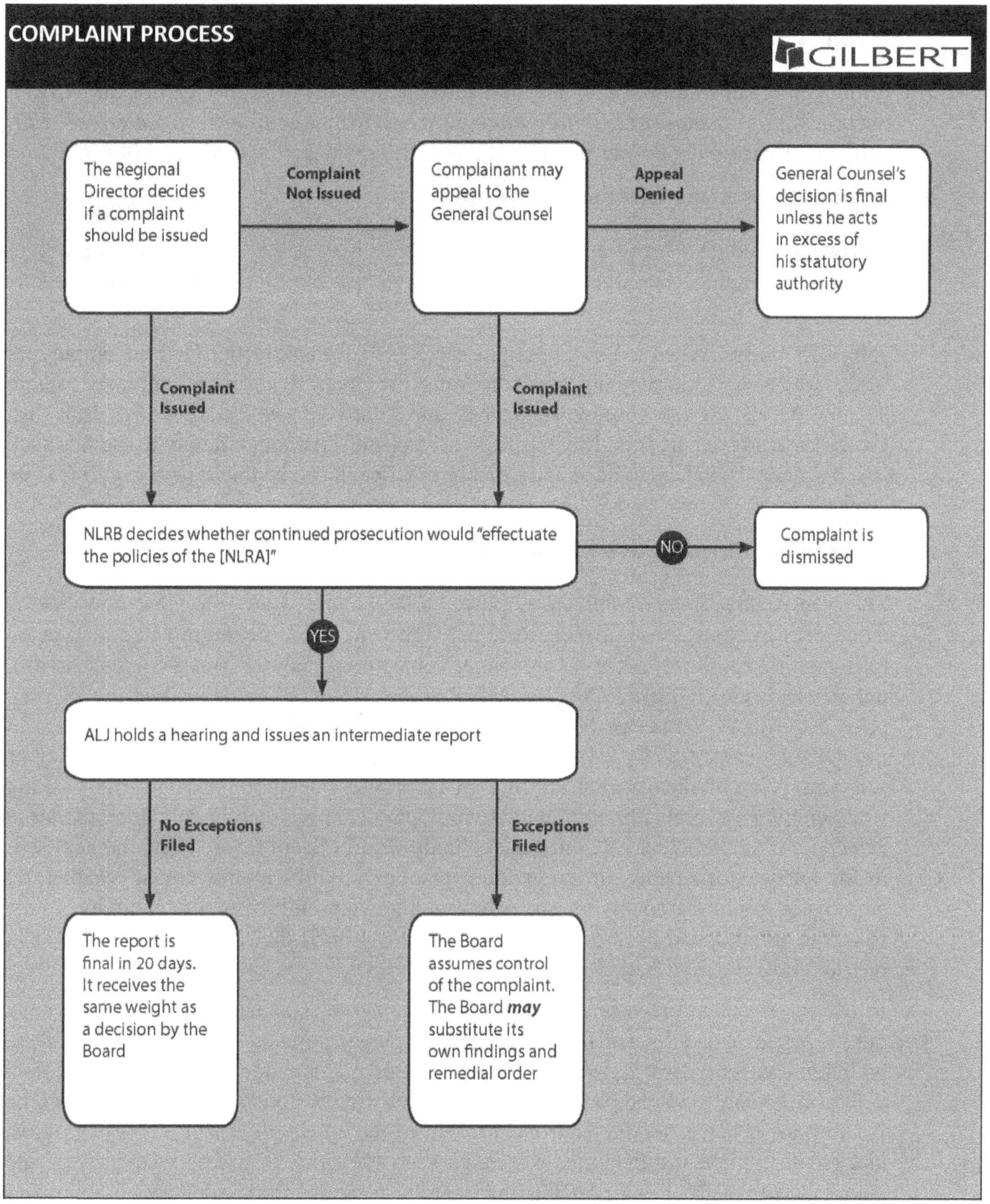

B. Protecting the Right to Self-Organization

1. Protection Against Employer Interference, Restraint, and Coercion—in General

Recognition of the right of employees to band together to form unions, to bargain collectively, and to engage in other concerted activities is the basic purpose of the NLRA. [NLRA § 7; *see supra*, p. 17]

a. Unfair Labor Practice

Employee organizational rights are protected by sections 8(a) and 8(e) of the NLRA. Section 8(a)(1) makes it an ***unfair labor practice*** for an employer "***to interfere with, restrain or coerce employees*** in the exercise of the rights guaranteed in section 7."

b. Conduct Upsetting Election Conditions

Moreover, conduct short of an unfair labor practice may still be enough to set aside an election if it inhibits choice and upsets the required "laboratory conditions" for elections [*infra,* p. 61]

e.g. **Example:** When a union petitions the NLRB for an election and the employees involved in the campaign are numerous, the Board requires the employer to give the union a list of the employees' names and addresses—a so-called *Excelsior* list. [**Excelsior Underwear, Inc.,** 156 N.L.R.B. 1236 (1966)] Although failure to provide such a list has never been held to be an unfair labor practice, it can be the basis for setting aside the election.

c. Not All Employer Activity Prohibited

The NLRA does not prohibit all employer policies and work rules that may coerce employees in the exercise of their section 7 rights. In 2017, the Trump Board reversed longstanding board precedent by agreeing to change its analysis in assessing such work policies and rules. [**Boeing Co.,** 365 N.L.R.B. No. 154 (2017), overruling the Board's prior decision in **Lutheran Heritage Village-Livonia,** 343 N.L.R.B. 646 (2004)] In *Lutheran Heritage*, the Board had identified its analysis when an employer's policy or rule was being challenged for limiting an employee's section 7 right by first asking whether the rule explicitly restricts activities protected by section 7. Under *Lutheran Heritage*, if the policy or rule did not explicitly restrict Section 7 activity, the next step in the analysis of finding an unfair labor practice requires a showing of whether: 1) employees would reasonably construe the language to prohibit Section 7 activity; 2) the rule was promulgated in response to union activity; or 3) the rule has been applied to restrict the exercise of Section 7 rights.

In *Boeing*, the Board reversed the "reasonably construe" standard in Lutheran Heritage out of various concerns that facially neutral employer policies had become difficult to maintain and function when subjected to this standard. The new test from *Boeing* now determines if any potential ban on Section 7 activity in the policy is not explicit, then the Board must balance "(i) the nature and extent of the potential impact on NLRA rights, and (ii) legitimate justifications associated with the rule" to assess whether the rule complies with the NLRA. In *Boeing*, the Board also created three categories of employer provisions that would be considered:

Category 1: This includes rules that the Board designates as lawful to maintain, either because i) the rule, when reasonably interpreted, does not prohibit or interfere with the exercise of NLRA rights; or ii) the potential adverse impact on protected rights is outweighed by the justifications.

Category 2: This includes rules that warrant individualized scrutiny in each case as to whether the rule, when reasonably interpreted, would prohibit or interfere with the exercise of NLRA rights, and if so, whether any adverse impact on the NLRA-protected conduct is outweighed by legitimate justifications.

Category 3: This includes rules that the Board will designate as unlawful to maintain because they would prohibit or limit NLRA-protected conduct, and the adverse impact on NLRA rights is not outweighed by justifications associated with the rule.

The Board clarified the categories it had created in *Boeing* by reclassifying Category 1 into Categories 1(a) and (b) based upon the subheadings previously established. The Board also clarified that its Boeing test starts by determining whether a facially neutral rule, as reasonably interpreted, may interfere with an employee's exercise of NLRA rights. [**LA Specialty,** 368 N.L.R.B. No. 93 (2019)] The Board must consider the rule from the perspective of "an objectively reasonable employee who is 'aware of his legal rights but who also interprets work rules as they apply to the everydayness of his job.' " The General Counsel now has the burden to prove the facially neutral policy would be reasonably interpreted to interfere with an employee's NLRA rights. If the General Counsel fails to meet this burden, the rule or policy is classified under Category 1(a) as a rule, when reasonably interpreted, does not prohibit or interfere with the exercise of NLRA rights.

General Counsel Abruzzo has identified *Boeing* and *LA Specialty* and other decisions involving purported doctrinal shifts that arose during the Trump Board as major considerations for her office. [General Counsel Memorandum, GC 21-04, at 2 (Aug. 12, 2021), https://www.nlrb.gov/guidance/memos-research/general-counsel-memos] Also, on January 6, 2022, the Board invited briefs from the parties and amici to consider a new standard for work rules to address *Boeing* and *LA Specialty*. [**Stericyle, Inc.,** 371 N.L.R.B. No. 48 (2021)] With the current Biden majority on the NLRB, further changes to the analysis of employer policies and work rules may be coming soon.

The NLRA also does not prohibit ***all*** employer activities that may obstruct organizing efforts by employees. The NLRA recognizes that an employer has certain rights, including freedom of speech, on matters affecting the operation of the business. Accordingly, section 8(c) provides that the mere expression of views, argument, or opinion does "not constitute an unfair labor practice . . . if such expression contains no threat of reprisal or force, or promise of benefit."

(1) But Note

Certain types of employer speech may be prohibited even if they do not contain a threat of reprisal or a promise of benefit.

e.g. **Example: *Inflammatory appeals to racial prejudice*** violate section 8(a)(1) and thus are not protected by section 8(c). [**NLRB v. Bush Hog, Inc.,** 405 F.2d 755 (5th Cir. 1968); *and see infra*, p. 62]

2. Employer Actions Affecting Right to Self-Organization

a. Interrogation of Employees

An employer's questioning of employees about union membership or activities, while not unlawful per se, is subject to very close scrutiny. [**NLRB v. Dale Industries, Inc.,** 355 F.2d 851 (6th Cir. 1966)]

(1) "Totality of Circumstances" Approach

Ad hoc or individual interrogation by an employer concerning an employee's union sentiments will be evaluated by the NLRB, considering the "totality of the circumstances." These would include, among other things, the employer's known attitudes about unions, the type of information sought, the rank or position of the interrogator, the time and location of the inquiry, and the nature of the employee's reply. [*See* **Blue Flash Express,** 109 N.L.R.B. 591 (1954); **Rossmore House,** 269 N.L.R.B. 1176 (1984), *enforced sub. nom.* **Hotel Employees Local 11 v. NLRB,** 760 F.2d 1006 (9th Cir. 1985)]

(2) Polling of Employees

An employer's polling of employees is ***unlawful, unless*** the following safeguards are observed:

(i) The purpose of the poll must be ***to determine the validity of a union's claim that it represents a majority*** of the employees;

(ii) The ***employees must be aware*** of this specific purpose;

(iii) ***Assurances against reprisals*** must be given;

(iv) The poll must be conducted by ***secret ballot;*** and

(v) ***The employer must not have engaged in previous unfair labor practices*** or otherwise created a "coercive atmosphere."

[**Struksnes Construction Co.,** 165 N.L.R.B. 1062 (1967)]

(a) Polls After Recognition of Union

Once a union has been recognized, the NLRB requires an employer to have a good-faith, reasonable doubt that the union still has majority support before it can conduct a poll. This is the same standard used for decertification petitions and for withdrawal of recognition (*see infra*, pp. 83, 114). The Supreme Court has approved this unitary approach. [**Allentown Mack Sales & Service v. NLRB,** 522 U.S. 359 (1998)—majority opinion found unitary standard somewhat puzzling and inconsistent, but nevertheless upheld it]

1) Evidence Required to Justify Poll

The NLRB looks closely at the ***objective evidence*** relied on by the employer to question majority support for the union. There must be significant objective evidence to justify the poll. The evidence must be more than assorted employee complaints about the union, although the percentage of the workforce to which the evidence must apply to justify an employer poll remains unclear. [**Wagon Wheel Bowl, Inc.,** 310 N.L.R.B. 915 (1993), *enforced*, 47 F.3d 332 (9th Cir. 1995)]

(b) Polling vs. Interrogation

The Board and the courts must determine when certain employer activity exceeds legitimate campaign tactics and constitutes improper polling or interrogation. This issue concerns photographing or otherwise attempting to identify union sympathizers. (*See infra,* p. 51.)

(3) Polls as Substitute for Election

If the employer and the union agree to be bound by the results of a poll, and the results show that the majority of employees in an appropriate unit favor the union, the employer may be ordered to bargain with the union ***without*** an election (or regardless of the outcome of an election)—*i.e.,* the poll would be considered a ***substitute*** for an election. [**Sullivan Electric Co.,** 199 N.L.R.B. 809 (1972); *and see* discussion *infra,* p. 115]

b. Distribution of Antiunion Campaign Items

An employer who distributes "Vote No" buttons, coffee mugs emblazoned "Vote No," or other such paraphernalia interferes with employee rights. Such activity has been judged to affect the free choice of employees and to be a potentially improper means of identifying which employees support the union. [*See* **Circuit City Stores,** 324 N.L.R.B. 147 (1997); **A.O. Smith Automotive Products Co.,** 315 N.L.R.B. 994 (1994)]

c. Surveillance of Employees

The use of spies or informers (whether concealed or overt) in connection with ***any*** phase of employee rights to self-organization is *prohibited.* [**Excelsior Laundry Co.,** 186 N.L.R.B. 914 (1970), *enforced,* 459 F.2d 1013 (10th Cir. 1972)]

(1) Effect of Surveillance

In such circumstances, a subsequent election lost by the union ***may be set aside.*** [**General Engineering, Inc.,** 131 N.L.R.B. 901 (1961)]

(2) Proof

There must be proof that the employer ***caused or authorized*** the surveillance before it can be found guilty of an unfair labor practice. [*See* **Montgomery Ward & Co. v. NLRB,** 385 F.2d 760 (8th Cir. 1967)]

(3) Videotapes and Photographs

The NLRB has tried to determine when videotaping or photographing employees constitutes an improper infringement on the right to self-organization.

e.g. **Example:** An employer who videotaped peaceful union rallies in support of collective bargaining demands for three months was found guilty of improper surveillance. The Board ruled that such videotaping was not justified by the alleged security concerns of the employer. [**National Steel and Shipbuilding Co.,** 324 N.L.R.B. 499 (1997), *enforced,* 156 F.3d 1268 (D.C. Cir. 1998)]

(a) Indirect Means of Polling

The NLRB also has found some employer videotaping to be an indirect (and improper) means of "polling" employees. Responding to court pleas to provide guidelines for conscientious employers (and unions) to follow in this area [*see* **Allegheny Ludlum Corp. v. NLRB,** 104 F.3d 1354 (D.C. Cir. 1997)], the Board has laid out rules by which an employer may properly solicit employees to participate in a campaign video. [**Allegheny Ludlum Corp.,** 333 N.L.R.B. 734 (2001)]

(b) Distinguish—When Unions Videotape or Photograph

While employer videotaping and photographing has been held improper, the Board has held that it is not improper for a ***union*** to photograph or videotape its organizers distributing literature outside an employer's plant—even though such photographs or film could potentially reveal which employees supported (or did not support) the union. [**Randall Warehouse of Arizona,** 328 N.L.R.B. 1034 (1999)]

d. Restricting Activities on Company-Owned Property—Solicitation and Distribution Rules

The right to organize comes into conflict with an employer's property rights when organizing activity is conducted on company property. Although the Supreme Court has held that an employer must tolerate some inconvenience in this respect to safeguard the employees' section 7 rights [*see* **Republic Aviation Corp. v. NLRB,** 324 U.S. 793 (1945)], the courts and the Board permit the employer to impose certain ***nondiscriminatory*** restrictions on solicitation and distribution of materials during working hours on company premises.

(1) Solicitation by Employees

An employer may ***limit*** prounion solicitation to an employee's ***free time*** (*i.e.,* before or after work, at breaks or mealtime), and may impose this limitation even after the start of a union campaign. [**Whitcraft Houseboat Division,** 195 N.L.R.B. 1046 (1972); **Our Way, Inc.,** 268 N.L.R.B. 394 (1984)—employer rule prohibiting solicitation during an employee's "working time" is permissible]

(a) "Solicitation"

"Solicitation" generally refers to verbal communication, but also includes the handing out of union authorization cards. [**Rose Co.,** 154 N.L.R.B. 228 (1965)] In 2020, the Board discussed prior rulings suggesting that solicitation was limited to asking someone to join a union by signing an authorization card and the Board found a broader definition of solicitation as it "encompasses the act of encouraging employees to vote for or against union representation." [**Wynn Vegas LLC,** 369 N.L.R.B. No. 91 (2020)] Further questions about what is protected solicitation continue to evolve especially as digital communications and social media have become major communication tools with the Board continuing to reverse itself regarding a balance of section 7 rights versus employer property interests when considering e-mail communications. The Board first addressed this issue of email communications in 2007 when it found that a policy prohibiting use of the employer's email system for non-job-related solicitations did not violate the NLRA. [**The Register-Guard,** 351 N.L.R.B. 1110 (2007)] However, in 2014, the Board reversed *Register Guard* and found an employee's section 7 right to use an employer's email system to make protected communications was presumptively permitted during nonworking times. [**Purple Communications, Inc.,** 361 N.L.R.B. 1050 (2014)] The employer could rebut this presumption by showing special circumstances warranting prohibition of nonwork email if needed for production or disciplinary reasons. In 2019, the Board reversed *Purple Communications* and found no employee section 7 right to communicate via an employer's email system because employees may typically communicate face-to-face or by other means. [**Caesar's Entertainment,** 368 N.L.R.B. No. 143 (2019)] The Board found in *Caesar's Entertainment* that an employer's property interest in controlling the use of its email and other information technology prevails unless employees would be deprived of any reasonable means of communicating with each other. Because current NLRB Chair McFerran dissented in *Caesar's Entertainment* and NLRB General Counsel Abruzzo has requested that regional offices seek advice before pursuing cases addressing an employee's right to use email or other electronic platforms as a section 7 right, one should consult the NLRB's website for updates on this issue.

(b) Retail Stores

More stringent rules regarding where an employee may solicit during her free time may be imposed by retail stores, where there is considerable contact with the general public. [**Marshall Field & Co. v. NLRB,** 200 F.2d 375 (7th Cir. 1953)]

(c) Health Care Institutions

The Supreme Court has ruled that Congress did not intend special treatment of health care institutions regarding union solicitation in the 1974 Health Care Amendments to the NLRA. Thus, a hospital cannot bar union distribution or solicitation in public areas (*e.g.,* cafeterias) unless such activity would disrupt health care operations or disturb patients, and the burden is on the hospital to prove that such a disruption or disturbance would exist. [**Beth Israel Hospital v. NLRB,** 434 U.S. 1033 (1978)]

1) But Note

A hospital can prohibit solicitation in corridors and sitting rooms on floors housing patient or operating rooms, since it could adversely affect the recovery of patients. [**NLRB v. Baptist Hospital, Inc.,** 442 U.S. 773 (1979)]

(d) Off-Duty Employees

A rule ***barring*** off-duty employees from soliciting on company premises may be upheld, as long as the rule is ***nondiscriminatory*** (*i.e.,* designed to prevent access by off-duty employees for any reason). [**GTE Lenkurt, Inc.,** 204 N.L.R.B. 921 (1973), *overruled on other grounds*, **Resistance Technology, Inc.,** 280 N.L.R.B. 1004 (1986)]

1) Limitations

The NLRB has construed *GTE* narrowly to prevent undue interference with an employee's statutory right to communicate with those who work on different shifts. Thus, for example, an employer's rule denying off-duty employees entry to parking lots, gates, and other outside nonworking areas has been held invalid. [**Tri-County Medical Center, Inc.,** 222 N.L.R.B. 1089 (1976)]

(2) Distribution by Employees

Distribution of written materials may be limited ***both*** to the ***nonworking time*** of employees ***and to nonworking areas*** (*i.e.,* exits, restrooms, cafeterias, parking lots, etc.). [**NLRB v. Walton Manufacturing Co.,** 289 F.2d 177 (5th Cir. 1961)]

(a) Discrimination Against Union Literature

The limitation must not discriminate against distribution of union literature. If ***other*** types of distribution (or solicitation) are permitted in such areas (or times), the limitation would be an unfair labor practice. [**Mason & Hanger-Silas Mason Co.,** 167 N.L.R.B. 894 (1967)]

(b) No Waiver of Right by Union

The Supreme Court has held that a union cannot waive by a contract provision the ***employee's*** right to distribute literature during nonworking time. [**NLRB v. Magnavox Co.,** 415 U.S. 322 (1974)]

(c) Distribution Outside Employer's Place of Business

The NLRB has upheld an employee's distribution of union leaflets to co-workers at a ***customer's*** facility, given that the employee worked regularly and exclusively at that facility and the distribution occurred during nonworking time and in a nonworking area. [**Southern Services,** 300 N.L.R.B. 1154 (1990)]

(3) Solicitation or Distribution by Nonemployees

An employer may ***prohibit*** solicitation or distribution by ***nonemployee*** organizers ***anywhere*** on company property, ***provided the union has other reasonable means of communicating with employees.*** [**NLRB v. Babcock & Wilcox Co.,** 351 U.S. 105 (1956)]

(a) Initial NLRB Approaches

During the period between the Supreme Court decision in *Babcock & Wilcox* and its 1992 opinion in Lechmere (*infra*, p. 54), the NLRB approach to nonemployee solicitation and distribution changed several times.

1) "Alternative Means Available"

At first, the Board tended to find that alternative means were available to organizers, thereby justifying a complete bar by employers of nonemployee activity. For example, a refusal to allow handbilling in a company parking lot was upheld by the Board, even though the union had been unsuccessful in its other attempts to reach employees (telephoning, etc.). [**Dexter Thread Mills, Inc.,** 199 N.L.R.B. 543 (1972)]

2) "Balancing Test"

After some intermediate revisions to this view [*see, e.g.,* **Fairmont Hotel Co.,** 282 N.L.R.B. 139 (1986)], the NLRB settled on an approach that would analyze the propriety of nonemployee activity on the employer's property by balancing the section 7 rights of employees against the property rights of the employer. [**Jean Country,** 291 N.L.R.B. 11 (1988)]

(b) Supreme Court Clarification—*Lechmere*

Reading the Board decision in *Jean Country* as an attempt to balance employee section 7 rights against employer property rights in deciding *all* nonemployee access cases, the Supreme Court ***disapproved*** this approach as an incorrect interpretation of its decision in *Babcock & Wilcox, supra.* The Court held that such a balancing test was appropriate ***only*** if nonemployee organizers had no reasonable access to employees other than on company property—usually just those rare instances in which the employees work in geographically remote or inaccessible locations. [**Lechmere, Inc. v. NLRB,** 502 U.S. 527 (1992)]

1) Limits Imposed by State Law

In a case after *Lechmere*, the Supreme Court observed that "the right of employers to exclude union organizers from their private property emanates from state common law, and while this right is not superseded by the NLRA, [likewise] nothing in the NLRA expressly protects it." [**Thunder Basin Coal Co. v. Reich,** 510 U.S. 200 (1994)] Thus, for example, broad rights of free speech protected by the California State Constitution could override the right of a private property owner to exclude nonemployee union representatives from picketing on store property—and *Lechmere* would not apply under those circumstances. [**NLRB v. Calkins,** 187 F.3d 1080 (9th Cir. 1999)] *But see* [**Cedar Point Nursery v. Hassid,** 141 S. Ct. 891 (2021)] (finding that a California law requiring union access to employees on private property violated the Fifth Amendment of the Constitution's Takings Clause).

EXAM TIP GILBERT

If an exam question involves distribution of union material, be sure to remember that there are competing rights: An ***employer*** has the right to restrict solicitation and distribution of prounion material to off-duty time and nonworking areas. However, an ***employee*** has a statutory right to communicate with other employees on different shifts. Therefore, an employee may have the right to off-duty access to outside nonworking areas. Note that the analysis is different for ***nonemployee*** union organizers. They have a right to come on company property only if they do not have reasonable access to employees other than on company property, and even in this case you must ***balance*** the employee's section 7 rights against the employer's state-law property rights.

And remember that a shopping center is a whole different ball game, as discussed below.

(4) Union Organizing on Other Private Property—"Shopping Center" Limitations

Attempts to restrict or prohibit solicitation in private shopping centers of substantial size and of a quasi-public nature may raise constitutional free speech issues.

(a) Former Rule—*Logan Valley*

In *Logan Valley*, the Supreme Court held that union free speech rights prevailed over the rights of property owners to control use of their property (*i.e.*, by prohibiting solicitation and distribution) where the walks, streets, and parking areas of a large shopping center had been "***dedicated to a public use***" similar to those of a normal city block. [**Amalgamated Food Employees Union, Local 590 v. Logan Valley Plaza, Inc.,** 391 U.S. 308 (1968)]

(b) Limitation—*Central Hardware Co.*

However, in *Central Hardware* Co. the Court limited such free speech rights ***solely*** to situations in which the private property had taken on the ***attributes of public property***. In *Central Hardware Co.*, rules prohibiting union solicitation and picketing in the parking lots of a large hardware store were upheld by the Court, which ruled that the mere fact of being "open to the public" did not bring the lots within the "shopping center" standards of *Logan Valley*. [**Central Hardware Co. v. NLRB,** 407 U.S. 539 (1972)]

1) "Alternative Means" Test

In *Central Hardware Co.* the Court specifically referred to the "alternative means" test for solicitation by nonemployees as governing the right to limit or prohibit solicitation [*see* **NLRB v. Babcock & Wilcox Co.,** *supra*, p. 54]; and the NLRB subsequently applied that test to solicitation ***near*** retail stores [*see* **Dexter Thread Mills, Inc.,** *supra*, p. 54]. The holdings were reinforced by the Supreme Court's decision in *Lechmere, supra.*

(c) Present View—*Logan Valley* Overruled

In 1976, the Supreme Court extended its criteria in *Central Hardware Co.* to shopping centers and overruled *Logan Valley.* [**Hudgens v. NLRB,** 424 U.S. 507 (1976)] In *Hudgens*, the Court held that, short of a "company town" situation, there was ***no constitutional right*** to enter on private property to engage in speech.

1) Statutory Right

The Court did recognize that employees might have a ***statutory*** right to picket at shopping centers (under NLRA section 7), provided they could satisfy the "***alternative means***" test set out in *Central Hardware Co., Babcock & Wilcox*, and *Lechmere.*

2) Scope of Restrictions Permitted

The NLRB has ruled that *Lechmere* precludes picketing and distribution of handbills by nonemployee union members even if the union is seeking to communicate with the public rather than trying to organize workers. [**Leslie Homes, Inc.,** 316 N.L.R.B. 123 (1995); **Makro, Inc. and Renaissance Properties Co.,** 316 N.L.R.B. 109 (1995)—both dealing with area-standards picketing (*see infra,* p. 170)] And the Sixth Circuit has applied *Lechmere* to uphold the right of an employer to eject nonemployee organizers from its public cafeteria. [**Oakwood Hospital v. NLRB,** 983 F.2d 698 (6th Cir. 1993)]

a) But Note

The Board also has required employers to administer "no solicitation" policies evenhandedly, so that nonemployee ***union*** members cannot be excluded from a retail outlet in a shopping plaza if nonemployee solicitation or distribution is allowed for other purposes. [**Riesbeck Food Markets, Inc.,** 315 N.L.R.B. 940 (1994)] The circuit courts of appeal are divided on this issue.

e. Employer Free Speech as Interference with Union Organization

An employer has a right of free speech under the First Amendment, and this right has been explicitly codified in NLRA section 8(c).

(1) Application of "Free Speech" Rules

Since an employer has considerable economic power over employees, its statements may influence employee conduct far more than statements outside the employer-employee relationship. This is important in determining whether an employer's communication with employees is legitimate "free speech" or an unfair labor practice. [**NLRB v. Gissel Packing Co.,** 395 U.S. 575 (1969)]

(a) Coercive Statements Not Protected

There is no "free speech" protection for ***threats*** of reprisal or force against employees exercising their rights to self-organization, or for a ***promise of benefits*** to those who do not exercise those rights.

EXAM TIP GILBERT

In dealing with an employer's right to free speech, you must consider whether the statement contains a ***threat of reprisal*** or a ***promise of benefit.*** If the statement contains a threat or promise, it is said to be ***coercive*** and may form the basis for setting aside an election and an unfair labor practice violation. Be sure to consider the circumstances in which the statement was made—an otherwise neutral statement may become coercive depending on the circumstances. For example, predictions of dire economic consequences must be founded on objective facts and be shown to be beyond the employer's control.

1) Employer's Assertion of Legal Rights

Coercion may be found whether the threats or promises are express or implied. But if the employer merely asserts how it legally intends to deal with the union, this has been held ***not*** to constitute coercion. [*See* **NLRB v. Herman Wilson Lumber Co.,** 355 F.2d 426 (8th Cir. 1966)—"I intend to deal hard with the Union" and "you may be replaced if you strike" held not impliedly coercive]

2) Employer's Prediction of Adverse Consequences

An employer's statements predicting adverse economic consequences from unionization may be held coercive if such predictions are based on factors over which the employer has control or that will result from the employer's own volition. On the other hand, predictions that are ***reasonably*** based on ***objective facts*** over which the ***employer has no control*** will be protected as employer "free speech." [**NLRB v. Gissel Packing Co.,** *supra,* p. 56]

e.g. **Example:** Under this standard, an employer's statements charging that the union was dominated by "strike-happy hoodlums" who would make impossible demands on the company and force it out of business were held not based on objective facts and hence coercive. [**NLRB v. Gissel Packing Co.,** *supra*]

cf. **Compare:** However, an employer's ***factual*** account of labor strife (including bombings, shootings, and the like) was protected where the employer also emphasized a willingness to bargain if the union won an election. [**Louisburg Sportswear Co. v. NLRB,** 462 F.2d 380 (4th Cir. 1972)]

e.g. **Example:** A prediction that the union would make certain demands on the employer that he would be forced to grant, at the cost of impairing existing employee benefits, has been held protected speech, where it is shown to be drawn from previous dealings with other unions in the same plant and thus based on objective facts. [**NLRB v. Lenkurt Electric Co.,** 438 F.2d 1102 (9th Cir. 1971)]

e.g. **Example:** Likewise, an employer's statement that it would "bargain from scratch" ("they [employees] would be guaranteed minimum wages and workers' comp[ensation] and that's where our collective bargaining process would begin") has been held to be noncoercive and indicative of an appropriate "give and take" attitude on the part of the employer. [**Shaw's Supermarkets v. NLRB,** 884 F.2d 34 (1st Cir. 1989)]

a) Plant Closings

In *Gissel Packing Co., supra,* the Court stated that an employer's prediction, even though sincere, that unionization "will or may" result in ***closing the plant*** (*i.e.,* as a result of union demands) is coercive, ***unless*** the likelihood of closing was ***capable of objective proof.***

1/ Distinguish—Absolute Right to Close

At the same time, the Court recognized that ***an employer has the absolute right to go out of business for any reason—including antiunion hostility.*** [**Textile Workers Union v. Darlington Manufacturing Co.,** 380 U.S. 263 (1965); *and see* discussion of partial vs. total closings, *infra,* p. 74]

2/ Distinguish—Statements Based on Objective Facts or on Decision Already Made

Reciting a history of closing stores for "economic" reasons after successful union organizing, or predicting layoffs and plant closings as a result of unionization, has been upheld as protected free speech by employers—as long as such statements are based on objective facts beyond the employer's control or reflect a decision already made to close down in the event of unionization. [**Crown Cork & Seal Co. v. NLRB,** 36 F.3d 1130 (D.C. Cir. 1994); **J.J. Newberry Co.,** 202 N.L.R.B. 420 (1973)]

(b) "Coerciveness" Determined by Context in Which Speech Is Made

Statements that ***on their face*** contain neither threats of reprisal nor promises of benefit may still be found coercive because of the context in which they are uttered. [**NLRB v. Virginia Electric & Power Co.,** 314 U.S. 469 (1941); *and see* **NLRB v. Pentre Electric,** 998 F.2d 363 (6th Cir. 1993)—comprehensive discussion of this issue]

e.g. **Example:** An employer's "suggestions" or "preferences" may be coercive if the employees, from prior experience, know the consequences of incurring the employer's strong displeasure. [**International Association of Machinists, Lodge 35 v. NLRB,** 311 U.S. 72 (1940)]

1) Approach

Former NLRB Chairman Miller suggested a helpful, three-question approach to assess the coerciveness of employer statements:

(i) What actions were threatened;

(ii) Were the threats, under all the circumstances, likely to be taken seriously; and

(iii) How widely were the threats disseminated?

As to the second question, the source, deliberateness, and generality of the threats would be important considerations. [**General Stencils, Inc.,** 195 N.L.R.B. 1109 (1972)]

(c) Noncoercive Speech Cannot Be Used as Evidence of Other Employer Violations

Statements that are protected under the free speech provisions of section 8(c) ***cannot*** be used as evidence of some other unfair labor practice by the employer (such as bad motives or antiunion bias). [**Pittsburgh S.S. Co. v. NLRB,** 180 F.2d 731 (6th Cir. 1950)]

(d) Noncoercive Speech Not Subject to State Defamation Laws

Federal labor laws preempt state defamation laws to the extent that the speech is protected under the NLRA. Hence, defamatory falsehoods stated by an employer in connection with union organizing activities are ***not actionable*** as defamation under state law—at least where the statements are not coercive and were made ***without knowledge of their falsity or reckless disregard of the truth***. [*See* **Linn v. United Plant Guard Workers, Local 114,** *supra,* p. 27]

1) But Note

An action under state tort law for ***intentional infliction of emotional distress*** might be possible in this situation [*see supra,* p. 27].

(e) "Captive Audiences"

An employer may give antiunion speeches to employees ***on company time and property*** (*i.e.*, to a "captive audience"), as long as the speech itself is not coercive. This is true even if the employer refuses to give the union an equal opportunity to reply on company property during work hours. [**NLRB v. United Steelworkers of America,** 357 U.S. 357 (1958)]

1) Rationale

An employer is entitled to use his property as a forum to express his own views and to address his employees during work hours, without sharing that forum with union organizers. [**Livingston Shirt Corp.,** 107 N.L.R.B. 400 (1953)]

2) Possible Limitation

The NLRB has warned employers that this rule may be changed if experience shows that it results in a lack of reasonably equal communications opportunities for the union. In that situation, the union would be given facilities necessary to respond to the employer's statements, such as bulletin boards, parking lot platforms, and the like. [**Livingston Shirt Corp.,** *supra; and see* **General Industries Electronics Co.,** 163 N.L.R.B. 38 (1967)] To date, however, no such inequality has been found by the Board.

(2) Ban on Speeches Within Twenty-Four Hours of Election

The NLRB has imposed a 24-hour cooling-off period before a representation election. During this period, the free speech privilege for ***both the employer and the union*** is curtailed. "Captive audience" speeches are forbidden, and violation of this provision is sufficient to set aside the election. [**Peerless Plywood Co.,** 107 N.L.R.B. 427 (1953); *and see* **Industrial Acoustics Co. v. NLRB,** 912 F.2d 717 (4th Cir. 1990)—union could not use a sound car outside employer's plant two days before certification election; **Bro-tech Corp.,** 330 N.L.R.B. 37 (1999)—union sound truck could not play tape-recorded music (including prounion songs) for 9½ hours on day of election]

(a) Exceptions

The 24-hour ban does not apply to:

(i) ***Employer speeches if employee attendance is voluntary and on the employee's own time***; or

(ii) ***The dissemination of campaign literature or other legitimate propaganda*** (*e.g.,* noncoercive radio messages within the 24-hour period).

[**Peerless Plywood Co.,** *supra*]

(b) And Note

The NLRB has also ruled that brief statements by a plant manager to ***individual employees at their work stations,*** advocating a vote against the union, are permissible even on the morning of the election.

EXAM TIP GILBERT

On your exam, be sure to remember that generally the free speech privilege is limited within the ***24 hours before an election.*** At that time, "captive audience" speeches are forbidden. However, employers can still make speeches as long as attendance is ***voluntary and on the employee's own time.*** They may even briefly talk to individual employees at their work stations. Moreover, campaign literature and other legitimate propaganda can be disseminated.

---

(3) "Eleventh Hour" Statements

For many years, the NLRB held that statements in ***any*** form made so late in the campaign that the other party had inadequate opportunity to reply would be viewed much more critically than those made earlier. If the "eleventh hour" statements contained ***factual misrepresentations***, the election would probably be set aside. [**Hollywood Ceramics Co.,** 140 N.L.R.B. 221 (1962)]

(a) Subsequent Shifts in Board Policy

The *Hollywood Ceramics* doctrine was overruled by the NLRB in **Shopping Kart Food Market, Inc.,** 228 N.L.R.B. 1311 (1977). One year later, the Board had second thoughts and revived *Hollywood Ceramics*, overruling *Shopping* Kart. [**General Knit of California, Inc.,** 239 N.L.R.B. 619 (1978)] Four years after that, the NLRB reversed itself again, overruling *General Knit* (and *Hollywood Ceramics* a second time) and reviving *Shopping Kart.* [**Midland National Insurance Co.,** 263 N.L.R.B. 127 (1982)]

(b) Current NLRB Position

At present, the Board will ***not*** set aside elections on the basis of misrepresentations of fact or law contained in last-minute campaign statements. [**Furr's, Inc.,** 265 N.L.R.B. 1300 (1982); **Riveredge Hospital,** 251 N.L.R.B. 196 (1980)] More specifically, in *Midland* the Board held that it was "returning to the sound principles espoused in Shopping Kart" to "also insure the certainty and finality of election results, and minimize unwarranted and dilatory claims attacking those results." From *Midland*, elections would not be set aside for misrepresentations unless they involved "a substantial departure from the truth, at a time which prevents the other party . . . from making an effective reply, so that the misrepresentation, whether deliberate or not, may reasonably be expected to have a significant impact on the election." The Board stated: "we rule today that we will no longer probe into the truth or falsity of the parties' campaign statements, and that we will not set elections aside on the basis of misleading campaign statements. We will, however, intervene in cases where a party has used forged documents which render the voters unable to recognize propaganda for what it is." [**Midland,** *supra*]

(4) Propaganda Otherwise Interfering with Elections

Although it is not NLRB policy to police or censor ***noncoercive*** preelection statements—even if the statements are exaggerated, inaccurate, or false—the Board ***will*** set aside an election if employer or union propaganda has so compromised the standards of campaigning that employees cannot be said to have made an uninhibited choice. ***The test*** is whether such propaganda has ***upset the "laboratory conditions" under which elections are to be conducted.*** [***In re*** **General Shoe Corp.,** 77 N.L.R.B. 124 (1948)]

(a) Antiunion Propaganda

The mere release of antiunion literature that contains false statements is not in itself an unfair labor practice, because employees are presumed capable of evaluating the employer's statements as campaign propaganda and are not necessarily misled thereby. [*See, e.g.,* **St. Margaret Memorial Hospital v. NLRB,** 991 F.2d 1146 (3d Cir. 1993)]

(b) Limitation

The more flagrant the misstatements and the more limited the union's opportunity to rebut them, the more likely it is that the NLRB will set aside the election results. [**Dal-Tex Optical Co.,** 137 N.L.R.B. 1782 (1962)]

e.g. **Example:** An employer's use of an outdated and misleading NLRB publication on the reemployment rights of strikers constituted grounds for setting aside an election. [**Thiokol Chemical Corp.,** 202 N.L.R.B. 434 (1973)]

e.g. **Example:** An employer was found to have interfered with the free selection of a bargaining representative by showing, on the eve of the election, a motion picture that falsely implied violence by union strikers. [**Industrial Steel Products Co.,** 143 N.L.R.B. 336 (1963)]

(c) Injection of Racial Prejudice

The Board has held that the employer's injection of ***racial prejudice*** into the election campaign by ***inflammatory methods*** required a new election, even though the employer's statements were not otherwise coercive, because this upset the required ***"laboratory conditions."*** [**Sewell Manufacturing Co.,** 138 N.L.R.B. 66 (1962)]

(d) Caution

The validity of the cases above may be open to some question, given subsequent Board decisions that indicate a more "laissez faire" attitude toward election propaganda. [*See* **DID Building Services v. NLRB,** 915 F.2d 490 (9th Cir. 1990)—religious and ethnic slurs made by worker against employer not sufficient to invalidate election; **NLRB v. Flambeau Airmold Corp,** 178 F.3d 705 (4th Cir. 1999)—racially inflammatory rumor by third party circulated one day before election would not invalidate election, given the source of the rumor was unclear and not so severe as to make "a reasoned basis for choice. . .impossible"; *but compare* **Zartic, Inc.,** 315 N.L.R.B. 495 (1994)—inflammatory appeal to Hispanic employees through use of leaflets falsely associating the employer with the Ku Klux Klan invalidated election]

EXAM TIP GILBERT

On an exam, review the employer's speech carefully to look for a ***threat of reprisal*** or a ***promise of benefit.*** If you find such coercive speech, note that the election may be set aside and unfair labor practices violations may be found. If you ***don't find coercive speech,*** continue your analysis to consider whether the speech has ***upset the requisite laboratory conditions,*** which can also overturn the election results.

---

f. Changing Employee Benefits to Influence Election

During a union organizing campaign, the employer must conduct "business as usual" with respect to existing personnel policies and practices. Failure to do so is likely to be an unfair labor practice, especially where new steps are undertaken for the purpose of influencing the campaign. [**NLRB v. Exchange Parts Co.,** 375 U.S. 405 (1964)]

(1) Conferring Economic Benefits

An employer may not confer economic benefits, such as additional paid holidays and vacation time or higher overtime pay, shortly before an election. Such conduct is an unfair labor practice in and of itself, despite the fact that such benefits are "permanent and unconditional." [**NLRB v. Exchange Parts Co.,** *supra*]

(a) Rationale

In *Exchange Parts,* the Court reasoned that benefits motivated by the threat of unionization were likely to be ephemeral and of little real value to employees, and would be interpreted by employees as a reminder that the employer controlled the employees' economic purse strings—*i.e.,* the proverbial iron fist in the velvet glove. Academics and judges have questioned this rationale, suggesting that employee free choice may not really be adversely affected. [*See, e.g.,* **Skyline Distributors v. NLRB,** 99 F.3d 403 (D.C. Cir. 1996)] Until a change by the Supreme Court, however, the rule continues to apply.

(2) Withholding General Wage Increase

An employer may not withhold a general wage increase customary at a specified time each year because his employees have elected to seek union representation. [**Pacific Southwest Airlines,** 201 N.L.R.B. 647 (1973)]

(a) Distinguish—Promotions

In **The Singer Company, Climate Control Division,** 198 N.L.R.B. 870 (1972), the NLRB held that the withholding of employee promotions during the period before a representation election was ***not*** coercive, even though such promotions "probably would have been granted" but for the union campaign. The Board distinguished this case on the ground that promotions by the employer ***had not previously been made on any regular or periodic basis,*** and that the employer had made no formal announcement concerning promotions.

(b) And Note—Benefits

An employer may be permitted under section 8(c) to announce during a campaign (in order to influence the election) benefits that would take effect later, as long as the benefits were planned or in motion before the campaign began. [*See* **Raleys, Inc. v. NLRB,** 703 F.2d 410 (9th Cir. 1983); **NLRB v. Tommy's Spanish Foods, Inc.,** 463 F.2d 116 (9th Cir. 1972)]

3. Protection Against Union Restraint or Coercion

Section 8(b) of the NLRA also prohibits the ***union*** from coercing employees in the exercise of their right to organize or engage in concerted activities.

a. Distinguish—Section 8(a)

Section 8(b) is similar to section 8(a), which prohibits employer interference, restraint, or coercion. The only difference is that section 8(a) includes the term "***interference***" in describing the type of activity prohibited to an employer, whereas section 8(b)(1)(A) does not include that term in proscribing union activity.

(1) Impact

This difference was recognized in **NLRB v. Drivers, Chauffeurs, Helpers, Local 639,** 362 U.S. 274 (1960), in which the Supreme Court declared that section 8(b)(1)(A) granted the Board only ***limited*** authority to proceed against union tactics involving violence, intimidation and reprisal, or threats. Thus, regarding organizing activities, the union has greater latitude than employers. [*See, e.g.,* **Kusan Manufacturing Co. v. NLRB,** 749 F.2d 362 (6th Cir. 1985)—preelection polling by a union is not inherently coercive; *but compare supra,* p. 50]

(2) Power over Membership Status

The union has even greater power over ***union membership status*** once organization is attained. (*See* discussion *infra,* pp. 208 *et seq.*)

(3) But Note—"Laboratory Conditions" Test Regarding Elections

Unions are subject to the same "laboratory conditions" test as employers with respect to election propaganda or other vote-getting activities. (*See supra,* p. 61.) Thus, even if union behavior is not severe enough to constitute an unfair labor practice under section 8(b), it can invalidate an election if it is found to upset the requisite laboratory conditions for that election.

Example: Distribution by the union of what appeared to be, but was not, an official NLRB document was held likely to mislead Spanish-speaking employees in the bargaining unit and hence invalidated a subsequent election in the unit. [**SDC Investment,** 274 N.L.R.B. 556 (1985)]

b. Union Coercion and Free Speech

The guarantees and restrictions that apply to employer speech also apply to the union. [**NLRB v. Triplex Manufacturing Co.,** 701 F.2d 703 (7th Cir. 1983)—inflammatory racial or ethnic slurs made during election campaign stated prima facie case for overturning an election]

(1) Union Expressions of Opinion Protected

Union announcements or publications that are merely expressions of opinion are protected.

Example: Placing an employer's name on a "do not patronize" list is permissible. [**NLRB v. International Association of Machinists, Lodge 942,** 263 F.2d 796 (9th Cir. 1959)]

(2) Coercive Statements Not Protected

However, statements that are coercive violate section 8(b)(1)(A).

Example: Statements by a union representative (in an attempt to organize workers) that "those who do not join the union will eventually lose their jobs" and "we have ways of handling people that argue against the union," are an unfair labor practice. [**Lane v. NLRB,** 186 F.2d 671 (10th Cir. 1951)]

(3) Noncoercive Speech Not Subject to State Defamation Laws

As long as the union statement is protected by the NLRA, no action for defamation lies under state law, provided that the union statement is noncoercive and is made ***without knowledge of its falsity or in reckless disregard of the truth*****.** [**Linn v. United Plant Guard Workers, Local 114,** *supra,* p. 59]

(a) Note

Mere ***expressions of opinion***, no matter how insulting [*e.g.,* calling a nonmember a "rotten scab") are absolutely protected under the NLRA. [**Old Dominion Branch No. 496, National Association of Letter Carriers v. Austin,** 418 U.S. 264 (1974)]

(b) And Note

Even where ***false statements of fact*** are made, no defamation action will lie if the statement is noncoercive and made without "knowledge or reckless falsity." [**Linn v. United Plant Guard Workers, Local 114,** *supra*—claims that plant manager had "lied" to employees and "robbed" them of pay increases]

c. Physical Restraint or Coercion

Section 8(b)(1)(A) prohibits ***physical threats or actual violence*** against employees who refuse to cooperate with the union. Thus, under this section, any overt threat of bodily harm is unlawful. [**Teamsters Local Union No. 5. v. NLRB,** 406 F.2d 439 (5th Cir. 1969)]

(1) Acts Directed Against Employer

Restraint or coercion may be found even where acts of violence are directed at the ***employer*** rather than employees. Hence, the destruction of company property by a union agent was held to violate section 8(b)(1)(A), since the acts constituted an ***implied threat*** of harm to any employee attempting to enter the plant. [**Local 542, International Union of Operating Engineers v. NLRB,** 328 F.2d 850 (3d Cir. 1964), *cert. denied,* 379 U.S. 826 (1964)]

(2) Possible Effect on Election

Union threats may also be grounds to set aside an election, even if the threats do not relate directly to the employees' votes (*e.g.,* threat of violent reprisals against strikebreakers). [**Industrial Disposal Service,** 266 N.L.R.B. 100 (1983)—*overruling* **Hickory Springs Manufacturing Co.,** 239 N.L.R.B. 641 (1978)]

d. Economic Coercion

Section 8(b)(1)(A) also applies to subtle forms of restraint or coercion.

Example—use of general fund for sole benefit of members: Union administration of a health trust fund (to which all employees were contributing) ***for the benefit of union members alone*** coerced nonmembers to join the union, thereby violating section 8(b)(1)(A). [**Indiana Gas & Chemical Corp.,** 130 N.L.R.B. 1488 (1961)]

Example—union causes employer to discriminate: If union pressure causes an employer to discriminate in any way on the basis of union membership (in violation of section 8(b)(2)), the union violates section 8(b)(1)(A), even if no force or violence has been used. [**Local 17, International Union of Operating Engineers,** 143 N.L.R.B. 29 (1963)] (This subject is considered in more detail *infra*, pp. 76 *et seq.*)

Example—waiver of initiation fees for some employees: A union may not attempt to influence membership by promising to waive normal union initiation fees for all ***employees who sign union authorization cards prior to the election.*** The restraints on employer promises of economic benefits also apply to unions, under the terms of NLRA section 8(c). [**NLRB v. Savair Manufacturing Co.,** 414 U.S. 270 (1973); **Teamsters Local 420,** 274 N.L.R.B. 603 (1985)]

Compare—waiver for all employees: An offer to waive initiation fees is valid if it is extended to ***all employees,*** not merely those who sign authorization cards. [**NLRB v. VSA, Inc.,** 24 F.3d 588 (4th Cir. 1994), *cert. denied,* 513 U.S. 1041 (1995)—enforcing NLRB order]

Compare—not all economic action is coercion: A union's reimbursing employees for ***wages*** lost while attending a representation meeting is ***not*** sufficient grounds for setting aside a subsequent election. Such reimbursement has been deemed not to impair the employees' right to make free election choices. [**Commercial Letter, Inc.,** 200 N.L.R.B. 534 (1972)]

e. Picketing and Coercion

Peaceful picketing by itself is not "coercion" under section 8(b)(1)(A), even though it constitutes direct economic pressure. [**NLRB v. Drivers, Chauffeurs, Helpers, Local 639,** *supra,* p. 63]

(1) Distinguish—Picketing to Deter Nonstrikers

On the other hand, mass picketing calculated to deter nonstrikers from working may violate section 8(b)(1)(A). [**American Newspaper Guild,** 151 N.L.R.B. 1558 (1965)]

(2) Blocking Plant Entrances

The tactic of blocking plant entrances and exits is unlawful, even if the picketing is otherwise peaceful. [**International Woodworkers Local Union 3-3,** 144 N.L.R.B. 912 (1963)]

EXAM TIP GILBERT

On your exam be sure to remember the law and not what you might have seen on the evening news. While peaceful picketing alone is not coercive, ***blocking plant entrances/exits***—even peacefully—is coercive and unlawful under section 8(b)(1)(A).

f. Coercion by Union Subordinates—Union "Agency" Concepts

In the organizational stage, or at other stages of labor relations, it may be necessary to charge the union with the acts of its alleged "agents." Rules governing the responsibility of labor unions for the unlawful activities of members and agents have varied over the years. Moreover, cases arising under the NLRA or LMRA (Taft-Hartley Act) are governed by ***different rules*** than cases arising under the Norris-LaGuardia Act or other federal statutes.

(1) Cases Arising Under NLRA and LMRA

The Taft-Hartley Act applies ***common law rules*** of agency in deciding whether a union is responsible for various unfair labor practices committed by others. [*See* NLRA § 2(13)—"actual authorization not essential"]

(a) Proving the Agency Relationship

Pursuant to section 2(13), the NLRB has established the following rules:

1) Burden of Proof

The burden of proof rests upon the party claiming that there is an agency relationship. That party must prove both ***existence*** of the agency ***and*** the nature and extent of the agent's ***authority***.

2) Apparent Authority Sufficient

While agency is a contractual relationship, calling for the mutual consent of principal and agent, such consent need not be express. It may be shown by a course of conduct, and its existence will be ***inferred*** whenever the conduct of the principal (*i.e.,* the union) indicates that it ***intended*** to confer authority. [**NLRB v. Urban Telephone Corp.,** 499 F.2d 239 (7th Cir. 1974); *and see* **Sunset Line & Twine Co.,** 79 N.L.R.B. 1487 (1948)]

(b) Liability for Acts of Agent

If the principal gives an agent power to represent him in a general area of activity, the principal is responsible for all acts of the agent within the scope of this general authority—even if the principal has ***not specifically authorized*** the acts in question. [**Sunset Line & Twine Co.,** *supra*]

(2) **Cases Arising Under Norris-LaGuardia Act**

A more ***restricted scope*** of union liability will apply in those rare cases where private individuals seek injunctive relief under the Norris-LaGuardia Act or similar state statutes.

4. Employer Domination or Assistance

NLRA section 8(a)(2) prohibits employer domination or interference with labor organizations and/or the contribution of financial or other support to such organizations. Determining whether an employer is guilty of "domination or undue interference or support" is a difficult task. Creating a company union, aiding the formation of a union, soliciting membership, financial assistance, use of company facilities, check-offs, and/or coercion in aid of a particular union have all been found to violate section 8(a)(2) (*see* below).

a. Test

When employer activity reaches a point where it is reasonable to infer that ***the union is not truly representing the employees in disputes arising between the employer and the employee***, the employer has violated section 8(a)(2). [**NLRB v. Brown Paper Mill Co.,** 108 F.2d 867 (5th Cir. 1940)]

(1) **Note—Not All Intervention Prohibited**

Of course, not all intervention by an employer is improper. Section 8(a)(2) provides that an employer "shall not be prohibited from permitting employees to confer with him during working hours without loss of time or pay." This means that an employer may pay the employee or his representative for time spent discussing grievances or other matters, without violating the statute. [***In re*** **Remington Arms Co.,** 62 N.L.R.B. 611 (1945)]

b. Actions by Subordinates

As in the case of unions (*supra,* p. 66), ordinary rules of agency govern the responsibility of employers for the actions of their subordinates.

(1) **Test of Agency**

If the acts of a subordinate could be interpreted by a reasonable person in the position of the employee as representing the attitude of the employer, the acts will be considered those of the employer. [**NLRB v. Pacific Gas & Electric Co.,** 118 F.2d 780 (9th Cir. 1941)]

(2) **Supervisors—"Management"**

Since supervisors are excluded by the NLRA from coverage as "employees" (*supra,* p. 39), they are deemed to be management representatives. The employer must therefore ***disavow*** any activity by such persons before it can be relieved of responsibility for their conduct. [**H.J. Heinz Co. v. NLRB,** 311 U.S. 514 (1941)]

c. Methods of Determining Unlawful Domination or Support

A wide variety of conduct has been held to constitute illegal "domination" or "support" of a union by an employer. The following major types of activity are likely to violate section 8(a)(2):

(1) Solicitation of Membership

An employer may not actively solicit union members (*e.g.,* for a union favored by the employer, as opposed to another union). However, the employer may establish rules permitting ***employees*** to solicit for a union, provided that such rules are ***not discriminatorily applied*** to prohibit antiunion arguments or solicitation by rival unions.

e.g. **Example:** An employer violated section 8(a)(2) by allowing one union to solicit on company time and property while prohibiting solicitation by a rival union. [**Stainless Steel Products, Inc.,** 157 N.L.R.B. 232 (1966)]

(2) Undue Assistance

If the employer takes an active part in the establishment of a union or in its affairs, the employer may be guilty of unlawful "domination or assistance." (Note that the employer need not take part ***personally***, since a supervisor or other party may be considered an agent acting for the employer (above).)

e.g. **Example:** A violation of the NLRA has been found where the employer merely aided in drafting the charter and bylaws that started the union. [***In re* Home,** 61 N.L.R.B. 742 (1945)]

e.g. **Example:** Similarly, an employer's antiunion campaign against one union, resulting in the formation of a company union, was found to be unlawful assistance. [**NLRB v. Daylight Grocery Co.,** 345 F.2d 239 (5th Cir. 1965)]

cf. **Compare:** However, an employer may continue to deal with an incumbent union despite a valid election petition from an outside union. [**RCA Del Caribe, Inc.,** 262 N.L.R.B. 963 (1982)] Moreover, it is not unlawful for a previously unorganized employer to recognize one of two rival unions, provided the union has demonstrated a clear, unassisted majority and the recognition occurs prior to the filing of any petition for an election. [**Bruckner Nursing Home,** 262 N.L.R.B. 955 (1982); *and see infra,* pp. 93–94]

(3) Use of Company Facilities

Supplying company facilities or services (such as legal counsel, office space, secretarial services, and printing or other equipment) to one union, ***while denying them to another***, would be unlawful support under section 8(a)(2).

e.g. **Example:** An employer violated the NLRA by granting one union the use of company premises, time to hold committee elections, and a motel room for use as a meeting place, while refusing to consider the claim of a rival union for recognition. [**Watkins Furniture Co.,** 160 N.L.R.B. 188 (1966)]

cf. **Compare:** Given that the employer merely introduced an employee to a union agent, allowed the agent to contact employees in nonpublic areas of the employer's premises during working hours, and then promptly recognized the union, the NLRB concluded that there was ***not enough evidence*** to support a finding of unlawful "assistance." [**Mace Food Stores, Inc.,** 167 N.L.R.B. 441 (1967)] *Rationale:* The Board found that the employer had permitted access to the premises by rival unions, had not solicited members for the union, and had not recognized the union in question before it represented a majority of the employees or after another union had filed a representation claim.

cf. **Compare:** In another case, the court held that an incidental benefit—in the form of receipts totaling $120 per year from a coffee machine operation on company premises—granted to one union over another, but not used to gain concessions from that union during bargaining sessions, did not constitute domination or assistance. [**NLRB v. Post Publishing Co.,** 311 F.2d 565 (7th Cir. 1962)] *Rationale:* The court distinguished between "support" and "cooperation." ***Mere cooperation*** would not be unlawful absent evidence that it had been calculated to (or did) coerce employees.

(4) Domination Through Union Bylaws or Constitutional Provisions

Provisions in a union constitution or bylaws that evidence ***employer control*** will violate section 8(a)(2). Moreover, the absence of any constitution, bylaws, or membership requirements other than employment at the employer's plant is considered evidence of employer domination. [**Muriel H. Rehrig,** 99 N.L.R.B. 163 (1952)]

e.g. **Example:** A bylaw that gives the employer equal representation on a "committee" governing the employee organization, plus the power to determine which employees would sit on the committee, would violate the NLRA. [**Dennison Manufacturing Co.,** 168 N.L.R.B. 1012 (1967)]

cf. **Compare:** An employer may be represented on employee committees ***if*** the employees so desire, ***and*** the representation was not thrust upon them and does not inhibit them from voicing their demands. [**Hertzka & Knowles v. NLRB,** 503 F.2d 625 (9th Cir. 1974)]

(5) Limitations on Innovative Workplace Methods

In an important and potentially far-reaching decision, the NLRB has held that experimental committees set up by management with employee participation—inspired to some extent by Japanese work methods—may constitute "labor organizations" and thus violate section 8(a)(2). [**Electromation, Inc.,** 309 N.L.R.B. 990 (1992), *relying on* **NLRB v. Cabot Carbon Co.,** 360 U.S. 203 (1959), *enforced,* 35 F.3d 1148 (7th Cir. 1994)]

(a) Criteria

The Board ruled that three conditions are required to find unlawful domination or support: (i) employees must be on the committee in question; (ii) the committee must "deal with" the employer; and (in) the subjects must include wages, hours, or other conditions of employment. Under these criteria, "quality work circles," "employee self-evaluation committees," "action committees," and the like would be open to challenge.

e.g. **Example:** The NLRB held that a nurses' committee was invalid under the *Electromation* principles, since (in the Board's view) the purpose of the committee was to deal with management or employment matters. The Fourth Circuit reached a contrary result, however, ruling that section 8(a)(2) required a "pattern or practice" of employee proposals and employer responses, which the court did not find with the nurses' committee. [**NLRB v. Peninsula Regional Medical Center,** 36 F.3d 1262 (4th Cir. 1994)—denying enforcement of NLRB order]

e.g. **Example:** The Board also held invalid an "Employees-Owners Influence Council" at Polaroid Corporation, given that the Council was established to address issues such as medical insurance benefits, the Employee Stock Option Plan, policies on employee termination, and family medical leave. [**Polaroid Corp.,** 329 N.L.R.B. 424 (1999)]

(b) Union Involvement Irrelevant

Electromation involved a nonunion plant, but the NLRB also has invalidated "employee participation committees" in organized plants—despite union involvement—where the committees dealt with safety (incentive awards) and benefits (jogging tracks, picnic areas), and made proposals to the employer through managerial employees who were on the committees. [**E.I. duPont & Co.,** 311 N.L.R.B. 893 (1988)—such committees might be approved if they were merely informational or discussion groups (making no proposals to management) or if they dealt only with subjects outside the scope of the duty to bargain]

EXAM TIP GILBERT

On your exam, be careful not to be "tricked" by an "innovative" employer that wants to work with employees by setting up management committees with employee participants to deal with wages, hours, or other employment conditions. Such committees ***could constitute illegal domination*** of a union and violate section 8(a)(2).

5. Employer Discrimination on Basis of Union Membership

NLRA section 8(a)(3) makes it unlawful for an employer to discourage or encourage membership in any labor organization by discrimination in regard to hiring or tenure of employment, or with respect to any term or condition of employment.

a. Proving Discrimination

To prove unlawful discrimination under section 8(a)(3), an ***improper motive*** (*i.e.*, an intent by the employer to affect union affiliation or activity on the part of the employees) must be demonstrated.

(1) Burden of Proof

Ordinarily, the General Counsel has the burden of proving all essential elements of an unfair labor practice. However, in a section 8(a)(3) case if employees are shown by the General Counsel to have been adversely affected by the employer's conduct, the burden of proof shifts to the ***employer*** to show that the conduct was justified by a legitimate and substantial business purpose and was not intended to affect union activity or affiliation. [**NLRB v. Great Dane Trailers, Inc.,** 388 U.S. 26 (1967)]

(a) If Employer's Conduct Is Inherently Destructive

If the employer's conduct is "inherently destructive" of union membership (*e.g.*, disparate wage and benefit scales for union and nonunion members), the Board may assume that the employer acted with an antiunion motivation and may ***disregard*** evidence of a business purpose and find a section 8(a)(3) violation ***without*** independent proof of motive. [*See* **Radio Officers' Union of the Commercial Telegraphers' Union v. NLRB,** 347 U.S. 17 (1954)]

(b) If Employer's Conduct Causes Lesser Harm

If the employer's conduct is less than inherently destructive of employee rights (*e.g.,* refusal to reinstate a validly replaced striker) and the employer presents a substantial business justification for the conduct, the General Counsel must overcome the employer's showing with ***independent*** evidence of an antiunion motive in order to prove a violation of section 8(a)(3). [*See* **NLRB v. Fleetwood Trailer Co.,** 389 U.S. 375 (1967)]

1) Scope of "Business Justification"

If the employer's conduct is not inherently destructive, a good faith interpretation of the collective bargaining contract, even if wrong, can qualify as a business justification. [**Vesuvius Crucible Co. v. NLRB,** 668 F.2d 162 (3d Cir. 1981)]

BURDEN OF PROOF UNDER *GREAT DANE TRAILERS* GILBERT

TYPE OF EMPLOYER CONDUCT	EMPLOYER OFFERS NO (OR INSUBSTANTIAL) EVIDENCE OF BUSINESS JUSTIFICATION	EMPLOYER OFFERS SUBSTANTIAL EVIDENCE OF BUSINESS JUSTIFICATION
"INHERENTLY DESTRUCTIVE" OF EMPLOYEE RIGHTS	General Counsel prevails	General Counsel can prevail ***without affirmative showing of motive***—Board may accept Employer's evidence, but ***need not do so***
"COMPARATIVELY SLIGHT" IMPACT ON EMPLOYEE RIGHTS	General Counsel prevails	General Counsel ***must establish motive*** affirmatively (by independent evidence) in order to prevail

(2) Circumstantial Evidence

Once the employer has presented evidence of a legitimate and substantial business justification for the conduct in question, *Great Dane Trailers* permits the General Counsel to establish the employer's antiunion motive independently through circumstantial evidence. Relevant factors would include:

(a) ***The percentage of union members affected*** by the conduct;

(b) ***The extent to which the affected employees were engaged in union activity;***

(c) ***The service record and efficiency of such employees;***

(d) ***The quantum of employer knowledge*** **of union activity;**

(e) ***Statements or conduct of the employer showing state of mind;***

(f) ***Disparate treatment*** **of union and nonunion employees;**

(g) ***Timing of any employee dismissals;***

(h) ***Consistency of reasons given for dismissals***; and

(i) ***Antiunion background*** of the employer.

(3) Proof in "Mixed Motive" Cases

The NLRB has also applied the approach in *Great Dane Trailers* to "dual motivation" cases. The Board has ruled that the General Counsel must establish a prima facie case that protected conduct was a "***motivating factor***" in the action taken by the employer—at which point the employer has the burden of proving that the action would have been the same even in the absence of the protected conduct. [**Wright Line,** 251 N.L.R.B. 1083 (1980); *and see* **NLRB v. Transportation Management Corp.,** 462 U.S. 393 (1983)—approving this allocation of the burden of proof]

(a) Note—Discharge and Hiring Distinction

The Sixth Circuit Court of Appeals has chosen to follow the Board approach in *Wright Line* only in cases in which an employee has been discharged. In cases involving a refusal to hire, the General Counsel's prima facie case must show there was a job vacancy for which the applicant was qualified, and that after rejecting the applicant, the employer continued to seek other candidates with the applicant's same qualifications. [**NLRB v. Fluor Daniel,** 102 F.3d 818 (6th Cir. 1996)]

EXAM TIP GILBERT

Remember that the central issue in discrimination cases is whether the employer acted with ***improper motive,*** which usually requires drawing inferences from circumstantial evidence. The NLRB can ***conclusively presume*** such a motive (because such actions "speak louder" than any other evidence) only if the employer's actions are ***inherently destructive of employee rights.***

b. Examples of Employer Discrimination

(1) Discrimination in Hiring or Firing

An employer may not hire or fire an employee on the basis of the employee's membership or lack of membership in a union, or to encourage or discourage union membership. [**Phelps Dodge Corp. v. NLRB,** 313 U.S. 177 (1941)]

e.g. **Example:** A violation of section 8(a)(3) has been found when an employer discharged a nonunion employee solely because he attended a union organizational meeting. [**B.M. Smith,** 132 N.L.R.B. 1493 (1961)]

e.g. **Example:** An employer's discharge of an employee who refused to join a company-dominated union was also found to be a violation of section (8)(a)(3). [**Hoisting and Portable Engineers, Local 302,** 144 N.L.R.B. 1449 (1963)]

cf. **Compare—union security agreements:** Agreements that permit an employer (at the request of the union) to discharge an employee for nonpayment of dues or initiation fees ***are*** allowed. (This exception is discussed *infra,* p. 212.)

(2) Discrimination in Tenure, Terms, or Conditions of Employment

It is an unfair labor practice under section 8(a)(3) for an employer "by discrimination in regard to tenure of employment or any term or condition of employment, to encourage or discourage membership in any labor organization." This means that an employer may not lay off, demote, transfer, etc., if his decision to do so is based on union considerations, or if the employer's action would have the inevitable ***effect*** of encouraging or discouraging membership in a labor organization.

(a) Strikebreakers

Thus, it is an unfair labor practice to offer 20 years of super-seniority to strikebreakers and permanent replacements of strikers. [**NLRB v. Erie Resistor Corp.,** 373 U.S. 221 (1963)]

(b) Discrimination Regarding Union Personnel

Likewise, super-seniority clauses for union stewards are unlawful unless limited to layoff and recall—because seniority beyond what is needed to keep stewards on the job (where they can help their fellow union members) would be undue favoritism and thus discrimination. [**Dairylea Cooperative, Inc.,** 219 N.L.R.B. 656 (1975)] Even clauses limited to layoffs and recalls are invalid if applied to union officers who do not perform steward-like duties, *i.e.,* engage in "immediate, on-the-job, at-the-plant representation activities" that would benefit all employees in the bargaining unit. [**Gulton Electro-Voice, Inc.,** 266 N.L.R.B. 406 (1983), *enforced sub nom.* **Electrical Workers IUE Local 900 v. NLRB,** 727 F.2d 1184 (D.C. Cir. 1984)]

1) And Note

An employer may not impose more severe discipline on union officers than on union members for violating a no-strike clause, unless the contract expressly waives protection for the officers or establishes a duty on the officers to take steps to prevent unlawful work stoppages. [**Metropolitan Edison Co. v. NLRB,** 460 U.S. 693 (1983)]

(c) Lockouts

It is not unlawful for an employer to lock out his employees for valid economic reasons. Ordinarily, this will occur after an impasse has been reached. [**American Ship Building Co. v. NLRB,** 380 U.S. 300 (1965); and *see infra,* pp. 125–126] A pre-impasse lockout also may be valid in some circumstances—for example, in response to "inside game" union tactics (*e.g.,* workers refuse all voluntary overtime) in an attempt to resolve negotiation issues. [**Central Illinois Public Service Co.,** 326 N.L.R.B. 928 (1998)]

1) Temporary Replacements

The hiring of temporary replacements during a lawful lockout also is permissible. [**Inter-Collegiate Press v. NLRB,** 486 F.2d 837 (8th Cir. 1973)]

2) Subcontracting During Lockout

During a lawful lockout, it is not inherently destructive of employee rights for an employer to permanently subcontract work previously done within the bargaining unit. Such subcontracting can be justified if it is done for legitimate and substantial business reasons. [**International Paper Co. v. NLRB,** 115 F.3d 1045 (D.C. Cir. 1997)]

3) Distinguish—Permanent Replacements

However, an employer violates section 8(a)(3) if he unilaterally hires permanent replacements during an otherwise ***lawful*** lockout. [**Johns-Manville Products Corp.,** 223 N.L.R.B. 1317 (1976), *rev'd on other grounds,* 557 F.2d 1126 (5th Cir. 1977), *cert. denied,* 436 U.S. 956 (1978); *and see infra,* pp. 164–169]

(d) Movement of Plant Operations

Changing the location of a business is not a violation of the NLRA if dictated by ***sound economic considerations.*** This is true even if the move has the effect of thwarting unionization. [**NLRB v. Rapid Bindery, Inc.,** 293 F.2d 170 (2d Cir. 1961)]

(e) Discontinuance of Business Operations

An employer's right to discontinue operations without violating the NLRA depends on the extent of discontinuance.

1) Total Discontinuance

So far as the NLRA is concerned, an employer has the right to terminate his entire business ***for any reason whatsoever,*** including antiunion sentiments. [**Textile Workers Union of America v. Darlington Manufacturing Co.,** *supra,* p. 58]

2) Partial Discontinuance

If the partial discontinuation is not bona fide, however, or if it involves only a part of the employer's total business operations, then discontinuing business with the ***purpose and foreseeable effect of discouraging unionization*** is a violation of section 8(a)(3). [**Textile Workers Union of America v. Darlington Manufacturing Co.,** *supra*]

a) Test

Under *Darlington,* there is a violation of section 8(a)(3) when: (i) the employer has continuing business operations significant enough to afford the employer a benefit from discouraging unionization; (ii) independent evidence exists that the partial closing was done for that reason; and (iii) it is reasonably foreseeable that employees at the remaining (continuing) operations will fear for their jobs if they support a union.

b) Remedies

An employer who closes a plant for reasons found to be discriminatory may be ordered to reopen, unless the employer can show that the reopening would be unduly burdensome or would threaten the continued viability of the company. [**Mid South Bottling Co. v. NLRB,** 876 F.2d 458 (5th Cir. 1989)] In the case of partial closures, the NLRB also has ordered reinstatement of the affected employees in another part of the business, together with back pay.

EXAM TIP GILBERT

On your exam, if an employer "closes" to ***prevent unionization,*** be sure to scrutinize the facts carefully. An employer can close his ***entire business*** based on antiunion sentiments. But if the employer ***continues to have significant business operations*** and it appears the closure was intended ***to discourage unionization*** of the employer's remaining employees, there likely is a violation of section 8(a)(3), and the employer may be ordered to reopen the closed plant.

c. Exceptions for Building and Trades Industry

Largely for historical reasons (such as the longstanding, extensive use of union hiring halls), the building and trades industry has been granted certain exceptions from section 8(a)(3). Section 8(f), added by the 1959 Landrum-Griffin Act, permits the employer and the union to enter a compulsory union agreement ***before*** employees have been hired. It also permits an agreement requiring union membership within seven (as opposed to the usual 30) days after the beginning of employment, permitting union referral of qualified applicants for job openings, and specifying minimum training or experience qualifications for jobs.

(1) Limitation

Section 8(f) does ***not*** permit an employer to discriminate against an employee for nonmembership in a union if the employer has reasonable cause to believe that membership was not available to the employee or was terminated for reasons other than nonpayment of union dues or initiation fees. In April 2020, the Board used rulemaking to address what it considered to be concerns that unions and employers might impose recognition through an 8(f) pre-hire agreement even if there was no majority support for the recognized union. The rule amends Board procedures to provide that where bargaining relationships are established under Section 8(f), proof of a Section 9(a) representative relationship will require positive evidence of majority employee support and cannot be based on contract language alone, overruling **Staunton Fuel,** 335 N.L.R.B. 717 (2001). This new rule applies to an employer's voluntary recognition extended on or after the effective date of the rule, and to any collective-bargaining agreement entered into after voluntary recognition after the effective date of the rule.

(2) Note—State Laws Apply

Furthermore, such agreements in the building and trades industry—like other compulsory union agreements—are subject to applicable ***state*** laws, a number of which prohibit (or rigorously restrict) compulsory unionism. (*See* discussion *infra,* pp. 213 *et seq.*)

(3) Antitrust Implications

An agreement prohibiting a contractor-employer from awarding jobs to nonunion subcontractors has also been held to violate the Sherman Act (thereby subjecting the union to damage suits under the antitrust laws). [**Connell Construction Co. v. Plumbers & Steamfitters Local Union No. 100,** 421 U.S. 616 (1975); *and see* discussion *infra,* p. 188]

6. Discrimination by Unions

Union practices that discriminate between members and nonmembers are prohibited by the Landrum-Griffin Act of 1959 as well as by the NLRA. Additionally, union practices that discriminate on the basis of race, religion, color, national origin, or sex violate Title VII of the 1964 Civil Rights Act. [78 Stat. 241 (1964)] The discussion here centers on practices prohibited by sections 8(b)(2), 8(b)(5), and 8(a)(3). (Conduct prohibited under the Landrum-Griffin Act is discussed *infra*, pp. 219 *et seq.*; activities barred by Title VII are mentioned *infra*, p. 203.)

a. Authority of NLRB

The NLRB has no authority to insist that a union admit to membership all of the employees it purports to represent. However, if a union is the authorized bargaining agent, it is under a ***duty to represent all employees*** in the bargaining unit fairly ***even though admission to membership cannot he required.*** [**Syres v. Oil Workers International Union Local No. 23,** 350 U.S. 892 (1955)]

b. Union Discrimination Through Coercion of Employer

As noted previously, NLRA section 8(a)(3) makes it unlawful for an employer to discriminate among or against employees if the motive for the discrimination is to encourage or discourage certain union activities. Similarly, section 8(b)(2) makes it ***unlawful for a union to cause, or attempt to cause, an employer to discriminate against an employee.*** (There is an exception for legitimate union shop clauses; *see* discussion *infra*, p. 77.)

(1) Union Hiring Hall Not Unlawful Per Se

The union may negotiate a collective bargaining agreement that grants the union exclusive control over the hiring hall from which the employer must obtain all employees. Such an agreement is not necessarily a violation of section 8(b)(2). [**Local 357, International Brotherhood of Teamsters, Warehousemen, Chauffeurs & Helpers v. NLRB,** 365 U.S. 667 (1961)]

(a) Rationale

The NLRB does not specifically ban hiring halls, and the Board may not do so by fiat. Rather, the NLRB must consider such agreements on an ad hoc basis.

(2) Coercing the Employer to Discriminate

Coercion of employers to discriminate may take the form of (i) union threats to strike or other pressure aimed at forcing the employer to discriminate against an employee out of favor with the union, or (ii) an attempt to require the employer to discriminate against an employee pursuant to the terms of a valid compulsory union contract (*see* "union security" agreements, *infra*, pp. 208 *et seq.*).

(a) Union Coercion Where No Compulsory Union Contract Exists

If no compulsory union contract exists, a union violates section 8(b)(2) when it seeks to force the employer to treat employees or applicants differently by reason of their union membership or lack thereof.

Example: If a union requests an employer to discharge an employee ***solely*** on the basis of the employee's lack of union membership, there is a violation of the NLRA.

1) **Note—Presumption**

The union is ***presumed*** to have intended the foreseeable consequences of its conduct. Hence, specific proof that the union actually intended the discriminatory consequences of its action is not required. [**NLRB v. Local 50, American Bakery & Confectionery Workers Union,** 339 F.2d 324 (2d Cir. 1964)]

EXAM TIP GILBERT

Remember, although unions need not accept all employees for membership, a union that is the ***authorized bargaining agent*** must fairly represent all employees, even those who are not union members. The union generally cannot discriminate in favor of union members and cannot coerce—through threat of strike or the like—employers to discriminate either.

(b) **Discrimination Where Valid Compulsory Union Contract Exists**

If a valid compulsory union contract exists, a union may legally seek the discharge of an employee, ***but only if the employee has refused to pay reasonable and nondiscriminatory membership fees or dues.*** If the discharge is sought for any other purpose, it may be held discriminatory.

e.g. **Example:** Discharging an employee merely because she failed to participate in union picketing, or to attend union meetings, is unlawful.

e.g. **Example:** Causing an employer to lay off an employee because the employee lacked "good standing" in the union is also unlawful unless there is a valid union-shop contract and the employee has not tendered the initiation fees or dues required of all members in the bargaining unit. [**Journeymen Plasterers Protective & Benevolent Society, Local No. 5 v. NLRB,** 341 F.2d 539 (7th Cir. 1965)]

e.g. **Example:** An employee cannot be discharged because of membership in a rival union, even if a compulsory union agreement exists. [N.L.R.B. Release R-4 (Sept. 23, 1947); *and see* **Ballas v. McKiernan,** 35 N.Y.2d 14 (1974)—decided by the New York Court of Appeals under LMRDA § 101(a)(2) (*infra*, p. 219); **Goldtex v. NLRB,** 14 F.3d 1008 (4th Cir. 1994)]

7. Judicial Remedies for Violation of the Right to Organize

If judicial relief is sought by the Board for refusal to abide by an NLRB order concerning violations of employee rights under section 7, the remedy generally takes the form of a ***cease and desist order*** and/or an order requiring ***affirmative action*** (such as reinstatement with back pay or preferential hiring). The scope of remedy imposed is determined by the circumstances of each case.

a. Cease and Desist Orders

Such orders are usually directed against ***specific*** conduct. If a long history of violations or antiunion sentiment exists, however, a blanket order may be imposed directing the employer to "cease and desist ***in any manner***" from interfering with employees' organizational rights. [*See* **NLRB v. California Date Growers Association,** 259 F.2d 587 (9th Cir. 1958)—in absence of history of antiunion practices, this type of order is too broad]

(1) Corporation-Wide Orders

If an employer has shown an extreme proclivity to violate the NLRA, the Board may issue a cease and desist order running to all of the employer's plants nationwide. [*See* **J.P. Stevens & Co.,** 240 N.L.R.B. 33 (1979); **Beverly California Corp.,** 326 N.L.R.B. 232 (1998), *enforced,* 227 F.3d 817 (7th Cir. 2000)]

b. Orders for Affirmative Action

In appropriate situations, the court may order affirmative action to correct the effects of past unfair labor practices.

(1) Reinstatement

In **J.P. Stevens & Co. v. NLRB,** 380 F.2d 292 (2d Cir. 1967), the court upheld a Board order directing reinstatement to offset an employer's "major campaign of illegal antiunion activity spearheaded by retaliatory discharges."

(a) Note

The NLRB could also require the employer to post a ***notice*** of reinstatement in all of the employer's plants and to mail a copy of the notice to all employees, but the Board could not require the employer to ***read*** the notice to his employees on company time. Moreover, the facts did not justify requiring the employer to make company bulletin boards available to the ***union*** for the posting of a notice of reinstatement.

(2) Notice to Employees

However, in **Textile Workers Union v. NLRB,** 388 F.2d 896 (2d Cir. 1967), involving the same employer (J.P. Stevens & Co.), an NLRB order that a company official read the Board's remedies for an unfair labor practice to employees on company time, and that the company make its bulletin boards available to the union, was ***upheld***. The court in *Textile Workers* pointed to facts demonstrating the need for such a remedy in that case, *i.e.,* an extremely coercive atmosphere at the plant in question.

(a) Note—Other Remedies

J.P. Stevens & Co. also has been ordered to reimburse both the union and the NLRB for expenses connected with the union's organizing campaign and subsequent litigation, in light of the employer's flagrant misconduct. [**J.P. Stevens & Co. v. NLRB,** 668 F.2d 767 (4th Cir. 1982)] The Board has meted out similar remedies in other extreme cases. [*See* **Dynatron/Bondo Corp.,** 324 N.L.R.B. 572 (1997)]

(3) Access to Employer's Premises

The Board may order access to the employer's premises by an organizing union to remedy employer unfair labor practices, whether or not the union would be able to reach employees through other available channels (*supra,* pp. 54–55), provided there is a sufficient showing that the employer's unlawful tactics had a "chilling effect" on employee organizing rights at the plant in question. [*See* **Florida Steel Corp. v. NLRB,** 713 F.2d 823 (D.C. Cir. 1983)—history of employer misconduct not enough by itself to permit union access to all of employer's plants after unfair labor practice at a single plant]

(4) Distinguish—No Order to Bargain After Plant Relocation

The Supreme Court has refused to enforce an NLRB order directing the employer to bargain with a union that lost its organizing campaign after the employer moved the plant to avoid the union. The Court reasoned that such an order would deprive employees at the new location of their right to a free choice of bargaining agent. [**Local 57, International Ladies Garment Workers' Union v. NLRB,** 387 U.S. 942 (1967)]

(a) Location of New Plant Determinative

The appropriateness of an order to bargain in the above situation depends on how far the employer moves the plant. If the distance is sufficiently far that a completely new set of employees will be hired, no bargaining order will issue. However, if the new plant is within range of the existing employees, an order to bargain may be proper.

(5) Order to Restore Department or Operations

Similarly, the courts have been hesitant to require an employer to reestablish a department or operation within the company that was closed down in response to union activity—even if the closure was clearly unlawful. Such orders by the NLRB are viewed as unduly burdensome, given the usual passage of time between the closure and a subsequent court proceeding for remedial action, and the practical difficulties in enforcing this type of order. [*See, e.g.*, **Coronet Foods, Inc. v. NLRB,** 158 F.3d 782 (4th Cir. 1998)]

SUMMARY OF SECTION 8 GILBERT

SECTION	SUBSTANTIVE RULE	PROVING A VIOLATION
8(a)(1)	Makes it an unfair labor practice for an employer "to interfere, restrain, or coerce employees in the exercise of the rights guaranteed in section 7."	Conduct short of an unfair labor practice may be sufficient to set aside an election if it inhibited choice and upset "laboratory conditions" of an election.
8(a)(2)	Prohibits employer domination or interference with employees' rights to organize.	The employer's conduct has reached a point where it is reasonable to infer that the union is not truly representing the employees in disputes between the employer and the employee.
8(a)(3)	Makes it unlawful for an employer to discourage or encourage union membership by discriminating in regard to employment or tenure.	Improper motive must be shown. Once the General Counsel shows that employees were adversely affected, the burden of proof shifts to the employer to show a legitimate and substantial business purpose. Once the employer presents such a purpose, the General Counsel can overcome that showing with

		independent evidence of an antiunion motive. However, if the employer's conduct is "inherently destructive" of union membership, the Board may assume an antiunion motive, disregard evidence of a business purpose, and find a violation without independent proof of motive.
8(b)	Prohibits the union from coercing employees in the exercise of their rights to organize or engage in union activity.	Physical threats and economic coercion are prohibited. A union is subject to a "laboratory conditions" test. Thus, even if the union's conduct does not constitute an unfair labor practice, the conduct may still upset the "laboratory conditions" of an election.
8(b)(2)	Prohibits the union from discriminating or attempting to discriminate on the basis of union membership.	If ***no compulsory union contract*** exists, a union violates this section when it seeks to force the employer to treat employees or applicants differently on the basis of union membership. If ***a compulsory union contract*** exists, the union may seek the discharge of an employee on the basis of failure to pay reasonable and nondiscriminatory fees or dues.
8(c)	Protects expression of views, argument, or opinion. Employers and the union are protected by this provision.	If the speech contains a promise of benefit or threat of reprisal or force, or if the speech in absence of a promise or threat upsets the "laboratory conditions" of an election, evidence of an unfair labor practice exists.

c. Temporary Injunctions

NLRA section 10(j) authorizes the Board in "***emergency***" situations to seek a temporary injunction restraining employer or union unfair labor practices, even before a hearing on the charges. (When an unfair labor practice charge involves a secondary boycott, hot cargo agreement (*see* discussion *infra,* p. 158), or improper organizational or recognition picketing, the NLRB ***must*** seek appropriate injunctive relief under section 10(j) if there is reasonable cause to believe the charge is true. *See* discussion *infra*, pp. 186–187.)

(1) Prerequisites for Injunctive Relief

To obtain a section 10(j) injunction, the NLRB must file a petition in federal court that alleges ***all*** of the following:

(a) ***The filing of an unfair labor practice charge;***

(b) ***Issuance of a complaint*** on the charge;

(c) ***Facts supporting the charge;*** and

(d) ***A likelihood that the unfair practice will continue*** unless restrained.

(2) Standard

Injunctive relief is proper if the above pleading requirements are met and the facts presented at the show cause hearing indicate that the Board had ***reasonable cause*** to believe the unfair practice had been committed. [**Johnston v. Evans,** 223 F. Supp. 766 (E.D.N.C. 1963)]

C. Selection of the Bargaining Representative—Elections and Bargaining Units

1. Introduction

NLRA section 8(a)(5) requires that an employer bargain collectively with the properly designated representative of employees in an appropriate bargaining unit. The first step in this process is selection of the bargaining representative and designation of the appropriate bargaining unit. (*See infra*, pp. 86–89.)

a. Elections

Both the NLRA and the Railway Labor Act provide for employee selection of the bargaining representative by secret ballot, in an election administered by the NLRB or the National Mediation Board, respectively. (The Railway Labor Act also provides for selection by "any other appropriate method.")

b. NLRB Authority

The powers and duties of the NLRB concerning elections are set forth in NLRA section 9, which authorizes the Board to determine the appropriate bargaining unit, to order a hearing on whether a representation question exists, to direct an election, and to certify the results.

(1) Delegation to Regional Directors

The NLRB has delegated these powers to its Regional Directors (pursuant to section 3(b), *supra,* p. 43). Under current procedure, therefore, the Regional Director decides all major issues in a representation case. If novel or complex issues are presented, the Director may seek the advice of the Board prior to a hearing, and the Director may also transfer cases to the Board for decision.

(2) NLRB Review

A determination by the Regional Director is final unless a party seeks review by the NLRB (i) on alleged departures from official Board precedents, (ii) to reconsider important rules or policies, or (iii) upon a claim of prejudicial error in determining the facts. And such review does not stay the Regional Director's action unless specifically so ordered by the Board.

c. Alternatives to the Election Process

NLRA section 9 provides that the bargaining representative shall be the one "designated or selected" by a majority of employees within an appropriate bargaining unit. However, it does not specify how the representative must be chosen. Although the election and certification procedure under NLRA section 9(c) is the most common method, it may not be the only route available to the union. Circumstances under which other selection processes may impose a duty to bargain are discussed *infra*, pp. 112 *et seq.*

d. Certification of Unions That Discriminate

At one time, the NLRB refused for constitutional reasons to certify unions shown to be guilty of racial discrimination. In 1977, however, the Board abandoned this view, concluding that questions of racial discrimination could be taken up by the NLRB only in the context of unfair labor practice proceedings, *e.g.*, in cases alleging a breach of the union's duty of fair representation (*infra,* pp. 197 *et seq.*). This latter approach was upheld in **Bell & Howell Co. v. NLRB,** 598 F.2d 136 (D.C. Cir.), *cert. denied,* 442 U.S. 942 (1979).

2. Representation Elections

a. Types of Elections

The following types of elections for a bargaining representative may be conducted by the Board:

(1) Agreed Elections

Agreed elections eliminate the time and expense of participating in pre-election hearings conducted by the NLRB. In 2020 after several iterations and court challenges to prior attempts to adopt improved election rules aimed at efficiency and shorter times to obtain election results, the Board adopted a final election rule. [NLRB General Counsel's Guidance Memorandum 20-07 on Representation Case Procedures Changes (June 1, 2020), available at https://www.nlrb.gov/guidance/memos-research/general-counsel-memos] There are now three types of election agreements: (1) a consent election agreement, which provides that the Regional Director's rulings on challenged ballots and election objections are final and binding; (2) a full consent agreement, which is utilized when the parties proceed to a hearing and provides for final Regional Director determination of both pre-election and post-election disputes; and (3) a stipulated election agreement, under which the Regional Director will resolve any post-election disputes subject to discretionary Board review.

(2) Contested Elections

If the parties cannot agree upon the matters just referred to, a contested election will be held if the various criteria for holding an election exist (*see infra,* pp. 85 *et seq.*).

(3) "Globe" Elections

If a particular group of employees could either bargain as a separate unit or be merged into an existing unit, the NLRB will allow the employees to choose between the two alternatives, unless there is a ***pattern or history*** indicating the appropriate unit. [***In re*** **Globe Machine & Stamping Co.,** 3 N.L.R.B. 294 (1937)]

(4) Certification Elections

Employers may—and frequently do—recognize and bargain with unions that prove with authorization cards, membership cards, applications for membership, dues receipts, dues record books, or petitions signed by employees that the union is authorized by a majority of employees to act as bargaining representative.

(a) Purpose of Election

In such cases, the union may still seek a "certification" election. This formality is desirable primarily because a certified union has a one-year period free from interference by rival unions within which to execute a collective bargaining agreement with the employer (*infra*, p. 92).

(b) Remedy for Unfair Labor Practice

Under the Landrum-Griffin Amendments to the NLRA, a certification election may be directed as a remedy for a meritorious unfair labor practice charge; *e.g.*, when recognitional or organizational picketing (*see* discussion *infra*, pp. 170–173) has continued for an unreasonable period without any petition for an election having been filed by the union, an expedited certification election will be ordered. [NLRA § 8(b)(7)(C); *and see infra,* p. 174]

(5) Decertification Elections

If employees contend that the union previously certified is no longer desired by a majority of the employees or that the employer is recognizing a union that does not represent a majority of the employees, a decertification election may be held. A tie vote results in decertification. (An "RD" election is one petitioned for by employees or a union; an "RM" election is one petitioned for by the employer.)

(a) Standards for Seeking Decertification

If at least 30% of the employees in a certified unit contend that the previously certified union no longer is desired by a majority of employees, an RD decertification (removal of representative) election may be held. Additionally, if an employer has a good faith, reasonable uncertainty about continued majority support for the union, the employer can petition for an RM decertification election. [**Levitz Furniture Co. of the Pacific, Inc.,** 333 N.L.R.B. 717 (2001)]

(b) Note

Decertification elections are also subject to the one-year bar on interference by rival unions (*infra*, p. 92).

(6) Deauthorization Elections

If employees wish to terminate the authority of their bargaining representative to enter into a union-shop or maintenance-of-membership agreement, they may petition for an election on that issue. A majority of eligible voters must vote for such deauthorization.

(7) Run-Off Elections

Run-off elections are conducted automatically if two or more unions are on the ballot and none of the available alternatives (including a choice of ***no*** union) receives a majority of the votes cast. Run-off elections can occur with respect to contested, consent, or "Globe" elections, but they are ***not*** possible in decertification or deauthorization elections (where only two alternatives exist).

b. Eligibility of Voters

The right to vote in a representation election depends on (i) whether the person is an "***employee***" within the meaning of the NLRA (*see supra,* pp. 39 *et seq.*), (ii) whether she is ***properly included in the bargaining unit*** for which the election is being held, and (iii) whether her job or position gives her a ***sufficient interest in employment conditions within that unit.***

(1) Payroll Period Determinative

Absent unusual circumstances, all employees in the appropriate bargaining unit (*see infra,* pp. 86–89) who were employed during the payroll period immediately preceding the date on which the election is ordered are eligible to vote.

(a) Eligibility Based on Other Payroll Periods

Unique circumstances, such as the seasonal character of an industry or a strike called after the voting eligibility date, may cause the NLRB to condition eligibility on some other payroll period (*e.g.*, the last pay period during the "season").

(b) Temporary Absence Does Not Destroy Status

A person's employee status does not terminate if she is temporarily absent from work during the payroll period in question (*e.g.*, on sick leave, vacation, or even laid off if it is expected that the employee will be recalled to work).

(2) Eligibility of Strikers to Vote

Prior to the 1959 Landrum-Griffin Amendments, striking employees not entitled to reinstatement (*see infra*, pp. 164 *et seq.*) were not eligible to vote in a representation election. The 1959 Amendments, however, provided that "[e]mployees engaged in an economic strike who are not entitled to reinstatement ***shall*** be eligible to vote under such regulations as the Board shall find are consistent with the purposes and provisions of this [LMRDA], in any elections conducted within 12 months after the commencement of the strike." [NLRA § 9(c)(3)]

(a) Rationale

Economic strikers run the risk of being permanently replaced (*see infra*, p. 164). Having risked their jobs to get an election, they should not be doubly penalized by being excluded from voting in the election.

(b) Criteria

Although each case is considered on its own merits, the NLRB has developed the following criteria in this area:

1) Presumption of Eligibility

The Board will ***presume*** that economic strikers ***are*** eligible to vote. This presumption can be rebutted only by objective evidence that the striker has "abandoned interest" in the struck job. The fact that a striker may have taken another job at a higher wage does not, by itself, rebut the presumption. [**Pacific Tile & Porcelain Co.,** 137 N.L.R.B. 1358 (1962)]

2) Replacements

Employees hired as ***permanent*** replacements for economic strikers may also vote, but those hired as ***temporary*** replacements may ***not*** vote. (Persons considered to be permanent replacements also benefit from the presumption in the previous paragraph.) [*See* **NLRB v. United Furniture Workers,** 337 F.2d 936 (2d Cir. 1964)] Employment status (*i.e.,* whether a person is a permanent or a temporary replacement) is a question of law.

3) Closure of Operations

Strikers who lose their jobs when an employer decides to *close* a certain operation are *not* eligible to vote, at least where such closure is made for valid economic reasons unrelated to the purpose of the strike. [**Lamb Grays Harbor Co.,** 295 N.L.R.B. 355 (1989)]

3. Election Procedure

Although a hearing on selection of a bargaining representative is considered "informal," certain steps must be taken before the NLRB will act at all. The first step is the filing of a petition. Next, the petition is evaluated by the Board to determine whether jurisdictional and other requirements are met; if they are, a hearing is set. At the hearing, all evidence for and against holding an election is presented and the Board (usually in the person of the Regional Director) either orders an election or dismisses the petition. Finally, the results of the election, if held, are formally recognized by the Board through certification, decertification, or (where the union loses the election) no certification.

a. Petitions

The representation procedure begins when a petition for certification is filed. Petitions may be filed by ***employees***, or by an ***employer*** when presented with a union demand for recognition.

(1) Limitation

Employers are prohibited from filing a petition to test the certification of an incumbent union seeking continued recognition, unless they have "reasonable grounds" for believing that the union has lost the support of a majority of employees within the unit. [**United States Gypsum Co.,** 157 N.L.R.B. 652 (1966)]

(a) Note

Union informational picketing alone will not suffice as grounds for employers to file a petition. [**Raymond F. Schweitzer, Inc.,** 165 N.L.R.B. 675 (1967); *see* discussion *infra*, p. 173]

(b) And Note

Employers may not file decertification petitions; these can be filed only by employees or employee organizations. [NLRA § 9(c)(*l*)]

(2) Withdrawing Petitions

If a union that requested recognition later disclaims such interest in a "clear and unequivocal" manner, the petition will be dismissed.

(a) **Limitation**

The disclaimer will not be recognized if the union engages in conduct incompatible with its disclaimer, as where the union continues to seek recognition by striking or making direct demands on the employer.

(b) **Waiting Period**

If the Regional Director permits a petition to be withdrawn, the same union may not file another petition for at least ***six months*** hereafter (unless good cause is shown).

(c) **Tactic**

Withdrawal of a petition is often used by the union as an effective organizing device. When a petition is filed and an election is ordered, the employer must submit to the union within seven days an ***"Excelsior" list***—containing the names and addresses of all eligible voters in the unit. [**Excelsior Underwear, Inc.,** *supra,* p. 48] Once the union has this list, it may withdraw its petition. Although the union is barred from refiling for six months, it can use the employee list to campaign during that period.

b. Requirements for NLRB Action on Petitions

The NLRB will not investigate a petition (or certify or decertify a representative) unless the following conditions are met:

(i) The Board must have ***jurisdiction*** over the employer's business;

(ii) The union must represent or claim to represent an ***appropriate bargaining unit;***

(iii) There must be evidence that ***at least 30% of the employees support the petition;***

(iv) There must be ***no unremedied unfair labor practice*** involving the parties to the election;

(v) There must be ***no prior certification or election*** within the preceding year; and

(vi) There must be ***no existing collective bargaining agreement that would bar the petition*** (*see infra,* pp. 92–93).

(1) **Jurisdiction**

For the NLRB to act on the petition, the employer's business must meet the requirements for NLRB jurisdiction as set forth in the NLRA (*see supra,* pp. 35 *et seq.*).

(2) **Appropriate Bargaining Unit**

The union must claim (or hold) recognition as the bargaining agent for the employees involved in a unit appropriate for collective bargaining.

(a) **Rationale**

Since an employer owes a duty to bargain only if the union involved represents the majority of employees in a unit "appropriate" for collective bargaining purposes, the NLRB must ascertain whether the group of employees in question is an "appropriate" one for bargaining with the employer. [NLRA § 9(b)]

(b) Determining "Appropriateness"—Matter of NLRB Discretion

Basically, this matter is committed to the discretion of the Board (in the person of the Regional Director). Its decision is not subject to judicial review except where it is alleged to be arbitrary, capricious, or otherwise "lacking in rational basis."

1) Challenge to Appropriateness

In unusual cases, a court may enjoin an election until the "appropriateness" of the unit has been finally determined. [NLRA § 9(d)] Typically, however, an employer who wishes to challenge a unit determination does so through the awkward procedure of refusing to bargain and then raising the unit issue in court when the NLRB seeks to enforce its order to bargain.

2) "Appropriateness" Defined

The NLRB has described the term "appropriate" as follows: "Nothing . . . requires that the unit be the only appropriate unit, or the ***ultimate*** unit, or even the most appropriate unit; the [NLRA] requires only that the unit be 'appropriate.' It must . . . ensure the employees in each case 'the fullest freedom in exercising the rights guaranteed by this [NLRA].' " [***In re* Morand Brothers Beverage Co.,** 91 N.L.R.B. 409 (1950)]

3) Relevant Factors

In determining "appropriateness," the Board normally considers the following factors:

a) Mutuality of Interest

Similarity of skills, wages, hours, and other working conditions (or the lack thereof) is probably the ***most important factor*** in deciding whether a particular group of employees constitutes an "appropriate" unit. [**Continental Baking Co.,** 99 N.L.R.B. 777 (1952)]

b) History of Collective Bargaining

The history of the unit's collective bargaining may be important, but it is not conclusive. It may be ignored if there are strong reasons for designating a unit different from the historical pattern (as where racial discrimination previously set the pattern for unit selection). [**Murray Company of Texas, Inc.,** 107 N.L.R.B. 1571 (1954)]

c) Desires of Employees

The employees' desires may be significant where other factors are evenly balanced and the question is decided by a "Globe" election (*see supra,* p. 82).

d) Extent of Employee Organization

The extent to which the employees have organized may be considered, but the Board is ***prohibited*** from giving this factor controlling weight in determining the appropriate unit. [NLRA § 9(c)(5)]

4) Statutory Limitations on NLRB Discretion

Section 9(b) places certain limits on the discretion of the Board to designate bargaining units. That section states that "the unit appropriate for the purposes of collective bargaining shall be the employer unit, craft unit, plant unit, or subdivision thereof," and further limits the Board's discretion in the following respects:

a) Professionals vs. Nonprofessionals

Professional employees may not be included in a unit of nonprofessional employees, unless a majority of the professional employees vote for such inclusion. [NLRA § 9(b)(*l*); *and see* **Pratt & Whitney,** 327 N.L.R.B. 1213 (1999)]

b) Prior Decisions Not Binding

A craft unit cannot be held inappropriate solely on the ground that a different unit was established by prior Board decision. [NLRA § 9(b)(2)]

c) Plant Guards

Plant guards who enforce rules for the protection of property or safety on an employer's premises may not be included in a unit with other employees. [NLRA § 9(b)(3)]

1/ Distinguish—Voluntary Recognition

Although section 9(b)(3) prohibits formal NLRB approval of a mixed unit of guards and non-guards, it does not prevent ***voluntary*** recognition by an employer—but an employer who withdraws such recognition may violate section 8(a)(5). [*See* **Loomis Armored Us, Inc.,** 364 N.L.R.B. No. 23 (2016). But the Board's rule requiring 45-day notice to allow an election petition may prevent a voluntary recognition from occurring]

d) Temporary Employees

Employees supplied to an employer by a temp agency can be combined in a bargaining unit with permanent employees within the parameters of section 9(b), provided that customary "community of interest" factors are present. [**Miller & Anderson, Inc.,** 364 N.L.R.B. No. 39 (2016)] Although joint employer status is currently determined by following the requirements of a final rule the Board adopted on February 26, 2020 when both employers share or codetermine the employees' essential terms and conditions of employment.

e) Health Care Employees

The legislative committee report on the 1974 Federal Health Care Amendments admonished the NLRB to avoid a proliferation of bargaining units in the health care field.

1/ Initial Approaches

In 1982, the NLRB identified certain classifications of employees that it considered generally appropriate to units in the health-care industry. [**St. Francis Hospital** ("*St. Francis I*"), 265 N.L.R.B. 1025 (1982)] Two years later, however, the Board discarded this approach in favor of a "disparity-of-interest" test, under which it would apply traditional criteria to designate a bargaining unit unless "sharper than usual" differences among employees could be demonstrated. [**St. Francis Hospital** ("*St. Francis II*"), 271 N.L.R.B. 948 (1984)] The circuit courts split on whether this latter test was proper. [*Compare* **Electrical Workers, IBEW, Local 474 v. NLRB,** 814 F.2d 697 (D.C. Cir. 1987), *with* **Southwest Community Health Services v. NLRB,** 726 F.2d 611 (10th Cir. 1984)]

2/ Current Standard

Exercising its *substantive rulemaking powers,* in 1989 the NLRB established eight units appropriate for bargaining in acute care hospitals: Registered nurses, physicians, all other professionals, technical employees, skilled maintenance employees, business-office clericals, all other nonprofessionals, and guards. The Board continues to use its adjudicatory process to determine the propriety of units of five or fewer hospital employees (regardless of category) and to determine appropriate bargaining units for other (nonacute) health care facilities. [*See* 131 Lab. L. Rep. ¶ 8 (1989); and *see* **American Hospital Association v. NLRB,** 499 U.S. 606 (1991)—approving these eight bargaining units for acute care facilities]

5) Judicial Limitations on NLRB Discretion

The courts generally defer to the NLRB in bargaining unit determinations. However, if the Board appears to depart without explanation from traditional criteria used in a particular industry, or if it fails to correctly apply such criteria to the proper evidence, the NLRB determination will be overturned. [*See, e.g.,* **Willamette Industries, Inc. v. NLRB,** 144 F.3d 877 (D.C. Cir. 1998); **Sundor Brands, Inc. v. NLRB,** 168 F.3d 515 (D.C. Cir. 1999)]

6) Multiemployer Bargaining Units

Multiemployer bargaining associations (such as the Pacific Maritime Association) must initially have the consent of the union and the various employers involved. Even if the parties agree to such an arrangement, the NLRB still must determine whether the proposed grouping constitutes an "appropriate" unit. In making this decision, the Board attaches primary importance to the desires of the parties and their previous bargaining history.

(3) Support of the Employees

Another requirement for NLRB action on a petition is evidence that at least 30% of the employees in the appropriate bargaining unit favor certification or decertification.

(a) Rationale

Before the Regional Director will commit NLRB time and money to an election, there must be some evidence that the purpose of the election (*i.e.*, selection of a bargaining representative) will be realized.

(b) Method of Proving Support

The petitioning union may demonstrate employee interest by submitting signed authorization cards, union membership cards, applications for membership, dues receipts, dues record books, or petitions signed by employees. Such proof must be produced within 48 hours after the filing of the petition.

(c) Degree of Support Required

The petitioner must present evidence that a substantial number (usually ***more than 30%***) of the employees support the petition.

1) Exception

This requirement does not apply in cases where section 8(b)(7) picketing (*i.e.*, recognitional or organizational picketing) is involved; *see* discussion *infra*, pp. 170 *et seq.*

2) Not Required if Employer Petitions

If the petition for certification is filed by the employer, no showing of employee support is required; it is presumed that the employer would not commit itself in this manner unless there is such support.

a) But Note

If the employer seeks to test the majority status of a ***certified*** union (under section 9(c)(1)(B)), it must demonstrate "reasonable, objective grounds" for believing that the union has lost its majority status. [**United States Gypsum Co.,** *supra,* p. 85]

(d) Intervening Unions

If one union has filed a petition for an election, another union may intervene to have its name placed on the ballot as well. In such cases, a ***5% showing of interest in*** the intervening union will suffice.

(4) No Charge of Unfair Labor Practice

The NLRB will normally refuse to proceed with an election if there is a pending unfair labor practice charge relating to organizing activity in the bargaining unit and the charging party is a party to the representation proceeding.

(a) Rationale

The effects of the unfair labor practice must be neutralized before the "laboratory" atmosphere conducive to a free election can be achieved.

(b) Waiver

If a petitioning union permits another union to enter an election where the latter union was alleged to have been assisted unlawfully by the employer in violation of section 8(a)(2), the petitioning union loses its right subsequently to challenge the validity of the election on that ground.

1) Note—Request to Proceed

Other charges related to the parties' behavior during the organizing campaign (usually under section 8(a)(1) or 8(a)(3)) will not block an election if the union files a request to proceed. Although the request "unblocks" the election petition, it does ***not constitute a waiver;*** *i.e.,* the union ***can*** subsequently challenge the election on the same grounds supporting the unfair labor practice charges.

2) Refusal-to-Bargain Charges

If a union's majority status has been lost due to unfair labor practices prior to an election, the union does not waive refusal-to-bargain charges under section 8(a)(5) if it proceeds with the election and loses. [**Bernel Foam Products Co.,** 146 N.L.R.B. 1277 (1964)]

e.g. **Example:** In *Bernel,* the union obtained authorization cards from a majority of employees and sought recognition from the employer. The employer refused to bargain and, when the union petitioned for an election, unlawfully promised various benefits to employees on the eve of the election. When the union lost the election and then filed refusal-to-bargain charges under NLRA section 8(a)(5), the Board found that the employer had denied recognition without good faith doubt as to the union's majority status and ordered the employer to bargain with the union ***despite*** the results of the election (which was a nullity because of the employer's misconduct). (*See* discussion on employer's duty to bargain, *infra,* pp. 112 *et seq.*)

(c) Unrelated Unfair Labor Practice

Of course, if the unfair labor practice charge is ***unrelated to organizing activities***—so that the alleged unlawful conduct would not interfere with the "laboratory conditions" in which an election must be held—the Board may allow the election to proceed while the charge is still pending.

e.g. **Example:** If the unfair labor practice involves an illegal "hot cargo agreement" (*infra,* p. 158) in the collective bargaining contract, the Board may order an immediate representation election. In such cases, the pending unfair labor practice usually does not involve any coercion of or interference with the organizing rights of employees, so that there is no reason to postpone the election. [**Holt Bros.,** 146 N.L.R.B. 383 (1964)]

(5) No Prior Certification

Section 9(c)(3) forbids holding an election for the same bargaining unit ***within 12 months of a prior valid election***, whether or not a union was certified in that election. Also, the Board requires an employer to continue bargaining with the certified union during the year following certification, ***regardless of any change in employee attitude about the representative during that year*** (*see* below).

(a) Voluntary Recognition by Employer

Occasionally, an employer will voluntarily recognize a union without any election or Board certification. In such cases, the NLRB has held that a ***recognition bar*** will protect the union for a reasonable time against any challenge that the union lacks majority support. [**Keller Plastics Eastern, Inc.,** 157 N.L.R.B. 583 (1966); **Sound Contractors,** 162 N.L.R.B. 364 (1966); **Josephine Furniture,** 172 N.L.R.B. 404 (1968)] The Board reversed this reasonable time rule for the recognition bar in 2007. [**Dana Corp.,** 351 N.L.R.B. 434 (2007) (finding that a 45-day window was allowed from the date of recognition during which employees could file a decertification petition supported by a 30 percent showing)] In *Dana Corp*., employers were also required to post a notice informing employees of the 45-day window. The Board later reversed and returned to finding a specific "reasonable period of time" to bar an election petition after voluntary recognition to be defined as "no less than six months and no more than one year after that date. [**Lammons Gasket Company,** 357 N.L.R.B. 739 (2011)] In 2020, the Board, in one of its multiple rulemaking efforts, returned to the *Dana Corp.* rule and rejected the *Lammons Gasket* decision by requiring an employer must post a notice of recognition and identify a 45-day window allowing election petitions to challenge any employer voluntary recognition action. *See* 85 Fed. Reg. 18,666 (April 1, 2020).

(6) No Valid Collective Bargaining Agreement in Existence

If there is a valid collective bargaining agreement between a union representing the bargaining unit and the employer, and it has not been in effect for an unreasonable amount of time, the Board will refuse to proceed further.

(a) "Contract Bar Rule"

Whenever a petition is filed by employees subject to an existing collective bargaining contract, the Regional Director must ***weigh the need for industrial peace and stability against the right of employees to change their bargaining representative***. The principle developed to balance these interests is the "contract bar rule." (*Note:* The contract bar rule does not apply unless it is ***specifically pleaded*** as a bar; otherwise, it is waived.)

1) "Three-Year Maximum Term" Rule

To bar a new election, the existing contract must (i) precede a rival claim (*i.e.,* become effective before any rival union has made a claim for representation), (ii) be fully executed, and (iii) be a written contract covering the usual conditions of employment for a ***fixed period*** (*see* below).

a) Contract for Three Years or Less

A contract between the union and the employer for a term of three years or less is an effective "bar" to the petition of a rival union only for the ***term of the contract*** itself (*i.e.,* a one-year contract will serve as a "bar" only for one year). [**General Cable Corp.,** 139 N.L.R.B. 1123 (1962)]

b) Contract for More than Three Years

A contract for a period of more than three years will "bar" the petition of a rival union *only for three years* (*i.e.,* a four-year contract would constitute a bar for three years). [**Pure Seal Dairy Co.,** 135 N.L.R.B. 76 (1962)]

c) Contract with No Fixed Term

Contracts that contain no fixed term will *not bar* an election for ***any*** period. [**Pacific Coast Association of Pulp & Paper Manufacturers,** 121 N.L.R.B. 990 (1958)]

d) Bar as to Parties for Complete Term

A contract between the union and the employer serves as a "bar" to a petition for certification or decertification by the ***parties*** thereto for the ***entire period of the contract*** (*i.e.,* a contract for a period of four years serves as a bar for the entire four years to any petition by the employer or the union). This rule binds the employer even if the contracting union is not certified. [**General Cable Corp.,** *supra,* p. 93]

2) "Substantial Claim" Requirement

If an employer is faced with claims by two competing unions, and thereafter recognizes and contracts with one of them, most courts have required that the recognition be based on a substantial claim (as opposed to a "bare" claim). That is, the employer must make a determination based on concrete evidence, such as authorization cards signed by a majority of the employees. If the employer fails to do so, the contract will not serve as a bar for any period. [*See, e.g.,* **NLRB v. Air Master Corp.,** 339 F.2d 553 (3d Cir. 1964)]

a) NLRB Policy

For 37 years, the NLRB followed the *Midwest Piping* doctrine, which insisted on a policy of complete neutrality by employers in rival union situations. [**Midwest Piping & Supply Co.,** 63 N.L.R.B. 1060 (1945)] In 1982, however, the Board sharply modified its approach as follows:

1/ If There Is an Incumbent Union

An employer must continue to deal with an incumbent union even if a valid election petition has been filed by a rival union. [**RCA Del Caribe,** *supra,* p. 68]

2/ If There Is No Incumbent

If there is no incumbent union, the Board has held the employer to a position of complete neutrality only ***after*** a valid election petition has been filed. Before that time, the employer is free to recognize a union that represents "an uncoerced, unassisted majority" of employees. [**Bruckner Nursing Home,** 262 N.L.R.B. 955 (1982); *and see supra,* p. 68; *but see* **Rollins Transportation System,** 296 N.L.R.B. 793 (1989)—election petition found valid even though employer was unaware of union's organizing campaign and recognized another union]

3) "Hot Cargo" Clauses

"Hot cargo" clauses in a contract (*infra,* p. 158), although clearly illegal, do *not* remove the contract as a bar to a petition for election.

4) Effect of "Union Security" Provisions

Contracts containing union security provisions (*infra,* pp. 208 *et seq.*) will not bar petitions for an election if the provisions are unlawful on their face. [**Paragon Products Corp.,** 134 N.L.R.B. 662 (1961)]

a) Distinguish

Contracts containing ***ambiguous,*** but not clearly unlawful, union security provisions will bar a petition.

b) And Note

Contracts with clearly unlawful security provisions can act as a bar if the unlawful union security clause is eliminated by a properly executed rescission or amendment to the contract.

(b) Removing the Bar

To remove the existing contract as a bar to an election, a rival petition **must be filed** *not more than 90 days or less than 61 days* **before** the date for termination of the contract or the expiration of three years, whichever is shorter. If no petition is filed within this period, and if the existing union negotiates a new contract with the employer during the 60 days prior to termination of the old contract, the renewed contract will again bar a rival petition for the period of the contract (subject to the qualifications discussed *infra,* p. 95). [**City Cab, Inc.,** 128 N.L.R.B. 493 (1960)]

1) "Automatic Renewal" Clauses

If the existing contract has a clause providing for automatic renewal of the agreement, the bar will renew with the contract *unless* a rival petition is timely filed (*see* above), or unless the parties themselves forestall the automatic-renewal clause—as where either party announces that it will seek to *change* certain terms in the existing contract. [**Deluxe Metal Furniture Co.,** 121 N.L.R.B. 995 (1958)]

(c) Situations in Which Existing Contract Is Not a Bar

An existing contract will not bar an election if:

1) ***The contract has no fixed term*** (*see* above);
2) ***The employer contracts with an uncertified union and that union seeks certification*** during the period of the contract;
3) ***The contracting union becomes defunct;***
4) ***A schism within the bargaining unit*** (*i.e.,* a basic intra-union policy conflict at the international-union level) ***develops*** [**Hershey Chocolate Corp.,** 121 N.L.R.B. 901 (1958)];
5) ***There are "changes in circumstances"*** (*i.e.,* employer expansion or merger, **or a change in job classifications) that justify disregarding the existing contract as bar to a new election;**
6) ***A clause in the existing contract involves racial discrimination;***
7) ***The existing contract has an illegal "closed-shop" provision*** (*infra*, p. 209); or
8) ***The existing contract was prematurely extended*** (*i.e.,* the parties agreed to an extension of the contract *prior to* the 90-day filing period for petitions by rival unions).

c. Judicial Review of Representation Proceedings

NLRA section 9(d) provides for judicial review of certification or decertification rulings only when such review is ***incidental to restraining an unfair labor practice*** (*e.g.,* refusal to bargain); and section 10 provides that only a "person aggrieved by a ***final order***" may obtain review. Consequently, such NLRB rulings are subject to review only after (i) a party to the election files an unfair labor practice charge with respect to the election, ***and*** (ii) the Board issues a "final order" with respect to that charge. [**NLRB v. International Brotherhood of Electrical Workers,** 308 U.S. 413 (1940)]

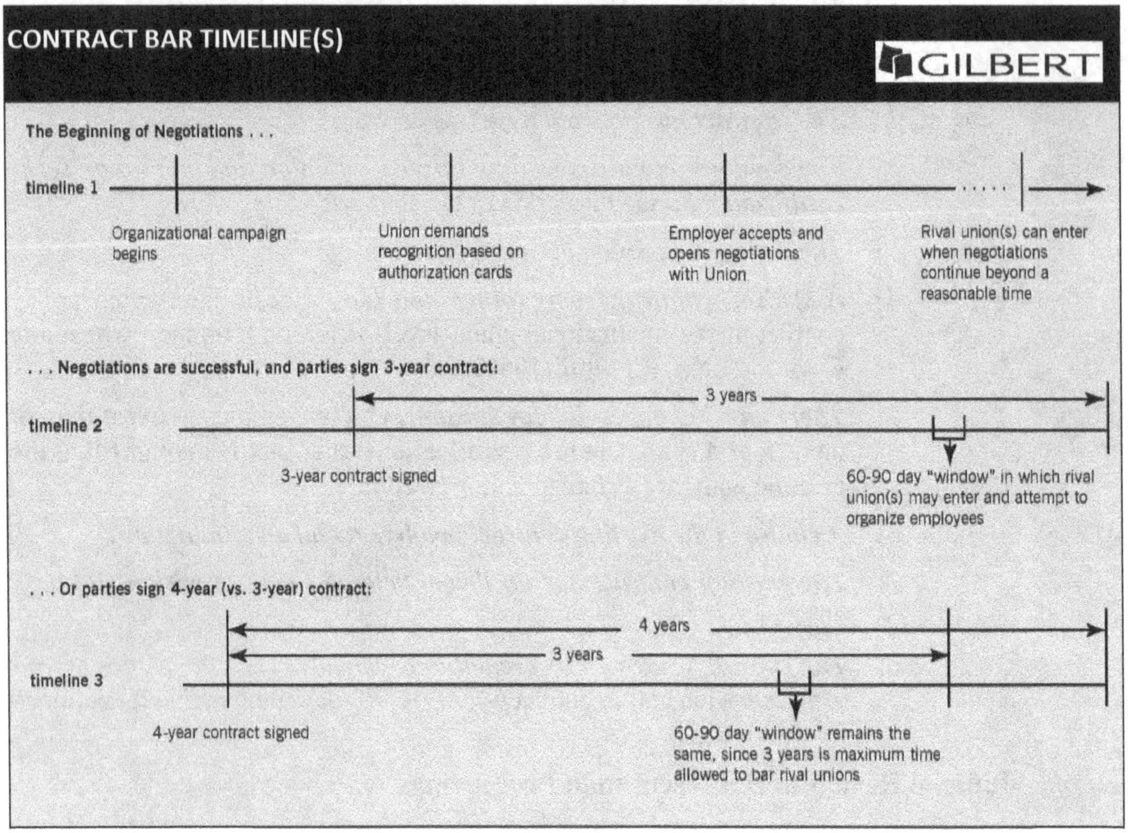

(1) Effect

If the Board refuses to hear the unfair labor practice charges, any direct review of the ruling on certification is foreclosed. [**NLRB v. National Broadcasting Co.,** 150 F.2d 895 (2d Cir. 1945)]

(2) Relief in Equity

Quite apart from judicial review under the NLRA, federal district courts have ***original jurisdiction*** (under 28 U.S.C. section 1337) to hear any claim "arising under the laws of the United States." Pursuant to that section, a court may compel or restrain an election upon a showing that the Board's action was ***contrary to the NLRA*** (a "law of the United States") and that it has caused or threatens to cause irreparable injury or deprivation of a right. [**Leedom v. Kyne,** 358 U.S. 184 (1958)]

(a) Rationale

Such a suit is not one for "review" of a decision by the Board within its jurisdiction. Rather, it seeks to strike down an order of the Board made contrary to a specific provision of the NLRA (and hence in excess of its delegated powers).

e.g. **Example:** In **Leedom v. Kyne,** *supra,* the Board had certified an employees' unit that consisted of both professional and nonprofessional personnel, without the consent of the professional employees. This was contrary to the express provisions of NLRA section 9(b)(1) (*supra*, p. 88) and hence justified equitable relief under 28 U.S.C. section 1337.

Chapter Three

Collective Bargaining

CONTENTS | PAGE

Chapter Approach

Once the bargaining unit and representative have been determined, the bargaining process must begin. The give and take of collective bargaining is relied upon to achieve economic stability and growth, and American labor law is designed to implement the process wherever possible.

For exam purposes you must understand two main themes of collective bargaining: (i) the ***duty to bargain*** once a union is certified as the bargaining representative; and (ii) the importance of the ***grievance and arbitration procedure*** in administering the collective bargaining contract.

1. **Duty to Bargain**

   An employer must bargain with the union if the union has won an election (and perhaps also if the union loses the election because of serious unfair labor practices by the employer). You should understand what happens to this duty to bargain if there is a sale, merger, or other transfer of the employer's business (the ***successorship*** doctrine).

   Remember that the duty to bargain has a ***qualitative*** side and a ***quantitative*** side, and you need to be familiar with both. The ***qualitative*** side requires bargaining in ***good faith,*** which includes:

   — Serious ***negotiation*** over mandatory subjects.

   — Providing ***information*** needed to make negotiation meaningful.

   The ***quantitative*** side provides that certain subjects ("wages, hours, and other terms and conditions of employment") are compulsory and ***must*** be bargained about, while other subjects are *permissive* (or in some cases, illegal). You must know the rules and decisions that determine which subjects fall within these respective categories.

   Your exam also may raise the issue of what the parties may do if negotiations break down (***impasse***). Employees in this situation may be able to ***strike,*** and employers may be able to ***lock out*** employees.

2. **Grievance Arbitration**

   This is the key to making a collective bargaining contract work. You should understand the role of the arbitrator in deciding disputes about interpretation or application of the contract, and the criteria for NLRB ***deferral*** to the arbitration process (one of the unstable areas of NLRB case law). Your exam may raise the applicability of LMRA section 301 (pp. 138 *et seq.*), and you should remember how it facilitates enforcement of arbitration procedures (including use of the injunction). Finally, you should understand the ***finality*** of arbitration awards, as emphasized in the "*Steelworker Trilogy*" (pp. 140 *et seq.*).

A. Negotiating the Collective Bargaining Agreement

1. Duration of Representative's Authority to Bargain

A bargaining representative selected by employees and certified by the NLRB must be recognized by the employer for a "reasonable period," even if a majority of employees ***disavow*** the representative immediately after certification. [**Brooks v. NLRB,** 348 U.S. 96 (1954)—employer guilty of unfair labor practice for refusal to bargain even though two-thirds of his employees had disavowed the union] *Rationale:* A newly elected union needs time to become established and carry out its programs. The underlying goal of industrial peace and stability would be thwarted if employees could change representatives capriciously and in rapid succession.

a. What Constitutes a "Reasonable Period"

Section 9(c)(3) of the LMRA requires that NLRB elections be held no more than ***once a year*** for any given unit of employees. If no union is certified, the year is measured from the date of the election. But when a union wins an election conducted by the Board, the union must be honored for a period of one year from the date of certification.

(1) Note

After one year has passed, the employees or the employer may petition for a new election.

(2) And Note

At one time, the NLRB recognized exceptions to the one-year rule for "unusual circumstances." However, this is no longer possible under the language of section 9(c)(3).

b. Extension of "Reasonable Period" Due to Employer Delay

If the employer delays bargaining in good faith with a certified union, the one-year period will be extended. Thus, a period of ***one year of actual bargaining*** may be required where an employer fails to bargain in good faith. [**Mar-Jac Poultry Co.,** 136 N.L.R.B. 785 (1962)]

2. Scope of Union Negotiating Authority

Once a union has been selected by a majority of employees in the bargaining unit, it has ***exclusive authority to represent all employees in the unit*** on matters that are properly the subject of collective bargaining. [NLRA § 9(a)]

a. Individual Contracts Superseded on Matters Covered by Collective Agreement

The employer may not negotiate individual contracts with employees, or use the existence of individual contracts prior to certification as grounds for refusing to bargain with the union. [**J.I. Case Co. v. NLRB,** 321 U.S. 332 (1944)]

(1) Rationale—the Majority Rules

All parties, including the employer, are bound by the election and must deal with and through the elected representative. The individual employee is a "third-party beneficiary" of the terms of the collective agreement, because she shares common benefits that she might not be able to obtain through individual negotiation with the employer. Moreover, individual employer-employee negotiations could be used to subvert the union's bargaining position, as when "favored" employees (or those hostile to the union) are offered better terms in return for opposition to the union.

(2) No Exceptions

Not even "exceptional circumstances" will justify negotiating with individuals where a certified representative and a collective agreement exist. [**Order of Railroad Telegraphers v. Railway Express Agency, Inc.,** 321 U.S. 342 (1944)]

e.g. **Example:** In *Order of Railroad Telegraphers,* the defendant-employer took over another company and assumed the company's obligations under a collective bargaining agreement. When the defendant instituted certain changes in freight handling, a few uniquely situated employees became entitled to huge salary increases under the existing agreement—a situation clearly not envisioned when that agreement was entered into. The employer proceeded to negotiate new individual contracts with the employees concerned ***without*** consulting the union. These individual contracts were held ***invalid.*** The Court reasoned that the "exceptional circumstances" affecting the individual employees might have permitted the union ***to obtain concessions on other matters of concern to all employees.***

(a) Note

Although *Order of Railroad Telegraphers* was decided under the Railway Labor Act, the result would be the same under the NLRA.

b. Individual Contracts Permitted if Not in Conflict with Collective Agreement

In both *J.I. Case Co.* and *Order of Railroad Telegraphers, supra,* the Supreme Court recognized that individual contracts between employer and employee might be valid in certain ***limited*** situations:

(1) If No Collective Bargaining Representative

Individual agreements are of course valid and enforceable if collective bargaining does not exist, *i.e.,* if no representative has been recognized.

(2) Matters Outside Scope of or Not Inconsistent with Collective Agreement

Even if a collective agreement exists, individual contracts on ***matters not covered by and/or not inconsistent with the agreement*** are permitted.

For example, the collective agreement might set minimum wage rates and permit individual negotiation for better terms by employees with special skills. [**Caterpillar, Inc. v. Williams,** *supra,* p. 29—individual employment contracts are not automatically superseded by collective agreement and can give rise to claims (on such contracts) under state law]

(a) But Note

At all times, the collective agreement is paramount. The employer may not use negotiations with individual employees to reduce his own obligations under the agreement, increase the obligations of the employees, or otherwise take away concessions obtained by the union. [**J.I. Case Co. v. NLRB,** *supra*]

c. Section 9(a) Supersedes Section 7 Rights of Individual Employees

If a union has exclusive authority under section 9(a) to represent all employees in the unit, an employee has no independent right to bargain with the employer. Thus, individual employees who engage in concerted activities without union approval are not protected by section 7 from discipline (including discharge). [**Emporium Capwell Co. v. Western Addition Community Organization,** 420 U.S. 50 (1975)]

e.g. **Example:** In *Emporium Capwell Co.,* certain employees picketed against alleged discriminatory hiring by the employer even though the union was already pursuing such charges through the grievance procedure established by collective bargaining. The Supreme Court held that discharging the workers was not an employer unfair labor practice, citing the union's right of exclusive representation under section 9(a).

(1) Title VII Violations Separate and Distinct

If employer discipline in such cases violates Title VII of the Civil Rights Act (*see infra,* pp. 203 *et seq.*), the employees affected may seek relief under the provisions of that Act, but the employer cannot be charged with an unfair labor practice under NLRA section 8(a)(1). [**Emporium Capwell Co. v. Western Addition Community Organization,** *supra*]

d. Limitations on Union Authority and Majority Rule

Recognizing that the power resulting from exclusive bargaining authority may invite abuse, the law provides certain safeguards against unfair treatment by the union of individuals or groups within the bargaining unit.

(1) Union Must Represent All Employees

While this topic is covered in detail (*see infra,* pp. 215 *et seq.*), it is important to note that the union has a ***duty to bargain fairly on behalf of all employees, including nonmembers,*** and that its failure to do so may be an unfair labor practice.

(2) Employee May Contact Employer Directly

An additional safeguard is provided by NLRA section 9(a), which permits employees to ***present and adjust grievances directly with the employer***, as long as (i) the adjustment is ***not inconsistent*** with the collective agreement and (ii) ***the union is given the opportunity to be present*** at the adjustment (*see infra,* p. 205).

(a) But Note

It is not clear whether an employee may seek assistance from a rival union in pressing a grievance.

e. No Duty to Bargain with Respect to Replacement Workers

Employees who strike over economic issues can be permanently replaced. (*See infra,* pp. 164–166.) When this happens, the replacement workers technically become active employees in the bargaining unit for which the union is certified. Nonetheless, the NLRB has held that the employer has no duty to bargain with the union about the terms and conditions of employment of such workers. [**Service Electric Co.,** 281 N.L.R.B. 633 (1986); **Detroit Newspaper Agency,** 327 N.L.R.B. 871 (1999)]

3. Duty to Bargain "in Good Faith"

NLRA section 8(d) requires the employer *and* the union to meet and confer at reasonable times and to bargain "in good faith."

a. Statutory Policy Behind "Good Faith" Requirement

Unless an employer was forced to bargain meaningfully with the union, it could simply "talk a weak union to death," thereby frustrating the goals of mutual negotiation and industrial peace. The same reasoning applies to unions.

b. "Good Faith" Standard

Each party must make ***a sincere effort to reach agreement, and must participate in negotiations*** to that end. [**NLRB v. Truitt Manufacturing Co.,** 351 U.S. 149 (1956)]

(1) "Good Faith"

"Good faith" requires more than merely going through the motions of bargaining. But the fact that an impasse is reached does not necessarily show lack of good faith (or "bad faith"). Section 8(d) does ***not*** compel either party to accept any proposal or make any concession. [**NLRB v. Truitt Manufacturing Co.,** *supra*]

(2) Good or Bad Faith Shown by Actions

"Good faith" ultimately depends upon the subjective intent of the parties. Since a party rarely declares its bad faith, the determination must be based on ***external manifestations*** of intent in each case. For example, "bad faith" may be demonstrated by the substantive proposals made by a party or by the tactics and conduct employed.

(a) Approach

The ***total course of conduct*** of the party, rather than isolated actions, must be considered. Thus, a violation of section 8(d) may result from the "sum" of several incidents which, looked at separately, might not establish bad faith. [**NLRB v. Cummer-Graham Co.,** 279 F.2d 757 (5th Cir. 1960)]

c. Inferences of Bad Faith

Although each case must be judged on its own facts, bad faith will be *inferred* under certain circumstances. In these situations, the actual motives of the party are irrelevant. [**NLRB v. Katz,** 369 U.S. 736 (1962)]

(1) Content of Proposals

The NLRB may look at the ***reasonableness*** of the proposal in determining whether the proposal was adopted for the purpose of frustrating negotiations and preventing agreement. [**NLRB v. Herman Sausage Co.,** 275 F.2d 229 (5th Cir. 1960)]

e.g. **Example:** An employer proposal that ***offers terms that no responsible employee representative could accept*** raises an inference of bad faith. [**Alba-Waldensian, Inc.,** 167 N.L.R.B. 695 (1967)—employer proposed to retain absolute authority over wages while depriving the union of any effective weapon to protest grievances]

e.g. **Example:** A proposal that would result in employees receiving less at the end of the year following certification than they had received before the union became their bargaining agent demonstrates a refusal to bargain in good faith. [**Stevenson Brick & Block Co.,** 160 N.L.R.B. 198 (1966)]

(2) Conduct or Tactics in Negotiations

Negotiating tactics by an employer also may constitute bad faith bargaining.

(a) Dilatory Tactics

When an employer uses dilatory tactics—such as repeatedly canceling scheduled negotiating sessions or continually shifting its position whenever an agreement appears to have been reached—it may be found guilty of "bad faith" bargaining. [**Calex Corp. v. NLRB,** 144 F.3d 904 (6th Cir. 1998); **Gopher Aviation, Inc.,** 160 N.L.R.B. 1698 (1966)]

1) But Note—Withdrawal of Offer

An employer's ***withdrawing*** earlier offers does not in itself indicate bad faith if none of the earlier proposals had been unconditionally accepted by the union. [**Perfect Service Gas Co.,** 146 N.L.R.B. 1686 (1964)]

(b) Demands That Union Drop Pending Charges

In **NLRB v. Southwestern Porcelain Steel Corp.,** 317 F.2d 527 (10th Cir. 1963), the court found that an employer was not bargaining in good faith when it made no effort to conclude an agreement and threatened to postpone negotiations until the union withdrew certain unfair labor practice charges it had lodged against the employer.

(c) "Take It or Leave It" Proposals

An employer who maintains a "take it or leave it" attitude in negotiations may have engaged in bad faith bargaining. [**NLRB v. General Electric Co.,** 418 F.2d 736 (2d Cir. 1969), *cert. denied,* 397 U.S. 965 (1970)—employer refused to deviate from its original offer throughout prolonged negotiations and engaged in vigorous publicity program to sell its offer to employees; held to be bargaining in bad faith]

1) Comment

These cases raise a difficult interpretive question under the NLRA, since the NLRA does not compel any party to make a concession in the bargaining process (*supra,* p. 102). Consequently, the NLRB and the courts often disagree as to whether an employer's actions in a particular negotiation constitute permissible "hard bargaining" or impermissible "surface bargaining." [*See e.g.,* **Pittsburgh-Des Moines Corp. v. NLRB,** 663 F.2d 956 (9th Cir. 1981); **Pease Co. v. NLRB,** 666 F.2d 1044 (6th Cir. 1981), *cert. denied,* 456 U.S. 974 (1982)]

(d) Refusal to Bargain About Racial Discrimination

An employer also violates section 8(a)(5) when it refuses to bargain meaningfully and in good faith about actual racial discrimination practices ***then in effect***—even though bargaining with the union about inclusion of a nondiscrimination clause in the contract. [**United Packinghouse, Food & Allied Workers v. NLRB,** 416 F.2d 1126 (D.C. Cir.), *cert. denied,* 396 U.S. 903 (1969)]

(e) Refusal to Furnish (or Delay in Furnishing) Information

The duty to bargain in good faith may require one party to provide the other with information at the bargaining table, and a refusal to furnish (or delay in furnishing) such information may be an unfair labor practice.

1) Information to Substantiate Bargaining Claims

Demands for increased wages or benefits tend to be compromised, often due to the employer's claim that it cannot meet the union's demands and remain profitable. If an employer argues "inability to pay," the union has a right (upon request) to sufficient information from the employer to substantiate that claim. [**NLRB v. Truitt Manufacturing Co.,** *supra,* p. 102]

a) What Constitutes an "Inability to Pay" Claim

If an employer merely complains that union demands would affect its future ability to compete, the *Truitt* requirement of substantiation has been held not to apply. Only when the employer asserts that it cannot pay the wages and benefits requested by the union, either at the time of the demand or within the term of the contract being negotiated, must the claim be substantiated. [**Nielson Lithographing Co.,** 305 N.L.R.B. 697 (1991), *review denied,* 977 F.2d 1168 (7th Cir. 1992); *and see* **ConAgra, Inc. v. NLRB,** 117 F.3d 1435 (D.C. Cir. 1997)—denying enforcement of an NLRB order to substantiate, given that the Board failed to properly apply its own standards as articulated in *Nielson Lithographing*]

b) Distinguish—Claim That Union Demands Exceed Industry Standards

An employer did not violate the NLRA by refusing to disclose his financial situation, because his argument was that union demands exceeded benefits prevailing in the industry, not an inability to pay. [**Teamsters Local 745 v. NLRB,** 355 F.2d 842 (D.C. Cir. 1966)]

2) Information Needed for Meaningful Bargaining

The NLRB and the courts have generally held that bargaining parties must have access to information sufficient to permit meaningful bargaining on mandatory topics. Information to substantiate bargaining claims (above) is presumptively necessary. In most situations, however, a showing of ***relevance*** on the particular facts of the case is required. [**Columbus Products,** 259 N.L.R.B. 220 (1981); *and see* **NLRB v. American National Can Co.,** 924 F.2d 518 (4th Cir. 1991)—union allowed access to plant to measure heat levels because employer allegedly failed to provide adequate heat-relief time]

a) Nature of Request

A request for information must be timely and reasonably specific, but it need *not* be in writing, and it is not prejudiced if accompanied by other requests that the employer lawfully may refuse.

b) Information Furnished

The information furnished by the employer must be current and sufficient in scope to permit effective bargaining. In addition, it should be prepared with such care and speed as the employer would exercise in other important business matters. [**J.H. Rutter-Rex Manufacturing Co.,** 86 N.L.R.B. 470 (1949)]

c) Limits on Disclosure

The NLRB has not been sympathetic toward defenses to disclosure based on alleged complexity, expense, or confidentiality. However, the Supreme Court has required that union access to relevant information be balanced against legitimate claims of confidentiality by the employer. [**Detroit Edison Co. v. NLRB,** 440 U.S. 301 (1979)]

e.g. **Example:** The NLRB could not require disclosure of questions, answers, and individual scores on standardized tests administered by the employer for employee selection and advancement. [**Detroit Edison Co. v. NLRB,** *supra*]

cf. **Compare:** However, the "balancing test" has been applied to require disclosure of (among other things) the generic names of substances with which employees work, and certain aggregate, nonpersonalized medical records on employees in the bargaining unit. [**Colgate-Palmolive Co.,** 261 N.L.R.B. 90 (1982); **Borden Chemical Co.,** 261 N.L.R.B. 64 (1982)]

WHEN BAD FAITH MAY BE INFERRED GILBERT

CONTENT OF PROPOSALS	CONDUCT OR TACTICS
• No terms that a ***responsible employee representative could accept*** are offered • Terms are offered that result in employees ***receiving less compensation after certification*** • ***"Take it or leave it" proposal*** is offered—unless it could be considered permissible "hard bargaining"	• Bargaining sessions are ***repeatedly canceled*** • Negotiations are ***threatened to be postponed*** until unfair labor practice charges are withdrawn • Bargaining position is ***repeatedly shifted*** • ***Refusal to bargain*** about racial discrimination practices then in effect • ***Refusal to furnish or delay in furnishing*** information to substantiate bargaining claims, or information needed for meaningful bargaining

d. Duty to Bargain or Honor Contract After Filing of Bankruptcy Petition

At one time, an employer undergoing reorganization under Chapter 11 of the Bankruptcy Act could unilaterally change the existing collective bargaining pact—subject to certain conditions—without violating section 8(a)(5). [**NLRB v. Bildisco & Bildisco,** 465 U.S. 513 (1984)]

(1) Unilateral Action No Longer Permitted

Under the Bankruptcy Amendments and Federal Act of 1984 (passed by Congress after *Bildisco*), an employer in reorganization may *not* unilaterally reject or revise a collective bargaining contract. Instead, the employer must first present its proposal(s) to the union and attempt in good faith to achieve a modification of the agreement. The Bankruptcy Court is permitted to approve a rejection of the contract only after finding that the union has refused to assent to a modification without good cause and that the balance of equities clearly favors rejection.

e. Duty of New Employer to Bargain—"Contractual Successorship"

Corporate mergers and acquisitions are common in American business. An important question relating to mergers is whether the new employer is bound by the terms of an existing collective bargaining agreement, and whether it must recognize and bargain with the existing union representative.

(1) If Successor Assumes Existing Contract in Acquiring Business

If the successor agrees to accept ("assumes") the existing contract as part of its acquisition of the business, it is bound by the terms of the contract and must bargain with the designated representative.

(2) If Successor Is Survivor Corporation in Statutory Merger

If the new employer is the survivor of a statutory merger, it may be bound as a matter of state corporation law to assume certain obligations of the disappearing entity. In any case, the purchaser must bargain with the representative and must honor the grievance and arbitration procedures of the existing contract with respect to grievances arising out of the merger. [*See* **John Wiley & Sons, Inc. v. Livingston,** 376 U.S. 543 (1964)]

(3) If Successor Acquires Business Other than by Merger or Purchase of Assets

One employer may occasionally replace another employer without a formal merger or sale of assets and yet be properly considered a "successor" in terms of continuity of the business, *e.g.*, a successful bidder for contracted services who retains most of the employees of the previous supplier of such services.

SUCCESSORSHIP: HYPOTHETICAL CASE

Sometimes, a preexisting company ("PC") will agree to sell its assets to, or merge with, another company (new company—"NC"). When this occurs, some or all of PC's operations may be temporarily discontinued. After the sale or merger, NC will then resume (sometimes partial) operations. At this point, the union that represented PC employees demands recognition by NC and demands that the pre-existing collective bargaining contract be honored. What result?

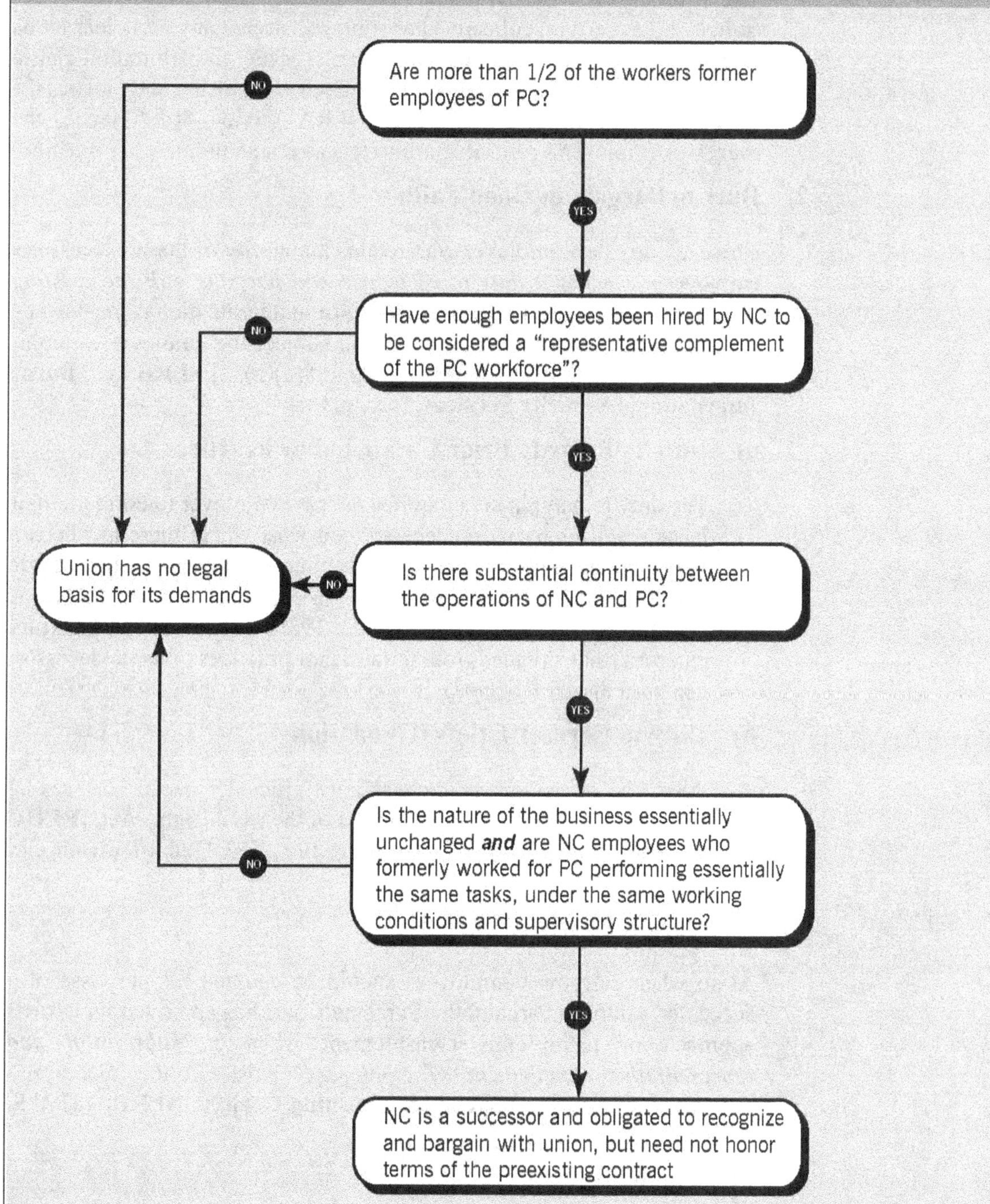

(a) Unfair Labor Practice Proceedings

In the leading case in this situation, an unfair labor practice charge was filed against a new bidder for security guard services for refusing to bargain with the union representing the former bidder's employees and for not honoring the existing contract. The Supreme Court held that the union could *not* enforce arbitration provisions in the contract despite a substantial continuity in business operations and work force between the prior employer and its successor. [**NLRB v. Burns International Security Services, Inc.,** 406 U.S. 272 (1972)]

1) Rationale

The NLRA—the basis for unfair labor practice proceedings—does not compel either party in collective bargaining to accept any particular terms or conditions. Requiring a new employer to accept the arbitration clause of a previous agreement is tantamount to such compulsion and violates the "fundamental policy" expressed in NLRA section 8(d). Hence, the successor employer's refusal to arbitrate was not an unfair labor practice.

2) Duty to Bargain in Good Faith

However, any new employer who retains a majority of the predecessor's employees is under *a duty to recognize and bargain* ***with the existing union representative.*** **The duty to bargain** in this situation is imposed by section 8(d), and failure to do so would subject the employer to unfair labor practice charges under section 8(a)(5). [**NLRB v. Burns International Security Services, Inc.,** *supra*]

a) Duty to Remedy Prior Unfair Labor Practices

The duty to bargain also requires the new employer to correct unfair labor practices by its predecessor—at least where there has been a Board ruling with respect to the former employer. [**Golden State Bottling Co. v. NLRB,** 414 U.S. 168 (1973); *and see* **NLRB v. Goodman,** 873 F.2d 598 (2d Cir. 1989)—successor to bankrupt enterprise not shielded from unfair labor practices of its predecessor; *compare* discussion *supra,* p. 105]

b) Duty to Correct Title VII Violations

Also, a successor employer must remedy racial or sexual discrimination that violates Title VII of the Civil Rights Act. [**EEOC v. MacMillan Bloedel Containers, Inc.,** 503 F.2d 1086 (6th Cir. 1974)]

3) Standard for Duty to Bargain

As to when carryover employees should be counted for purposes of a successor's duty to bargain, the Supreme Court has approved the NLRB approach of taking this measurement when a "***substantial and representative complement of employees***" exists in the successor's operations. [**Fall River Dyeing & Finishing Corp. v. NLRB,** 482 U.S. 27 (1987)]

a) Application

In at least one case, the Board has found a purchaser to be a successor despite a 16-month hiatus in operations and a resumption of business with only 50 of the 500 persons employed at the time of sale. [**Tree-Free Fiber Co.,** 328 N.L.R.B. 389 (1999)]

(b) Section 301 Suit to Compel Arbitration

Following the decision in **John Wiley & Sons, Inc. v. Livingston** (*supra,* p. 106), numerous lower federal courts have required successor employers to arbitrate under the existing contract even when there was no statutory merger, provided the union sought enforcement of the arbitration provisions in a section 301 lawsuit.

1) Duty to Arbitrate if "Substantial Continuity in Workforce"

The new employer generally has been considered a "successor" (and therefore required to arbitrate) if a *majority* of the purchaser's employees worked for the predecessor. [**NLRB v. Bachrodt Chevrolet Co.,** 468 F.2d 963 (7th Cir. 1972)]

a) Scope of Duty

The duty to arbitrate may require the new employer to accept other terms in the agreement as well. For example, when the arbitration clause covers a union's claim that the whole agreement remains in force (as is often the case), the arbitrator could compel acceptance of the previous contract *en toto.* [**United States Gypsum Co. v. United Steelworkers of America, AFL-CIO,** 384 F.2d 38 (5th Cir. 1967), *cert. denied,* 389 U.S. 1042 (1968)]

b) Arbitrator's Discretion

On the other hand, the arbitrator has discretion to decide which portions of the existing contract would be inequitable if imposed on the successor (*i.e.,* due to changed circumstances, etc.). [**United Steelworkers of America v. Reliance Universal Inc.,** 335 F.2d 891 (3d Cir. 1964)]

SUCCESSOR'S DUTIES TO HONOR CONTRACT AND BARGAIN WITH EXISTING UNION REPRESENTATIVE GILBERT

METHOD OF ACQUISITION	BOUND BY CONTRACT/BARGAIN WITH REPRESENTATIVE?
SUCCESSOR ASSUMES EXISTING CONTRACT DURING ACQUISITION	Successor is ***bound*** by the contract and ***must*** bargain with representative.
SUCCESSOR IS SURVIVOR CORPORATION IN STATUTORY MERGER	Successor ***may or may not*** be deemed to have assumed contract, ***depending on state corporation law.*** Successor must bargain with representative and honor grievance procedure for those grievances stemming from merger.
SUCCESSOR ACQUIRES BUSINESS OTHER THAN BY MERGER OR PURCHASE OF ASSETS	If there is a substantial continuity in work force, successor ***must honor grievance procedure.*** Arbitrator could then impose other contract conditions—***arbitrator will look to equities***.

2) Duty When Business Is Terminated

The Supreme Court has held that a claim for severance pay raised by employees after the closing of a plant and termination of the collective bargaining agreement was arbitrable under the arbitration clause of the terminated contract. [**Nolde Bros., Inc. v. Local No. 358, Bakery & Confectionery Workers Union,** 430 U.S. 243 (1977)] While not directly presented with a successorship issue, the Court relied heavily on *John Wiley & Sons, supra,* p. 109, in reaching this decision. [*See also* **American Sink Top & Cabinet Co.,** 242 N.L.R.B. 408 (1979)]

a) But Note

The Supreme Court also held that an employer is *not* required to arbitrate the grievances of employees who were laid off almost a year after the collective bargaining agreement had expired, when—unlike the situation in *Nolde Bros., Inc.*—the grievances did not have their real source in the expired agreement. [**Litton Financial Printing Division v. NLRB,** 501 U.S. 190 (1991)]

3) Continuing Presumption of Majority Status for Union

An established union carries forward the presumption of its majority status beyond the one-year certification period, and a new employer has a duty to bargain with the union as long as that employer is a successor (*i.e.,* if there is a continuity of the business enterprise, as in *John Wiley & Sons*) and the majority of its employees were employed by the predecessor employer. [**Fall River Dyeing & Finishing Corp. v. NLRB,** *supra,* p. 108]

(c) Limitations on Section 301 Duty to Arbitrate

Following its decisions in *John Wiley & Sons, supra,* and *Burns, supra,* p. 108, the Supreme Court stated that successorship cases should *not* turn on whether they are brought under section 301 or as unfair labor practice proceedings. [**Howard Johnson Co. v. Detroit Local Joint Executive Board, Hotel & Restaurant Employees & Bartenders International Union,** 417 U.S. 249 (1974)] In *Howard Johnson Co.,* the district court and court of appeals (citing *John Wiley & Sons*) compelled a successor employer to arbitrate under the existing contract on the basis of "substantial business continuity" of the operation, even though only a small minority of former employees were retained by the new employer. The Supreme Court reversed, rejecting any duty to arbitrate under such circumstances.

1) Merger or Sale of Assets

At a minimum, *Howard Johnson Co.* requires a substantial continuity in work force, probably in the context of a merger or sale of assets, before any duty to arbitrate under section 301 will be found. In this respect, the Court stressed that the purpose of *John Wiley & Sons* was to protect employee interests during a change in ownership.

a) Rationale

If a merger or sale of assets occurs, the right to compel arbitration may be necessary to ensure that the union has some means of enforcing the contract obligations of the predecessor employer.

b) But Note

If (as in *Howard Johnson Co.*) the new employer chooses not to retain the former employees, there is no obligation to arbitrate—provided the former employees were not dismissed because of their union activities.

(4) Application of *Burns* Doctrine to Section 301 Lawsuits

The Supreme Court in *Howard Johnson Co.* declined to decide whether there was any "irreconcilable conflict" between *John Wiley & Sons and Burns* (choosing instead to distinguish *Wiley* from the case at bar). Nevertheless, the Court *strongly reaffirmed Burns* and its section 8(d) policy considerations (above), noted the requirement of consistent section 301 determinations under **Textile Workers Union v. Lincoln Mills,** 353 U.S. 488 (1957) (*see infra*, p. 140), and urged the development of "successor employer" law on a "careful, case-by-case basis." [*See* **Fall River Dyeing & Finishing Corp. v. NLRB,** *supra,* p. 110—again reaffirming the doctrine in *Burns*]

(a) Comment

The *Burns* doctrine might well be applied in future section 301 cases to hold that a successor employer need not arbitrate under the prior agreement (unless obligated to do so by contract or by state corporation law). One federal court reached precisely this conclusion in the sale of another Howard Johnson franchise where a majority of the employees were retained by the purchaser. [*See* **Bartenders & Culinary Workers Union, Local 340 v. Howard Johnson Co.,** 535 F.2d 1160 (9th Cir. 1976)]

(5) "Successor Bar"

Once a successor's duty to bargain attaches, the NLRB has ruled that the incumbent union is protected from any challenges to its continued majority status—by either employees or the successor employer—for a reasonable period of time. This is the same standard applied for unions that have been voluntarily recognized by the employer (the "recognition bar" discussed *supra*, pp. 92 *et seq.*). [*See* **St. Elizabeth Manor, Inc.,** 329 N.L.R.B. 341 (1999)] The Board reversed *St. Elizabeth Manor, Inc.*, in 20002. [**MV Transportation, Inc.,** 337 N.L.R.B. 770 (2002)] However, the Board reversed that case and returned to the establishment of a successor bar in 2011. [**UGL-UNICCO Service Co,** 357 N.L.R.B. 801 (2011) (reversing *MV Transp.*). In *UGL-UNICCO*, the Board found a successor bar that establishes an irrebuttable presumption of majority status for a reasonable period of bargaining. That reasonable period will be a minimum of six months and a maximum of one year. The actual period will be measured from the date of the first bargaining meeting between the union and the employer, and ending by applying a multi-factored test to determine when this reasonable period of time has elapsed]

f. Duty of Employer to Bargain with "Noncertified" Majority Representative

Section 8(a)(5) makes it an unfair labor practice for an employer to refuse to bargain with the representative "designated" by a majority of employees in the unit. The duty to bargain is clear where the representative has been selected and certified in an NLRB election. However, a union may present the employer with evidence (*e.g.,* authorization cards) purporting to show majority support among employees and, ***without*** seeking an election, demand to negotiate. The employer in this situation may of course petition the NLRB for an election. Whether, in the alternative, the employer may simply refuse to bargain with the union depends on the employer's own conduct during the organizing period.

(1) When Employer Unfair Labor Practices Have Impaired Electoral Process

When an employer has so interfered with the union's organizing drive that a fair election seems unlikely, the employer will be ordered to bargain based upon union authorization cards signed by a majority of employees (provided the cards "clearly state their purpose on their face"). [**NLRB v. Gissel Packing Co.,** 395 U.S. 575 (1969)] Failure to bargain in this situation would also be an employer unfair labor practice.

(a) Strike Vote

Although the opinion in ***Gissel Packing,*** *supra,* dealt only with authorization cards, ***other evidence*** of majority support, such as a union-called strike or strike vote approved by a majority of employees, would probably also suffice. [*See* **NLRB v. Dahlstrom Metallic Door Co.,** 112 F.2d 756 (2d Cir. 1940)]

(b) Odious Practices

At one time, the NLRB was willing to issue a bargaining order, even without a showing of majority support, where the employer's behavior was so flagrant that it blocked an effective opportunity to generate such support. However, the Board has now concluded that issuing a bargaining order absent a showing of majority support would be outside its discretion. [**Gourmet Foods, Inc.,** 270 N.L.R.B. 578 (1984)]

(c) Criticism of NLRB Approach

A growing number of circuit courts criticized what they considered to be a mechanical application of *Gissel Packing* by the NLRB, suggesting that the Board take into account, among other things, the effect of employee turnover and the elapsed time since the original election. [*See, e.g.,* **NLRB v. K & K Gourmet Meats, Inc.,** 640 F.2d 460 (3d Cir. 1981); **HarperCollins San Francisco v. NLRB,** 79 F.3d 1324 (2d Cir. 1996); **Be-Lo Stores v. NLRB,** 126 F.3d 268 (4th Cir. 1997); **Flamingo Hilton-Laughlin v. NLRB,** 148 F.3d 1166 (D.C. Cir. 1998)]

(d) *Gissel Packing* or *Joy Silk* Bargaining Order Guidelines

Responding to such criticism, the NLRB General Counsel issued a detailed Guideline Memorandum Concerning *Gissel* in 1999 concerning the application of *Gissel Packing.* [Memorandum GC No. 99–08, 1999 W.L. 33313998 (Nov. 10, 1999), https://www.nlrb.gov/guidance/memos-research/general-counsel-memos] A more recent General Counsel Memorandum covers *Gissel* matters. [*See* General Counsel Memorandum, Mandatory Submissions to Advice, GC 21-04 (Aug. 12, 2021), https://www.nlrb.gov/guidance/memos-research/general-counsel-memos] The Board had previously ruled before *Gissel* that an employer can refuse union recognition on the basis of authorization cards ***only if it has a good faith doubt as to the union's majority status***. [**Joy Silk Mills, Inc.,** 85 N.L.R.B. 1263 (1949)] In oral argument at the Supreme Court in *Gissel*, the Board's counsel announced the Board's current position to be that the employer's good faith was largely irrelevant (in essence orally abandoning a *Joy Silk* position of requiring an employer have good faith to reject authorization cards); the propriety of a bargaining order would turn solely on whether the employer had engaged in substantial unfair labor practices interfering with the union's election efforts. In a September 8, 2021 memorandum focused on seeking full remedies as a matter of policy, NLRB General Counsel Abruzzo announced that she would now "consider *Joy Silk*-type bargaining orders." [*See* General Counsel Memorandum, Seeking Full Remedies, GC 21-06 (Sep. 8, 2021), https://www.nlrb.gov/guidance/memos-research/general-counsel-memos]

1) Categories of Cases

The 1999 Guideline Memorandum and the *Gissel* case identified three categories related to possibly reviewing card checks for majority determinations. The Memorandum classified *Gissel-type* cases where cards might be considered as category I or category II. Category I cases (relatively rare) involve unfair labor practices by the employer that are so "outrageous" and "pervasive" as to make a fair and reliable election impossible. Most situations are category II cases, in which there are less pervasive but "serious" actions that nonetheless tend to undermine the majority strength and impede the election process. Category III cases are those that involve minor actions that do not justify a *Gissel* bargaining order because those actions do not preclude the holding of a fair rerun election.

2) Relevant Considerations for Category II Cases

In determining if remedial action is necessary in a category II case, the Guideline Memorandum provided that eight factors should be considered:

a) ***The presence of any "hallmark" violations***—such as plant closures or threats to close, unlawful discharge of union supporters, threats of job loss, or the granting of significant benefits to employees;

b) ***The number of employees affected by the violation***—either directly or indirectly by dissemination of knowledge of the occurrence among the workforce;

c) ***The size of the bargaining unit*** (the smaller the unit, the greater the likelihood that the employer's conduct would be coercive);

d) ***The identity of the perpetrator of unfair labor practices*** (*i.e.*, high-ranking officials versus first-line supervisors);

e) ***The timing*** of the unfair labor practice;

f) ***Direct evidence of an effect*** upon the majority status of the union;

g) ***The likelihood that violations will recur;*** and

h) ***Any change in circumstances*** after the violations (such as the passage of time or employee turnover).

3) **Emphasis on Injunctive Relief**

The Guideline Memorandum also emphasizes the effectiveness of section 10(j) injunctions in *Gissel*-type cases, and recommends that the propriety of seeking a section 10(j) *Gissel* order automatically be a part of any such bargaining investigation.

(e) Commencement of Order

The NLRB has ruled that a *Gissel-type* order can be made ***retroactive*** to the date the employer refused to bargain, as well as prospective from the date of the Board's order. [**Trading Port, Inc.,** 219 N.L.R.B. 298 (1975)] Several circuits have approved, at least where the union has demonstrated majority support within the bargaining unit. [*See, e.g.,* **Road Sprinkler Fitters Local 669 v. NLRB,** 681 F.2d 11 (D.C. Cir. 1982), *cert. denied,* 459 U.S. 1178 (1983); **Hedstrom Co. v. NLRB,** 629 F.2d 305 (3d Cir. 1980) (en banc), *cert. denied,* 450 U.S. 996 (1981); and *see* **Amazing Stores, Inc. v. NLRB,** 887 F.2d 328 (D.C. Cir. 1989), *cert. denied,* 494 U.S. 1029 (1990)—high turnover rate in years following order to bargain is not per se reason to overturn that order]

(f) Successor Employers

If a *Gissel* bargaining order has issued against an employer, and that employer is taken over by a successor before the bargaining order has been complied with, new circumstances may permit a fair election. Thus, the Board is *not* entitled to automatic enforcement of the *Gissel* order against the successor. [**NLRB v. Cott Corp.,** 578 F.2d 892 (1st Cir. 1978)]

(2) If Electoral Process Not Impaired

If the employer is not guilty of unfair labor practices interfering with an election, it ***need not recognize or bargain with the union*** on the basis of authorization cards or other nonelection evidence of majority support. The only recourse here for a union denied recognition is to seek an NLRB election. [**Linden Lumber Division, Summer & Co. v. NLRB,** 419 U.S. 301 (1974)]

(a) "Good Faith" Doubt by Employer Immaterial

The Supreme Court in *Linden Lumber, supra,* rejected a requirement that the employer's refusal to bargain be based on a good faith doubt as to employee support of the union. Instead, it approved the NLRB policy of not examining employer motives when there are no unfair labor practices affecting conditions for a fair election. Will the 2021 General Counsel's focus on *Joy Silk* lead to a good faith doubt requirement?

1) **Caution**

"Good faith doubt" still may be a valid requirement for an employer to ***withdraw recognition*** from a union certified for more than one year. The Board has held that such withdrawal must be based on a showing that the union ***in fact*** has lost majority status. [**Levitz Furniture Co. of the Pacific, Inc.,** 333 N.L.R.B. 717 (2000)] The Board recently modified its anticipatory withdrawal doctrine under *Levitz Furniture* in two respects.

First, the "reasonable period of time" prior to contract expiration within which recognition may be anticipatorily withdrawn is now defined as no more than 90 days before the parties' contract expires. Second, once an employer announces that it is withdrawing recognition anticipatorily, the incumbent union may file, within 45 days from the date of that announcement, an election petition (and a rival union may intervene in that representation case based on a sufficient showing of interest). [**Johnson Controls, Inc.,** 368 N.L.R.B. No. 20 (2019)] Before *Levitz Furniture*, the Supreme Court approved of the Board's prior withdrawal of recognition standard of establishing the employer had an objective, good faith grounds for doubting the union's continued majority status. [*See* **Allentown Mack Sales & Service, Inc. v. NLRB,** 522 U.S. 359 (1998)—approving this view]

a) Withdrawal Due to Violence

And, the circuit courts have upheld an employer's withdrawal of recognition when strikes involved "intolerable levels of violence." [*See* **Texas Petrochemicals Corp. v. NLRB,** 923 F.2d 398 (5th Cir. 1998); **Johns-Manville Sales Corp. v. NLRB,** 906 F.2d 1428 (10th Cir. 1990)]

2) Replacement Workers

One common situation leading to withdrawal of recognition is where an employer hires permanent replacements for most of the striking employees in an economic strike (*see* discussion *infra,* p. 164). However, the NLRB does not allow the employer to ***presume*** that all the replacement workers are antiunion, and the Supreme Court has endorsed this Board policy. [**NLRB v. Curtin Matheson Scientific, Inc.,** 494 U.S. 775 (1990)]

(b) Possible Exception When Parties Agree on Nonelection Method to Select Representative

In some cases, an employer may agree that majority status may be determined by means other than a Board election. The NLRB has suggested that an employer who breaches such an agreement by refusing to recognize a representative selected in the agreed fashion could be guilty of an unfair labor practice. [*See* **Wilder Mfg.,** 198 N.L.R.B. 998 (1972)] (The Supreme Court expressly declined to decide this question in *Linden Lumber, supra.*)

1) Right to Withdraw from Agreement

Note, however, that the employer may withdraw from any such agreement up until the time the agreement is executed. [**Georgetown Hotel v. NLRB,** 835 F.2d 1467 (D.C. Cir. 1987)]

g. Remedies in the Event of Failure to Bargain in Good Faith

Where the employer or the union refuses to bargain in good faith, the NLRB may take "such action as will effectuate the policies of [the NLRA]." [NLRA § 10(c)] This may consist of a cease and desist order to the offending party, or it may entail ***affirmative*** steps to remedy the situation.

(1) Order to Bargain

The Board may order the recalcitrant party to bargain in good faith on a specific subject and may enforce its order in the courts through the contempt procedure. [**H.K. Porter Co. v. NLRB,** 397 U.S. 99 (1970)]

(2) Compensatory Relief

At one time, the NLRB would award attorneys' fees and litigation expenses to the aggrieved party when a refusal to bargain was "clear and flagrant," and this view was approved by the D.C. Circuit Court of Appeals. [**Tiidee Products, Inc.,** 194 N.L.R.B. 1234 (1972), *enforced sub nom.,* **International Union of Electrical Workers v. NLRB,** 502 F.2d 349 (D.C. Cir. 1974)]

(a) Limits on Relief

A bit later, however, the D.C. Circuit Court concluded that—although reimbursement of negotiating expenses might be proper—NLRB awards of attorneys' fees and costs were beyond the Board's remedial powers under NLRA section 10(c) and inconsistent with American rules of "fee-shifting" as articulated by the Supreme Court. [**Unbelievable, Inc. v. NLRB,** 118 F.3d 795 (D.C. Cir. 1997)]

1) The circuit court left open whether the NLRB might have power to make such awards under the "bad-faith" exception to the American rule against awarding litigation expenses.

2) In any event, the Board has continued to award fees and costs in extreme cases. [*See, e.g.,* **Alwin Manufacturing Co.,** 326 N.L.R.B. 646 (1998); **Lake Holiday Associates, Inc.,** 325 N.L.R.B. 469 (1998)]

(b) And Note

Compensatory relief is *not* appropriate when a refusal to bargain is less than brazen or flagrant, even though it may constitute an unfair labor practice. [**Culinary Alliance & Bartenders Union, Local 703 v. NLRB,** 488 F.2d 664 (9th Cir. 1973)]

(3) Acceptance of Agreement Cannot Be Ordered

The Board cannot force a party to ***accept*** any particular agreement. Thus, the NLRB is not "effectuating NLRA policies" under section 10(c) when it orders an employer to accept a check-off provision on which the parties could not independently agree. [**H.K. Porter Co. v. NLRB,** *supra,* p. 116]

(4) No "Make Whole" Orders

With the possible exception of cases in which an employer's refusal to bargain is "patently frivolous" [*see* **Heck's, Inc.,** 215 N.L.R.B. 765 (1974)], the NLRB does not consider itself to have authority to issue a "make whole" order in refusal to bargain cases. (Such an order would make wage and other benefits ultimately obtained by the union retroactive to the date of the employer's refusal to bargain.) [**Tiidee Products, Inc.,** *supra,* p. 116]

4. Subjects of Collective Bargaining

a. Mandatory, Permissive, and Illegal Subjects of Bargaining

Possible subjects for collective bargaining fall into three categories: (i) those over which bargaining is ***required by statute*** (mandatory); (ii) those over which the parties may bargain ***if they choose*** (permissive); and (iii) those over which the parties ***may not bargain*** under any circumstances (illegal).

(1) Mandatory Subjects

NLRA section 8(d) requires employers and unions to bargain collectively on "***wages, hours and other terms and conditions of employment,*** or the negotiation of an agreement, or any question arising thereunder." Since the NLRA does not define "wages, hours, and other terms and conditions of employment," the NLRB and the courts must determine what subjects are within the statutory requirement.

SCOPE OF DUTY TO BARGAIN (MANDATORY VS. PERMISSIVE SUBJECTS)

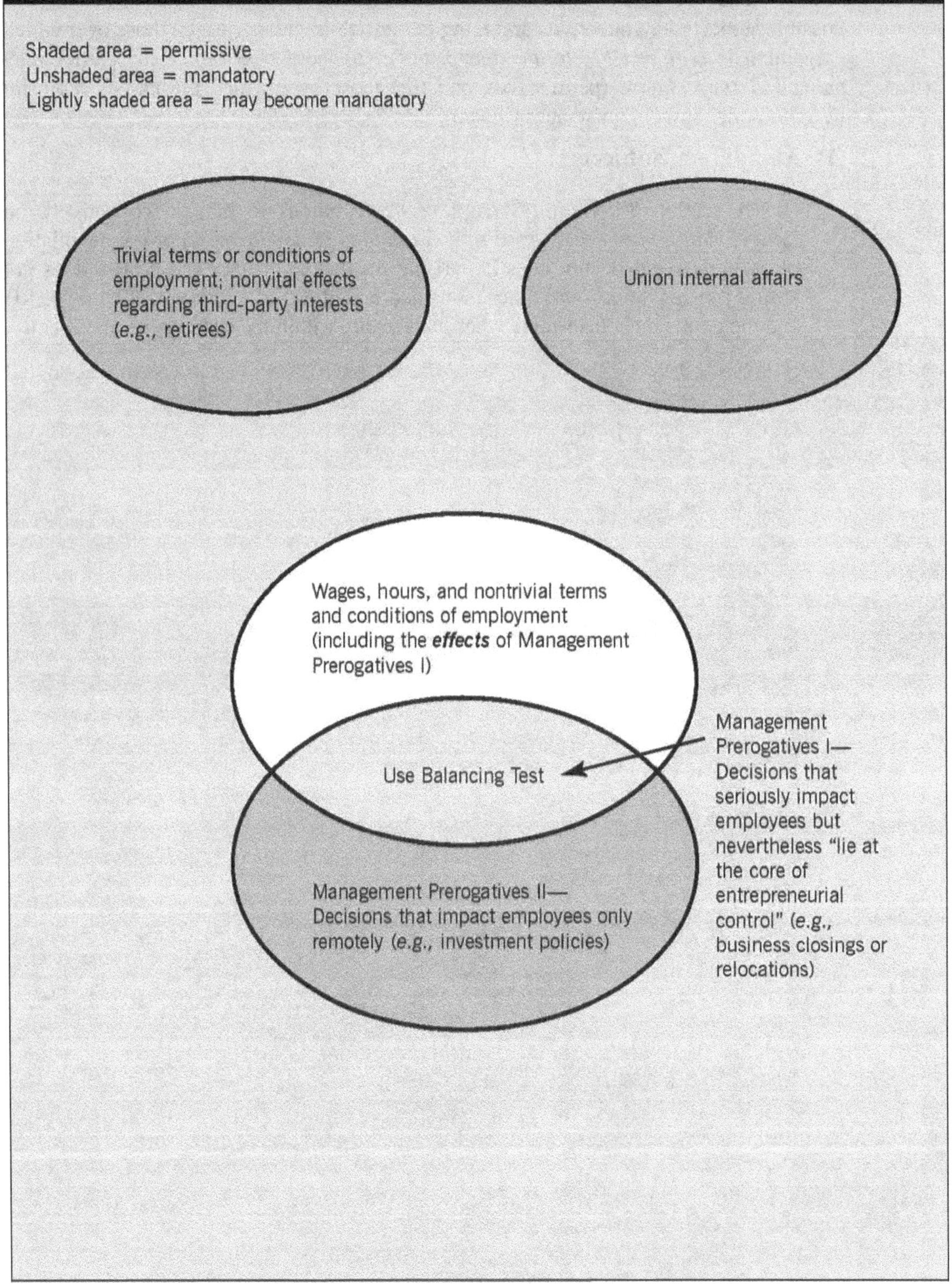

(a) Retirement Plan Benefits

Retirement benefits fall within the meaning of "wages, rate of pay, hours of employment or other conditions of employment," and hence are mandatory bargaining subjects. [**Inland Steel Co. v. NLRB,** 170 F.2d 247 (7th Cir. 1948); *but see* **Toledo Typographical Union No. 63 v. NLRB** ("*Toledo Blade Co.*"), 907 F.2d 1220 (D.C. Cir. 1990), *cert. denied,* 498 U.S. 1053 (1991)—contract provision concerning employer's right to offer retirement and/or separation incentives held ***not*** to be a mandatory subject of bargaining]

1) But Note

The ***manner*** in which retiree health benefits are paid by the employer (*i.e.,* whether through a union-negotiated insurance plan or a supplemental Medicare premium initiated by the employer) is not a mandatory subject for bargaining since it does not "vitally affect" the terms and conditions for active employees. [**Allied Chemical & Alkali Workers, Local Union No. 1 v. Pittsburgh Plate Glass Co.,** *supra,* p. 40]

(b) In-Plant Food Prices

Resolving a sharp disagreement between the NLRB and the circuit courts, the Supreme Court has approved the Board's view that "in-plant" food services and prices are within the scope of mandatory bargaining. [**Ford Motor Co. v. NLRB,** 441 U.S. 488 (1979)]

1) Rationale

The Court reached this conclusion because food prices were a significant aspect of the relationship between employer and employees, there was a widespread industry pattern of bargaining over them, and the Board's judgment was entitled to deference. In response to the argument that such food prices did not "vitally affect" employees, the Court distinguished *Pittsburgh Plate Glass, supra,* p. 119, stating that the "vital effect" test applied only where the interests of third parties outside the bargaining relationship were involved.

(c) Work Assignments

An employer's refusal to bargain over reclassification and transfer of employees and work assignments violates section 8(d), since a "condition of employment" is involved. [**Brotherhood of Locomotive Firemen & Enginemen,** 168 N.L.R.B. 677 (1967)]

(d) Grievances

The area of grievances normally concerns work conditions and is therefore a mandatory subject of bargaining. However, a special provision permits the settlement of ***individual grievances*** without collective bargaining, under certain circumstances. [NLRA § 9(a); *see infra,* p. 205]

(e) Safety Rules and Practices

The phrase "other terms and conditions of employment" also includes safety rules and practices, and this area is a mandatory subject of bargaining. [**NLRB v. Gulf Power Co.,** 384 F.2d 822 (5th Cir. 1967)]

1) Prior Application

Prior to 1970, however, very few substantive protections were incorporated in collective bargaining agreements. Most contracts contained a "management rights" clause that gave the employer unilateral control over safety and health, and employees were obliged to seek relief "after the fact" for injuries sustained on the job.

2) Occupational Safety and Health Act ("OSHA")

In 1970, Congress passed the Occupational Safety and Health Act [29 U.S.C. §§ 651 *et seq.*] in response to increasing industrial accidents and health hazards. Basically, OSHA empowers the Secretary of Labor to establish health and safety standards, to investigate complaints of employees and issue citations to employers for violation of such standards, and to seek penalties from the Occupational Safety and Health Review Commission for uncorrected violations. Commission rulings are subject to judicial review by federal courts of appeal.

a) Effect

As a result of OSHA, it is not uncommon for collective bargaining agreements to incorporate OSHA (and related state) standards by reference, thereby creating the possibility of grievance arbitration for violations thereof. (*See* discussion of arbitration process, *infra,* pp. 129 *et seq.*)

3) Drug and Alcohol Testing

The NLRB has held that such testing of employees who suffer work-related injuries requiring medical treatment is a mandatory subject of bargaining, but that the testing of job applicants is not. Applicants are not considered "employees," nor does their testing "vitally" affect employees' work conditions. [**Johnson-Bateman Co.,** 295 N.L.R.B. 180 (1989)]

(f) Monitoring Employees in Workplace

The Board likewise has required employers to bargain over the use of ***surveillance cameras in the plant*** [**Colgate-Palmolive Co.,** 323 N.L.R.B. 515 (1997)], ***mandatory physical examinations*** [**Lockheed Shipbuilding & Construction Co.,** 273 N.L.R.B. 171 (1984)], and *polygraph testing* [**Austine-Berryhill, Inc.,** 246 N.L.R.B. 1139 (1979)]. Employers have contended that such measures are within their "exclusive entrepreneurial control" [*see* **Fibreboard Paper & Products Corp. v. NLRB,** 379 U.S. 203 (1964), (Stewart, J., concurring)—discussed *infra,* p. 122], but the NLRB has not accepted this argument.

(g) No Duty to Bargain if Subject Is Covered by Existing Agreement

Neither party need bargain on a subject that is covered by an existing agreement, *e.g.,* when the union seeks to ***modify*** some term or provision before the time provided in the contract for renegotiation. [NLRA § 8(d)]

(h) No Duty to Bargain on Policy Objectives

Likewise, a union demand that the employer contribute to a fund used exclusively to promote the industry is ***not*** a mandatory bargaining subject. [**NLRB v. Detroit Resilient Floor Decorators, Local Union No. 2265,** 317 F.2d 269 (6th Cir. 1963)]

1) **Rationale**

To hold that a party ***must*** bargain over any matter that might conceivably enhance prospects for the industry would turn collective bargaining into a debate on policy objectives.

(2) Permissive Subjects

If a subject is "bargainable" (*i.e.*, if bargaining upon the subject is ***not foreclosed***) ***and*** if it is ***not mandatory,*** the employer and the union may bargain collectively about the subject only if ***both elect*** to do so.

(a) Applications

Areas such as corporate organization, size and composition of the supervisory force, general business practices, and location of plants are generally considered to be management prerogatives (*see* below). However, they may become subjects for bargaining at the option of the employer.

(b) Note

The union may not require an agreement to bargain on such voluntary subjects as a precondition to bargaining on ***mandatory*** subjects. [**NLRB v. Wooster Division of Borg-Warner Corp.,** 356 U.S. 342 (1958)]

(c) Effect of Inclusion in Collective Agreement

The mere fact that the parties bargained over a permissive subject and included it in their collective bargaining agreement does ***not*** convert the subject from "permissive" to "mandatory." Thus, an employer is ***not guilty of an unfair labor practice*** if it thereafter unilaterally changes or modifies such terms in the agreement without consulting the union. The union's remedy in such cases is a ***breach of contract*** action or a grievance. [**Allied Chemical & Alkali Workers, Local Union No. 1 v. Pittsburgh Plate Glass Co.,** *supra,* p. 119—employer and union had agreed on manner of paying retirement benefits, but employer unilaterally changed this; held not an unfair labor practice because subject matter was only permissive]

(3) Nonbargainable Subjects

Finally, bargaining may be prohibited on a topic either because the subject ***must be included*** in the contract in every case, or because it ***cannot lawfully be included*** in any case.

Example: A subject that ***must*** be included in the contract, and is therefore nonbargainable, is recognition of the union—because an employer, upon request, must include such a provision in the contract. [**Simplicity Pattern Co.,** 102 N.L.R.B. 1283 (1953)]

Example: Subjects that ***cannot*** lawfully be made part of the contract, and hence are equally nonbargainable, are demands by the union for a "closed shop," preferential hiring for union members, or a "check off" system (when the employer deducts union dues from an employee's paycheck and remits the money to the union) that does not meet statutory requirements. [*See* NLRA § 8(a)(5), (b)(3), (d), *and see infra*, p. 209]

Example: An employer may not bargain with a union to waive the right to distribute literature on company property. Such a waiver would violate the

employees' section 7 rights, and would be illegal. [**NLRB v. Magnavox Co.,** 415 U.S. 322 (1974); *and see supra,* p. 47]

(a) **Remedy**

If a subject is nonbargainable, the courts may ***enjoin*** either party from insisting upon that subject as part of the collective bargaining contract. [**Pennello v. International Union, UMW,** 88 F. Supp. 935 (D.D.C. 1950)]

b. Management Prerogatives and Union Participation

Most managerial prerogatives—such as expansion of company facilities, production decisions, and the like—are considered ***permissive*** subjects of bargaining. Under certain circumstances, however, an area generally considered to be the prerogative of management may become a ***mandatory*** subject.

(1) Unit Work by Supervisors

The performance of production work by a supervisor has been held to be a mandatory bargaining subject (and not a management prerogative) when the union contends that the supervisor is ***depriving union employees of overtime pay.*** [**Crown Coach Corp.,** 155 N.L.R.B. 625 (1965)]

(2) Subcontracting of Work Covered by Collective Bargaining Agreement

An employer may have a duty to bargain with the union before making such economically motivated decisions as ***contracting out work formerly done on the premises by its employees,*** because such decisions deprive employees of their employment. [**Fibreboard Paper & Products Corp. v. NLRB,** *supra,* p. 120] In an influential concurring opinion, however, Justice Stewart emphasized that matters "at the core of entrepreneurial control" (*e.g.,* decisions central to the scope and direction of the enterprise) are management prerogatives and need *not* be bargained about.

(a) **Note**

The application of *Fibreboard* to particular fact situations has been somewhat inconsistent. For a number of years, the NLRB gave a wide scope to this duty to bargain (finding it in nearly every employer decision that impaired employment security), while most courts of appeal imposed a much narrower standard. In 1971, however, the Board acquiesced in the narrow standard reflected in Justice Stewart's concurring opinion in *Fibreboard.* [**General Motors Corp.,** 191 N.L.R.B. 951 (1971); *and see* **Collateral Control Corp.,** 288 N.L.R.B. 308 (1988)]

(3) General Approach—"Balancing Test"

In 1981, the Supreme Court reviewed this area and interpreted *Fibreboard* to require a ***case-by-case balancing*** of the employer's need for "unencumbered decisionmaking" against the benefits to labor-management relations and the bargaining process from bargaining over a particular management decision. [**First National Maintenance Corp. v. NLRB,** 452 U.S. 666 (1981)]

EXAM TIP GILBERT

Note that management prerogatives can become mandatory subjects under certain circumstances. For example, unit work performed by supervisors becomes a mandatory topic when the union contends that the practice deprives union employees of overtime pay. To determine if a topic normally considered a management prerogative has become mandatory, apply the *Fibreboard* test—*i.e.,* balance the ***employer's need for unencumbered decisionmaking*** against the ***benefits to labor-management relations and the bargaining process*** from bargaining over the topic.

(a) Closure of Business

The Court in *First National Maintenance* held that bargaining was ***not*** required over an employer's decision to partially close a business, since it involved a change in the scope or direction of the enterprise "akin to the decision of whether to be in business at all."

1) Distinguish

The NLRB *has* required the employer to bargain over a decision to close and subcontract one of five departments in its food processing business, where capital expenditures were insubstantial, the overall nature of the business continued unchanged, and the increased production costs prompting the decision intimately involved wages and other issues susceptible to collective bargaining. [**Bob's Big Boy Family Restaurants, Division of Marriott Corp.,** 264 N.L.R.B. 1369 (1982); *and see* **Collateral Control Corp.,** *supra*; **Storer Cable TV,** 295 N.L.R.B. 295 (1989); **Cone Mills Corp.,** 298 N.L.R.B. 661 (1990)]

2) Statutory Notice Period for Plant Closings

Under the Worker Adjustment and Retraining Notification Act ("WARN") [21 U.S.C. § 2101], employers must provide ***60 days' advance notice*** of plant closings and layoffs. WARN applies to employers with 100 or more employees and requires notice in the following situations:

a) When 50 or more employees at one site are to lose their jobs because of a plant ***shutdown;***

b) When a ***layoff*** will cause 50 or more employees to lose their jobs, if the affected employees constitute one-third or more of the total workforce at the site; ***or***

c) When a ***layoff will affect*** *500* or more employees (regardless of the percentage of the workforce they represent).

(b) Sale of Business

The decision to sell all or part of a business presumably would be analyzed in the same manner as closure of a business as lower courts have done. [*See* **NLRB v. Transmarine Navigation Corp.,** 380 F.2d 933 (9th Cir. 1967)]

(c) Transfer of Business

Reacting to criticism from the courts that it was prone to accept an employer's decision to transfer or relocate business, rather than analyze that decision [*see, e.g.,* **Food & Commercial Workers Local 150-A v. NLRB** ("*Dubuque*

Packing Co."), 880 F.2d 1422 (D.C. Cir. 1989)], the Board has shifted the burden of proof to the ***employer*** in determining whether a decision to relocate is a mandatory subject of bargaining. Once the NLRB establishes a prima facie case for bargaining by showing that the relocation does not involve a change in the nature of the business, the employer must rebut by showing that (i) the relocated work varies significantly, (ii) the existing work was discontinued and not relocated, (iii) the new work involves a change in the scope and direction of the business, (iv) labor costs were not a factor in the decision, or (v) union concessions could not have affected the decision to relocate. [**Dubuque Packing Co.,** 303 N.L.R.B. 386 (1991), *enforced sub. nom.* **United Food & Commercial Workers Union Local 150-A v. NLRB,** 1 F.3d 24 (D.C. Cir. 1993), *cert. dismissed,* 511 U.S. 1138 (1994)]

1) Earlier Approach

The NLRB had applied *First National Maintenance* to find that bargaining was *not* required over an employer's decision to transfer research and development work from a unionized location to a new, nonunion research center, where the transfer was part of an overall corporate consolidation. [**Otis Elevator Co.** ("*Otis Elevator I*"), 269 N.L.R.B. 891 (1984)] But this decision was effectively overruled by *Dubuque Packing Co., supra.*

2) And Note

If a transfer of work is shown to be in conflict with a *work protection clause* in the collective bargaining contract, which prohibits the transfer of work from the unit, the employer may be required to bargain about it. [*See* **Brown Co.,** 121 L.R.R.M. 1250 (N.L.R.B. 1986); *and see* discussion *infra*, p. 129]

(4) Duty to Bargain over Impact of Managerial Decisions

Even when a managerial decision (*e.g.*, sale or closure of business) is outside the scope of mandatory bargaining, the employer still must bargain over the *effects* of that decision on employees. This would include bargaining about severance pay, accumulated or "earned" fringe benefits, pensions, and the like, at such time as the bargaining would be meaningful. [**First National Maintenance Corp. v. NLRB,** *supra,* p. 122; **Otis Elevator Co.** ("*Otis Elevator II*"), 283 N.L.R.B. 223 (1987); **Town & Country Manufacturing Co.,** 136 N.L.R.B. 1022 (1962)]

c. Waiver of Bargaining Rights by Union

Unless there is a clear and *specific* waiver by the union of its bargaining rights on a particular subject, *no waiver will be implied.* As a general policy matter, the NLRB is reluctant to deprive employees of their right to bargain over a subject.

(1) Union Silence on Subject Not Waiver

No waiver will be implied from the mere fact that a contract entered into by the union is silent on the subject matter; the union is free to raise the matter at a later time. (But failure to include some demand or provision sought by the employer may be evidence of the employer's intent to waive it.)

(2) Fundamental Employee Rights Cannot Be Waived

And, even an explicit waiver by the union may be ineffective if ***fundamental*** employee rights are concerned. For example, the right of employees to be represented in bargaining with the employer is a ***public right***, rather than a private right, and unions do not have the power to waive that right—even explicitly. [**NLRB v. Magnavox Co.,** *supra,* p. 121]

EXAM TIP GILBERT

Beware of fact patterns in which the union agrees to a broad waiver provision (commonly called a "zipper" clause) that purports to waive the right to bargain. The Board would probably view such a provision as a waiver only of the right to bargain over entirely new subjects unless it ***specifically*** mentions topic areas.

5. Employer Economic Weapons—"Lockout"

An employer engages in a "lockout" when it closes a plant to workers ***in anticipation of*** (*i.e.,* prior to) a strike. The lockout traditionally has been one of the most powerful weapons available to an employer in combatting union pressure. By shutting down the plant prior to a strike and preventing employees from coming to work, the employer gains the initiative: It can decide when the work stoppage begins and which plants or plant sections will be closed. Furthermore, the employer can control which (and how many) employees will be out of work, and this may discourage strike activity. Since Congress has never expressly prohibited the use of "lockouts" by employers, the NLRB and the courts have had to analyze this weapon as a possible violation of sections 8(a)(1) or 8(a)(3), *i.e.,* as an employer unfair labor practice.

a. Permissible "Lockouts"

An employer may lawfully "lock out" employees if:

(i) Collective bargaining negotiations have reached an *impasse*; or

(ii) *"Special circumstances" are* present, such as the threat of imminent and irreparable economic loss to the employer (*e.g.,* lack of profitable work).

(1) Note

The Court in *American Ship Building* (*supra,* p. 73) ruled that the NLRA does not protect unions from the economic consequences of a bargaining dispute, and that a lockout is ***not*** an "inherently destructive" act automatically prohibited by sections 8(a)(1) or 8(a)(3). Thus, where a bargaining impasse is reached, a temporary layoff is permissible, even if used solely to create pressure in support of the employer's bargaining position.

(2) Replacements

The NLRB and several circuit courts have held that the employer may hire temporary replacements for locked-out employees as a means of applying further bargaining pressure on the employees. [**Harter Equipment, Inc.,** 280 N.L.R.B. 597 (1986), *enforced sub nom.* **Operating Engineers Local 825 v. NLRB,** 829 F.2d 458 (3d Cir. 1987); *and see* **International Brotherhood of Boilermakers, Local 88 v. NLRB,** 858 F.2d 756 (D.C. Cir. 1988); **Inter-Collegiate Press v. NLRB,** *supra,* p. 73]

(a) **But Note**

At least one court has held that a lockout accompanied by the hiring of temporary replacements is per se an interference with protected employee rights and an unfair labor practice. [**Inland Trucking Co. v. NLRB,** 440 F.2d 562 (7th Cir.), *cert. denied,* 404 U.S. 858 (1971)]

(b) **Distinguish—Permanent Replacements**

The employer may not hire *permanent* replacements without first consulting the union. [**Johns-Manville Products Corp.,** *supra,* p. 74]

b. **Unlawful Lockouts**

Lockouts become an employer unfair labor practice if the employer is evading the duty to bargain in good faith (*supra,* pp. 101 *et seq.*) or was *intending to injure the union.* [*See* **American Ship Building,** *supra,* p. 125; *and see* **Tonkin Corp.,** 165 N.L.R.B. 607 (1967)]

e.g. **Example:** Where the employer announces that union activity is the reason for the shutdown, the lockout clearly is unlawful. Likewise, declaring an "impasse" in bargaining with the union after one day of negotiations, and locking out and replacing employees, is an employer unfair labor practice, since there has been no real exploration of the issues and only the employer believed that an impasse had been reached. [**Teamsters Local Union No. 639 v. NLRB,** 924 F.2d 1078 (D.C. Cir. 1991)]

(1) **Evidence of Intent**

Extrinsic evidence may be used to show an antiunion motivation on the part of the employer. [**NLRB v. Norma Mining Co.,** 206 F.2d 38 (4th Cir. 1953)—employer claimed mine was shut down due to road conditions, but Board found intent to "break" the union was the real motive]

6. Effect of a Strike on the Bargaining Process

The general subject of strikes, boycotts, and picketing is covered *infra,* pp. 151 *et seq.* However, it is useful to assess the possible effect of a strike on the policies, rules, and duties relating to the bargaining process.

a. **Employer's Duty**

The employer has a duty to bargain until (i) an agreement has been reached, (ii) a genuine impasse has developed, or (iii) a breach in negotiations occurs without its fault. Therefore, unless a strike violates the contract between the parties or some provision of the law, *the strike does not automatically relieve the employer of a duty to bargain.* Furthermore, if the strike was not initiated by the union in bad faith, the employer remains under a duty to bargain. [**NLRB v. J.H. Rutter-Rex Manufacturing Co.,** 245 F.2d 594 (5th Cir. 1957)]

(1) **And Note**

The duty to bargain continues during a shutdown, lockout, or layoff. [**International Ladies Garment Workers' Union v. NLRB,** 374 F.2d 295 (D.C. Cir.), *cert. denied sub. nom.* **Garwin Corp. v. NLRB,** 387 U.S. 942 (1967)]

b. Employer-Employee Relations During an Impasse

Once an impasse has developed between the parties and a strike occurs, the employer may—under certain circumstances—hire replacements, poll the striking employees, and unilaterally increase wages.

(1) Implementation of Terms by Employer

Moreover, an employer is permitted to *implement* his final offer package after an impasse in negotiations has occurred—provided that the impasse is an overall stalemate. [**Duffy Tool & Stamping LLC v. NLRB,** 233 F.3d 995 (7th Cir. 2000)—employer cannot implement final offer on a single issue at impasse when negotiations continue on other issues]

EMPLOYER OPTIONS AT AN IMPASSE	GILBERT
IMPLEMENTATION	An employer may implement his final offer package, provided that negotiations on other issues are not taking place.
LOCKOUT	An impasse ***or*** special circumstances (*i.e.,* imminent and irreparable economic harm) are required. An unlawful lockout becomes an unfair labor practice if the employer is evading the duty to bargain in good faith or was intending to injure the union.
LOCKOUT PLUS REPLACEMENTS	An employer ***may*** hire ***temporary*** replacements (conflicting case law whether this is per se an unfair labor practice). An employer may ***not*** hire permanent replacements without first consulting the union.

(2) Replacements

If the strike is not a result of employer unfair labor practices, the employer has a right to hire replacements to carry on the business without bargaining with the union over this matter. [**Pacific Gamble Robinson Co. v. NLRB,** 186 F.2d 106 (6th Cir. 1950)]

(3) Polls

It is not an unfair labor practice for the employer to send a letter to striking employees to determine how many are willing to return to work on *terms formerly offered by the employer and rejected by the union,* especially where the letter states that no compulsion to return will be exerted and that the legal rights of strikers will be protected. [**NLRB v. Penokee Veneer Co.,** 168 F.2d 868 (7th Cir. 1948)]

(4) Wage Increase

It ***would*** be an unfair labor practice for an employer, while negotiations with the union are deadlocked, unilaterally to *increase wages above the level offered* in its proposal during negotiations. *Rationale:* The employer's paying more than previously offered to the union impairs the union's stature with employees and hence may prejudice subsequent negotiations. [**NLRB v. Crompton-Highland Mills, Inc.,** 337 U.S. 217 (1949)]

(a) **Unilateral Merit Increase**

Similarly, when an employer proposes during negotiations that it be given unlimited discretion to award merit increases to employees, the employer cannot unilaterally implement that proposal during an impasse. [**McClatchy Newspapers, Inc. v. NLRB,** 131 F.3d 1026 (D.C. Cir. 1997)]

(5) **And Note—Impasse Between Union and Multiemployer Association**

A bargaining impasse between a multiemployer association (*supra,* p. 89) and the union does not justify a unilateral withdrawal from the association by a member. *Rationale:* An impasse is a temporary condition that does not necessarily signify a breakdown of the multiemployer bargaining format, and permitting unilateral withdrawal at such a point would eliminate the usefulness of such a format as a practical matter. [**Charles D. Bonanno Linen Service, Inc. v. NLRB,** 454 U.S. 404 (1982)]

7. Modifying or Terminating an Existing Agreement—Union-Employer Bargaining Duties

a. Procedure

If *either party* wishes to modify or terminate a collective bargaining agreement, that party must take the following steps:

(1) *It must notify the other party in writing* of this intention (i) *60 days* prior to the expiration date of the contract, or (ii) 60 days prior to the time it proposes to terminate or modify, if the contract contains no expiration date;

(2) ***It must offer to meet and confer with the other party*** for the purpose of negotiating a new contract or a contract containing the proposed modifications;

(3) ***It must notify the appropriate federal, state, or territorial mediation agency*** within 30 days of the first notice, unless an agreement has been reached by that time; and

(4) ***The terms and conditions of the existing contract must continue in full force and effect,*** without resort by any party to a strike or lockout, for a period of 60 days after the first notice is given or until the expiration date of the contract, whichever occurs later. [NLRA § 8(d)] (For discussion of strikes and lockouts during renegotiation of the contract, *see infra,* p. 157.)

b. Qualifications

Section 8(d) provides two qualifications to the above procedure:

(1) **NLRB Certifies Another Union**

Where the NLRB certifies another union during the stated period, thereby superseding the contracting union, the second, third, and fourth steps (above) would not apply.

(2) **Modification Prior to Time for Renegotiation**

Neither party is required to consider a proposal to modify an existing agreement if the modification would become effective ***prior to the time provided in the agreement for renegotiation*** (*see supra,* p. 120).

c. What Constitutes a "Modification"

It is not always clear whether unilateral action by one party modifies the terms of a contract. For example, would the ***transfer of work*** by an employer from a unionized plant to a nonunion plant (to reduce labor costs) modify the recognition clause in its collective bargaining agreement with the union? For many years the NLRB held that this constituted a "modification" under section 8(d). In 1984, however, the Board overruled its prior decisions and held that such transfers in and of themselves would *not* modify the agreement. [**Milwaukee Spring Division of Illinois Spring Co.,** 268 N.L.R.B. 601 (1984), *enforced sub. nom.* **United Auto Workers v. NLRB,** 765 F.2d 175 (D.C. Cir. 1985); *and see* discussion *supra,* p. 123]

B. Administering the Collective Bargaining Agreement

1. Introduction

The duty to bargain in good faith includes bargaining over the interpretation (as well as the establishment) of a collective agreement. Settlement of disputes that arise under collective bargaining agreements can take three basic forms:

a. ***The parties may reach agreement informally*** (*i.e.,* a supervisor or other management official may deal directly with the employee and/or the union representative to arrive at a settlement);

b. ***The issue may be settled by an arbitrator*** (provided the matter in question is arbitrable); or

c. ***The issue may be taken to court when there is an alleged breach of the agreement*** (*e.g.,* a refusal by one of the parties to arbitrate).

2. Arbitration Process

Most collective bargaining agreements contain a grievance-arbitration procedure for settling disputes that arise under the agreement. Typical provisions would include: (i) a *definition* of what constitutes a "grievance"; (ii) the *standing* of union officials and individual employees, jointly or separately, to initiate a grievance; (iii) some *time limitation* for initiating grievances or for disposing of them through the grievance process; and (iv) the *scope of the arbitrator's authority,* remedies available to the arbitrator, and methods for selecting the arbitrator.

a. Distinguish—Mediation and Conciliation

In ***arbitration,*** the parties submit issues for ***decision*** by a mutually agreed-upon third party. ***Mediation and conciliation,*** on the other hand, attempt to ***persuade*** the disputants to reach an agreement on their own initiative. Mediators typically do not propose settlements, and they never reach a "decision." Instead, they function as intermediaries between the parties, helping to create a proper atmosphere for settlement.

b. Arbitration of Grievances

A collective bargaining agreement usually provides steps that must be taken by the parties to resolve the dispute before calling in an arbitrator. Generally, the aggrieved party is represented by the union throughout this series of steps, which is referred to as the "grievance machinery." If the dispute cannot be resolved at the initial level or "step" in the procedure, the grievance passes from lower managerial personnel to higher levels of management and ultimately to arbitration. Normally, the union, as the exclusive bargaining representative, has ***complete control*** over processing of the grievance for the employees (*see* discussion *infra,* pp. 205 *et seq.*).

(1) Initiating Arbitration

Most agreements provide that arbitration is mandatory if requested by either party.

(2) Selecting the Arbitrator

An arbitrator may be selected ad hoc for each dispute, or a permanent arbitrator can be designated by the agreement. Arbitration may be conducted by one person agreed upon by both parties, or by a tripartite board in which one member is chosen by management, one member by the union, and the third member by both parties.

(a) Note

Neutral agencies, such as the FMCS and the American Arbitration Association, can help the parties to select qualified, impartial arbitrators.

(3) Hearings

The time and place for arbitration usually is left to the parties, but the arbitrator normally determines hearing procedures. (The American Arbitration Association publishes suggested procedures for arbitrators.)

(a) Nature of Hearings

As a general rule, hearings are informal. The more controversial the issue or the more formalized the grievance procedure, however, the stricter the adherence to constitutional due process and rules of evidence will be considered.

(b) Parties May Regulate

Of course, any and all details of the arbitration procedure can be spelled out by the parties in the collective bargaining agreement.

(4) Other Procedures Illegal

If arbitration of a grievance is called for by the collective bargaining agreement, any resort to a strike or other pressure to resolve the dispute, without first using the contractual grievance procedure, violates the collective bargaining agreement.

c. Authority of the Arbitrator

The arbitrator's authority to decide the merits of disputes arising under a collective bargaining agreement is controlled by the arbitration clause of the agreement. Usually, however, the contract will contain a general clause requiring arbitration of disputes involving the "***interpretation***" or "***application***" of contract provisions.

(1) Authority Broadly Construed

Clauses authorizing the arbitration of disputes involving the "interpretation" or "application" of the agreement are construed ***very broadly***—to cover all disputes other than those ***explicitly*** withdrawn from arbitration by the terms of the contract itself. [**United Steelworkers of America v. Warrior & Gulf Navigation Co.,** 363 U.S. 574 (1960); *and see supra,* p. 130]

e.g. **Example:** In *Warrior & Gulf Navigation, supra,* the question was whether a clause excluding "disputes arising strictly from functions of management" prevented arbitration of a dispute growing out of a management decision to contract out work. The Court held that the clause did not ***explicitly*** cover such a dispute, and hence it had to be arbitrated.

e.g. **Example:** In **International Union of Operating Engineers, Local 150 v. Flair Builders, Inc.,** 406 U.S. 487 (1972), a provision binding the parties to arbitrate "any dispute" was held to cover the issue of whether the union was guilty of "laches" in instituting the grievance procedure. And in **Gateway Coal Co. v. UMW,** 414 U.S. 368 (1974), a provision requiring arbitration of "any local trouble of any kind" was held to encompass safety disputes involving falsification of records on safe air flow in mining operations.

(2) Effect of Precedent

(a) Participation Is Not a Waiver as to Subsequent Disputes

If a party (employer or union) participates in arbitration, it does not thereby waive its right to object to arbitration of a subsequent dispute on the same type of issue under the same contract, [***In re*** **Towns and James, Inc.,** 197 Misc. 1022 (1950)]

(b) Prior Awards Not Binding

Arbitrators are not bound to follow prior awards, even awards under the same agreement. But arbitrators generally ***will*** follow an earlier award involving the same parties, the same agreement, and the same general fact situation, [*See, e.g.,* **NFL Players Ass'n v. NFL,** 831 F.3d 985, 995–96 (8th Cir. 2016) (discussing arbitrator's consideration of prior arbitral precedent involving the same parties and same agreement as the "law of the shop")]

d. Deferral by NLRB to the Arbitration Process

The NLRB has jurisdiction to resolve unfair labor practices in whatever context they arise. It may happen that a dispute that falls within the contractual grievance and arbitration machinery of the parties also involves an unfair labor practice (*e.g.,* work assignment disputes). In this area, the Board has developed certain rules on when (and to what extent) it will defer to arbitration of the dispute.

(1) Post-Award Deferral—*Spielberg* Doctrine

Since 1955, in unfair labor practice disputes, the NLRB has deferred to existing arbitration awards ***only if*** (i) all parties ***acquiesced*** in arbitration of the dispute, (ii) the arbitration proceedings ***on their face were "fair" and "regular,"*** (iii) the ***factual issues*** underlying the unfair labor practice charge before the Board ***were heard and determined*** by the arbitrator, and (iv) the arbitrator's award was ***not "clearly repugnant to the purposes and policies"*** of the Taft-Hartley Act. [**Spielberg Manufacturing Co.,** 112 N.L.R.B. 1080 (1955)]

(a) Application of *Spielberg*

In a 1984 decision, the Board issued the following guidelines in applying the *Spielberg* criteria:

(i) ***The arbitrator will be deemed to have adequately considered*** the unfair labor practice issue if the facts relevant to that issue were presented before the arbitrator and paralleled the facts relevant to the contractual issue; and

(ii) ***The award need not be totally consistent*** with NLRB precedents, and will not be considered repugnant to the Taft-Hartley Act unless it is "palpably wrong."

[**Olin Corp.,** 268 N.L.R.B. 573 (1984)]

1) Status of Guidelines Since Olin

More recently, the Board attempted to address the appropriate balance to exert when considering the Board's role in protecting employee rights versus respecting the parties' agreement to let an arbitrator resolve their disputes. *See* [**Babcock & Wilcox Construction Co.,** 361 N.L.R.B. 1127 (2014)] Prior to *Babcock*, the Board tended to defer to arbitration under *Spielberg* and *Olin* and its progeny.

In *Babcock*, the Board changed that approach by agreeing to only defer to arbitral decisions if 1) the arbitrator was explicitly authorized to decide the unfair labor practice; 2) the arbitrator was presented with and considered the statutory issue, or was prevented from doing so by the party opposing deferral; and 3) Board law reasonably permitted the award. The Board wanted to make sure that some statutory claims did not slip through the cracks un-der the Spielberg standard which allowed deferral as long as the award was not repugnant.

The Board overruled *Babcock* and readopted the *Olin/Spielberg* standards in 2019. [**United Parcel Service,** 369 N.L.R.B. No. 1 (2019)] The Board claimed the overruling of *Babcock* was necessary because that decision had relied on two faulty premises: 1) a distrust of arbitrators to handle statutory matters and 2) an inappropriate desire to make the Board the primary resolution process despite the parties" agreement to arbitrate. This is probably not the end of the issue. General Counsel Abruzzo has identified deferral cases as one of the issues warranting further consideration. [*See* General Counsel Memorandum 21-04 (August 12, 2021), at 6, https://www.nlrb.gov/guidance/memos-research/general-counsel-memos]

(b) Additional Requirements

At least one court also has held that the issue before the arbitrator must be clearly within her competence to decide, and that the arbitrator must indicate the reasons for her decision with sufficient particularity to permit NLRB assessment thereof, before deferral is proper. [**Banyard v. NLRB,** 505 F.2d 342 (D.C. Cir. 1974); *but see* **V.I. Nursing Association v. Schneider,** 668 F.2d 221 (3d Cir. 1981)—courts should not impose such additional requirements on the private arbitration process negotiated by the parties]

(c) Deferral to Settlement Agreement

In line with its *Spielberg* standards, the NLRB likewise will defer to a pre-arbitral settlement agreement when it finds that (i) the settlement agreement is "fair and regular"; (ii) the parties agreed to be bound by the settlement; (iii) the settlement is not "palpably wrong," in that each side made concessions; and

(iv) the unfair labor practice issue paralleled the contractual issue and was "considered" in the settlement process, the facts being known to both parties. [**Alpha Beta Co.,** 273 N.L.R.B. 1546 (1985); **United States Postal Service,** 300 N.L.R.B. 196 (1990)] One circuit court has accepted this approach, but questioned the absence of any coherent rationale for applying the "palpably wrong" criterion, referring to it as a potential "recipe for arbitrary action." [**Plumbers & Pipefitters Local Union 520 v. NLRB,** 955 F.2d 744 (D.C. Cir.), *cert. denied,* 506 U.S. 817 (1992)]

(2) Pre-Award Deferral—*Collyer* Doctrine

In 1971, the Board substantially broadened its deferral policies. Faced with an alleged employer violation of section 8(a)(5), the NLRB held that it would dismiss charges involving refusals to bargain filed *prior* to an arbitration award—even prior to submission of the dispute to arbitration—*if* (i) the dispute were *contractual* in nature; (ii) the agreement called for *final and binding arbitration*; and (iii) a *"reasonable"* construction of the agreement would preclude a finding that the disputed conduct violated the NLRA. [**Collyer Insulated Wire,** 192 N.L.R.B. 837 (1971)]

(a) Last Requirement Eliminated

In decisions subsequent to *Collyer,* the Board eliminated the last requirement, holding that deferral is appropriate even if no construction of the collective bargaining agreement would justify the conduct in question. [*See* **Great Coastal Express, Inc.,** 196 N.L.R.B. 871 (1972)]

(b) And Note—Reactivation of Charges Possible

The NLRB retains jurisdiction to *reactivate* the charges if the eventual arbitration does not comply with the *Spielberg* requirements described above. [**Collyer Insulated Wire,** *supra*]

(3) Scope of *Collyer* Doctrine

In a number of decisions since *Collyer,* the Board has elaborated on the areas in which deferral to arbitration is appropriate.

(a) Refusal to Bargain Cases

When the dispute concerns a ***refusal to bargain***, the NLRB has deferred to arbitration in virtually every case. Typical disputes in this area involve unilateral wage changes, subcontracting, and reassignment of work; failure to implement agreed-upon warning rules regarding employee discipline; and unilateral union orders to driver-members to cease making cash collections (together with threats of intraunion discipline). [*See, e.g.,* **Roy Robinson, Inc.,** 228 N.L.R.B. 828 (1977)]

(b) Interference or Discrimination Based on Union Activity

In a companion case to *Roy Robinson, supra,* the NLRB held that *Collyer* should not apply to cases involving individual rights, such as alleged discrimination under section 8(a)(3). [**General American Transportation Corp.,** 228 N.L.R.B. 808 (1977)] However, the Board has overruled this decision and has held the *Collyer* doctrine applicable to cases involving alleged violations of section 8(a)(1), 8(a)(3), 8(b)(1)(A), or 8(b)(2). [**United Technologies Corp.,** 268 N.L.R.B. 557 (1984)]

(c) Arbitration Hostile to Employee Interests

The NLRB has refused to defer to arbitration where deferral would "relegate the [charging employees] to an arbitral process authored [and] administered by parties [both union and employer] hostile to their interests." [**Kansas Meat Packers,** 198 N.L.R.B. 543 (1972)] (This is still valid policy after *United Technologies, supra,* according to a prior advisory memorandum of the NLRB General Counsel; parties should continue to consult changing views of the NLRB about arbitration.)

DEFERRAL BY THE BOARD TO THE ARBITRATION PROCESS GILBERT

POST-AWARD DEFERRAL (*SPIELBERG* AND *OLIN AND UNITED PARCEL SERVICES*)	PRE-AWARD DEFERRAL (*COLLYER*)
The NLRB will defer resolution of an unfair labor practice dispute to an ***existing arbitration award*** if:	The NLRB will dismiss charges involving refusal to bargain filed ***prior to an arbitration award*** only if:
— All parties acquiesced in arbitration; — The arbitration proceedings were ***fair and regular on their face***; — The ***factual issues*** underlying the unfair labor practice charge were ***heard and determined*** by the arbitrator. The arbitrator will be deemed to have considered the unfair labor practice if the facts of the unfair labor practice and the contractual issue are similar; and — Award by the arbitrator was ***not clearly repugnant to the purposes and policies*** of the Taft-Hartley Act. The award does not have to be completely consistent with NLRB precedent.	— The dispute was ***contractual*** in nature; and — The agreement called for ***final and binding arbitration.***

Note: The NLRB will defer resolution of an unfair labor practice dispute to an existing ***settlement agreement*** under conditions similar to those under which it will defer to an existing arbitration award (*see* column 1, above).

e. Deferral by the Courts to Arbitration

While the question of deferral to arbitration arises more frequently in connection with NLRB unfair labor practice charges, the courts—in line with the general Board policy favoring arbitration—may decline jurisdiction on matters where arbitrable issues are involved. [**Carey v. Westinghouse Electric Corp.,** 375 U.S. 261 (1964)]

Example: In *Carey, supra,* the Supreme Court ruled that the union was entitled to arbitration of a work assignment dispute. The employer had resisted arbitration claiming that there was a jurisdictional dispute between two rival unions (*i.e.,* a controversy over which union should represent the particular employees involved) and that this issue could not be resolved by an arbitrator, since only one of the unions was a party to the agreement to arbitrate. According to the employer, it was entitled to resolve the dispute on its own, and the aggrieved union could then challenge its decision by filing a section 8(a)(5) charge alleging that the employer had refused to bargain. However, the Supreme Court sent the case to the arbitrator, reasoning that if the matter was merely a work assignment dispute, it had to be resolved by arbitration under the contract; and if it was a jurisdictional dispute, "resort to arbitration may have a pervasive, curative effect" even though one union was not a party to the agreement to arbitrate. In either case, the NLRB could review the decision of the arbitrator should it so choose.

(1) Exhaustion of Remedies Doctrine

If the collective bargaining agreement contains a mandatory arbitration provision, no independent court action can be maintained to enforce the agreement without first going through the arbitration process. Therefore, even though courts have jurisdiction to enforce collective bargaining agreements (under Taft-Hartley section 301, *infra,* pp. 138 *et seq.*), they will ***decline to exercise jurisdiction*** when a party attempts to bypass the contract grievance procedure. [**Republic Steel Corp. v. Maddox,** 379 U.S. 650 (1965)]

Example: In *Maddox, supra,* an individual employee sought to sue his employer for severance benefits under the collective bargaining agreement. The Supreme Court held that the employee was bound by the union's agreement to submit all grievances to arbitration, and that no independent action could be permitted under section 301 because of the strong public interest favoring arbitration.

(a) Exhaustion Doctrine Applies Under Railway Labor Act

The exhaustion of remedies doctrine applies to agreements covered by the Railway Labor Act, as well as the NLRA. [**Andrews v. Louisville & Nashville Railroad,** 406 U.S. 320 (1972)]

(b) Exception—Union Failure to Provide Representation

If an employee presents her grievance for arbitration and the union ***refuses to represent her or fails to provide adequate representation***, the employee is relieved of any further duty to pursue remedies under the collective bargaining agreement and may file suit under section 301. [**Hines v. Anchor Motor Freight, Inc.,** 424 U.S. 554 (1976); **Petersen v. Rath Packing Co.,** 461 F.2d 312 (8th Cir. 1972)]

1) But Note

If the employee has *internal union procedures* open to her after the union allegedly fails to represent her adequately, it is a matter of judicial discretion whether the employee will be required to exhaust such procedures before suing under section 301. In exercising this discretion, the court will consider:

(i) The ***degree of hostility*** of union officials toward the employee;

(ii) The ***potential remedial effectiveness*** of the union procedures; and

(iii) The ***extent of delay*** likely to be caused by the procedures. [**Clayton v. UAW,** 451 U.S. 679 (1981); *and see* *infra,* p. 140]

(2) Arbitration of Statutory Claims

Collective bargaining contracts frequently contain protections for employers that overlap external statutory provisions, or even incorporate such statutes by reference. The question then arises whether employees in this situation can or must have their rights under the statute determined by arbitration.

(a) "Just Cause" Provisions Generally Not Relevant

Virtually all contracts provide that covered employees may not be disciplined or discharged except for just cause. It could be argued that any discipline or discharge in violation of a statutory protection would not be for just cause. However, such a broad reading of the "just cause" clause generally is not intended by the parties, and a more specific reference is required before an arbitrator would be authorized to take statutory protections into account.

(b) Nondiscrimination Clauses—Rights Are Independent

Many collective bargaining contracts contain a provision precluding the employer from discriminating against employees on the basis of union activities, or on grounds protected by ***Title VII of the Civil Rights Act of 1964***—*i.e.,* race, color, religion, sex, or national origin. The Supreme Court had held that an employee's rights under Title VII and under the contract are ***independent.*** Thus, employees can file a grievance under the contract for arbitration of an alleged violation of such rights, and they can obtain a trial de novo in federal court under Title VII for the same claim—either independently and simultaneously, or if unsuccessful in the grievance procedure. [**Alexander v. Gardner-Denver Co.,** 415 U.S. 36 (1974)]

(c) Extension to Other Statutory Rights

The Supreme Court has extended the rule in *Alexander* to employee rights under the *Fair Labor Standards Act* and under *Section 1983, a provision of the Civil Rights Act of 1871.* [**Barrentine v. Arkansas-Best Freight System, Inc.** 450 U.S. 728 (1981); **McDonald v. City of West Branch,** 466 U.S. 284 (1984)]

(d) Waiver of Statutory Rights

The extent to which a union can, in a collective bargaining agreement, *waive* the right of covered employees to independently pursue their statutory rights and require all such claims be resolved exclusively through the grievance and arbitration procedure is a difficult question. Court decisions have shed some light on this issue, however. [**14 Penn Plaza LLC v. Pyett,** 556 U.S. 247 (2009)] In *Pyett*, an employer brought a claim seeking to compel arbitration of a statutory age discrimination claim arising under a collective bargaining agreement's provisions for arbitration. The Court reviewed the broad language in the collective bargaining agreement's arbitration clause referring to antidiscrimination statutes and providing that the arbitrator would have responsibilities similar to a judge. The Court held that if the arbitration clause of a collective bargaining agreement covered statutory discrimination claims and if it "clearly and unmistakably" waived a bargaining unit member's opportunity to pursue those claims in court, then the waiver was enforceable. The Court specifically stated that it was not overruling *Alexander*, *supra,* p. 136, as there was no finding of a clear and unmistakable waiver in the collective bargaining agreement in the *Alexander* case. Any broader application of *Alexander* and its progeny by lower courts to limit arbitration of statutory employment discrimination claims pursuant to a collective bargaining agreement had misconstrued that case.

1) Non-Labor Law Situation—Rights Waived

In one case not involving a collective bargaining contract, a financial manager was subject to a broad arbitration clause in a registration statement that he was required to file with the New York Stock Exchange. The Supreme Court held that all of the manager's statutory rights, including claims under the Age Discrimination in Employment Act of 1967, had to be arbitrated. [**Gilmer v. Interstate/Johnson Lane Corp.,** 500 U.S. 20 (1991)] Subsequently, some circuit courts questioned whether the result in *Gilmer* was consistent with the holding in *Alexander, supra.* The most recent Supreme Court case addressing the arbitration of statutory claims occurred in 2018. [**Epic Systems Corp. v. Lewis,** 138 S. Ct. 1612 (2018)] The Supreme Court found that employer policies, including arbitration agreements that prohibited class actions, ostensibly including wage and hour statutory claims, did not interfere with the NLRA's protection of an employee's right to engage in "concerted activity for the purpose of collective bargaining or other mutual aid or protection." 29 U.S.C. § 157. Allowing a defense based on the NLRA to defeat agreed-upon collective/class action waivers uniquely harms the arbitration process and does not treat it similarly to "any" other contract. Blocking the effect of class and collective waivers "interfere[s] with a fundamental attribute of arbitration . . . by effectively permitting any party in arbitration to demand classwide proceedings despite the traditionally individualized and informal nature of arbitration.' " *Id.* at 1622–23. In addition, Justice Gorsuch explained, NLRA § 7 does not grant a right to pursue a particular litigation strategy of a class or collective action. In summary, Justice Gorsuch wrote: "The policy may be debatable but the law is clear: Congress has instructed that arbitration agreements like those before us must be enforced as written." *Id.* at 1632.

2) Labor Law Situation—"Clear and Unmistakable Waiver" Required

In another case, the Supreme Court held that a plaintiff longshoreman was covered by a collective bargaining contract that provided for arbitration of "all matters in dispute." The Court held that plaintiff's claim under the ADA was *not* waived by the contract provision. While acknowledging some "tension" between the *Alexander* and *Gilmer* cases, the Court found that in this case the contract did not contain "a clear and unmistakable waiver of [the employee's] rights to a judicial forum for federal claims of employment discrimination." [**Wright v. Universal Maritime Corp.,** 525 U.S. 70 (1998)] The *Wright* decision was a precursor to the Court's later decision in *Pyett, supra,* p. 136, where the Court held that if the arbitration clause of a collective bargaining agreement covered statutory discrimination claims and it "clearly and unmistakably" waived a bargaining unit member's opportunity to pursue those claims in court, the waiver was enforceable. Lower courts have applied *Pyett* to both uphold and deny waiver of an employee's right to sue while focusing on the terms of the collective bargaining agreement.

a) Enforceability of Agreement to Arbitrate

In a case involving the scope of the "contracts of employment" exception to the Federal Arbitration Act (*see infra,* p. 142), the Supreme Court did find a clear waiver of the right to pursue claims in litigation. The Court held that "arbitration agreements can be enforced under the [Federal] Arbitration Act without contravening . . . congressional enactments giving employees specific protection against discrimination prohibited by federal law," and it reiterated its position in *Gilmer* that "[b]y agreeing to arbitrate a statutory claim, a party does not forgo the substantive rights afforded by statute; it only submits to their resolution in an arbitral, rather than a judicial, forum." [**Circuit City Stores, Inc. v. Saint Clair Adams,** 532 U.S. 105 (2001)]

3. Judicial Enforcement of Collective Bargaining Agreements

a. Federal Court Jurisdiction Under Taft-Hartley Section 301

Section 301 of the Taft-Hartley (Labor Management Relations) Act provides that suits between an employer and a labor organization representing employees in an industry affecting commerce, or between two such labor organizations, may be brought in any federal district court having jurisdiction over the parties—***regardless of diversity of citizenship or federal jurisdictional amount.***

EXAM TIP GILBERT

Remember that a section 301 case falls under "federal question" jurisdiction. Therefore, diversity of citizenship and amount in controversy are ***irrelevant.***

(1) Federal Forum for Contract Actions

By enacting this section, Congress intended to create a federal forum for suits involving alleged breaches of collective bargaining agreements. [**Association of Westinghouse Salaried Employees v. Westinghouse Electric Corp.,** 348 U.S. 437 (1955)]

(2) Suits by Employees Permitted

Although section 301 expressly authorizes only "employers and unions" to sue one another for breach of the collective agreement, the Supreme Court has held that ***individual employees*** also may bring suit against their employers to vindicate "uniquely personal rights" under the contract, *e.g.,* special conditions of employment, or special rates of pay. [**Smith v. Evening News Association,** 371 U.S. 195 (1962); *and see infra,* pp. 205–207]

(3) Suits on Other Contracts

Section 301 also encompasses labor disputes arising out of contracts ***other than*** the traditional collective bargaining agreement.

e.g. **Example:** A local union can sue its parent to enforce the contractual obligations contained in the union constitution. [**United Association of Journeymen & Apprentices v. Local 334,** 452 U.S. 615 (1981)] And, a union may enforce an employer's monetary obligations contained in a *prehire agreement* authorized by section 8(f) of the NLRA, even though the union did not obtain majority support in the relevant unit. [**Jim McNeff, Inc. v. Todd,** 461 U.S. 260 (1983)]

b. Concurrent Jurisdiction in State Courts

Federal court jurisdiction under section 301 is not exclusive. Rather, state courts have *concurrent jurisdiction* so that section 301 cases may be brought in either federal or state court. [**Wolko v. Highway Truck Drivers & Helpers Local 107,** 232 F. Supp. 594 (E.D. Pa. 1964)]

(1) Federal Law Applies

Of course, state courts that assume jurisdiction must apply ***federal substantive law*** to the issues involved. [**Local 174, Teamsters, Chauffeurs, Warehousemen, & Helpers v. Lucas Flour Co.,** 369 U.S. 95 (1962)]

(a) Exception

The *statute of limitations* is governed by state law. This is true whether the action is filed in federal or state court, because there is no federal limitations period applicable to collective bargaining agreements. [**UAW v. Hoosier Cardinal Corp.,** 383 U.S. 696 (1966)]

(2) Power of State Courts

State courts have power to enforce a collective bargaining agreement even where the dispute involves an activity that is "arguably protected" under the NLRA, and would otherwise be exempt from state regulation (*see supra,* pp. 26–30). The rationale is that where the parties have covered the subject by collective agreement, the preemption doctrine is not relevant. [**William E. Arnold Co. v. Carpenters District Council,** 417 U.S. 12 (1974); *see* below]

c. Judicial Enforcement of Agreements to Arbitrate

As previously discussed, collective bargaining agreements normally contain a grievance procedure—usually, a commitment by both parties to submit any grievance or dispute arising under the contract to binding arbitration by a third party, and to abide by the decision of the arbitrator.

(1) Exhaustion of Remedies Doctrine

No action will lie to enforce any claim under the collective bargaining agreement by one who has not first exhausted his remedies under the contract grievance procedure. [**Republic Steel Corp. v. Maddox,** *supra,* p. 135]

(2) Court May Compel Specific Performance of Agreement to Arbitrate

However, if either party has refused to arbitrate as provided in the agreement, and the grievance procedure has been followed, the other party may sue under Taft-Hartley section 301 to compel arbitration. [**Textile Workers Union v. Lincoln Mills,** *supra,* p. 111]

(a) Rationale

Enforcement of arbitration clauses is crucial to industrial peace, and specific performance is the most direct and immediate way of assuring enforcement.

(b) And Note

Lincoln Mills held that section 301 authorizes federal courts to fashion a body of substantive law (federal common law) for the enforcement of collective bargaining agreements.

d. Judicial Review of Arbitration Awards—the "*Steelworker Trilogy*" and Finality Doctrine

The "hands off" attitude of the courts toward arbitrable disputes also extends to the scope of judicial review afforded to arbitration awards. In the famous "*Steelworker Trilogy*" (three opinions issued on the same day involving the Steelworkers' Union), the Supreme Court held that ***the merits of either the grievance or the arbitration award are irrelevant*** when a federal court is asked to enforce an arbitration agreement or an award thereunder. Judicial review is limited to whether the award "draws its essence" from the collective agreement—*i.e.,* whether the award was ***within the authority conferred upon the arbitrator by the agreement.*** If so, the award traditionally has been held **to be *final and binding*.** [**United Steelworkers of America v. American Manufacturing Co.,** 363 U.S. 564 (1960); **United Steelworkers of America v. Warrior & Gulf Navigation Co.,** *supra,* p. 130; **United Steelworkers of America v. Enterprise Wheel & Car Corp.,** 363 U.S. 593 (1960)]

(1) Court Determines Arbitrability

Under this approach, it is always proper for the court to determine whether the dispute or grievance in question falls within the agreement to arbitrate—*i.e.,* whether there is "substantive arbitrability." If not, the arbitrator would have no authority and any award would be void. [*See, e.g.,* **Carpenters 46 Northern California Counties Conference Board v. Zcon Builders,** 96 F.3d 410 (9th Cir. 1996)]

(a) Claim Judged on Its Face

It is sufficient if the claim ***on its face*** falls within the scope of the arbitration agreement—and all inferences are to be drawn in favor of arbitration.

(b) "Substantive" vs. "Procedural" Arbitrability

While the courts determine substantive arbitrability, it is customary for arbitrators to decide questions of procedural arbitrability—for example, whether a grievance was properly filed within the time limits specified in the collective bargaining agreement.

JUDICIAL REVERSAL OF ARBITRATION AWARDS

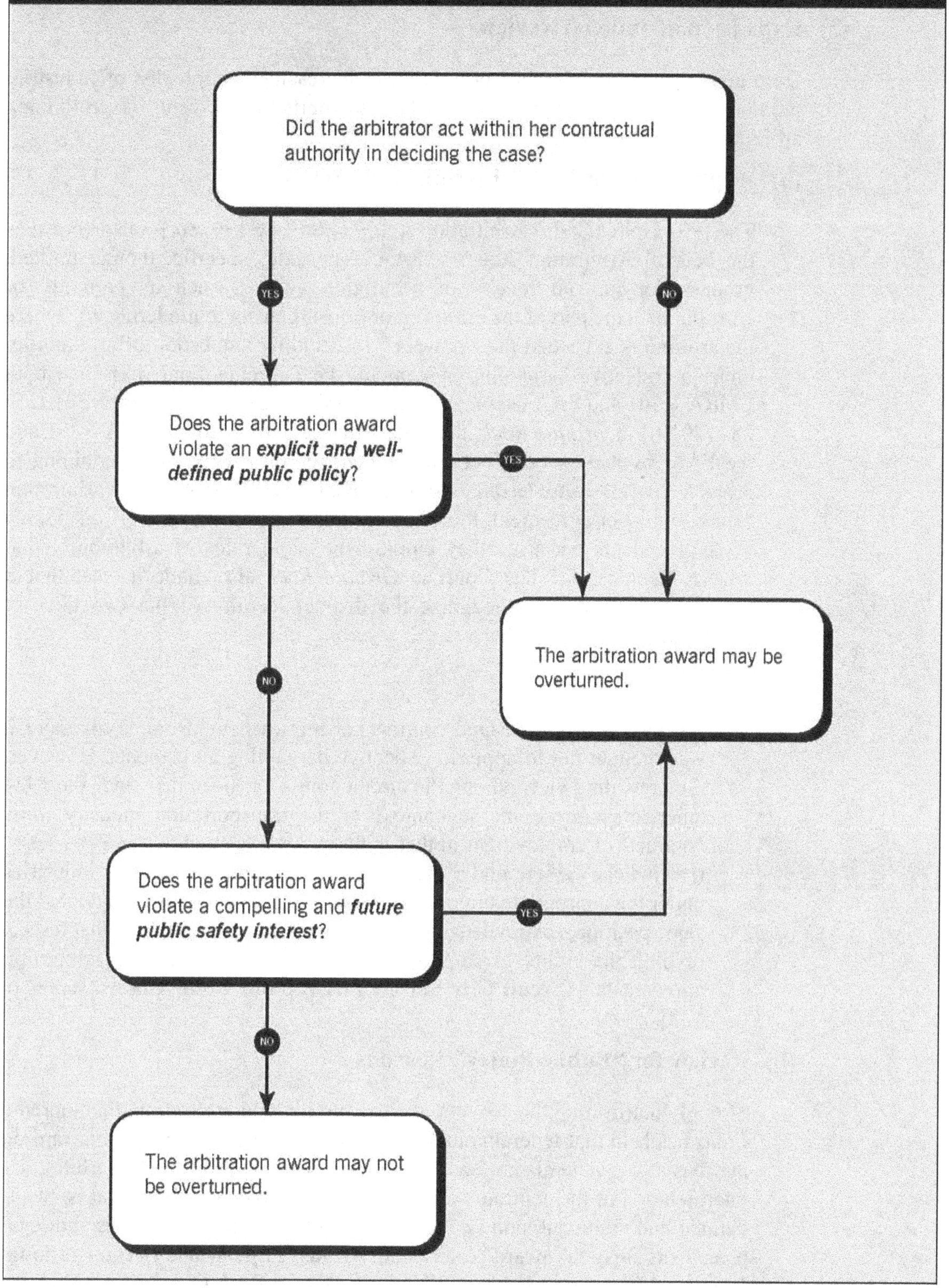

(c) Waiver of Judicial Review

Note that the parties may voluntarily submit the issue of arbitrability to the arbitrator, in which case they *waive* any right to subsequent judicial review of arbitrability. [**Ficek v. Southern Pacific Co.,** 338 F.2d 655 (9th Cir. 1964), *cert. denied,* 380 U.S. 1988 (1965)]

(2) Expansion of Judicial Review

Despite the traditional finality doctrine, the increasing complexity of industrial problems and the relevant statutory law has led courts to seek ways of scrutinizing arbitration awards more closely.

(a) Applicability of Federal Arbitration Act

The 1924 United States Arbitration Act [9 U.S.C. §§ 1 *et seq.*]—also known as the Federal Arbitration Act, or "FAA"—provides specific, though limited, grounds for judicial review of arbitration awards, such as partiality or corruption on the part of the arbitrator or (most relevant to modern law) "where the arbitrators exceeded their powers." In deciding a question of arbitrability under a collective bargaining agreement, the Supreme Court has cited both LMRA § 301 and FAA cases. [*See* **Granite Rock Co. v. Teamsters,** 561 U.S. 287 (2010)] In *Granite Rock,* the Court emphasized that the LMRA § 301 and the FAA involve two distinct enforcement regimes with cases pertaining to separate laws. Because *Granite Rock* involved the enforcement of an arbitration clause in a labor agreement, the Court explained that it was merely discussing FAA precedents because "they employ the same rules of arbitrability that govern labor cases." The Court in *Granite Rock* also made it clear that it planned to continue to recognize the distinct identity of the two lines of precedent "even in LMRA cases."

1) Scope of Statute

Because the FAA ***excepts*** "contracts of employment" from its coverage, it was thought not to apply to collective bargaining agreements. However, the prevailing view among the circuit courts has been that since the 1924 amendment arose in the context of the transportation industry, ***only*** contracts of employment in that industry are excepted by the FAA—*i.e.,* that judicial review under the FAA would be proper in other industries under the appropriate circumstances. The Supreme Court has adopted the same position, acknowledging that this will preempt state laws that restrict or limit the ability of employers or employees to enter into arbitration agreements. [**Circuit City Stores, Inc. v. Saint Clair Adams,** *supra,* p. 138]

(b) Review for "Public Policy" Reasons

Strongly reaffirming the concept of final and binding arbitration, the Supreme Court has held that federal courts should not overturn an arbitration award on the basis of general notions of public policy. Only if an arbitrator's interpretation of the contract violates an "explicit public policy" that is "well-defined and dominant, and . . . ascertained by reference to the laws and legal precedents" may the award be set aside. [**United Paperworkers International Union v. Misco, Inc.,** 484 U.S. 29 (1987); *and see* **W.R. Grace Co. v. Rubber Workers,** 461 U.S. 757 (1983)]

e.g. **Example:** In *Misco, supra,* an award ordering reinstatement of an employee who had been discharged for the alleged use or possession of marijuana on company property was upheld, even though the reviewing court might disagree with the arbitrator's findings of fact. Absent bad faith or dishonesty, an award is to be honored if the arbitrator "is even arguably construing or applying the contract and acting within the scope of his authority."

1) Distinguish—Cases Involving Public Safety

While acknowledging that a "public policy" rationale for overturning awards is narrowly limited by *Misco*, lower courts nonetheless have relied on it when *future* public safety is deemed to be an issue.

e.g. **Example:** An arbitrator's reinstatement of a nuclear power plant machinist who was discharged for deliberately violating a safety system at the plant has been rejected [**Iowa Electric Power & Light Co. v. Local 204,** 834 F.2d 1424 (8th Cir. 1987)], as has the reinstatement of an airline pilot discharged for operating an aircraft while intoxicated [**Delta Airlines v. Airline Pilots Association International,** 861 F.2d 665 (11th Cir. 1988), *cert. denied,* 493 U.S. 871 (1989)].

cf. **Compare:** The Supreme Court has upheld an arbitration award reinstating a truck driver who was discharged after failing a random drug test required by the Department of Transportation for workers engaged in "safety-sensitive" tasks. The Court found that the award did not violate any specific law or regulation, and that it was in keeping with the "remedial aims" of the drug-testing statute (even though the employee had failed two previous drug tests). [**Eastern Associated Coal Corp. v. United Mineworkers of America,** 531 U.S. 57 (2000)] This decision suggests that overturning arbitration awards based on public safety grounds may be proper only if the safety risk is compelling.

2) Distinguish—Cases in Which Arbitrator Exceeds Authority

Courts likewise have distinguished *Misco* in setting aside arbitration awards where the arbitrator is found to have ignored or exceeded the unambiguous terms of the collective bargaining contract—*i.e.,* when the award is not "drawn from the essence of the agreement."

e.g. **Example:** An award that reduced to a suspension the discharge of employees who had sold drugs on company property was overturned, because the contract specifically precluded the arbitrator from determining penalties for violation of disciplinary rules under the agreement. [**S.D. Warren Co. v. Paperworkers Local 1069,** 845 F.2d 3 (1st Cir. 1988); *and see* **Georgia-Pacific Corp. v. Local 27, United Paperworkers International Union,** 864 F.2d 940 (1st Cir. 1988); **Hawaii Teamsters & Allied Workers Union, Local 996 v. United Parcel Service,** 241 F.3d 1177 (9th Cir. 2000)]

(c) Caution—"Finality Doctrine" Still Applies

In **Garvey v. Roberts,** 203 F.3d 580 (9th Cir. 2000), the circuit court refused to enforce the decision of a baseball arbitrator, concluding that the arbitrator had "dispensed his own brand of industrial justice" beyond the scope of his contractual authority. The Supreme Court summarily reversed, finding that the lower court had based its decision on a disagreement with the arbitrator's ***findings of fact***—which is not permitted under the "*Steelworker Trilogy*"—and holding that because the award was within the arbitrator's authority, the decision was final and binding. [**Major League Baseball Players Association v. Garvey,** 532 U.S. 504 (2001)]

EXAM TIP GILBERT

Note the ***similarity*** between the *Spielberg and United Parcel Services* ***deferral doctrine*** and the *Misco* ***public policy doctrine.*** Although both doctrines indicate that arbitration awards should not be overturned lightly, the doctrines are ***not*** interchangeable. *Misco* applies to a review of an arbitrator's decision by a ***federal court*** and holds that the arbitrator's decision should generally not be overturned on "public policy" grounds, whereas *Spielberg* applies to the ***NLRB*** and sets forth guidelines for the NLRB to use to determine if it should overturn an arbitration award.

e. Judicial Enforcement of No-Strike Agreements

As part of the consideration for an agreement by the employee to arbitrate any disputes or grievances arising under the contract, the union normally agrees not to strike (or cause any work stoppage or slowdown) because of such disputes or grievances. This no-strike obligation is such a necessary ingredient of the commitment to arbitrate that it will be ***implied*** in the absence of any express provision to this effect—on the rationale that it must have been the quid pro quo for the employer's agreement to arbitrate. [**Local 174, Teamsters, Chauffeurs, Warehousemen, & Helpers v. Lucas Flour Co.,** *supra,* p. 139] If there is a no-strike agreement (express or implied), what happens if a dispute arises and the union calls a strike or work stoppage instead of invoking arbitration?

(1) Right to Injunctive Relief

(a) Prior Rule—No Injunctions

Initially, the Supreme Court held that federal courts could only award damages against a union that violated a no-strike agreement; *i.e.,* they ***could not enjoin*** the union from striking. The rationale was that Norris-LaGuardia Act section 4 [29 U.S.C. § 104] prohibited federal courts from issuing injunctions in labor disputes. [**Sinclair Refining Co. v. Atkinson,** 370 U.S. 195 (1962)]

1) Comment

This left the employer with no real remedy against a union that breached its no-strike agreement. A damage award did not necessarily end the strike. Moreover, if the agreement contained a broad arbitration clause (covering employer grievances), the union could *stay* the damage action pending arbitration over the union's right to strike—while the strike continued.

2) Application

As a result of these deficiencies, few employers bothered to sue in federal court. Considerable forum shopping and litigation in state courts followed, until the Supreme Court held that such state court actions could be removed to federal court. [**Avco Corp. v. Aero Lodge 735, International Association of Machinists & Aerospace Workers,** 390 U.S. 557 (1968)]

(b) Present Rule—Injunction Permissible

The Supreme Court later reversed itself and held that federal courts ***could*** enjoin a union from striking in violation of a no-strike clause if the dispute was arbitrable under the collective bargaining contract. [**Boys Markets, Inc. v. Retail Clerks Union, Local 770,** 398 U.S. 235 (1970)]

1) Rationale

The Court reasoned that in conferring jurisdiction on federal courts with respect to breaches of the collective agreement, Taft-Hartley section 301 ***impliedly repealed*** the anti-injunction provisions of Norris-LaGuardia in this area.

2) Limitation—Must Be Arbitrable Issue

Boys Markets has been held to apply only to strikes over an ***arbitrable issue.*** Thus, for example, a federal court may not enjoin a sympathy strike. [**Buffalo Forge Co. v. United Steelworkers,** 424 U.S. 906 (1976)] *Rationale:* The question of whether a strike violates the collective bargaining agreement may be arbitrable. However, the strike itself is not over an arbitrable issue, so the arbitrator cannot resolve the labor dispute.

a) Note

If the underlying dispute is arbitrable, *Buffalo Forge* has been held not to preclude either injunctive or monetary relief to an employer. [**Republic Steel Corp. v. UMW,** 570 F.2d 467 (3d Cir. 1978)]

b) And Note

An injunction is not precluded to prevent a corporation from completing the sale of its assets pending arbitration, where a contract provision required the corporation to have any purchaser assume existing obligations under the collective bargaining contract. [**International Association of Machinists, Local 1266 v. Panoramic Corp.,** 668 F.2d 276 (7th Cir. 1981)—contract provision gave rise to arbitrable issue]

c) Distinguish

However, *Buffalo Forge* has been held to preclude an injunction when longshoremen refused to load cargo onto Soviet-bound ships following the 1979 intervention by the Soviet Union in Afghanistan. Despite the political nature of the protest, the longshoremen's action was found to be a labor dispute under Norris-LaGuardia, and thus no injunction could issue. [**Jacksonville Bulk Terminals, Inc. v. International Longshoremen's Association, Local 1408,** 457 U.S. 702 (1982); *compare* **International Longshoremen's Association v. Allied International, Inc.,** 456 U.S. 212 (1982)] Likewise, it has been held that peaceful picketing to protest the cancellation of a collective bargaining contract during bankruptcy proceedings (*see supra,* p. 105) cannot be enjoined. [**Briggs Transportation Co. v. International Brotherhood of Teamsters,** 739 F.2d 341 (8th Cir.), *cert. denied,* 469 U.S. 917 (1984)]

d) Contract Must Provide for Binding Arbitration

Even if the labor dispute is a typical one subject to a multistep grievance process, a *Boys Markets* injunction will not issue unless the collective bargaining contract provides for binding arbitration before a neutral third party (if requested by the union) should the grievance process fail to resolve the matter. [**American Telephone & Telegraph Co. v. Communications Workers,** 985 F.2d 855 (6th Cir. 1993)]

3) Preliminary Injunctions

One circuit court has held that a preliminary injunction to maintain the status quo pending arbitration will *not* issue if there is no express promise to maintain the status quo. Such a promise will not be implied, even though a no-strike obligation can be implied from a broad arbitration clause. [**Amalgamated Transit Union, Division 1384 v. Greyhound Lines, Inc.,** 529 F.2d 1073 (9th Cir. 1976)]

a) But Note

Another circuit has held that a preliminary injunction might issue where irreparable harm could occur to employees if the employer did not maintain the status quo. [**Lever Brothers Co. v. International Chemical Workers Union, Local 217,** 554 F.2d 115 (4th Cir. 1976)]

(2) Showing Required to Obtain Injunctive Relief

The holding in *Boys Markets* (*supra,* p. 145) does not authorize injunctive relief in every case. Rather, an injunction may issue only where the employer establishes:

(i) ***A mandatory grievance and arbitration procedure*** in the collective bargaining contract;

(ii) ***A dispute that is arbitrable*** thereunder;

(iii) ***A likelihood of irreparable harm*** to the employer if the strike continues; ***and***

(iv) ***Injury to the employer that will exceed any harm to the union*** from being enjoined.

[**Boys Markets, Inc. v. Retail Clerks Union, Local 770,** *supra*]

(3) Even Unfair Labor Practice Strikes May Be Enjoined

If the above requirements are met, any strike that violates a no-strike agreement may be enjoined, even though the strike itself (or the conduct to which it is a response) is also an unfair labor practice. [**William E. Arnold Co. v. Carpenters District Council,** *supra,* p. 139—union's calling a jurisdictional strike was concededly a violation of NLRA § 8(b)(4) (*infra,* pp. 162–163); but it was also in direct violation of no-strike provision in the collective agreement, and hence subject to court injunction]

(a) Rationale

Parties who have agreed to arbitrate their disputes should be compelled to do so and should not be allowed to bypass such procedures by categorizing objectionable conduct as an "unfair labor practice" and calling a strike.

1) **Comment**

NLRB jurisdiction over unfair labor practices is not exclusive, and it does not oust courts from their section 301 jurisdiction to enforce the terms of the collective bargaining agreement. Moreover, the NLRB policy is to *refrain* from exercising jurisdiction in such cases and to defer to contractual mechanisms for settling the dispute.

(b) **Preemption Doctrine Does Not Apply**

Likewise, the doctrine that state courts cannot regulate conduct protected under the NLRA (*supra,* pp. 23 *et seq.*) does not apply where suit is brought under section 301. In such cases, the state court is properly exercising the concurrent jurisdiction conferred upon it (*supra,* p. 139). [**William E. Arnold Co. v. Carpenters District Council,** *supra*]

(4) **Employer's Right to Terminate Collective Bargaining Agreement**

When the union breaches a no-strike clause, several courts of appeal have recognized the employer's right to terminate the entire agreement under common law contract principles. [*See, e.g.,* **Children's Rehabilitation Center, Inc. v. Service Employees International Union, Local No. 227,** 419 U.S. 1090 (1974); **Boeing Airplane Co. v. Aeronautical Industrial District Lodge No. 751,** 188 F.2d 356 (9th Cir.), *cert. denied,* 342 U.S. 821 (1951)]

(a) **No Right to Damages if Contract Terminated**

However, the employer cannot terminate the agreement and then seek recovery of damages caused by the strike. [**Children's Rehabilitation Center, Inc. v. Service Employees International Union, Local No. 227,** *supra*] The basic policy favoring industrial peace and stability prevents encouragement of such terminations (which could occur by allowing employers the additional right to monetary relief). The employer must choose between termination and damages.

(b) **Limitation**

Violation of the no-strike clause does not in itself relieve the employer of obligations under the contract. The employer must abrogate the entire agreement and clearly inform the union of its intention to **do so. [Children's Rehabilitation Center, Inc. v. Service Employees International Union, Local No. 227,** *supra*]

(5) **Right to Damages from Unauthorized Strikes**

By its terms, section 301 authorizes damage suits against unions for breach of contract. A common issue here is union liability for unauthorized "wildcat" strikes (*infra,* p. 168).

(a) **Local Union**

Liability in this situation often is assessed against a local union that is a party to a collective bargaining contract with a no-strike obligation, if the union made little or no effort to forestall the strike.

(b) International Union

However, an international union is not liable for damages without a clear contractual undertaking on its part to attempt to prevent or end unauthorized strikes. [**Carbon Fuel Co. v. UMW,** 444 U.S. 212 (1979)]

(c) Individual Union Members

Section 301 does not authorize damage actions against individual union members who participate in wildcat strikes violating a no-strike clause. [**Complete Auto Transit, Inc. v. Reis,** 451 U.S. 401 (1981)]

Chapter Four

Strikes, Boycotts, and Picketing

CONTENTS	PAGE

Chapter Approach

You will most likely encounter a strike or a picket line, or both, on your exam. In regulating strikes, picketing, and the like, Congress and the courts have tried to balance the somewhat vague, but vital, right of employees to engage in such activity against the public's right to be protected from potentially destructive conduct. When you encounter a strike or picketing on your exam, check the facts to see the stage at which this has occurred:

1. **Campaigning Stage Picketing**

   At the campaigning stage, a union may engage in *organizational or recognition picketing.* Here, you need to know under what circumstances, and how long, such picketing may continue under the statutory formula in section 8(b)(7)(C). Among other things, consider:

   — What is ***area standards*** picketing?

   — What is ***informational*** picketing?

   — What are the ***limits*** on each of these?

   — What happens if the NLRB finds a ***violation*** of section 8(b)(7)(C)?

2. **Post-Certification Picketing**

   Strikes and picketing most often occur ***after the union has been certified*** and bargaining is underway (or has broken down). In this case, you should understand the rules on ***when*** and ***where*** a union may strike or picket, and what *risks* the union members (or the employer) take when there is a strike. In particular, consider:

   — Who are ***economic*** strikers, and who are ***unfair labor practice*** strikers?

   — What are the rules concerning ***permanent replacement*** of strikers?

   — What is the difference between ***primary*** and ***secondary*** picketing?

   — Who are "***allies***" of a primary employer?

   — How does section 8(b)(4) ***restrict secondary picketing***?

   — How does the statute govern more than one employer at the same job site ("***common situs***" problems)?

   — What difference does it make if the common situs is a ***construction project***?

   — How does the ***publicity proviso*** affect section 8(b)(4)?

   — When (and why) may a ***consumer boycott*** be legal under section 8(b)(4) (as secondary picketing)?

This chapter also notes the ***antitrust exemption*** for union activity, a subject which may or may not be covered in your course.

A. Constitutional Rights and Limitations on Concerted Activity

1. Right to Strike

a. Sources of Claimed Constitutional Right

The Supreme Court has never determined whether there is an ***absolute*** constitutional right to strike. The sources most often claimed for such a right are:

(1) ***The First Amendment*** guarantees of free speech, press, and assembly;

(2) ***The Fifth Amendment*** prohibition against deprivation of life, liberty, or property without due process of law;

(3) ***Those provisions of the Fourteenth Amendment*** that make the First and Fifth Amendments applicable to the states; and

(4) ***The prohibition in the Thirteenth Amendment*** against slavery and involuntary servitude.

b. Possible Parameters of Right

Although it did not expressly decide whether a constitutional right to strike exists, the Supreme Court in **Dorchy v. Kansas,** 272 U.S. 306 (1926), reviewed certain criteria in determining that a particular strike was not constitutionally protected. The Court found that the strike in question did ***not involve a controversy over "wages, hours or conditions of labor, discipline or discharge of an employee, or the employment of nonunion labor," nor was it a sympathetic strike "in aid of others engaged in any such controversy."*** On that basis, the Court held that neither common law guarantees nor any rights under the Fourteenth Amendment would protect the strike.

(1) Comment

Neither *Dorchy* nor any other opinion has discussed the parameters for strikes that ***would*** enjoy constitutional protection.

2. Picketing

The constitutional protection afforded picketing depends on the purposes for which it is used and the manner in which it is conducted. To be constitutionally protected, the picketing must be conducted in a *peaceful manner* and for a *lawful objective.* [**Thornhill v. Alabama,** 310 U.S. 88 (1940); *and see* Constitutional Law Summary]

a. "Lawful Objective"

Picketing on behalf of an unlawful objective (*i.e.,* an objective that violates federal or state law or public policy) is not constitutionally protected, even if it is conducted in a peaceful manner. [**International Brotherhood of Teamsters, Local 695 v. Vogt,** 354 U.S. 284 (1957)—upholding power of states to enjoin peaceful picketing designed to coerce employer to force employees to join the union, such coercion being unlawful under state law]

(1) Injunction Permitted

Picketing may be *enjoined* when it violates federal law (*e.g.*, an unfair labor practice) or state legislation or judicial decisions. [**Hughes v. Superior Court,** 339 U.S. 460 (1950)—upholding contempt convictions against pickets who violated state court injunction banning picketing aimed at forcing employer to hire blacks in proportion to his customers, although state policy against such involuntary employment on racial lines was expressed in judicial decisions rather than statute]

(2) Typical Violations

Cases enjoining picketing often concern the violation of state laws that are equivalent to the NLRA; *i.e.*, when the activity in question would be prohibited by the NLRA but occurs in some area beyond the coverage of the NLRA (*e.g.*, purely intrastate commerce). [*See* **American Radio Association v. Mobile Steamship Association, Inc.,** 419 U.S. 215 (1974)]

e.g. **Example:** In *American Radio Association, supra,* the union was engaged in picketing directed at a foreign-flag ship that paid its foreign crew less than American scale wages. The picketing resulted in the refusal of American longshoremen to unload the ship. An Alabama state court enjoined the picketing based on a state public policy against the wrongful interference with business. In upholding the injunction and rejecting the union's claim that their conduct was prohibited—if at all—by the NLRA's ban on secondary boycotts, the Supreme Court held that the longshoremen contracted to unload a foreign ship's cargo were not engaged, ***for the purposes of NLRA jurisdiction,*** in commerce or in activities affecting commerce; thus, state action was not preempted.

(3) Limitation—Legitimate Governmental Interest

Note, however, that the state or federal statute in question must be protecting a legitimate governmental interest. For example, a sweeping state statute that outlawed all peaceful picketing on public property would be invalid. [**International Brotherhood of Teamsters, Local 695 v. Vogt,** *supra,* p. 151]

b. "Peaceful Means"

Picketing is not protected to the same extent as communication by spoken word. Regardless of the message being communicated, the mere *presence* of a mass picket line may induce violent action, even though the picketing itself is conducted in a peaceful manner. Consequently, the *entire setting* must be peaceful in order to bring constitutional guarantees into play. [**Thornhill v. Alabama,** *supra,* p. 151]

c. Forms of Picketing

Assuming that it meets the "objectives" and "means" test, the protection afforded picketing may also depend on the form that it takes.

(1) Primary Picketing

Primary picketing results when the pickets are employees of the employer being picketed. Primary picketing enjoys the ***greatest degree of constitutional protection,*** subject to the "means" and "objectives" limitations. [**Thornhill v. Alabama,** *supra,* p. 152]

(2) Stranger Picketing

Nonemployees may picket an employer on behalf of a union with whom the employer has no bargaining relationship (as when the picketing is part of a union campaign to organize the employer's plant). This is "stranger" picketing, and it is constitutionally protected ***if*** carried on for a lawful objective and in a peaceful manner. [**AFL v. Swing,** 312 U.S. 321 (1941)—mere fact that pickets were nonemployees does not strip picketing of constitutional protection]

(a) Statutory Restrictions

Of course, there is no constitutional protection when the picketing is for an objective that is unlawful under state or federal statutes. Since many states have tight limitations on stranger picketing, and the NLRA also regulates stranger picketing in certain situations (*see* discussion below on secondary boycotts), such picketing is subject to considerable legislative restriction.

(3) Secondary Picketing

"Secondary" picketing is carried on at the business of ***someone other than the employer with whom the union has its labor dispute***—usually to pressure that employer by embarrassing and inconveniencing customers. (*See* discussion of "secondary activity," *infra,* pp. 175 *et seq.*)

e.g. **Example:** Cafe Owner hires Contractor to build a new restaurant at a different location. Contractor uses nonunion help. Union puts a picket line in front of Cafe, several miles from construction site, for the avowed purpose of forcing Cafe Owner to pressure Contractor to use union help. [*See* **Carpenters & Joiners Union, Local No. 213 v. Ritter's Cafe,** 315 U.S. 722 (1942)]

(a) Generally Illegal

This type of picketing is ***generally prohibited by statute***, so it fails the "objectives" test and is not entitled to protection. [**Carpenters & Joiners Union, Local No. 213 v. Ritter's Cafe,** *supra*]

1) Exception

Secondary picketing ***may*** be permitted when the "primary" and "secondary" employers are allies or otherwise linked in their position against the union (*see* discussion *infra,* p. 180).

EXAM TIP GILBERT

Picketing questions should be answered in a three-part analysis: First, you should determine if the picketing is done ***in pursuit of a lawful objective.*** Look for compliance with or violations of state and/or federal law. Then, discuss whether the picketing is done in a ***peaceful manner.*** Finally, you should remember that the ***form of the picketing*** is also relevant—primary picketing receives ***greater constitutional protection,*** stranger picketing receives ***less*** (and is often restricted by state law and the NLRA), while secondary picketing is ***almost always*** illegal.

---

d. Impact of Preemption Doctrine

Most state court cases complaining of picketing in violation of a state statute will involve activity that is arguably protected or prohibited by the NLRA. Thus, since the advent of the preemption doctrine (*supra,* pp. 23 *et seq.*), few cases have addressed the scope of free speech protection to be afforded to picketing. Occasionally, such a case occurs in which neither the parties nor the court raises the preemption issue. [*See, e.g.,* **Amalgamated Food Employees Union, Local 590 v. Logan Valley Plaza, Inc.,** *supra,* p. 55]

B. Statutory Regulation of Strikes, Boycotts, and Picketing

1. Statutory Sources of Right to Strike and Picket

Federal regulation of strikes, picketing, and boycotts is based principally on the NLRA, as amended by the Taft-Hartley and Landrum-Griffin Acts. Certain other statutes, such as the Norris-LaGuardia Act and the Sherman Antitrust Act, also affect this area.

a. NLRA Provisions

(1) Right to Strike and Picket

NLRA sections 7 and 13 provide for the right to strike and picket. Section 7 grants employees the right to "engage in concerted activity," and this language is held to guarantee the right to strike and to picket. Section 13 expressly grants employees the right to strike, subject to certain qualifications discussed below, and by implication grants the right to picket. [*See* **NLRB v. International Rice Milling Co.,** 341 U.S. 665 (1951)]

(2) Employee Status Retained by Strikers

NLRA section 2(3) provides that strikers retain their status as "employees" even while on strike, provided certain conditions are met (*see infra*, pp. 164–169). Therefore, section 2(3) is also an important source of the right to strike.

b. Waiver of Right to Strike

These statutory rights can be *waived.* The typical "no-strike" clause in a collective bargaining agreement (by which the union binds itself to arbitrate grievances with the employer, rather than strike) is an effective waiver of the right to strike during the term of the collective bargaining agreement. [**Boys Markets, Inc. v. Retail Clerks Union, Local 770,** *supra,* p. 145]

(1) Broad Construction

Such waivers are broadly construed—so that a union agreement not to cause a work stoppage "of any kind" has been held a waiver of the right to strike and picket, even as to disputes outside the grievance and arbitration machinery provided in the collective bargaining agreement. [**Alliance Manufacturing Co.,** 200 N.L.R.B. 697 (1972)]

(2) Waiver as to Sympathy Strikes

A broad "no-strike" clause likewise has been held by the NLRB to ban sympathy strikes, ***unless*** the collective bargaining contract or extrinsic evidence shows that the parties did not agree to the waiver of such strikes. [**Indianapolis Power & Light Co.,** 273 N.L.R.B. 1715 (1985) ("*Indianapolis Power I*"); **Indianapolis Power & Light Co.,** 291 N.L.R.B. 1039 (1988) ("*Indianapolis Power II*")]

c. Leaving Unsafe Conditions Not a "Strike"

Taft-Hartley section 502 provides that employees who quit work in good faith because of "abnormally dangerous conditions for work" are ***not*** engaged in a strike within the meaning of the NLRA. However, the quitting of work must be based on more than an honest belief; *i.e.,* there must be ***ascertainable, objective evidence*** of dangerous working conditions. [**Gateway Coal Co. v. UMW,** 414 U.S. 368 (1974)—general concern about competency of co-workers is insufficient basis to invoke protection under section 502]

d. Special Notice Provisions for Health Care Institutions

Ten days' notice must be given to the FMCS and to the health care institution in question before any strike or picketing directed at such institutions may commence. [NLRA § 8(g)]

e.g. **Example:** This provision has been applied to rear-entrance picketing of a hospital to protest the hospital's use of nonunion painters in its administrative services building. [**Painters District Council,** 243 N.L.R.B. 609 (1979)]

(1) Union Must Strike Promptly After Notice

When a 10-day notice is given under section 8(g), the union must commence its strike or picketing ***promptly,*** as indicated in its notice. Delay beyond 72 hours would be unreasonable, according to the legislative history of section 8(g)—and even within 72 hours, 12 hours' notice of a new time of commencement should be given. [**District 1199-E, Hospital & Health Care Employees,** 243 N.L.R.B. 23 (1979)]

2. Regulation of Concerted Activity—in General

a. Criteria

The test used to measure the constitutional protection afforded concerted activity—*i.e.,* whether the "***means***" and "***objectives***" of the activity are lawful (*supra,* pp. 151–152)—also determines the lawfulness of such activity under the NLRA.

(1) Unlawful Objective

It follows that strikes, picketing, or boycotts generally are illegal if their objective is to enforce what would be an ***unfair labor practice*** (*e.g.,* a strike to enforce a union security agreement illegal under the NLRA; or a strike to force discrimination against employees on the basis of race).

(2) Unlawful Means

Likewise, concerted activity is illegal where the objective is lawful, but the means employed are unlawful (*e.g.,* use of violence).

b. Categories of Activity

Concerted activity typically falls into one of two general categories—primary or secondary.

(1) **Primary Activity**

This type of activity is aimed at a party ***directly involved with the employees*** in question, *i.e.,* the employer or some other party with whom the union or the employees have a bona fide dispute.

(2) **Secondary Activity**

This is activity directed at a ***third party*** with whom there is no dispute, and the activity is aimed at persuading or coercing the third party to cease doing business with the primary party.

(3) **Legality**

As a general rule, primary activity is lawful under the federal statutes, whereas ***secondary activity, with few exceptions, is unlawful*** [NLRA § 8(b)(4)]

(a) **When Illegal "Secondary" Objective Is Sought**

If primary activity is engaged in for the purpose of accomplishing an illegal "secondary" objective, the primary activity is also illegal under section 8(b)(4). For example, a strike designed to compel the primary employer to execute or enforce a "hot cargo" agreement (*see infra,* p. 158) is not permitted.

3. Regulation of Strikes

a. Primary Activity

(1) **Violent Strikes**

Strikes that are violent in nature receive no protection under the NLRA.

e.g. **Example: *Sitdown strikes***, in which workers occupy the employer's premises, and refuse to work or leave, have been found illegal as "the ousting of the owner from lawful possession is not essentially different from an assault upon the officers of an employing company, or the seizure and conversion of its goods, or the despoiling of its property or other unlawful acts in order to force compliance with demands." [**NLRB v. Fansteel Metallurgical Corp.,** 306 U.S. 240 (1939)]

(a) **Note**

Strikers who engage in acts of violence during a strike may be *discharged,* notwithstanding NLRA section 2(3) (*supra,* p. 154). However, the ***degree of culpability*** may be important in determining whether an employee may be discharged for violent conduct during a strike. [**NLRB v. Thayer Co.,** 213 F.2d 748 (1st Cir.), *cert. denied*, 348 U.S. 883 (1954)]

EXAM TIP GILBERT

When taking your exam, don't be fooled by popular notions of what is "nonviolent." Some tactics that might be considered "pacifist" in other contexts—such as sitdowns—***are considered to be violent and illegal*** under the NLRA.

(2) Strikes During Sixty-Day Cooling-Off Period

Under NLRA section 8(d), a union may not strike to terminate or change a collective bargaining agreement without first giving the employer 60 days' notice and offering to negotiate a new (or modified) contract. The purpose of section 8(d) is to create a cooling-off period, which hopefully will prevent hasty strikes over contract disagreements.

(a) Computing the Sixty-Day Period

1) Fixed-Term Contracts

If the contract is for a fixed term, the union cannot strike prior to the termination date, and then only if 60 days' notice is given before the strike is called. If notice is given less than 60 days prior to expiration of the fixed term, the union must wait a ***full 60 days*** to strike. [**Snively Groves, Inc.,** 109 N.L.R.B. 1394 (1954)]

2) Contracts for Indefinite Term

If the contract has no fixed term, the union may give 60 days' notice ***at any time*** during the term of the agreement. [**Lion Oil Co.,** 109 N.L.R.B. 680 (1954)]

(b) Cases in Which Cooling-Off Is Not Required

The 60-day cooling-off period applies only to strikes aimed at ***terminating or modifying*** the contract. It does not affect other types of strikes (*e.g.,* strikes over unfair labor practices). Neither does section 8(d) apply to a union that is not a party to the contract in question, except to the extent of the "contract bar" rule (*supra,* pp. 92–95). [**NLRB v. Wagner Iron Works & Bridge Structural & Ornamental Iron Workers Shopmen's Local 471,** 220 F.2d 126 (7th Cir. 1955), *cert. denied,* 350 U.S. 981 (1956)]

(c) Cooling-Off Is also Applicable to Employers

Section 8(d) cooling-off requirements also apply to employers. Thus, an employer must give 60 days' notice of a lockout designed to exert pressure with respect to contract modification or termination. However, notice is not required where the lockout is used to ***enforce*** (rather than change or abolish) the contract.

(3) Partial or Intermittent Strikes

Partial or intermittent strikes or work stoppages are not protected activities. Employees may either continue to work and negotiate, or strike, but they may not stay on the job and sporadically disrupt or shut down the employer's operations. [**NLRB v. Kohler Co.,** 220 F.2d 3 (7th Cir. 1955)—paint shop employees refused to work full shifts until exhaust fans installed; *and see infra,* p. 168]

(a) Distinguish

This situation should be distinguished from "wildcat" strikes (strikes not authorized in advance by the union), which are discussed *infra,* pp. 168–169.

(4) Strikes Seeking to Compel Discrimination Against Certain Employees

A union may not strike to force an employer to compel nonunion employees to join the union. Such strikes are unfair labor practices in violation of section 8(b)(2) (*supra*, p. 76) and clearly are not protected by the NLRA. [**NLRB v. Lexington Electric Products Co.,** 283 F.2d 54 (3d Cir.), *cert denied*, 365 U.S. 845 (1960)]

(5) Strikes Seeking to Compel "Featherbedding" Agreements

NLRA section 8(b)(6) makes it an unfair labor practice for an employer to pay for "services which are not performed or not to be performed." It follows that a union may not strike to force payment by an employer for "featherbedding," *i.e.*, work not performed.

(a) Problems in Regulating "Featherbedding"

Section 8(b)(6) contains a rather narrow definition of "featherbedding" and leaves unanswered the question of unnecessary workers who still perform some services. Moreover, it does not resolve the extent to which unions should be permitted to resist automation or seek to preserve traditional services or operations in the face of technological change.

(b) "Featherbedding" Narrowly Construed

The Supreme Court has also read section 8(b)(6) narrowly to avoid finding that union efforts to "make work" are illegal attempts at featherbedding. Thus, section 8(b)(6) has been held not to apply as long as some actual services are performed—provided the services are more than "nominal" or "token." [**NLRB v. Gamble Enterprises, Inc.,** 345 U.S. 117 (1953)]

e.g. **Example:** In *Gamble Enterprises, Inc., supra,* the Musicians Union would not permit traveling bands to play at local theaters unless the employer agreed to hire local bands to play during intermissions or other breaks. The Supreme Court held that the agreement did not violate section 8(b)(6), since the local bands would be rendering "substantial services." However, a previous agreement giving "standby pay" to local musicians (who rendered no services) was prohibited by section 8(b)(6).

b. Secondary or Primary Activity—Regulation Under NLRA Section 8(b)(4)

NLRA sections 8(b)(4)(A)–(D) govern secondary or primary strikes that involve certain prohibited means or objectives. The following types of strikes are ***illegal*** under section 8(b)(4) and its subsections:

(1) Strikes Compelling Employer to Execute Collective Agreement Containing "Hot Cargo" Provisions

It is an unfair labor practice for the employer or the union to enter any agreement that *requires the employer not to do business with some other person* with whom the union has (or might have) a dispute. (This type of clause is commonly called a "hot cargo" clause.) [NLRA § 8(e); *and see* discussion of secondary boycotts, *infra*, p. 176]

(a) **Note**

Any pressure, including strikes, that is designed to force an employer to accept such a clause violates the prohibition in section 8(b)(4)(A) against coercing an employer to "cease doing business with any other person." [**Puget Sound District Council,** 153 N.L.R.B. 547 (1965)]

(b) **And Note**

A strike to enforce such an agreement violates the prohibition in section 8(b)(4)(B) against secondary strikes, since the strike would be directed at a neutral party.

(c) **Distinguish—Work Preservation vs. Work Acquisition Clauses**

Section 8(e) does not preclude a union from ***preserving*** the work of its own members by direct negotiation with the ***primary*** employer; *i.e.,* unions may legitimately negotiate work preservation clauses. However, an attempt to acquire *new* work through a work acquisition clause would violate section 8(e). [**National Woodwork Manufacturers Association v. NLRB,** 386 U.S. 612 (1967); **NLRB v. International Longshoremen's Association** ("*ILA II*"), 473 U.S. 61 (1985)]

1) **Test**

A critical factor in deciding whether the union objective is work acquisition or work preservation is the "right-to-control" test, *i.e.,* whether the employer picketed has the right to assign the work in dispute. If the employer does not, a secondary objective may be inferred. [*See* **NLRB v. Enterprise Association of Pipefitters, Local 1408,** 429 U.S. 507 (1977); **NLRB v. International Longshoremen's Association** ("*ILA I*"), 447 U.S. 490 (1980)—Shipper who owns or leases shipping containers and supplies them to secondary employers has the right to control loading and unloading of containers]

EXAM TIP GILBERT

It isn't always easy to distinguish between permissible "work preservation" and impermissible "hot cargo" clauses. A typical exam question may have union members displaced by innovations in workplace technology or methods. The union will seek to preserve the jobs of its members by negotiating for a clause that prohibits the employer from dealing with companies utilizing the new technology or methods. Assuming that the work was traditionally done by union members (regardless of where performed) and that the ***employer has the right to control such work,*** such a clause is permissible.

(2) **Strikes Against Neutral Employer Aimed at Coercing Primary Employer to Recognize Union**

Section 8(b)(4)(B) also prohibits an uncertified union from inducing work stoppages against, or threatening or coercing, a neutral employer for the purpose of pressuring the primary employer to recognize or bargain with the union. [*See* **Carpenters & Joiners Union, Local No. 213 v. Ritter's Cafe,** *supra,* p. 153]

(3) Strikes Coercing Recognition Despite Prior Certification of Rival Union

Section 8(b)(4)(C) makes it an unfair labor practice to call a strike or induce work stoppages against (or to threaten or coerce) an employer to obtain recognition as bargaining agent where another union has been certified.

(a) Against any Employer

Unlike section 8(b)(4)(B), which is directed at secondary activity, section 8(b)(4)(C) applies to conduct directed against ***either primary or secondary employers***.

(b) Requirements

There are three requirements to establish a violation of section 8(b)(4)(C): (i) a ***valid, currently effective certification;*** (ii) ***unlawful coercive tactics;*** and (iii) a ***prohibited objective*** (*i.e.*, recognition of the uncertified union).

1) Current Certification

A union is considered currently certified unless the contrary can be shown, and for one year following the initial certification, this presumption is ***conclusive***. (*See* discussion of certification, *supra,* p. 92.) Courts are split on whether section 8(b)(4)(C) prevents a rival union from coercing recognition after the one-year period, where the certified union no longer represents a majority of employees but the certification still exists. The better rule seems to be that section 8(b)(4)(C) bars such coercion until certification has been ***officially vacated*** by the **NLRB** or the certified union becomes defunct. [**NLRB v. Teamsters Local 901,** 314 F.2d 792 (1st Cir. 1963)]

2) Unlawful Tactics

Under section 8(b)(4)(C), unlawful tactics include the inducement of strikes or work stoppages through visits, letters to employees, or picketing. If the picketing is not intended to induce a work stoppage, there is no violation of the section. But if the purpose is to induce a work stoppage, there is a violation ***whether or not a stoppage actually occurs***. [**NLRB v. Knitgoods Workers Union, Local 155,** 267 F.2d 916 (2d Cir. 1959)]

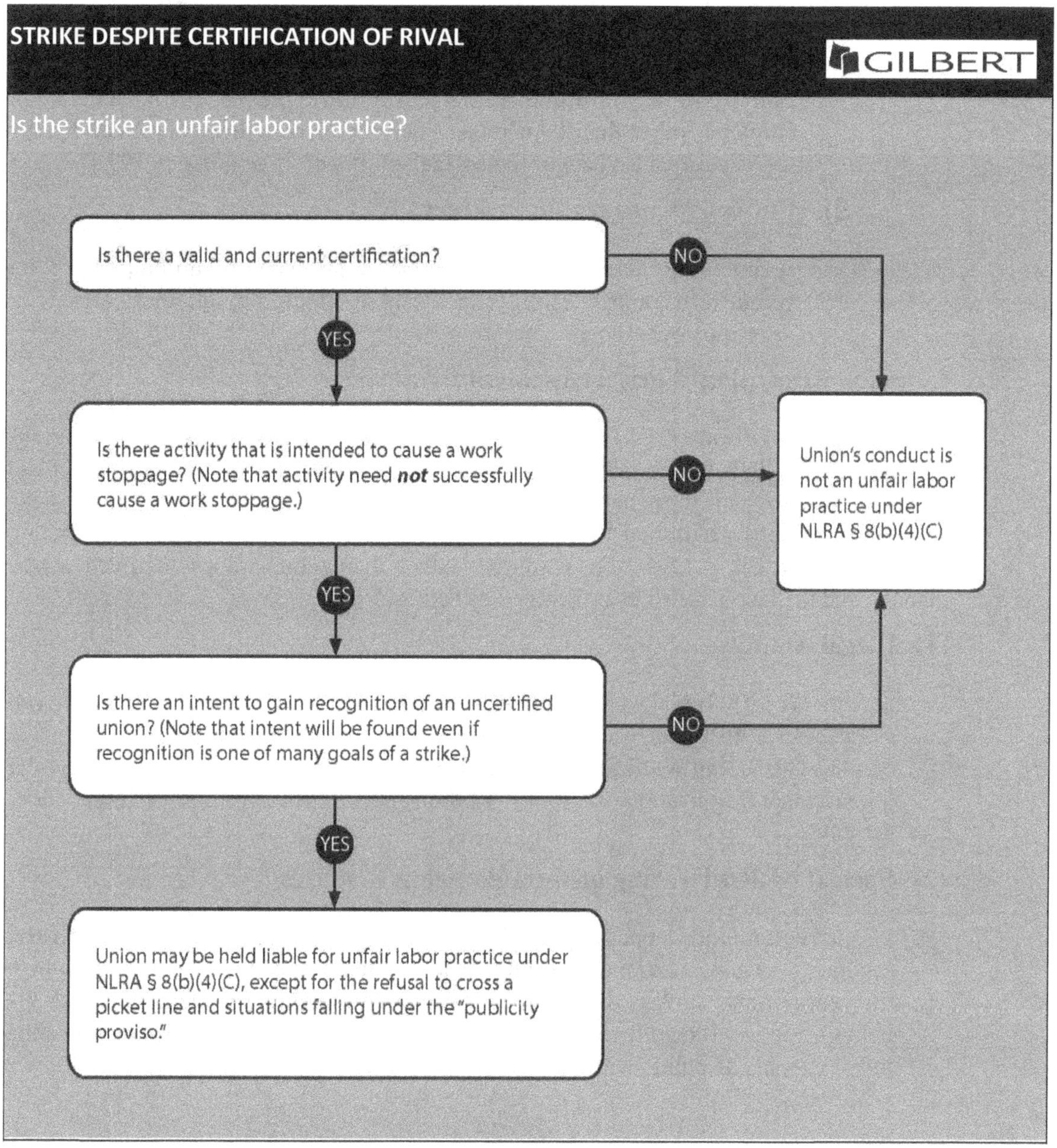

3) Prohibited Objective

The objective of the coercive activity must be recognition of an uncertified union in order for a violation of section 8(b)(4)(C) to be found. However, recognition as a partial objective violates section 8(b)(4)(C), as does recognition of a portion of employees in the bargaining unit. [**McLeod v. International Longshoremen's Association, Independent,** 177 F. Supp. 905 (E.D.N.Y. 1959)]

(c) Exempt Conduct

Section 8(b)(4) exempts certain conduct that might otherwise be unlawful under 8(b)(4)(C).

1) Refusal to Cross Picket Line

Employees may refuse to cross a picket line at the place of business of an employer other than their own, where there is a strike approved by the union entitled to recognition by that employer. (*See infra,* p. 175.)

2) Publicity Concerning Product

A union may publicize that a product is produced by an employer with whom it has a primary dispute and is distributed by another party. (*See infra,* pp. 182–183.)

c. Coercion Regarding Work Assignment Disputes

Work assignment disputes arise when a union wants the employer to assign certain jobs to its members. The term "jurisdictional dispute" is used where two or more rival unions seek the right to such jobs, but pressure may also occur where a single union seeks assignment of jobs performed by nonunion employees. In either case, the competing union generally will pressure the employer rather than other unions involved in the dispute, and the law is directed at this type of activity.

(1) Illegal Activity

Section 8(b)(4)(D) makes it an unfair practice for a union to strike or induce work stoppages, or to threaten or coerce an employer, with the object of forcing the employer to assign work to one class of employees (*i.e.,* members of a particular union) rather than to another. This prohibition applies to both primary and secondary activity.

(2) Special NLRB Hearing on Jurisdictional Disputes

Whenever an unfair labor practice charge under section 8(b)(4)(D) is filed, NLRA section 10(k) authorizes the Board to "hear and determine" the dispute from which the charge arose (unless the parties subsequently reach a private settlement; *see* below). Section 10(k) thus creates a *special **preliminary hearing*** designed to settle jurisdictional disputes without resort to the full-blown unfair labor practice procedure.

(a) Criteria

The NLRB in a section 10(k) hearing should adjudicate the merits fully and make a determination in favor of one union or the other, based on the following criteria: (i) ***skills required*** to perform the job in question; (ii) ***prior certification*** by the NLRB; (iii) ***common practices*** in the company or industry; (iv) any ***existing agreements*** between the unions (or between either union and the employer) concerning the disputed work; (v) ***awards by arbitrators*** or joint boards; and (vi) ***assignments made by the employer*** in the interest of efficient business operations. [**NLRB v. Radio & Television Broadcast Engineers Union, Local 1212, International Brotherhood of Electrical Workers,** 364 U.S. 573 (1961)]

ILLEGAL STRIKES	GILBERT
THE FOLLOWING TYPES OF STRIKES ARE ILLEGAL UNDER THE NLRA:	
PRIMARY ACTIVITY	**SECONDARY OR PRIMARY ACTIVITY**
— ***Violent*** strikes — Strikes during the ***60-day cooling-off period*** — ***Partial or intermittent*** strikes — Strikes seeking to compel ***discrimination against certain employees*** — Strikes seeking to compel ***"featherbedding" agreements***	— Strikes seeking to coerce the employer to execute an agreement containing ***"hot cargo" provisions*** — Strikes seeking to coerce ***recognition of a bargaining agent in defiance of certification*** — Strikes seeking to coerce employer ***to assign certain jobs to its members***

(3) Voluntary Settlement of Work Disputes

Many industries have set up private means for settling jurisdictional disputes (*e.g.,* by establishing joint arbitration boards for this particular problem). Section 10(k) provides for dismissal of a section 8(b)(4)(D) charge if, within 10 days after the charge is filed, all parties to the dispute submit evidence of a voluntary settlement.

(a) Note

Section 10(k) requires "***all*** parties" to agree to the settlement, and this includes the employer. Thus, a voluntary settlement between rival unions does not resolve the matter unless the employer also accepts it. Otherwise, the NLRB must proceed with a section 10(k) hearing. [**NLRB v. Plasterers Local Union No. 79, Operative Plasterers' & Cement Masons' International Association,** 404 U.S. 116 (1971)]

(b) And Note

If there is an effective voluntary settlement, but a ***subsequent dispute*** or noncompliance with the terms of the settlement, the NLRB will proceed directly to a full hearing on the unfair labor practice charge (*i.e.,* no section 10(k) hearing at this late date). [**Wood, Wire & Metal Lathers International Union,** 119 N.L.R.B. 1345 (1958)]

d. Rights of Strikers and Discrimination Against Strikers

Although section 7 grants employees the right to strike (*i.e.,* the right to engage in "concerted activities"), the NLRA has *no express provisions* governing the rights of employees who actually strike. However, the NLRB and the courts have read various rights into the terms of NLRA section 8(a)(1).

(1) Employer "Interference" as an Unfair Labor Practice

Section 8(a)(1) makes it an unfair labor practice for an employer to "interfere with" an employee's rights under section 7. Since section 7 guarantees the right of employees to engage in legitimate concerted activities, it follows that employer interference with such activity may violate section 8(a)(1). [***In re* Crosby Chemicals, Inc.,** 85 N.L.R.B. 791 (1949)]

(2) Job Tenure of Strikers Protected

Under section 8(a)(3), it is an unfair labor practice for an employer to discriminate on the basis of union membership with respect to the job tenure of "employees." When workers engage in a strike, ***they are still considered employees***. (*See supra,* p. 154.) Thus, it violates section 8(a)(3) to discharge or discriminate against an employee because of union membership or having engaged in a strike or picketing. [**NLRB v. MacKay Radio & Telegraph Co.,** 304 U.S. 333 (1938)—strikers remain "employees" for all remedial purposes of NLRA]

(3) Discharge and Reinstatement of Strikers

Whether strikers are entitled to reinstatement in jobs filled with replacements during a strike is a key factor, from the union's standpoint, in determining whether the strike can be successful. Workers understandably are reluctant to strike if they believe their jobs may be lost. At the same time, the employer has a legitimate interest in being able to continue business operations during a strike. The courts have attempted to balance these competing interests in dealing with the issue of reinstatement.

(a) Reinstatement Depends on Category of Strikers

Strikers generally fall into one of two basic categories: "***unfair labor practice*" *strikers*** (those striking because of an employer unfair labor practice, such as the discriminatory firing of employees) and ***economic strikers*** (all other strikers, but most commonly those striking for an increase in benefits).

1) "Economic Strikers"

Those giving up their jobs to strike for increased benefits or other issues not related to an unfair labor practice receive little protection with respect to reinstatement. The employer is not compelled to discharge replacements hired during the strike or otherwise create jobs for such strikers. The strikers are ***entitled only to non-discriminatory review and disposition of their job applications*** for rehiring. [**NLRB v. MacKay Radio & Telegraph Co.,** *supra; and see* **Trans World Airlines v. Flight Attendants,** 489 U.S. 426 (1989)—applying the same rule under the Railway Labor Act]

a) Refusal to Cross Picket Line

Employees such as deliverymen who refuse to cross a legitimate picket line at the place of business of their employer's customer have been treated by some courts as economic strikers, under certain circumstances. [**NLRB v. Browning-Ferris Industries,** 691 F.2d 1117 (7th Cir. 1983); *but see infra,* p. 175]

b) Where Position Abolished

Whether the employer has hired a replacement or not, an economic striker may not be entitled to reinstatement if, ***due to changed economic or business conditions***, the employer has abolished her job. Thus, the employer need not create a new job or revive the old one for an economic striker. [*See* **NLRB v. R.C. Can Co.,** 328 F.2d

974 (5th Cir. 1964); *and compare* discussion of management prerogatives and union participation, *supra,* p. 122]

c) Seniority

One court has held that an employer may structure a seniority system so that permanent replacements can be rehired before economic strikers in the event of a layoff after the strike (and a resumption of hiring thereafter). [**Giddings & Lewis, Inc. v. NLRB,** 675 F.2d 926 (7th Cir. 1982)] However, the NLRB has required an employer to reinstate returning economic strikers to the positions they formerly held on the company seniority list, despite the continued employment of strike replacements. [**Harrison Ready Mix,** 272 N.L.R.B. 331 (1984); *but see* **Trans World Airlines v. Flight Attendants,** *supra*—employer need not lay off strike replacements so that strikers with greater seniority may be reinstated]

d) Reinstatement May Not Be Made Contingent on Degree of Activity

The employer may ***not*** use the degree of activity by a striker to determine whether it will reinstate the striker. [**NLRB v. MacKay Radio & Telegraph Co.,** *supra,* p. 164—employer's refusal to reinstate those most active in forming strike held discriminatory and an unfair labor practice under § 8(a)(1), (3)] But if strikers use intimidating threats against nonstriking employees, this may be a valid reason to refuse reinstatement. [**Clear Pine Mouldings,** 268 N.L.R.B. 1044 (1984)] The Board in 2020 rejected prior cases that had applied a narrow reading of *Clear Pine Mouldings* to protect abusive, hostile, and potentially illegal employee actions of harassment and instead found that an employer may still justify its responses to such picket line misconduct even if it is short of becoming a threat or a violent act by showing the discipline taken would have occurred regardless of any related protected activity. [**General Motors, LLC,** 369 N.L.R.B. No. 127 (2020)]

e) Duty to Consider Application

Failure to consider existing job applications by strikers when vacancies do occur also is discriminatory and an unfair labor practice. [**Laidlaw Corp. v. NLRB,** 414 F.2d 99 (7th Cir. 1969), *cert. denied,* 397 U.S. 920 (1970)] In this situation, the hiring of someone other than a striker-applicant is ***presumptively*** a violation of the NLRA, unless the employer can show a "legitimate and substantial business reason" for the failure. [**Laidlaw Corp. v. NLRB,** *supra; and see* **David R. Webb Co. v. NLRB,** 888 F.2d 501 (7th Cir.), *cert. denied,* 495 U.S. 956 (1989)—employer also violated the NLRA by rehiring economic strikers for positions different from their jobs before strike and then terminating them for inability to perform in their new positions]

f) Duty to Reinstate When Jobs Resume After Shutdown

If the jobs of economic strikers are eliminated during the strike but are recreated after the strike ends, the strikers are entitled to reinstatement unless the employer can show "legitimate and substantial business justifications" not to do so. [**NLRB v. Great Dane Trailers,** *supra,* p. 70; **NLRB v. Fleetwood Trailer Co.,** 389 U.S. 375 (1967)] In this regard, the Board has held that offers of reinstatement are ***not*** necessary where a plant shutdown during a strike, and its post-strike reopening, are shown to have occurred for economic or other reasons wholly unrelated to the strike. [**Weyerhaeuser Co.,** 274 N.L.R.B. 972 (1985)]

2) "Unfair Labor Practice Strikers"

If employees strike because of employer unfair labor practices and the strike itself is not unlawful, the strikers are ***entitled to reinstatement*** during or after the strike, even if it is necessary to discharge replacements hired during the strike. [*See* **Mastro Plastics Corp. v. NLRB,** 350 U.S. 270 (1956); **NLRB v. MacKay Radio & Telegraph Co.,** *supra*] However, the strikers must submit unconditional applications for reinstatement before the employer is obligated to rehire them.

a) Back Pay

For many years, the Board also required strikers to make unconditional applications for reinstatement before the employer would incur any liability for back pay. However, in 1979, the NLRB overruled this requirement, so that a striker's rights to back pay run automatically from the ***date of discharge***. [**Abilities & Goodwill, Inc.,** 241 N.L.R.B. 27 (1979)]

b) Discharge Before Replacement

An employer who ***discharges an "economic striker" before hiring a permanent replacement*** may have committed an unfair labor practice by discriminating against employees for lawful union activity. The discharge thus converts the "economic striker" into an "unfair labor practice striker," so the discharged employee is ***unconditionally entitled to reinstatement*** (a right he would not have had as an "economic striker"). [**NLRB v. International Van Lines,** 409 U.S. 48 (1972)]

c) Limitations

The *Mastro Plastics* doctrine has been refined by the NLRB so that only strikes protesting "***serious***" unfair labor practices, as determined on a case-by-case basis, are entitled to the foregoing protections. [**Arlan's Department Store,** 133 N.L.R.B. 802 (1961)] Moreover, strikers protesting unilateral action by the employer that might constitute a breach of contract as well as a violation of section 8(a)(5) may not be protected under the doctrine. [**Dow Chemical Co. v. NLRB,** 636 F.2d 1352 (3d Cir.), *cert. denied,* 454 U.S. 818 (1980)]

EXAM TIP GILBERT

What is considered a "serious" unfair labor practice against which a union may strike notwithstanding a no-strike provision is determined on a case-by-case basis. Generally, it would be wise for you to discuss the ***negative effect*** the unfair labor practice has on the collective-bargaining agreement and on union representation.

3) Risks to Both Parties

Employees who strike take the risk of being permanently replaced if the dispute is deemed to be an economic strike, even though they believed in good faith that they were protesting an unfair labor practice. However, an employer who hires replacements with the promise of permanent jobs also takes a risk, since it may be sued for breach of contract or misrepresentation in state court if ***it*** misjudged the character of the strike and is forced to put the strikers back to work. [**Belknap, Inc. v. Hale,** *supra,* p. 28]

EXAM TIP GILBERT

On your exam, don't be fooled by a striker who, based on what his union told him, reasonably believes he is striking to protest an unfair labor practice. He still runs the risk of being replaced ***if the strike is deemed to be an "economic strike."*** The reverse is also true—an employer who honestly and reasonably believes a strike is "economic" may be sued by replacement workers who lose their jobs to returning strikers after the strike is ***deemed a protest against an unfair labor practice.***

4) Restriction on Reinstatement Rights

Both economic strikers and unfair labor practice strikers lose their protected status if the strike is conducted in an unlawful manner or for any illegal, additional purpose. As to both categories of strikers, NLRA section 10(c) (added by Taft-Hartley) provides that the Board may not order reinstatement or back pay for striking employees who were suspended or discharged "for cause."

5) Tactic—Reinstatement Agreement

If there is a danger that strikers may lose their jobs, the union will usually bargain for and obtain a reinstatement agreement from the employer, thereby removing any need to resort to the foregoing rules.

PROTECTION OF STRIKERS	GILBERT
THE LEVEL OF PROTECTION AFFORDED A STRIKER DEPENDS ON HER CLASSIFICATION:	
ECONOMIC STRIKERS	**"UNFAIR LABOR PRACTICE" STRIKERS**
— Not entitled to reinstatement if position abolished — May lose seniority to replacement workers — Entitled to have job application fairly considered by employer — If replacement is hired before striker's discharge, striker is converted to an "unfair labor practice" striker	— Entitled to reinstatement, even if replacements must be discharged — Entitled to back pay from date of discharge — Unfair labor practice must be serious—if not serious, striker may lose protection
Note: Both categories lose protection if strike is conducted in an ***unlawful manner*** or for any additional, ***illegal purpose.***	

(b) Distinguish—Discharge for Partial Strikes or Slowdowns

As discussed *supra,* p. 157, "partial" or "intermittent" strikes or slowdowns are ***illegal.*** Section 7 does not protect employees who seek to remain on the payroll and at the same time disrupt production as if they were on strike. Consequently, an employer can properly discharge and ***refuse to reinstate*** workers who take part in such illegal activities. This activity constitutes "just cause" for discharge within the meaning of section 10(c), above. [*See* **NLRB v. Montgomery Ward & Co.,** 157 F.2d 486 (8th Cir. 1946)]

(c) "Wildcat Strikes"

A "wildcat strike" is a work stoppage undertaken by a minority of union members ***without official authorization or sanction*** from the union. (This might take the form of a walkout by a dissident group within a bargaining unit, or a walkout by an entire bargaining unit that has not been sanctioned by the international union.) Like slow-downs or partial strikes, wildcat strikes are *not protected by section* 7, and thus are grounds for discharge under section 10(c).

1) Rationale

An employer should not have to deal with "splinter groups" or dissident elements within the union. [**NLRB v. Sunbeam Lighting Co.,** 318 F.2d 661 (7th Cir. 1963)—upholding employer's refusal to reinstate 50 employees (out of 120 in bargaining unit) who walked off the job before union membership had even voted on employer's final offer]

2) Exception

At least one decision has held that a wildcat strike ***might*** be protected if it were directed toward ***"a specific, previously considered and articulated union objective."*** [**NLRB v. Shop Rite Foods, Inc.,** 430 F.2d 786 (5th

Cir. 1970)] However, this holding may be questionable in light of the Supreme Court opinion in **Emporium Capwell Co. v. Western Addition Community Organization** (*see supra,* p. 100).

3) **Further Exception**

"Wildcat" activity may also be protected if the action is ***quickly ratified*** by a majority of union members.

(d) **Impact of No-Strike Clause in Collective Agreement**

Where the parties have included a no-strike clause and arbitration provisions in the collective bargaining agreement, the employer's right to discharge strikers for violating the no-strike clause is a ***matter of contract interpretation only***, and thus one for arbitration. This is true whether an "economic" or an "unfair labor practice" strike is involved. [**Mastro Plastics Co. v. NLRB,** *supra,* p. 166]

4. Regulation of Picketing

a. Scope of "Picketing"

The term "picketing" is not defined in the NLRA, and the determination of what constitutes picketing is determined on a case-by-case basis. Generally, there must be a ***confrontation between employees of the picketed employer and those purportedly engaged in picketing*** before "picketing" will be found. [**NLRB v. United Furniture Workers,** 337 F.2d 936 (2d Cir. 1964)—merely affixing signs to poles may not be enough]

e.g. **Example:** Picketing was held to occur when signs describing the union's dispute with an employer were placed in a snowbank next to the employer's premises—the necessary "confrontation" being found in the fact that the persons placing the signs remained nearby where employees could see them. [**NLRB v. Local 182, International Brotherhood of Teamsters, Chauffeurs, Warehousemen & Helpers,** 314 F.2d 53 (2d Cir. 1963)]

(1) **Note**

A threat to engage in organizational or recognition picketing may be equated with actual picketing in calculating the 30-day tolling period under section 8(b)(7)(C). (*See infra,* p. 170.)

EXAM TIP GILBERT

On your exam, before discussing the protection of and the restrictions on picketing, be sure to discuss ***whether there is in fact "picketing"***—*i.e.,* a confrontation between the employees and employer. Remember also that confrontation has a physical element—the employer must know who is doing the picketing.

b. Regulating the Means by Which Picketing Is Carried out

NLRA section 8(b)(1)(a) prohibits both ***mass picketing,*** which deters employees from entering or leaving a plant, and picketing accompanied by ***threats of violence.*** [**American Newspaper Guild,** 151 N.L.R.B. 1558 (1965)]

(1) Obstructing Entrances

Obstructing plant entrances with the intent of prohibiting nonstrikers from entering or leaving is unlawful, whether or not the attempts are successful. [**International Woodworkers, Local Union 3-3,** 144 N.L.R.B. 912 (1963)] However, the mere presence of mass picketers who do not obstruct entrances or exits does not in itself violate section 8(b)(1)(A). [**United Steelworkers of America,** 137 N.L.R.B. 95 (1962)]

(2) Isolated Misconduct

Minor, isolated instances of misconduct along a picket line may not amount to the ***degree*** of violence prohibited by the NLRA.

c. Regulating the Objectives of Picketing—Recognition and Organizational Picketing

Picketing for organizational or recognition purposes is regulated by the following NLRA sections (each of which is discussed further *infra*):

(i) ***Section 8(b)(7),*** which restricts primary picketing by uncertified unions for recognition or organizational purposes;

(ii) ***Section 8(b)(4)(C),*** which regulates secondary picketing in defiance of the certification of another union; and

(iii) ***Section 8(b)(4)(B),*** which deals with secondary picketing for recognition of an uncertified union.

(1) Picketing to Force Recognition of an Uncertified Union

Section 8(b)(7)(A), (B), and (C) make it unlawful for an uncertified union to picket (in an otherwise lawful manner), cause to be picketed, or threaten to picket any employer, if (i) the employer is ***currently recognizing another union,*** (ii) a valid election pursuant to section 9(c) has been held ***within the preceding 12 months,*** or the picketing union has not filed an NLRB election petition within a reasonable time (not to exceed 30 days after commencement of the picketing), and (iii) the object of the picketing is to ***force the employer to recognize or bargain with*** the uncertified union or to force employees to accept the union as their bargaining agent.

(a) Objective

To constitute a violation of section 8(b)(7), the picketing in question must have ***recognition or organization*** as one of its immediate objectives. [**Department & Specialty Store Employees' Union, Local 1265 v. Brown,** 284 F.2d 619 (9th Cir. 1960), *cert. denied,* 366 U.S. 934 (1961)—fact that picketing was also for "informational and advisory" purposes did not make it lawful, since one of its objects was unlawful]

1) "Area Standards" Exception

Picketing by a union to induce an employer to raise wages to union scale (*i.e.,* to the "area standard") is outside the scope of section 8(b)(7) since it does not have a prevailing objective of recognition or organization. [**Houston Building & Construction Trades Council,** 136 N.L.R.B. 321 (1962)—picketing allowed to continue despite substantial interruption of deliveries]

a) But Note

The NLRB has ruled that the Supreme Court decision in *Lechmere* (*supra,* p. 54) precludes even area-standards picketing by nonemployee union representatives on an employer's private property. [**Makro, Inc. and Renaissance Properties Co.,** *supra*, p. 56; **Leslie Homes, Inc.,** *supra*, p. 56]

APPROACH TO RECOGNITION/ORGANIZATIONAL PICKETING

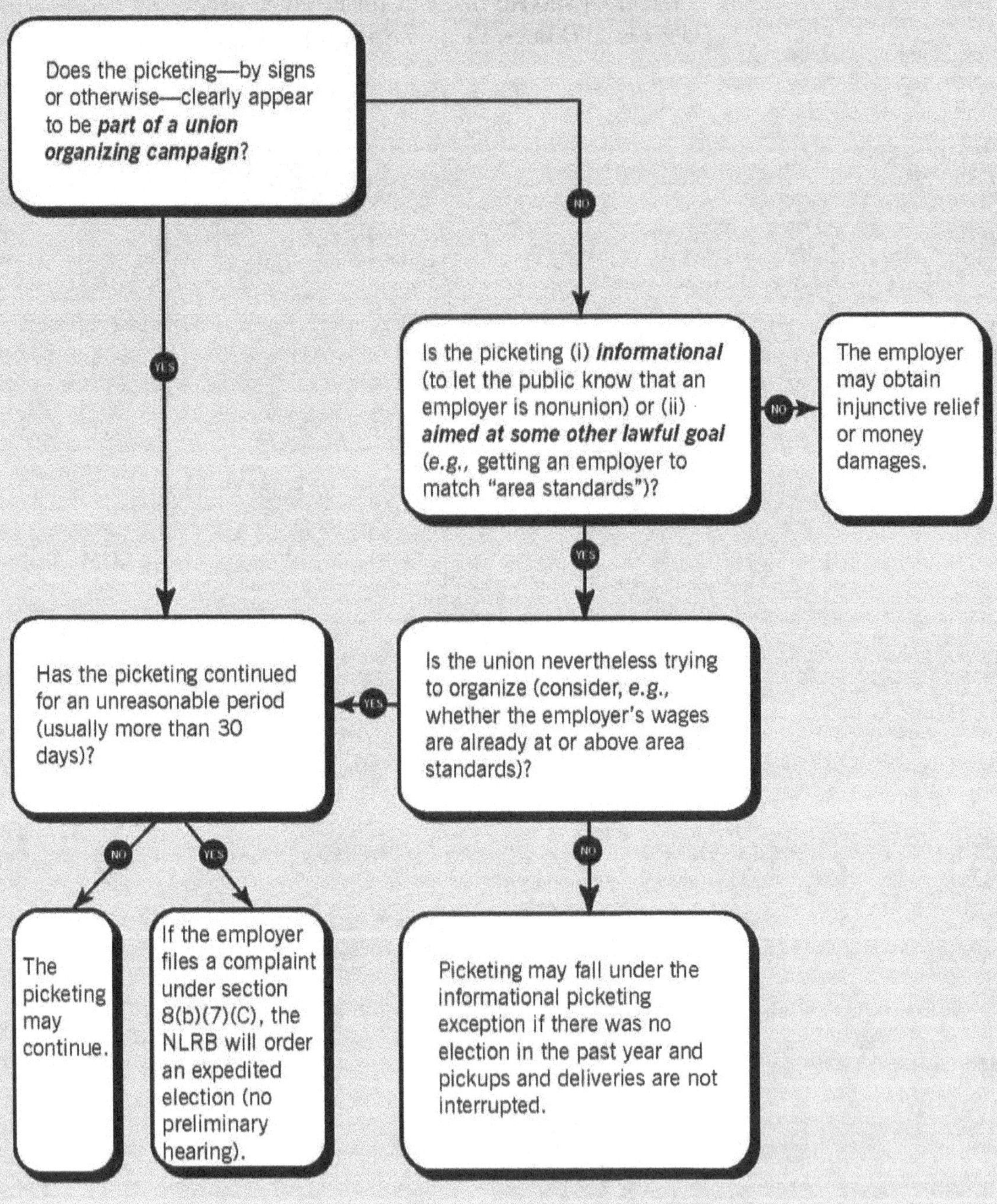

2) Immediacy of Objective

Likewise, picketing that does not have an *immediate* recognition or organizational objective may be lawful under section 8(b)(7). [**Houston Building & Construction Trades Council,** *supra*]

3) Note—Construction Union

A construction union permitted by section 8(f) to enter into a pre-hire agreement with an employer (*supra,* p. 75) is ***not exempt*** from the requirements of section 8(b)(7)(C). Thus, picketing to enforce a pre-hire agreement cannot continue for an unreasonable period, since it is viewed as the equivalent of recognitional picketing. [**NLRB v. Local Union No. 103, International Association of Bridge, Structural & Ornamental Iron Workers,** 434 U.S. 335 (1978)]

(b) Exception for "Informational Picketing"

However, the requirement that a union file an election petition within 30 days does not prohibit the union from attempting to induce a consumer boycott by picketing (or other publicity) by advertising the nonunion conditions, even if the picketing extends beyond 30 days. Furthermore, this exception applies even if the picketing has an additional organizational or recognition objective, provided that the picketing (i) is addressed mainly to the public, (ii) is truthful, and (iii) does not significantly interfere with deliveries or with services performed by other employers. [NLRA § 8(b)(7)(C); **Smith v. NLRB** ("*Crown Cafeteria* Case"), 327 F.2d 351 (9th Cir. 1964)]

1) Limitations

Such informational picketing may only take place if (i) no other union is lawfully recognized and (ii) no valid election has occurred within one year of the picketing. Moreover, pickets will lose the protection if their picketing interrupts pickups or deliveries at the employer's place of business.

e.g. **Example:** In the *Crown Cafeteria* Case, *supra,* the union picketed an employer for more than 30 days before filing for a representation election—ostensibly a violation of section 8(b)(7)(C). The picketing was restricted to consumer entrances to the employer's premises, and its announced objective was to advise the public that the employer did not have a contract with the union. There were no work stoppages or interferences with deliveries. The court found the picketing to fall within the "informational picketing" exception.

a) And Note

Where the union loses a representation election, it may subsequently picket the employer's premises if the placards clearly indicate the informational nature of the picketing (and there are accompanying instructions to picket only the customer entrances and not to interfere with deliveries). [**NLRB v. Local 239, International Brotherhood of Teamsters, Chauffeurs, Warehousemen & Helpers,** 340 F.2d 1020 (2d Cir. 1965)]

(c) Remedies for Unlawful Organizational Picketing

1) Speedy Elections

An alleged violation of section 8(b)(7) (or of section 8(b)(4)(A), (B), or (C)) is given priority treatment by the NLRB. [*See* NLRA § 10(1)] Where the employer files an unfair labor practice complaint under section 8(b)(7)(C), the NLRB may direct an expedited election under a proviso to that section. If the union wins the election, the restrictions of section 8(b)(7) no longer apply. If it loses, picketing for recognition or organization is barred for one year under section 8(b)(7)(B). If the election is challenged, the union may continue picketing until the dispute is resolved. [**Retail Store Employees' Union, Local No. 692,** 134 N.L.R.B. 686 (1961)]

a) Note

Where an election is not ordered by the Board, section 8(b)(7) charges are processed under the usual unfair labor practice procedures.

2) Injunctions

If the Board has ***reasonable cause*** to believe that the employer's section 8(b)(7) charge is true, it ***must*** seek an injunction against the picketing unless the union has filed a section 8(a)(2) charge of illegal domination or support by the employer and that charge also appears to be true. In the latter situation, no injunction against the 8(b)(7) conduct will be sought. (If the 8(a)(2) charge does not appear to be true, the NLRB may enjoin picketing on the 8(b)(7) charge.) (*See* further discussion of remedies, *infra,* pp. 186 *et seq.*) "Reasonable cause" is determined on the particular facts of each case.

(2) Picketing in Defiance of Prior Certification of Rival Union

NLRA section 8(b)(4)(C) makes it unlawful for an uncertified union to coerce the primary employer to recognize it as bargaining agent where another union has been certified (*see supra,* pp. 160 *et seq.*). The same three requirements applicable to strikes—***valid certification, prohibited objective,*** and ***coercive tactics***—also govern picketing that is the subject of an 8(b)(4)(C) charge.

(a) "Coercive Tactic"

Whether picketing is a "coercive tactic" is usually the issue in dispute.

1) Intent Relevant

Where there is no evidence that the picketing was intended to induce work stoppages, it does not violate section 8(b)(4)(C). [**NLRB v. Local 50, Bakery & Confectionery Workers International Union,** 245 F.2d 542 (2d Cir. 1957)]

2) Picketing Limited to Customer Entrance

Moreover, the union may picket ***customer entrances only*** without violating section 8(b)(4)(C). [**Retail Clerks International Association,** 122 N.L.R.B. 1264 (1959)]

(b) Limitation

As in the case of strikes, picketing by an uncertified union is subject to an ***exemption*** for "crossing the picket line." [*See* NLRA § 8(b)(4)(B); *and see infra,* p. 175] Also, certain product boycott picketing and publicity may be protected under section 8(b)(4) (*see infra,* pp. 182 *et seq.*).

(3) Secondary Picketing for Recognition of Uncertified Union

Section 8(b)(4)(B) is in the general nature of a ban on secondary boycotts, which includes secondary picketing for recognition or organizational purposes. This section focuses on picketing, while the broader implications of section 8(b)(4)(B) are discussed *infra,* pp. 176 *et seq.*

(a) General Ban on Secondary Picketing

Under section 8(b)(4)(B), a union may not picket a secondary employer to force the primary employer to recognize an uncertified union. Thus, if Union A pickets Employer B to pressure Employer C to recognize Union A ***or any other uncertified union,*** there is a violation of section 8(b)(4)(B).

(b) Exceptions

1) Lawful Primary Activity

Section 8(b)(4)(B) does not prohibit ***primary activity that is otherwise lawful.*** Thus, if Union A in the preceding paragraph engages in primary picketing of Employer C at Employer C's premises, the fact that the picketing may induce employees of Employer B (a secondary employer) to stop making deliveries to Employer C's premises—due to an unwillingness to cross the picket line—is simply a legitimate byproduct of primary picketing. Similarly, if Employer B were an "ally" of Employer C (*infra,* p. 180), both employers could be picketed at their places of business since the picketing would be primary in both cases.

2) Refusing to Cross Picket Lines

Section 8(b)(4)(B) does not prohibit any person from refusing to enter the premises of an employer other than his own, if the employees of that employer are engaged in a strike approved by their recognized bargaining agent and are picketing for that purpose. This insures the right of third parties (*e.g.,* the delivery people) to refuse to cross the picket line without prompting a charge of secondary boycott. [NLRA § 8(b)(4)(i); *but see supra,* p. 158]

a) Caution

It ***does*** violate section 8(b)(4)(B) (as well as section 8(b)(1)(A)) for a union involved in a dispute with a general contractor to prohibit union members from working for neutral subcontractors on the construction project. [**NLRB v. Glaziers & Glass Workers Local 1621,** 632 F.2d 89 (9th Cir. 1980)]

3) Construction and Garment Industry Exceptions

Section 8(e) provides exemptions for secondary picketing in the construction and garment industries. The construction industry exemption has been strictly construed by the NLRB, and is limited to activity ***on the job site*** (excluding, for example, ready-mixed concrete brought ***to*** the job site). The garment industry exemption permits employees in that industry to refuse to work for employers who attempt to subcontract work to nonunion employers.

a) Note

In at least one situation, the construction industry exemption has been read somewhat more broadly. The exemption has been held to shelter collective bargaining provisions that require employers to subcontract only to unionized subcontractors, even when such provisions are not restricted to job sites where both union and nonunion workers are employed. [**Woelke & Romero Framing, Inc. v. NLRB,** 456 U.S. 645 (1982)]

5. Secondary Pressure—Regulation of Boycotts

Section 8(b)(4) also applies to union action directed ***exclusively*** at secondary employers. A "secondary boycott" is defined as union pressure—in the form of strikes, picketing, threats, or other coercion—***aimed at an employer or other person with whom the union has no labor dispute,*** with the object of persuading or coercing that neutral party ***to stop dealing with a primary party*** with whom the union has a dispute, and thus ultimately persuading the primary party to meet union demands.

a. Activities Proscribed

Section 8(b)(4) proscribes two types of activity: (i) ***engaging in a strike, refusing to handle goods, or inducing another individual to strike or refuse to handle goods*** [NLRA § 8(b)(4)(i)]; or (ii) ***threatening, or otherwise coercing, an employer for any of the illegal objects discussed below,*** including purely verbal threats [NLRA § 8(b)(4)(ii)].

b. Illegal Objects

Both types of secondary activity described above are prohibited by section 8(b)(4) if they are undertaken for any of the following purposes:

(1) ***To force an employer to enter into a "hot cargo" agreement*** [NLRA § 58(b)(4)(A)] (*see supra,* p. 158);

(2) ***To force a third party to cease handling the employer's goods,*** or to force the third party to cease doing business with the employer [NLRA 58(b)(4)(B)]; or

(3) ***To compel an employer to assign work to one union rather than another*** [NLRA § 8(b)(4)(D)]. (Section 8(b)(4)(D) is analytically distinct from the other provisions of section 8(b)(4) and is treated separately, *supra,* pp. 162 *et seq.*)

c. Judicial Interpretation of Section 8(b)(4)

Legislative history clearly shows that section 8(b)(4) was designed to curtail secondary pressure, yet the statute itself never refers directly to secondary pressure. Moreover, it does not clearly specify which activities are prohibited. If the section were enforced literally, it would prohibit almost all strike activity, since one object of any strike is to induce persons not to do business with the primary employer.

(1) Protection Limited to Innocent Secondary Employer

The Supreme Court has held that section 8(b)(4) is limited to protecting an innocent secondary employer from the effects of a labor dispute involving another employer. In other words, the statute does not apply to strike activity unless the employees of a secondary employer are induced to strike (or to use other economic weapons) against their employer in order to aid a union striking another employer. [**Local 761, International Union of Electrical, Radio & Machine Workers v. NLRB** ("*G.E.* Case"), 366 U.S. 667 (1961)]

(2) Case-by-Case Approach

However, the opinion in the *G.E.* Case refused to promulgate any broad rules beyond the foregoing. Absent a specific legislative standard for determining whether particular secondary activity is prohibited by section 8(b)(4), the substantive law has developed on an ad hoc, case-by-case basis.

d. Specific Problems Involving Secondary Pressure

(1) "Political Protest" Cases

Conduct by union members designed to serve as a political protest may violate section 8(b)(4), despite First Amendment connotations of such activity. Thus, longshoremen who refused to unload cargo arriving from or destined for the Soviet Union as a protest against the Russian invasion of Afghanistan were found to be engaged in activity "in commerce" that imposed a heavy burden on neutral employers. Since this burden was at least one object of the activity, the activity was illegal secondary pressure under the NLRA. [**International Longshoremen's Association v. Allied International, Inc.,** *supra,* p. 145; **International Longshoremen's Association, Local 414,** 261 N.L.R.B. 1 (1982); *but compare* **Jacksonville Bulk Terminals, Inc. v. International Longshoremen's Association,** *supra,* p. 145]

(2) Common Situs Situations

Where more than one employer occupies the same physical location (plant site, construction site, etc.), it may be difficult to determine whether a union is engaged in illegal secondary action because any strike activity directed toward one employer at the site may well affect all.

(a) Conflicting Interests Involved

Common situs problems occur where the union and the secondary employer have legitimate but opposing interests. The union must be able to reach the primary employer at a place where its picketing and other economic activity will have an effect on that employer. At the same time, the secondary employer has an interest in avoiding the dispute between the union and the primary employer, and as a neutral (and innocent) third party, it should not be put "in the middle" or forced to suffer economic harm as a result of the primary dispute.

(b) *Moore Drydock* Rules

The NLRB was called upon to balance these competing interests in the so-called *Moore Drydock* Case. [***In re* Sailors' Union of the Pacific,** 92 N.L.R.B. 547 (1950)] There, the Sailors' Union commenced a strike against a shipowner while the ship was in a drydock facility owned by the secondary employer. The

Union began picketing the drydock, and the NLRB had to decide the extent to which such picketing would be permitted. In doing so, it formulated the following criteria (commonly referred to as the *Moore Drydock* rules).

1) Picketing at Situs Owned by Secondary Employer

Picketing at a situs owned by the secondary employer is allowed only if ***all*** of the following conditions are met, ***and*** there is no independent overriding evidence of a secondary motive:

a) ***The picketing is limited to times at which the primary employer is actually located at the secondary site;***

b) ***The primary employer is engaged in his ordinary business*** at the secondary site;

c) ***The picketing is reasonably close to the actual location of the primary employer*** (*i.e.,* if the primary employer is using only one corner of the site, picketing must be limited to that corner); ***and***

d) ***Any picketing signs clearly state that the dispute is only with the primary employer.***

2) Ownership of the Site Is Not Determinative

The *Moore Drydock* criteria have been applied to picketing at a site owned by the primary employer [**Local Union No. 55,** 108 N.L.R.B. 363 (1954)], and to a pre-dawn crowd of strikers who gathered at a motel housing replacement workers, calling for "the scabs" to go home [**District 29, United Mine Workers of America v. NLRB (New Beckley Mining Corp.),** 977 F.2d 1470 (D.C. Cir. 1992)].

(3) "Separate Gate" Cases

When labor disputes occur at premises occupied or serviced by more than one employer, attempts are frequently made to isolate the employees and employer involved in the dispute from other employers at the location. The device most commonly used is the creation of separate gates or entrances to the premises, one for employees of the primary employer and another (or others) for the remaining employees. The theory is that picketing then can be confined to the gate reserved for the primary employer.

(a) Limitation—Picketing Allowed Where Work Related to Primary Employer

In the *G.E.* Case (*supra,* p. 177), the Supreme Court approved the general concept of separate gates but held that picketing cannot be limited to the gate reserved for the primary employer where employees of secondary employers perform work ***related to or essential for*** the normal operations of the primary employer. In such cases, picketing is ***permitted*** at the gates where these employees enter the premises.

1) Rationale

Employers should not be allowed to use separate gates to defeat the traditional objectives of a strike.

2) "Related Work"

Typical examples of work related to operations of the primary employer include making deliveries for the primary employer and making repairs on the employer's plant or equipment.

(b) No Other Picketing

In all other situations, picketing at a separate gate is ***prohibited*** if the separate gate is ***clearly marked*** as being for outside employees only. [**Nashville Building & Construction Trades Council,** 164 N.L.R.B. 280 (1967); *and see* **Carpenters Local 33 (CB Construction Co.),** 289 N.L.R.B. 528 (1988)—location of primary gate at allegedly "remote and inconvenient" location would not justify picketing at neutral separate gate]

(4) Contractor-Subcontractor Relationships in Construction Industry

Construction sites pose a particularly difficult problem in separating legal secondary activity from illegal conduct, due to the presence on most sites of a general contractor and several different subcontractors. Each subcontractor may have a different degree of independence from the general contractor, and there may be complicated relationships between or among the various subcontractors.

(a) Picketing Entire Site Is Illegal

In **NLRB v. Denver Building & Construction Trades Council,** 341 U.S. 675 (1951), the Supreme Court held that a strike at a construction site, aimed at forcing the unionized general contractor to terminate his contract with a nonunion subcontractor, was illegal secondary activity prohibited by section 8(b)(4). The Court dismissed the union's argument that the close working relationship between the contractor and subcontractor created a "joint-employer" relation between the two. Note: The Board implemented a new rule in 2020 identifying how joint employers are determined including establishing how these entities must share or codetermine the employees' essential terms and conditions of employment through substantial and direct control. [85 Fed. Reg. 11, 184 (Feb. 26, 2020)] Given the substantial and direct control component, it is likely that the result in *Denver Building* would not be any different under this rule.

(b) Use of Separate Gates at Construction Sites

After the Supreme Court approved the use of separate gates in the *G.E.* Case (*supra,* p. 178), the NLRB had to consider the possible use of this device at construction sites.

1) *G.E.* Separate Gate Doctrine Does Not Apply

In **Building & Construction Trades Council,** 155 N.L.R.B. 319 (1965), the Board ruled that it would *not* apply the *G.E.* "separate gate" doctrine at construction sites. One reason given was that it would be difficult to find that the work of general contractors and subcontractors was not "related." Yet to call the work "related" would permit picketing the entire site under the *G.E.* doctrine, a result inconsistent with the decision in *Denver Building & Construction Trades Council, supra.*

a) *Moore Drydock* Will Apply

The NLRB thus held that separate gates at construction sites would be evaluated under the *Moore Drydock* standards (*see supra,* p. 177).

b) **Must Allow Reasonable Opportunity to Inform**

Even under the *Moore Drydock* rules, however, the union must be given a reasonable opportunity to inform the public about its dispute with the primary employer. Thus, if the area reserved for picketing is hidden from public view, the union may be able to picket elsewhere without violating the Act. [**Electrical Workers Local 501 v. NLRB,** 756 F.2d 888 (D.C. Cir. 1985)]

2) **Ownership of Job Site Irrelevant**

The Board has also ruled that ownership of the job site is not a relevant factor in construction cases (despite contrary language in *Denver Building & Construction Trades Council* and *Building & Construction Trades Council*). [**Carpenters Local Union No. 470, United Brotherhood of Carpenters & Joiners,** 224 N.L.R.B. 315 (1976)]

EXAM TIP GILBERT

In these situations, remember it is the separate gate ***doctrine*** that does not apply. ***The use of separate gates*** at ***construction*** sites is quite common. But picketing at such sites is governed by the *Moore Drydock* rules (rather than the *G.E.* "separate gate" doctrine) because of the Supreme Court's opinion in *Denver Building & Construction Trades.*

(c) **Possible Antitrust Violations**

Where secondary pressure by the union results in an agreement by the contractor not to award jobs to nonunion subcontractors, the union may also be liable under the antitrust laws. [**Connell Construction Co. v. Plumbers & Steamfitters Local Union No. 100,** *supra,* p. 75; *and see infra,* p. 188]

1) **Distinguish—Construction Contracts**

Legitimate "pre-hire" contracts between an employer and a union, permitted in the construction industry under NLRA section 8(f), have a sufficient "collective bargaining relationship" to avoid antitrust problems under *Connell.* Nor do such limitations on subcontracting to nonunion firms constitute unlawful "hot cargo" provisions under sections 8(b)(4) or 8(e). [**Donald Schriver, Inc. v. NLRB,** 635 F.2d 859 (D.C. Cir. 1980), *cert. denied,* 451 U.S. 976 (1981)—this result harmonizes construction industry proviso in § 8(e) with pre-hire concept in § 8(f)]

(5) **"Employer Allies"**

In many situations, the secondary employer is not a neutral or innocent third party—it may be linked economically to the primary employer, or be aiding the primary employer in some fashion. Although section 8(b)(4) does not expressly require that the secondary employer be an innocent or neutral third party, the courts have read this requirement into the statute. Thus, any secondary employer who "aids or abets" the primary employer in a dispute with the union is afforded *no protection from secondary pressures* under section 8(b)(4). [*See* **Douds v. Metropolitan Federation of Architects, Engineers, Chemists, & Technicians, Local 231,** 75 F. Supp. 672 (S.D.N.Y. 1948); **NLRB v. Business Machine & Office Appliance Mechanics Conference Board, Local 459,** 228 F.2d 553 (2d. Cir. 1955), *cert. denied*, 351 U.S. 962 (1956)]

e.g. **Example:** If a secondary employer arranges with the primary employer to do the work that striking workers would otherwise have done, the secondary employer is effectively aiding the primary employer and cannot claim protection under the secondary boycott ban. [**Laborers International Union, Local 859 v. NLRB,** 446 F.2d 1319 (D.C. Cir. 1971)]

e.g. **Example:** A secondary employer may also be an "ally" of the primary employer if its business operations are *closely related* to those of the primary employer. [***In re*** **National Union of Marine Cooks & Stewards,** 87 N.L.R.B. 54 (1949)—union was allowed to picket two companies **because both were** *owned and controlled by the same parties* **and** the functions performed by the two were part of the same horizontal business operation]

(6) Individual Coercion as "Boycott Activity"

As noted, a union violates section 8(b)(4) only when it causes "employees" of the secondary employer to put economic pressure on the secondary employer. Problems frequently arise where only one employee has been approached: Is this sufficient to constitute boycott activity?

(a) Background

Under the original language of section 8(b)(4) (enacted by the Taft-Hartley Amendments of 1947), three factors had to be present before union activity would violate the statute:

1) ***The activity had to induce or encourage*** employees of the neutral employer.
2) ***The activity had to cause a concerted refusal*** by employees of the neutral employer to perform their jobs. The Supreme Court interpreted this to mean that ***"more than one" secondary employee*** had to be involved. [**NLRB v. International Rice Milling Co.,** 341 U.S. 665 (1951)—no violation where pickets merely induced the driver of a single truck not to make deliveries at struck plant]
3) ***Those persons induced by the union had to be "employees,"*** as defined in section 2(3) of the NLRA. Thus, for example, the union would not violate section 8(b)(4) if it induced only supervisors or other managerial personnel to refuse to work for their employers.

(b) Impact of Landrum-Griffin Amendments

The 1959 Landrum-Griffin Amendments to section 8(b)(4) (*i.e.*, section 8(b)(4)(i)) deleted the word "concerted" from the initial language of the statute and changed the word "employee" to "individual."

1) Effect

A violation of section 8(b)(4)(i) now requires only that the union "***induce an individual***" to refuse to work for his secondary neutral employer.

2) Application

The Supreme Court interpreted these modifications in **NLRB v. Servette, Inc.,** 377 U.S. 46 (1964). Union representatives in *Servette* had asked the manager of a supermarket not to handle the goods of a primary employer with whom the union had a dispute. Under the original (Taft-Hartley) language of section 8(b)(4), such activity would have been outside the section, both because the union was not seeking "concerted" action (*i.e.,* action by more than one person) and because no "employee" was involved. Under section 8(b)(4) as amended, neither of these two defenses was available to the union.

a) Section 8(b)(4)(i) Test

Even so, the Court found that such union activity did ***not*** violate section 8(b)(4)(i) because the "inducement" requirement had not been met. Merely asking the manager to refuse to handle the goods, in the Court's view, did not constitute "inducement."

b) Section 8(b)(4)(ii) Test

Moreover, the union action in *Servette* did not violate section 8(b)(4)(ii) (*supra,* p. 176), added by Landrum-Griffin in 1959, because the union had not ***threatened*** the store manager. Thus, the crux of the matter here is whether the union is ***"asking" or "coercing."***

e. Exceptions to Section 8(b)(4)—"Legal Boycotts"

Express provisos in section 8(b)(4) exempt two types of conduct from the ban on boycotts:

(1) Request Not to Cross Picket Lines

Activity that may cause employees of a neutral employer not to cross a picket line to make deliveries to the primary employer ***where a strike is in progress*** is specifically permitted.

(a) But Note

To comply with this exception, the union picketing and carrying on the strike must be ***duly certified,*** and the strike must be an ***authorized*** one (ratified by members of the union).

(2) "Publicity Proviso"

Another exception to section 8(b)(4) allows the union to ***advise the public, by "means other than picketing," that a "product or products" are being "produced" by an employer with whom the union has a dispute,*** and that such products are being distributed by another secondary employer (*e.g.,* newspaper advertisements or handbills asking the public to refrain from buying farm produce packed by nonunion growers and distributed through supermarkets). [NLRA § 8(b)(4)(ii)(B)]

(a) Application

Section 8(b)(4)(ii)(B) has been held to permit a union to distribute handbills at a shopping mall urging customers not to patronize mall tenants because of a labor dispute between the union and a construction company building a department store, provided there is no violence, picketing, patrolling, or intimidation. [**Edward J. DeBartolo Corp. v. Florida Gulf Coast Building & Construction Trades Council,** 485 U.S. 568 (1988); *and see* **Schwab Foods, Inc.,** 125 L.R.R.M. 1225 (N.L.R.B. 1987)] Also, the Board has found *DeBartolo*'s handbilling analysis also protects any form of peaceful and expressive conduct including the display of a 12-foot tall inflatable rat ("Scabby") and two stationary banners. [**Lippert Components, Inc.,** 371 N.L.R.B. No. 8 (2021)]

(b) Limitations

The "publicity proviso" is subject to the following limitations:

1) ***There is no protection if the "publicity" induces a work stoppage or interferes with deliveries to secondary employers*** (*e.g.*, the supermarkets). [**NLRB v. Fruit & Vegetable Packers & Warehousemen Local 760** ("*Tree Fruits* Case"), 377 U.S. 58 (1964)]

2) ***The publicity must not stray from the message permitted by the proviso*** onto other (albeit related) matters. [**Service Employees Local 399 v. NLRB,** 743 F.2d 1417 (9th Cir. 1984)—handbills which included information about customer complaints and safety records did not fall under "publicity proviso" exception]

(c) Who Qualifies as a "Producer"

There has been considerable litigation over which employers can be regarded as the "producer" of a product, so as to permit union publicity urging a boycott against persons dealing with that employer. Basically, the courts hold that a "producer" is anyone who ***enhances the economic value*** of the product ultimately sold or consumed, meaning that the union in effect may urge a public boycott against ***anyone in the marketing chain.*** [**Great Western Broadcasting Corp. v. NLRB,** 356 F.2d 434 (9th Cir.), *cert. denied,* 384 U.S. 1002 (1966)—television station that advertised services and products of others held a "producer"]

WHO IS A "PRODUCER"?	GILBERT
"PRODUCER" IS ANYONE WHO ADDS *ECONOMIC VALUE*	
EXAMPLES—PRODUCERS	**EXAMPLES—NOT PRODUCERS**
A general contractor who is constructing a shopping center is a producer of the goods to be sold in the department store	The other tenants in the shopping center and the owner of the shopping center are not producers
Wholesaler of a product—union can therefore handbill retailer supplied by that wholesaler	Manufacturer of commercial and industrial equipment
Subcontractors—permitting union to boycott the prime contractor	Subsidiaries of a conglomerate—thus, a union cannot extend boycott to products of parents or of parent's subsidiaries

(d) "Means Other than Picketing"

Despite the apparent ban in section 8(b)(4)(ii)(B) on picketing as a means of publicizing a dispute, the Supreme Court in *Tree Fruits, supra,* held that Congress had not intended to ban all picketing at secondary sites. Only picketing that unduly coerces the secondary employer is prohibited, so ***noncoercive picketing is protected by the publicity proviso.*** In *Tree Fruits,* for example, the Court held that the peaceful picketing of retailers selling apples produced by the primary employer with whom the union had a dispute was lawful, since it was designed to induce consumers to cease purchasing the apples (*i.e.,* the product) rather than cease dealing altogether with the retailer.

1) Rationale

The Court ruled that in employing the term "means other than picketing" in section 8(b)(4)(ii)(B), Congress had not used the "requisite clarity" necessary to effect a broad ban against peaceful picketing (which would limit First Amendment guarantees of free speech).

2) Impact—Product Boycotts by Picketing

Thus, the union may lawfully picket a secondary employer for the purpose of imposing a ***partial,*** as opposed to a total, consumer boycott—*i.e.,* a boycott aimed at the struck product rather than at all of the products sold by the secondary employer.

a) "One Product" Employer

One difficulty discussed in *Tree Fruits* was how to deal with a "one product" secondary employer. A product boycott against such a business would be little different in practical effect from an effort to shut down the business.

1/ Note

In *Dow Chemical,* an NLRB order proscribing product picketing in this type of situation was denied enforcement by the D.C.

Circuit Court of Appeals, only to be vacated in turn by the Supreme Court, without opinion. [**Local 14055, United Steelworkers v. NLRB** ("*Dow Chemical*"), 524 F.2d 853 (D.C. Cir. 1975), *vacated,* 429 U.S. 807 (1976)]

2/ **And Note**

Subsequently, the Supreme Court resolved the issue more clearly in *Safeco Title Insurance.* There, a union engaged in negotiations with a title insurance under-writer was found to have violated section 8(b)(4)(ii)(B) by picketing five neutral insurance companies whose business came almost entirely (90%) from the under-writer. [**NLRB v. Retail Store Employees' Union, Local 1001** ("*Safeco Title Insurance*"), 447 U.S. 607 (1980)]

EXAM TIP GILBERT

On your exam remember that a boycott at a secondary employer/producer (*e.g.,* grocer) must be directed against the ***product of the primary employer*** (*e.g.,* apples of grower) with whom the union has a dispute.

3) What Constitutes a "Product" Boycott

Picketing a secondary employer to effectuate a product boycott may be unlawful if the appeal to the consumer is so broad that it amounts to a total boycott of the secondary employer.

e.g. **Example:** Union picketing of a secondary employer with signs urging consumers not to buy "products produced by nonunion manufacturers" is ***unlawful*** because there is no identification of the manufacturer or product. The effect is to induce a stoppage of all trade with the secondary employer, and therefore, such picketing is not protected under the decision in *Tree Fruits.* [**Bedding, Curtain & Drapery Workers Union, Local 140 v. NLRB,** 390 F.2d 495 (2d Cir.), *cert. denied,* 392 U.S. 905 (1968)]

a) "Merged Product" Exception

A more difficult problem occurs when the "product" of the primary employer is merged into the total product sold by the secondary employer. The courts and the Board have differed on this issue, but the problem is illustrated by **K & K Construction Co. v. NLRB,** 592 F.2d 1228 (3d Cir. 1979) (enforcement denied). There, a union having a dispute with a carpentry subcontractor picketed the housing project where the subcontractor was working. Pickets were stationed at the main gate where prospective customers entered the housing site and at the project developer's sales office in a nearby shopping mall. The NLRB found that the "merged product" exception to *Tree Fruits* did not apply in this situation. The court of appeals ruled otherwise, however, concluding that the consumer could not separate the carpentry work from the developer's product (so that the consumer was being asked, in effect, not to deal with the developer).

C. Remedies for Illegal Strikes, Boycotts, and Picketing

1. Unfair Labor Practice Proceeding

The most expedient remedy for an employer faced with an illegal strike or other illegal union activity is to file an unfair labor practice charge against the union. (*See* discussion of NLRB complaint procedure, *supra,* pp. 44 *et seq.*)

a. Priority Handling

The investigation of such charges is entitled to priority over all other cases in the office where it is filed. [NLRA § 10(1)]

b. If "Reasonable Cause" Exists, NLRB Must Seek Immediate Injunction

If, after the preliminary investigation, the Regional Director has "reasonable cause" to believe that the charge is true—*i.e.,* that the union has violated section 8(b)(4)(A), (B), or (C) (illegal strikes, picketing, and secondary boycotts)—he ***must*** seek an immediate injunction against the union activity pending final adjudication of the unfair labor practice charge. [NLRA § 10(1)]

(1) Distinguish—Other "Unfair Labor Practice" Proceedings

In other unfair labor practice proceedings, the NLRB is authorized, but is not required, to seek immediate injunctive relief. [NLRA § 10(j); *see supra,* pp. 80–81]

(2) Issuance of Injunction

Normally, there is a court hearing before issuance of an injunction. But the court may issue a restraining order ***ex parte*** (without notice or hearing) if there is sufficient showing that a delay might cause substantial and irreparable injury to the employer. If the court issues an injunction, the injunction will remain in effect until final disposition of the unfair labor practice charge.

(3) Other Cases in Which NLRB Must Seek Immediate Injunction

(a) "Hot Cargo" Provision

The NLRB ***must*** seek an immediate injunction where "reasonable cause" exists to believe that the union is attempting to obtain or enforce a "hot cargo" provision in a collective bargaining contract (in violation of NLRA section 8(e)).

(b) Unlawful Organizational Picketing

The NLRB ***must*** also seek an immediate injunction where there is "reasonable cause" to believe that the union has violated section 8(b)(7) (unlawful organizational picketing) unless the union has filed a countercharge that the employer has violated section 8(a)(2) (illegal employer domination or support of a certified union). If there is "reasonable cause" to believe that the countercharge is true, the NLRB will not seek to enjoin the organizational picketing (*see supra,* p. 174).

(4) No Injunction Against Secondary Picketing

Note that an employer may *not* obtain an injunction against secondary picketing by a union that arises from an otherwise lawful strike against another employer. The Norris-LaGuardia Act (*supra,* p. 15) generally precludes any such injunction against secondary activity, and applies to cases under both the National Labor Relations Act and the Railway Labor Act. [**Burlington Northern Railroad v. Brotherhood of Maintenance of Way Employees,** 481 U.S. 429 (1987)]

2. Injunctive Relief Against Acts of Violence

Quite apart from unfair labor practice proceedings, an employer (or any party for that matter) may sue the union to restrain acts of *violence or coercion.* Such activity is never protected.

a. Jurisdiction

Suits to restrain union violence or coercion are proper in *either* state or federal courts (*see supra,* p. 27).

b. Union "Agency" Concepts

The courts and the NLRB generally apply common law rules of agency in determining whether the union is responsible for acts of violence or coercion by individual members or subordinates. (*See* detailed discussion, *supra,* pp. 66–67.)

3. Injunctive Relief Under Collective Bargaining Agreement

Even where no violence is involved, if the illegal strike or other union activity is also a breach of a ***"no-strike" provision*** in the collective bargaining agreement, the employer may sue to enjoin the strike as long as the dispute with the union is ***subject to arbitration*** under the collective bargaining agreement. (*See supra,* pp. 144–147.)

4. Private Damages Action Against Union

In addition to injunctive relief, the employer or any other party suffering economic loss as the result of an illegal strike or other illegal union activity may seek damages against the union under Taft-Hartley section 303.

a. Federal Jurisdiction

The Taft-Hartley Act confers "federal question" jurisdiction on federal courts, so that the damage action can be maintained there regardless of diversity of citizenship. The only jurisdictional requirement is that the industry involved be within or "affect" interstate commerce. [LMRA § 301(a)]

b. State Jurisdiction

State courts have concurrent jurisdiction of section 303 damage actions, and such courts may also exercise jurisdiction under any state statutes or common law applicable to illegal union activities.

(1) Distinguish—Preemption

Keep in mind that state law can be applied in these cases only if the strikes, boycotts, or picketing are illegal under the NLRA. If the union activity is even "arguably" protected by the NLRA, the ***preemption doctrine*** applies, and state courts have no power to regulate the activity (*supra,* p. 23).

c. Employer or Other Injured Party May Recover Damages

The civil damage action authorized by section 303 may be maintained not only by the employer, but also by ***customers, suppliers,*** or other persons doing business with the employer, provided they can show a direct economic loss as the result of the illegal union activity.

(1) Limitation

However, no action is allowed where the relationship to the union activity is deemed ***too remote.*** [**UMW v. Osborne Mining Co.,** 279 F.2d 716 (6th Cir.), *cert. denied,* 364 U.S. 881 (1960)—corporation that was only partially supplied by struck employer not entitled to sue union for damages]

5. Right to Terminate Contract

An employer may be entitled to terminate the entire collective bargaining agreement if the union has violated a no-strike provision in the agreement (*see supra,* p. 147). However, an employer who elects to terminate forfeits any right to damages from the union. [**Children's Rehabilitation Center, Inc. v. Service Employees International Union, Local No 227,** *supra,* p. 147]

D. Impact of the Antitrust Laws on Union Concerted Activities

1. Legitimate Union Activities Exempt from Antitrust Laws

The Supreme Court in **United States v. Hutcheson,** 312 U.S. 219 (1941), held that a union acting in its own self-interest and using only lawful means was ***not*** subject to attack under the antitrust laws. The basic policy favoring legitimate concerted activities, as expressed in the Norris-LaGuardia Act, was held to warrant this interpretation of the Sherman and Clayton Antitrust Acts. (*See supra,* p. 16.)

2. Present Judicial Interpretation of Exemption

Generally speaking, the antitrust laws are now held to apply to a union only when (i) the union combines with ***nonlabor groups*** (*e.g.,* employers), and (ii) such combinations result in a ***restraint of interstate trade or commerce.*** [**UMW v. Pennington,** 381 U.S. 657 (1965)]

e.g. **Example:** There was no violation of the antitrust laws when a group of unions insisted that an employer sign the same contract they had negotiated with several other employers. [**Local Union No. 189, Amalgamated Meat Cutters & Butcher Workmen v. Jewel Tea Co.,** 381 U.S. 676 (1965)] *Rationale:* As long as the union and employer are bargaining over subjects as to which they were required to bargain—*i.e.,* wages, hours, and terms and conditions of employment—the activities are exempt from the antitrust laws.

cf. **Compare:** But where a union obtained contracts with all electrical equipment manufacturers and contractors in New York City, and used such contracts to restrain trade by refusing to allow union members to install equipment manufactured outside the city, there was a violation of the Sherman Act. [**Allen Bradley Co. v. Local Union No. 3, International Brotherhood of Electrical Workers,** *supra,* p. 16]

a. Note

A collective bargaining agreement that prohibited union contractors from awarding jobs to nonunion subcontractors has been held to violate the Sherman Act. [**Connell Construction Co. v. Plumbers & Steamfitters Local Union No. 100,** *supra,* p. 180]

(1) Insufficient Relationship to Bargaining

The Supreme Court in *Connell Construction Co.* distinguished the union-subcontractor clause from the antitrust exemption recognized in *Jewel Tea, supra,* on the ground that the former imposed direct restraints on competition among subcontractors that would ***not*** have resulted simply from eliminating competition based on differences in wages, hours, or terms and conditions of employment.

(2) Distinguish—"Pre-Hire" Contracts

However, a legitimate "pre-hire" contract between an employer and a union has a sufficient collective bargaining relationship to avoid anti-trust problems under the *Connell* decision. Only where the union allies itself with entities outside the collective bargaining relationship may antitrust issues arise. [**Donald Schriver, Inc. v. NLRB,** *supra,* p. 180]

(3) Distinguish—"Gig Economy" Workers

Seeking labor protections for workers in the so-called gig economy resulting from technology platforms may lead to antitrust concerns. [**Chamber of Commerce v. Seattle,** 890 F.3d 769 (9th Cir. 2018) (finding Seattle's local ordinance establishing collective bargaining for Uber and Lyft for-hire drivers was not preempted as more specificity needed to circumvent antitrust claims)]

Chapter Five

Protection of Individual Rights

CONTENTS	PAGE

Chapter Approach

Another possible area of examination concerns individual rights in the context of labor law. The basic sources of such rights are the NLRA, the Landrum-Griffin Act ("LMRDA"), and Title VII of the 1964 Civil Rights Act. The following are general guidelines for reviewing these acts:

1. **NLRA**

   Under the NLRA, you should understand:

   — What is ***protected concerted activity,*** and how the concept extends even to workers in ***unorganized*** shops.

   — The scope of the ***union duty of fair representation*** (owed to ***all*** employees in the bargaining unit).

   — How this duty can be ***enforced*** against the union (and the employer) through unfair labor practice or section 301 proceedings.

   — Employee rights to union representation at ***investigatory interviews.***

   — The rules governing ***union security agreements*** and employees who prefer not to join or contribute to the union.

   — The extent to which unions may restrict members' rights in the pursuit of ***legitimate union interests,*** and the enforceability of such rules by fines or expulsion.

2. **Landrum-Griffin Act**

   The LMRDA has been called the union member's "Bill of Rights" against undemocratic practices by union leaders. Whether your course (or exam) deals with the mechanics of the LMRDA will depend on your instructor. If it does, you should be familiar with the basic provisions regulating ***union elections*** (*i.e.,* election of union officers) and those guarding against ***improper financial practices.***

3. **Title VII**

   Title VII and related civil rights legislation generally are treated in a separate course, and are mentioned only briefly in this Summary.

A. Concerted Activity Protected Under the NLRA

1. Statutory Source

Section 7 of the NLRA grants employees the right to engage in (or to refrain from) "concerted activities for the purpose of collective bargaining and for other mutual aid or protection."

a. If There Is a Union

If a union has been recognized as the exclusive representative for employees in a bargaining unit, the employees must channel their grievances and activities through the union. This is true even for nonunion employees in an open shop. [**Emporium Capwell Co. v. Western Addition Community Organization,** *supra,* p. 168]

b. If There Is No Union

Note, however, that section 7 applies ***even though union activity is not involved*** and the employees do not contemplate collective bargaining. [**NLRB v. Phoenix Mutual Life Insurance Co.,** 167 F.2d 983 (7th Cir.), *cert. denied,* 335 U.S. 845 (1948)]

e.g. **Example:** An employer was held to violate the NLRA by discharging a group of unorganized employees who walked off the job to protest extreme cold in the shop. [**NLRB v. Washington Aluminum Co.,** 370 U.S. 9 (1962); *and see* **Roseville Dodge v. NLRB,** 882 F.2d 1355 (8th Cir. 1989)—employer could not discharge employees for refusing to work until employer agreed to discuss pay, supplies, and alleged improper treatment, where company had no grievance procedure and other methods of communication had proved futile]

2. Requirements for Protection Under Section 7

a. Concert of Action

For an activity to be protected under section 7, there must be some element of "concert" pertaining to more than one employee. Individual complaints or "griping" about working conditions are not protected. [**NLRB v. Office Towel Supply Co.,** 201 F.2d 838 (2d Cir. 1953)]

(1) Basic NLRB Standard—Assertion of Contract Issue

The basic NLRB interpretation of the "concert" requirement is the *Interboro* doctrine, which holds that the assertion by an individual employee of a right based on a provision of the collective bargaining agreement is deemed to be collective in nature and therefore concerted activity. [**Interboro Contractors, Inc.,** 157 N.L.R.B. 1295 (1966), *enforced,* 388 F.2d 495 (2d Cir. 1967)]

(a) Extension to Noncontract Issues Overruled

In 1975, the Board ruled that an employee's complaint to a state health and safety agency had the requisite collective character even though it was not based on any contract provision. [**Alleluia Cushion Co.,** 221 N.L.R.B. 999 (1975)] But in 1984, the NLRB ***overruled*** this expansion to noncontract issues, expressly finding that the *Interboro* doctrine applied to contract rights alone. [**Meyers Industries,** 268 N.L.R.B. 493 (1984) ("*Meyers I*")]

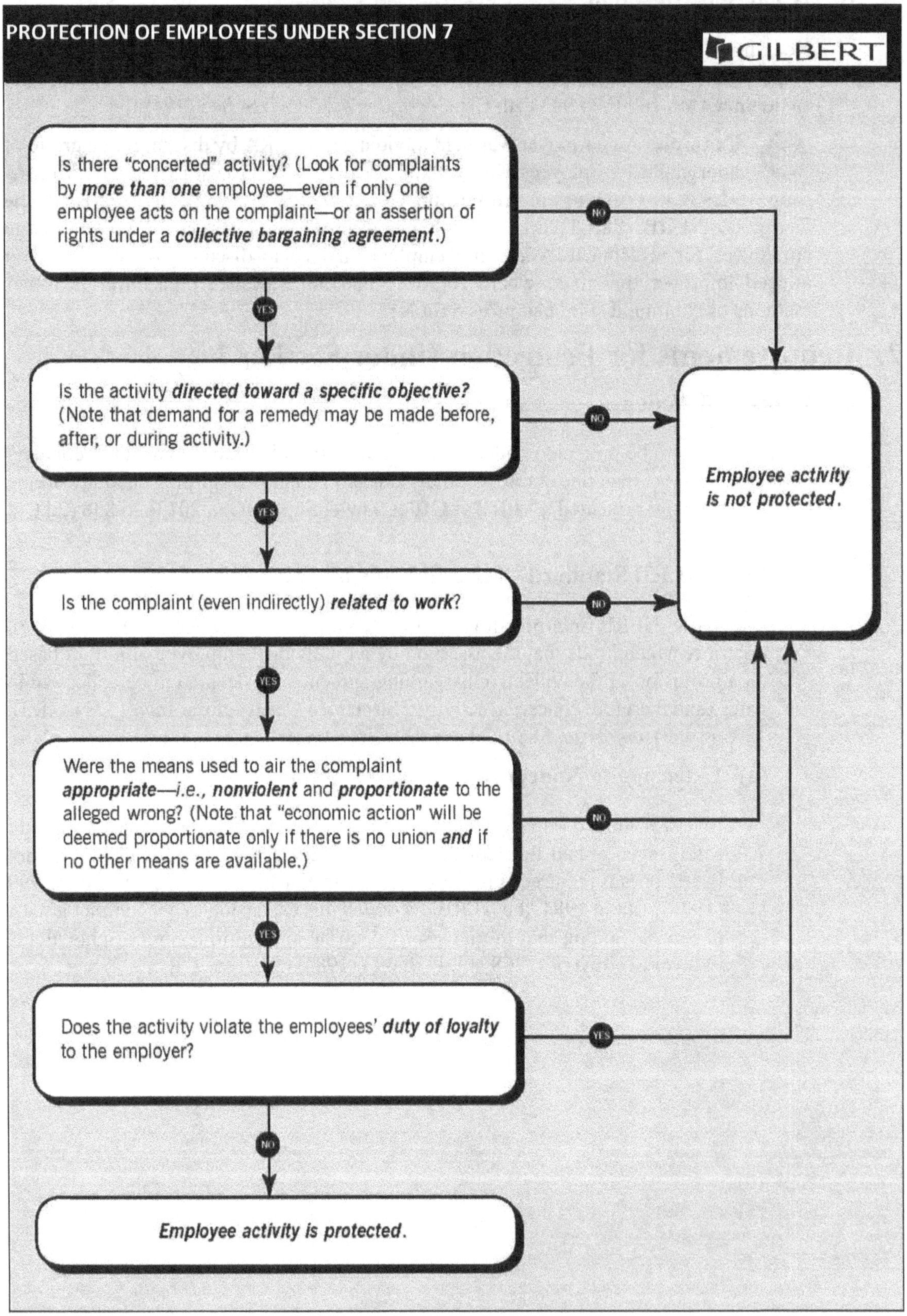

1) Note

The D.C. Circuit initially refused to enforce the Board's order in *Meyers* I, ordering the NLRB to reconsider. [**Prill v. NLRB,** 755 F.2d 941 (D.C.

Cir. 1985) ("*Prill I*")] Upon reconsideration of its position in *Meyers I*, the Board reaffirmed *Meyers I* by finding that position consistent with the Supreme Court holding in *City Disposal Systems, infra.* This time, the NLRB order was enforced. [**Meyers Industries,** 281 N.L.R.B. 882 (1986) ("*Meyers II*"), *enforced sub nom.* **Prill v. NLRB,** 835 F.2d 1481 (D.C. Cir. 1987) ("*Prill II*"), *cert. denied,* 487 U.S. 1205 (1988)]

(2) Supreme Court Interpretation

In 1984, the Supreme Court applied the *Interboro* doctrine to the case of an employee who refused to drive a truck he asserted to be unsafe, citing a contract right to refuse to operate any vehicle "not in safe operating condition." The Court noted that such assertions were very similar to (and might become) a grievance under the contract and that filing a grievance clearly is concerted activity. [**NLRB v. City Disposal Systems, Inc.,** 465 U.S. 822 (1984)] On remand, the circuit court concluded that the employee's refusal to drive the truck did constitute concerted activity. [**City Disposal Systems, Inc. v. NLRB,** 766 F.2d 969 (6th Cir. 1985)]

(a) Note

Even though such actions are held to be concerted activity, the employee still must act in good faith and advance his claim with propriety in order to be protected under section 7 (*see infra,* p. 196).

(3) A View of "Concerted Activity"

After *City Disposal Systems* and its own more restrictive approach in *Meyers,* the NLRB appears once again to be broadening the scope of "concerted activity."

Example: An employee who made an individual follow-up call to the Wage and Hour Division of the Department of Labor after several employees had made initial inquiries was held by the Board to have been engaged in protected concerted activity, even though the follow-up call was not made in any authorized or representative capacity. [**Every Woman's Place, Inc.,** 282 N.L.R.B. 413 (1986)]

Example: In **Salisbury Hotel, Inc.,** 283 N.L.R.B. 685 (1987), a group of employees became upset over a change in the scheduling of work hours and discussed the change among themselves. Thereafter, one employee, on her own, contacted the Department of Labor and was subsequently discharged by the employer. In ordering her reinstatement, the NLRB seemed to revive the notion that action addressed to matters of concern to more than one employee is "concerted" even when it is not commissioned by (or even known to) the other employee or employees in question. The Board found that the action of the employee "grew out of" and was "a continuation of" the group concern over the rescheduling of work shifts.

Example: The CEO of a nonunion computer company sent an e-mail message to employees about a proposed change in vacation policy. One employee responded by e-mail, disputing the CEO's claims about the change, whereupon the CEO discharged the employee for making an "inappropriate" response. The NLRB held that the employee had engaged in protected concerted activity. [**Timekeeping Systems, Inc.,** 323 N.L.R.B. 244 (1997)]

Example—a more recent and limited view: In **Alstate Maintenance, LLC,** 367 N.L.R.B. No. 68 (2019), a skycap at Kennedy International Airport was approached by a supervisor about a request from Lufthansa Airlines to assist passengers arriving with soccer equipment. Skycaps received most of their wages from tips. One of the skycaps responded to the request for help with the soccer equipment by saying "We did a similar job a year prior and we didn't receive a tip for it." When the soccer equipment arrived, the skycap who made the comment and the three other skycaps working with him all walked away. The employer fired the skycap for the comment. The Board found that the statement was not concerted and the employee agreed that it was " 'just a comment' and was not aimed at changing. . . policies or practices" of the employer. Also, even if the statement had involved concerted activity as it induced other workers to act, it did not seek mutual aid or protection. The statement was aimed at griping about customer behavior in not tipping rather than seeking a change in the employer's behavior in providing wages. The employee agreed that he was not dissatisfied with the employer's practice of compensating employees through tipping. The NLRB held the employee had not engaged in protected activity.

b. Specific Purpose

Employees need not make a specific demand on their employer in order to be protected, but the activity must be directed toward some specific objective.

c. "Work Relatedness"

Protected activity must pertain to a work-related matter. However, the connection between the activity and the employee's immediate job may be very indirect.

e.g. **Example:** The distribution of a union newsletter was held to constitute protected activity when the newsletter (i) urged employees to oppose incorporation of a state "right to work" law into the revised state constitution, and (ii) criticized the President's veto of an increase in the federal minimum wage. [**Eastex, Inc. v. NLRB,** 434 U.S. 1045 (1978)]

(1) Must Concern Employees as Employees

The activity in question must relate to the interests of employees in their capacity as employees. Thus, for example, concerted activity regarding an employee's proposal that the Employee Stock Ownership Plan be given an increased ownership interest in the employer company has been held ***not*** to be protected. [**Harrah's Lake Tahoe Resort Casino,** 307 N.L.R.B. 182 (1992)]

d. Propriety

The means used by employees must be appropriate. Unlawful or violent activities are not protected under section 7, nor are activities that constitute a breach of contract. [**NLRB v. Washington Aluminum Co.,** *supra,* p. 193] Methods of protest such as petitions, e-mail communications, brief visits to the boss's office, and the like are generally not objectionable. But when employees take concerted *economic* action, the results are less predictable.

(1) Limited Use of "Economic Action" Permitted as Last Resort

Economic actions may be permitted if there is no union and employees see no other way to make their position known, as in *Washington Aluminum* (*supra*). But at least one court has cautioned that "the right to disrupt. . . is tempered by an inherent proportionality requirement . . . . [R]easonableness of the means of protest is one of a variety of factors that are examined in order to determine whether an employee activity is protected." [**Bob Evans Farms v. NLRB,** 163 F.3d 1012 (7th Cir. 1998)]

e.g. **Example:** In *Bob Evans,* employees had staged a walkout to protest the discharge of a supervisor. The court held that while the discharge was a matter of legitimate concern to the employees on the facts of the case, the walkout was a disproportionate—and therefore unprotected—activity. In so ruling, the court rejected an NLRB finding to the contrary.

e. Loyalty

The Supreme Court has indicated that employees owe a certain degree of loyalty to their employer as an inherent part of the contractual relationship between them, and activity that transgresses this "duty of loyalty" will not be protected. [**NLRB v. International Brotherhood of Electrical Workers Local 1229 (Jefferson Standard Broadcasting Co.),** 346 U.S. 464 (1953) ("*Jefferson Standard*")]

e.g. **Example:** In *Jefferson Standard,* employees of a television station circulated handbills disparaging the television programs of their employer (a local television station) without indicating to the public that the employees were seeking any benefits for themselves. Such activity was held not to be protected under section 7.

(1) Note

The Supreme Court did not further elaborate on when the "duty of loyalty" is breached, but one lower court has held that public disparagement of the employer's product must be shown. [**NLRB v. New York University Medical Center,** 702 F.2d 284 (2d Cir. 1983)] Moreover, the NLRB has held that *Jefferson Standard,* permits employee communications that ***relate to an ongoing labor dispute*** and are not "so disloyal, reckless or maliciously untrue as to forfeit statutory protection." [**Cincinnati Suburban Press,** 289 N.L.R.B. 966 (1988)—employer could not discharge reporter for article in outside publication on an unsuccessful campaign to organize employer's editorial staff]

cf. **Compare:** A bit later, the NLRB and the D.C. Circuit Court of Appeals ruled that ***any*** product disparagement—as in quietly but publicly supporting a boycott of the employer's products—violates the duty of loyalty, at least when there is no labor dispute to which the activity relates. [**George A. Hormel & Co. v. NLRB,** 962 F.2d 1061 (D.C. Cir. 1992)]

B. Union or Employer Discrimination—NLRA Standards

1. Union Duty of Fair Representation

a. Duty Owed to All Employees in Unit

NLRA section 9(a) provides that the union selected by the majority of employees in the appropriate bargaining unit shall be the ***exclusive representative of all employees*** in the unit—whether members of the union or not. This right to exclusive representation carries with it the duty to represent all members fairly, including minority and nonunion members.

(1) Origin of Duty

Unlike most other labor law doctrines (which are based on statutes), the duty of fair representation was created by the courts as an accompaniment to the union's ***exclusive*** representation rights. Hence the scope of the doctrine is defined by case law rather than by statutory language.

(2) Scope of Duty

The duty of fair representation extends not only to negotiation of the collective bargaining agreement, but also to administration of the agreement, *e.g.*, to grievance and arbitration procedures established by the agreement. [**Conley v. Gibson,** 355 U.S. 41 (1957)]

b. Background—Racial Discrimination Cases

The union's duty to represent all members of the bargaining unit was first recognized in cases in which the union itself was involved in racial discrimination.

(1) Union Members

In **Steele v. Louisville & Nashville Railroad,** 323 U.S. 192 (1944), the union negotiated a collective bargaining agreement that discriminated against black union members. The Supreme Court granted injunctive relief against enforcement of the agreement, holding that the union had breached its statutory duty (under the Railway Labor Act) to represent the interests of ***all*** of its members. (The same result has also been reached under NLRA section 9(a). [*See* **Wallace Corp. v. NLRB,** 323 U.S. 248 (1944)])

(2) Nonunion Employees

Later, the Court applied the same doctrine where the union had pressured the employer to discharge black workers who were not union members, but who held jobs in the bargaining unit that the union purported to represent. The Court stressed that the duty of fair representation extended to ***all*** employees in the bargaining unit, specifically including non-union members. [**Brotherhood of Railroad Trainmen v. Howard,** 343 U.S. 768 (1952)]

(3) State or Federal Action Proper

Duty of fair representation suits may be brought in either federal or state court. [**Humphrey v. Moore,** 375 U.S. 335 (1964)] When such suits involve contract rights, they are commonly lodged under LMRA section 301 against the employer and the union jointly.

(a) Suit Against Union Alone

Where a suit is brought solely against the union and there is no contract claim against the employer under section 301, federal jurisdiction still may be derived from 28 U.S.C. section 1337(a), since the National Labor Relations Act is a "statute regulating commerce" within the scope of that provision. [**Breininger v. Sheet Metal Workers Local 6,** *supra,* p. 29]

c. Breach of Duty as Unfair Labor Practice

Under modern decisions, the union's failure to represent fairly an individual employee or group of employees in the bargaining unit may also be a violation of NLRA section 8(b)(1)(A), *i.e.,* a union unfair labor practice. [**Vaca v. Sipes,** *supra,* p. 29]

(1) Development of Doctrine

The NLRB first announced this rule in **Miranda Fuel Co.,** 140 N.L.R.B. 181 (1962). The Board's order in *Miranda* was denied enforcement [*see* **NLRB v. Miranda Fuel Co.,** 326 F.2d 172 (2d Cir. 1963)], but later court decisions adopted the NLRB doctrine, and in **Vaca v. Sipes,** *supra,* the Supreme Court clearly approved it.

d. What Constitutes "Breach" of Duty of Fair Representation

A union breaches its duty of fair representation only when its conduct toward a member of the collective bargaining unit is "arbitrary, discriminatory, or in bad faith." [**Vaca v. Sipes,** *supra; and see* discussion *infra,* p. 207]

EXAM TIP GILBERT

Always keep in mind that a union selected by the ***majority*** is the exclusive representative of ***all*** employees in the unit—even the employees who are not in the union—and that the union has a duty to refrain from treating a member of the unit in an ***arbitrary*** or ***discriminatory manner,*** or in ***bad faith.***

---

(1) Rationale

The process of labor-management relations involves continuous dealings between the union and the employer, and it is inevitable that the union may propose changes in work conditions or terms of employment that will benefit some employees and prejudice others. Moreover, the union is constantly confronted with complaints and grievances by individual union members. Thus, ***considerable discretion*** must be vested in the union, both in its dealings with management and its dealings with individual union members. [*See* **Air Line Pilots Association v. O'Neill,** 499 U.S. 65 (1991)]

(2) Application

(a) Negotiating the Contract

A union unfair labor practice cannot be predicated solely on the fact that the collective bargaining agreement negotiated by the union prejudices a particular employee or group of employees, as long as it appears that the union negotiated the provision in question in good faith. [**Bleier v. NLRB,** 457 F.2d 871 (3d Cir. 1972)]

(b) Conduct Regarding Grievance Procedures

Fair representation questions most frequently arise with respect to the union's role in advocating an employee's case through the grievance and arbitration procedures provided in the collective bargaining contract. The union need not take up every grievance or take every grievance to arbitration, nor must the union seek judicial review of an award unfavorable to the employee or judicial enforcement of a favorable award. [*See, e.g.,* **Camacho v. Ritz-Carlton Water**

Tower, 786 F.2d 242 (7th Cir. 1986)] In all such cases, however, the union's decision not to act must be in good faith (*i.e.,* not arbitrary, discriminatory, or in bad faith). [*See* **Freeman v. Teamsters Local 135,** 746 F.2d 1316 (7th Cir.), *cert. denied,* 477 U.S. 908 (1986); **Sear v. Cadillac Automobile Co.,** 654 F.2d 4 (1st Cir. 1981)]

(c) Arbitrary Classification—Race or Alienage

The duty of fair representation is breached where the union induces the employer to discriminate against an employee on the basis of an "invidious or arbitrary classification," ***such as race or citizenship.*** [**NLRB v. International Longshoremen's Association,** 489 F.2d 635 (5th Cir.), *cert. denied,* 419 U.S. 1040 (1974)—union induced employer to give preference in job referrals to U.S. citizens over Mexican nationals, although both were members of same bargaining unit]

(d) Sex Discrimination

Likewise, unions who determine membership solely on the basis of sex (and who refuse to process grievances on that basis) violate section 8(a)(1)(A). [**Local No. 106, Glass Bottle Blowers Association,** 210 N.L.R.B. 943 (1974)] Any attempt to cause the *employer* to discriminate on the basis of sex would presumably violate section 8(b)(2). [**Local No. 106, Glass Bottle Blowers Association,** *supra*]

(e) Discrimination Against Nonunion Employees

The union may breach the duty of fair representation where it acts **for the *purpose of intimidating nonunion employees, e.g.,* making** an "example" of a nonunion employee to encourage other non-union employees to join the union. [*See* **NLRB v. International Longshoremen's Association,** *supra,* p. 187]

(f) Political Actions

A breach of the duty occurs where the union acts ***solely out of political expediency.*** [**Truck Drivers & Helpers Local 568 v. NLRB,** 379 F.2d 137 (D.C. Cir. 1967)—union seeking recognition made campaign pledge that it would give preferential treatment to a numerically larger group of employees over another group in the same bargaining unit]

(g) Negligence

Ordinary negligence by the union in handling grievances or other duties does not constitute a breach of the duty of fair representation. [**United Steelworkers of America v. Rawson,** 495 U.S. 362 (1990)—union negligently performed safety inspections]

1) Distinguish—Hiring Halls

Because the union occupies an employer-like position in operating a hiring hall, circuit courts of appeals have found that ***mere negligence*** by the union in administering the hall can breach its duty of fair representation. [*See, e.g.,* **Jacoby v. NLRB,** 233 F.3d 611 (D.C. Cir. 2000)—union breached duty of fair representation by inadvertently dispatching less-senior union member before plaintiff, court thereby imposed almost a "no fault" duty on the union]

2) Gross Negligence or Indifference

Gross negligence or "reckless disregard" of an employee's rights ***can*** breach the duty of fair representation. [**Dutrisac v. Caterpillar Tractor Co.,** 749 F.2d 1270 (9th Cir. 1984)—union failed to timely request arbitration as planned; *but see* **Grant v. Burlington Industries,** 832 F.2d 76 (7th Cir. 1987)] And handling grievances in a "***perfunctory***" manner is prohibited—since this demonstrates indifference and apathy sufficient to breach the duty of fair representation. [*See* **O'Neill,** *supra,* p. 199; **Webb v. ABF Freight Systems, Inc.,** 155 F.3d 1230 (10th Cir. 1998)—union representative failed to review evidence and obtain information requested by plaintiff]

(3) Scope of "Breach" Violating the NLRA

There is some disagreement as to whether a breach of the duty of fair representation occurs only with respect to arbitrary, discriminatory, or bad faith action by the union that differentiates one employee (or one group of employees) from others within the bargaining unit, or whether it can also occur where such conduct affects all members of the unit equally. The NLRB and most courts of appeals extend the duty of fair representation to cover both situations, while the Sixth Circuit has limited the duty to cases of differential treatment within the unit. [*See* **NLRB v. Teamsters Local 299,** 782 F.2d 46 (6th Cir. 1986)]

EXAM TIP GILBERT

For your exam, remember that unlike most other labor law doctrines (which are based on statutes), the duty of fair representation was created by the courts—as an accompaniment to the union's ***exclusive*** representation rights. Thus, the scope of the doctrine is ***defined by case law*** rather than by statutory language.

---

c. Measure of Damages

When an employee brings a fair representation action based on wrongful discharge, damages must be ***apportioned*** between the employer and the union, with the union primarily liable for that portion of the employee's damages attributable to the union's breach of duty. [**Bowen v. United States Postal Service,** 459 U.S. 212 (1983)—award of $30,000 against union upheld, with employer responsible for additional $22,954 to make employee whole]

(1) No Punitive Damages

However, punitive damages apparently are not a permissible remedy against unions that breach the duty of fair representation. [**International Brotherhood of Electrical Workers v. Foust,** 442 U.S. 42 (1979)—case decided under Railway Labor Act]

(2) Right to Trial by Jury

An employee who sues a union for compensatory damages for breaching the duty of fair representation has the right to a jury trial. [**United Transportation Union Local 74 v. Consolidated Rail Corp.,** 881 F.2d 282 (6th Cir. 1989); *and see* **Chauffeurs, Teamsters & Helpers, Local No. 391 v. Terry,** 494 U.S. 558 (1990)—employee also may seek ***back pay*** (equitable relief under Title VII) in fair representation claim before a jury]

f. Statute of Limitations

In duty of fair representation suits against unions or employers, the applicable statute of limitations is the six-month period specified in NLRA section 10(b) for the filing of unfair labor practice charges. [**Del Costello v. Teamsters,** 462 U.S. 151 (1983)] This eliminates the former practice of applying state limitations periods, which had produced widely varying results.

(1) Note

The six-month limitations period applies whenever a duty of fair representation claim is at issue—even in "hybrid" cases where the claim is brought as a breach of contract action under section 301, or as a suit to vacate an arbitration award. [**Taylor v. Ford Motor Co.,** 761 F.2d 931 (3d Cir. 1985)] However, state limitations periods may still apply to suits against unions that are ***unrelated*** to the duty of fair representation, such as a claim for damages stemming from an unlawful secondary boycott. [**Monarch Long Beach Corp. v. Soft Drink Workers Local 812,** 762 F.2d 228 (2d Cir. 1985), *cert. denied,* 474 U.S. 1081 (1986)]

(2) And Note

In a suit to set aside an arbitration award, at least one court has applied the ***three-month*** statute of limitations of the United States Arbitration Act or Federal Arbitration Act. [**Occidental Chemical Corp. v. International Chemical Workers Union,** 853 F.2d 1310 (6th Cir. 1988)—policy dictating rapid resolution of such disputes outweighs normal six-month limitations period under NLRA]

g. Not Affected by Civil Rights Legislation

An unfair labor practice claim against a union for racial discrimination can be brought before the NLRB despite the fact that Title VII also prohibits such discrimination (*see* below). The NLRB has concurrent jurisdiction with the EEOC in this area. [**Local Union No. 12, United Rubber, Cork, Linoleum & Plastic Workers v. NLRB,** 368 F.2d 12 (5th Cir. 1966), *cert. denied,* 389 U.S. 387 (1967)]

2. Employer Discrimination

One circuit court opinion advanced the theory that an employer commits an unfair labor practice under section 8(a)(1) when the employer engages in racial discrimination. [**United Packinghouse Food & Allied Workers v. NLRB,** *supra,* p. 103] However, the NLRB has *rejected* this view, and no federal circuit court currently espouses it. [*See* **Jubilee Manufacturing Co.,** 202 N.L.R.B. 272 (1973)]

C. Union or Employer Discrimination—Civil Rights Legislation

1. Introduction

In addition to being an unfair labor practice under the NLRA, union or employer discrimination on the basis of race may violate the Civil Rights Act of 1866 and on the basis of race and/or sex may violate Title VII of the 1964 Civil Rights Act (as amended in 1972). An employee's rights under these statutes are ***independent*** of any claims under the NLRA or the collective bargaining contract (*see infra,* p. 203). While civil rights and employment discrimination law plays an important and ever-increasing role in the workplace, it is outside the scope of basic law school courses in labor law—which focus on union organization and collective bargaining—and it is too voluminous to treat adequately in a Labor Law Summary. Accordingly, the discussion in this section merely notes the major pieces of civil rights legislation and the possible impact of the collective bargaining contract on an employee's rights under that legislation.

2. Civil Rights Act of 1866

Section 1 of the Civil Rights Act of 1866 [42 U.S.C. § 1981] also referred to as "Section 1981" provides that all persons in the United States "shall have the same right . . . to make and enforce contracts, to sue, to be parties, to give evidence, and to the full and equal benefit of all laws and proceedings for the security of persons and property as is enjoyed by white citizens." Early cases found that only actual enslavement violated Section 1981, but it is now held to encompass strictly private rights in property or contract as well. [**Jones v. Alfred H. Mayer Co.,** 392 U.S. 409 (1968)] Section 1981 applies to discrimination by ***either*** the union or the employer, and also applies to racial discrimination against ***whites.*** [**McDonald v. Santa Fe Trail Transportation Co.,** 427 U.S. 273 (1976)]

3. Title VII, Civil Rights Act of 1964—Fair Employment Practices Act

Title VII of the 1964 Civil Rights Act [42 U.S.C. §§ 2000 *et seq.*] as amended by the Equal Employment Opportunity Act of 1972 (often referred to as the "Fair Employment Practices Act") prohibits discrimination by labor organizations, employers, or employment agencies on the basis of ***race, color, religion, sex, or national origin.*** The scope of activities covered is ***very broad,*** and includes hiring; discharge; compensation; promotion; classification; training; apprenticeship; referrals for employment; union membership; and terms, conditions, and privileges of employment.

4. Impact of Collective Bargaining Contract on Rights Under 1866, 1871 or 1964 Civil Rights Acts

Collective bargaining agreements often contain nondiscrimination clauses, together with procedures for arbitrating grievances under the contract. Moreover, a discriminatory discharge also might be said to be without just cause. In either event, the employee grievance may conceivably violate both the contract and the civil rights statutes.

a. Employee May Pursue Both Remedies

An employee in this situation properly may seek arbitration of his claim under the contract and, if not successful, subsequently start proceedings under Title VII or under Section 1 of the **Civil Rights Act of 1871** (also known as the Ku Klux Act of 1871) and now known today as "Section 1983" [42 U.S.C. § 1983] (if applicable). [**Alexander v. Gardner-Denver Co.,** *supra,* p. 136; **McDonald v. City of West Branch,** *supra,* p. 136; *see supra,* p. 136 and **Wilmington v. J.I. Case Co.,** 793 F.2d 909 (8th Cir. 1986). (applying *Alexander* and *McDonald* to a Section 1981 (Section of the Civil Rights Act of 1866) claim); *but see* **14 Penn Plaza v. Pyett,** *supra,* p. 136, where clear and unmistakable waiver could prevent a court action]

b. Rationale—Independent Rights

The Supreme Court in *Gardner-Denver* ruled that an employee's Title VII rights are ***independent*** of rights under the contract, so the employee may properly pursue both. In *McDonald* (a Section 1983 case), *supra,* the court determined that a prior arbitration award had no res judicata or collateral estoppel effect in these circumstances, nor was it a "judicial proceeding" entitled to full faith and credit under 28 U.S.C. section 1738.

EXAM TIP GILBERT

Remember on exam questions that if an aggrieved employee loses his discrimination claim under the contract, it "ain't necessarily over." The employee has an ***independent right*** under Title VII, and the prior arbitration hearing has no res judicata or collateral estoppel effect unless there was **a clear and unmistakable waiver** of that **independent right**.

5. Other Civil Rights Legislation

Additional civil rights legislation has been passed by Congress in connection with the 1964 Civil Rights Act. The following statutes have generated considerable litigation in the employment area and deserve mention.

a. Equal Pay Act

As a prelude to Title VII of the 1964 Civil Rights Act, Congress passed the Equal Pay Act ("EPA") in 1963. The EPA requires equal pay for equal work, regardless of sex. However, the EPA allows wage differentials if based on a seniority system, a merit system, a system that measures earnings by quantity or quality of production, or any factor other than sex.

b. Age Discrimination in Employment Act

As originally enacted in 1967, the Age Discrimination in Employment Act ("ADEA") covered only those employees aged 40 to 65 who worked for private employers. However, the ADEA was amended in 1978 to cover employees up to age 70 as well as federal government employees. In structure, the ADEA is patterned after Title VII.

c. Title IX, Educational Amendments of 1972

This Title has been construed to prohibit employment discrimination in federally funded education programs. [**North Haven Board of Education v. Bell,** 456 U.S. 512 (1982)]

d. Americans with Disabilities Act of 1990

The Americans with Disabilities Act of 1990 ("ADA") [42 U.S.C. §§ 12101 *et seq.*] was enacted to remedy discrimination based on an individual's disability (*i.e.,* a physical or mental impairment). The ADA applies to employment, public services, public accommodations, and telecommunications. The ADA was amended by the Americans with Disabilities Act Amendments Act of 2008 to make it easier for an individual seeking protection under the ADA to establish the existence of a disability within the meaning of the ADA.

(1) Outcome Where ADA Conflicts with Collective Bargaining Contract

Most issues in the growing volume of ADA litigation are beyond the scope of this Summary. One such matter *is* relevant, however—namely, what to do when the requirements of the ADA conflict with provisions in a collective bargaining agreement (such as those dealing with seniority). The Supreme Court addressed the issue in 2002 and found that ***ordinarily*** the collective bargaining provisions will prevail if a requested accommodation conflicts with the terms of seniority; but the plaintiff may still show evidence of special circumstances that would warrant an exception to applying the seniority rule in a particular case. [*See* **US Airways Inc. v. Barnett,** 535 U.S. 391 (2002)]

D. The Individual and the Grievance

1. Right to Adjust Grievances Directly with Employer

Normally, individual grievances under the collective bargaining contract are presented to the union, and the union presses the claim on behalf of the employee. However, it is not essential that the employee act through the union. Section 9(a) provides that the employee may seek to adjust grievances directly with the employer—without intervention by the union—as long as the adjustment is not inconsistent with the terms of the collective agreement, and the union has an opportunity to be present.

EXAM TIP GILBERT

Note that although employees may air their ***individual*** grievances with an employer without the aid of the union, they ***must*** channel their "***concerted activity***" against an employer through the union. (*See* discussion *supra,* p. 192.)

2. Right to Union Representation at Investigatory Interviews

An employee is entitled to have a union representative present at any investigatory interview by the employer that the employee reasonably believes might result in disciplinary action. The employer's refusal of a request for such representation would violate NLRA section 8(a)(1). [**NLRB v. J. Weingarten, Inc.,** 420 U.S. 251 (1975)]

a. Rights of Nonunion Employees

The NLRB extended this right to nonunion employees, allowing them to have a co-worker present at disciplinary interviews and permitting a brief pre-interview consultation to familiarize the co-worker with the employee's circumstances. [**Materials**

Research Corp., 262 N.L.R.B. 1010 (1982)] The Board subsequently reversed its view and limited such rights to unionized employees. [**Sears, Roebuck & Co.,** 274 N.L.R.B. 230 (1985); **E. I. duPont & Co.** ("*Walter Slaughter*"), 289 N.L.R.B. 627 (1988)] However, the NLRB reversed itself again a bit later and re-extended these rights to nonunion workers. [**Epilepsy Foundation of Northeast Ohio,** 331 N.L.R.B. 676 (2000)] Under its most recent approach, the NLRB decided to overrule *Epilepsy Foundation* and returned to the Board's approach under *Walter Slaughter*. [**IBM Corp.,** 341 N.L.R.B. 1288 (2004)]

b. When Does Right Arise

It may be difficult to determine in advance whether a particular meeting between employees and the employer portends disciplinary action.

e.g. **Example:** A general shop meeting to discuss company rules and infractions thereof is not considered one at which employees are entitled to a union representative—even where an employee at such a meeting is singled out as having violated a particular rule. [**Northwest Engineering Co.,** 265 N.L.R.B. 190 (1982)]

e.g. **Example:** Likewise, a meeting of security guards to discuss vandalism against company property is not a disciplinary investigation permitting representation. [**Bridgeport Hospital,** 265 N.L.R.B. 421 (1982)]

c. Right to Pre-Interview Consultation

The holding in *Weingarten, supra,* has been extended to allow an employee to consult with a union steward *before* being interviewed about conduct that could result in discipline or criminal prosecution. [**United States Postal Service v. NLRB,** 969 F.2d 1064 (D.C. Cir. 1992)]

d. Role of Union Representative

The NLRB has ruled that the union representative is not entitled to turn the employer interview into an adversary hearing. Thus, for example, the representative has no right to stop the employer from repeating questions to the employee being interviewed. [**New Jersey Bell Telephone,** 308 N.L.R.B. 277 (1992)]

e. Waiver of Right by Union

One court has held that the right to representation at investigatory interviews can be waived by the union in the collective bargaining agreement, provided the waiver is "clear and unmistakable." The NLRB has accepted this view. [**Prudential Insurance Co. v. NLRB,** 661 F.2d 398 (5th Cir. 1981); **Prudential Insurance Co.,** 275 N.L.R.B. 208 (1985)]

f. Limitation on Remedy for Employee

The NLRB has held that an award of reinstatement and back pay for violation of the right to representation is beyond the Board's discretion. [**Taracorp,** 273 N.L.R.B. 221 (1984); *and see* **Communication Workers Local 5008 v. NLRB,** 784 F.2d 847 (7th Cir. 1986)—upholding Board's position]

3. Right to Judicial Relief Against Employer

The fact that an employee has the right to present a grievance directly to the employer does not mean that the employer has to act on it.

a. Exhaustion of Contract Remedies Required

If the employer fails or refuses to act on the grievance, the employee first must ask the union to institute whatever *grievance procedure* is provided in the collective bargaining agreement. The employee cannot sue the employer unless she has attempted to exhaust the remedies provided in the collective agreement. [**Schuyler v. Metropolitan Transit Commission,** 374 N.W.2d 453 (Minn. 1985)—employee must exhaust grievance procedures in contract before commencing action for wrongful discharge]

(1) Note

The individual employee has no absolute right to have the grievance arbitrated under the collective bargaining agreement. She cannot compel the employer to arbitrate directly with her, nor can she compel the union to act on her behalf. [*See* **Vaca v. Sipes,** *supra,* p. 199]

EXAM TIP GILBERT

This is an important point to remember: An employee is required to ***exhaust the remedies*** provided in the collective bargaining agreement, even if the employee decided to air his complaint ***without the aid of the union***. Thus, if the employer refuses to act on a complaint brought to its attention by an individual employee, the employee must ask the union to institute formal grievance procedures.

---

b. Contract Action Against Employer

If the union "arbitrarily" refuses to press an employee's grievance under the procedures outlined in the agreement, or otherwise fails to represent her fairly, the employee may then bring suit against the employer to enforce the collective bargaining agreement—on the theory that, as a member of the bargaining unit, she is a *third-party beneficiary* of the agreement. [**Jenkins v. W. M. Schluderberg-T. J. Kurdle Co.,** 144 A.2d 88 (Md. 1958)—individual employee could sue because union had "arbitrarily" failed to take the case to arbitration; *and see* **Vaca v. Sipes,** *supra*; **Hines v. Anchor Motor Freight, Inc.,** *supra,* p. 135]

4. Right to Judicial Relief Against Union

If the union's failure to act on an employee's behalf amounts to a breach of its duty of fair representation (*i.e.,* if its refusal was "*arbitrary, discriminatory or in bad faith*"), the aggrieved employee can (i) file an unfair union labor practice charge with the NLRB, (ii) file a private damages action against the union under Taft-Hartley section 301, or (iii) initiate procedures under Title VII, where applicable [*supra,* p. 203]. (*See* discussion *supra,* pp. 197–202.)

5. Independent Remedies Under Civil Rights Acts

As noted previously, the Title VII rights of an aggrieved employee are independent of rights under the collective bargaining agreement. Hence, the employee can pursue those remedies in addition to unfair labor practice or section 301 proceedings. [**Alexander v. Gardner-Denver Co.,** *supra,* p. 204; unless a clear and unmistakable waiver has occurred, **14 Penn Plaza v. Pyett,** *supra,* p. 204]

CHECKLIST OF EMPLOYEE REMEDIES
IF UNION AND EMPLOYER FAIL TO ACT ON THE GRIEVANCE, EMPLOYEE MAY BRING:
☑ Contract Action Against Employer — ***Theory:*** Employee is third-party beneficiary of the collective bargaining agreement — Collective bargaining remedies must be exhausted — Union must have refused to act ☑ Lawsuit against the union based on a breach of its duty of fair representation ☑ Unfair labor practice against the union ☑ Title VII Lawsuit — Independent of any other rights under the collective bargaining agreement

E. Devices Insuring Union Security

1. Introduction

Unions have long sought to obtain agreements from employers that would effectively make all workers in the bargaining unit members of the union. The basic argument is that compulsory membership and the "checkoff" of union dues (whereby the employer deducts union dues directly from the employee's paycheck and forwards them to the union) are necessary to secure the union's bargaining position.

2. Federal Regulation of Compulsory Union Membership Arrangements

NLRA section 8(a)(3) prohibits employer discrimination on the basis of union membership (*supra,* p. 70). The statute is qualified, however, to allow certain union security devices to be negotiated by the parties (*see* below).

a. Background

Under the original NLRA (1935), union security agreements, including agreements for a "closed shop," were legal as long as the union had majority support. This led to serious abuses, including situations where the union could dictate who would and who would not be hired.

b. Present Law

To rectify such abuses, section 8(a)(3) and section 7 were amended by the Taft-Hartley Act in 1947. These sections now provide that employees may refrain from union activity, except that if the union is the exclusive bargaining agent for the unit, the union may negotiate for union security clauses (requiring union membership and/or the payment of union dues after the employee has been hired). [NLRA § 8(a)(3); *and see* **Marquez v. Screen Actors Guild, Inc.,** 525 U.S. 33 (1998)—union does not breach its duty of fair representation by negotiating a union security clause using exact wording of section 8(a)(3), although only dues and fees can be demanded (*see infra,* p. 209)]

c. Types (and Legality) of Compulsory Union Membership Agreements

(1) Closed Shop

In a closed shop, membership in the union is a condition of employment; *i.e.,* membership is required before hiring. This type of arrangement is ***illegal.*** [NLRA § 8(a)(3), (f)]

(2) Preferential Hiring

In this situation, the employer must hire only workers recommended or referred by the union.

(a) Membership Required Before Hiring

If the arrangement demands union membership before the employee is hired, it also is ***illegal.*** [*See* **NLRB v. Houston Maritime Association,** 337 F.2d 333 (5th Cir. 1964)]

(b) Hiring Halls and Work Permits

However, a system of job referrals (hiring halls) operated by the union or a system of union work permits is ***legal, provided*** that in **making referrals there is *no discrimination on the basis of membership*** in the union. [**Local 357, International Brotherhood of Teamsters, Chauffeurs, Warehousemen & Helpers v. NLRB,** *supra,* p. 76]

(3) Union Shop

Under this arrangement, membership in the union is ***compulsory after employment.*** Such arrangements are legal provided the union is the majority representative. The theory is that unions are entitled to avoid "free riders" (nonunion employees who enjoy union-won benefits without any cost to them).

(a) Grace Period

Section 8(a)(3) provides a ***30-day "grace" period,*** after hiring, before membership becomes mandatory. Thus, a collective agreement is lawful if it requires, as a condition of employment, that every new employee join the union "on or after" the 30th day of employment.

(b) Full Membership Not Compulsory

Full-fledged union membership cannot be required even though the collective bargaining contract contains a union-shop clause. Only the payment of dues and initiation fees can be demanded. [**NLRB v. Hershey Foods Corp.,** 513 F.2d 1083 (9th Cir. 1975)]

1) Application

In effect, this allows antiunion employees in a union shop to treat the agreement as if it created an agency shop (*see infra,* p. 210).

2) **And Note**

An employee may also resign full-fledged membership and thereby avoid the union's power to assess fines and enforce rules against him (*see infra,* pp. 216–218).

(c) **Exception for Religious Objectors**

An employee with a bona fide religious objection to financial support of labor organizations cannot be required to remit dues and initiation fees under a union shop clause, but may instead pay an equivalent sum to a nonreligious, nonlabor, tax-exempt charitable fund. [NLRA § 19]

1) **Judicial Interpretation of Exception**

One Circuit has found the religious objectors exception unconstitutional because it violates the Establishment Clause of the First Amendment to the Constitution. [**Wilson v. NLRB,** 920 F.2d 1282 (6th Cir. 1990), *cert. denied,* 505 U.S. 1218 (1992)] In earlier decisions, two other Circuits seemed to accept that the exception was constitutional, but did not squarely address the issue. [*See* **Tooley v. Martin-Marietta Corp.,** 648 F.2d 1239 (9th Cir. 1981), *cert. denied,* 454 U.S. 1098 (1981); **Machinists Lodge 751 v. Boeing Co.,** 833 F.2d 165 (9th Cir. 1987), *cert. denied,* 485 U.S. 1014 (1988)]

(4) **Agency Shop**

The "agency shop" is also legal. Here, full membership in the union is not required, but all employees must pay dues and initiation fees, regardless of whether they join. [**NLRB v. General Motors Corp.,** 373 U.S. 734 (1963)]

(a) **Note**

Agency shops are also subject to the section 19 exception for religious objectors (above).

(5) **Maintenance of Membership**

Under a maintenance of membership arrangement, union membership is not required, but current members can renounce their membership only within a time period fixed in the agreement. Any new employees who become members must retain their membership status for the duration of the agreement. These arrangements are legal.

TYPES OF COMPULSORY UNION MEMBERSHIP ARRANGEMENTS—A SUMMARY		GILBERT
TYPE	**ATTRIBUTES**	**LEGALITY**
CLOSED SHOP	Union membership required ***before*** hiring	Illegal
PREFERENTIAL HIRING	Employer may only hire employees recommended or referred by the union	Legal, unless union membership is demanded before hiring
HIRING HALLS/WORK PERMITS	Union refers employee to employer	Legal, unless there is discrimination on basis of union membership in making referrals
UNION SHOP	Union membership required 30 days after hiring	Legal, provided the union is the majority representative
AGENCY SHOP	Full membership is not required, but all employees must pay dues and initiation fees regardless of whether they join the union	Legal
MAINTENANCE OF MEMBERSHIP	Union membership is not required, but current union members can renounce their membership only within a time set by the agreement, and new members must retain union membership for the duration of the agreement	Legal

d. Objections to Use of Dues and Fees by Union

Nonunion employees who pay union dues and fees under union shop and agency shop clauses may object to (and prevent) the use of their monies for purposes other than those germane to collective bargaining, contract administration, or the processing of grievances. Thus, for example, the use of such fees for ***general organizing efforts,*** *political lobbying,* or *social and charitable events* can be precluded. [**Communication Workers of America v. Beck,** 487 U.S. 735 (1988)—rule applies under NLRA and Railway Labor Act; *and see* **Lehnert v. Ferris Faculty Association,** 500 U.S. 507 (1991)—identifying that the rule also applies to public sector unions] But more recently, the Supreme Court has found that public sector unions cannot require nonmember employees to pay *any* expenses to the union. [**Janus v. Am. Fed'n of State, Cnty., & Mun. Emps.,** 138 S. Ct. 2448 (2018)]

(1) Union Organizing Expenses

Citing the opinion in *Beck,* the Ninth Circuit has held that unions with union-shop clauses cannot require nonmembers to pay for union organizing expenses—rejecting a contrary view by the NLRB and the economic analysis supporting it. [**United Food & Commercial Workers Local 1036 v. NLRB,** 249 F.3d 1115 (9th Cir. 2001)]

(2) Formulation of NLRB Guidelines

After *Beck,* the NLRB General Counsel issued a memorandum for assessing challenges to union spending of dues and fees. [Memorandum GC 98–11, Guidelines Concerning Processing of *Beck* Cases] Under the memorandum, the fee objector has the initial burden of producing evidence (or promising leads to evidence) that the union's expenditures were not chargeable. The burden then shifts to the union to establish that the expenditures were chargeable. If the union fails to meet this burden, a complaint should issue. After the complaint is issued, the General Counsel has the initial burden of specifying the expenditures to which the member objects and the reasons why the objection is proper. Thereafter, the burden again shifts to the union to prove the validity of the fees and expenditures.

(3) Union Must Provide Information on Spending

When requested, unions are required to give new employees or potential objectors sufficient information to allow them to assess the allocation of dues and fees between "representational" and "nonrepresentational" activities. [**Chicago Teachers Union, Local 1 v. Hudson,** 475 U.S. 292 (1986); **Adams v. Communication Workers of America,** 59 F.3d 1373 (D.C. Cir. 1995); **Penrod v. NLRB,** 203 F.3d 41 (D.C. Cir. 2000)]

e. Enforcement of Union Security Agreement

Section 8(a)(3) provides for the enforcement of lawful union security agreements. The employer (generally acting at the request of the union) has the *right to discharge* an employee for lack of union membership where a valid compulsory membership agreement exists, *provided that:*

(i) The employer *has no reasonable grounds for believing that membership was unavailable to the employee* "on the same terms and conditions generally applicable to other members"; or

(ii) The employee's *union membership was denied or terminated for failure of the employee to tender the periodic dues and initiation fees uniformly required of all persons* as a condition of acquiring or retaining membership (subject to the limitations of NLRA section 19, *supra,* p. 210).

[NLRA § 8(a)(3)(A), (B); and *see* **Radio Officers' Union of the Commercial Telegraphers Union v. NLRB,** *supra,* p. 70; **NLRB v. Hershey Foods Corp.,** *supra,* p. 209]

(1) Note

Employees need not become full-fledged members to be protected from discharge; they are merely obliged to tender dues and initiation fees. [**NLRB v. Hershey Foods Corp.,** *supra*]

f. Authority to Negotiate Union Security Agreements

The union may negotiate union security agreements without explicit authority from employees in the bargaining unit. However, if employees wish to rescind the union's authority to negotiate a union security agreement, they may vote to do so in a special "deauthorization" election. [NLRA § 9(e); *supra,* p. 83]

3. State Regulation of Compulsory Membership Agreements—"Right to Work" Laws

NLRA section 14(b) allows the states, if they so choose, to prohibit those union security agreements otherwise legal under section 8(a)(3). Thus, agreements that are valid under federal law may still violate a more stringent state provision. (*Note:* The Railway Labor Act does not have a provision comparable to section 14(b); hence, federal law *preempts* any state "right to work" laws as to railroad or airline employees.)

a. Present Scope of Regulation

Pursuant to section 14(b), 19 states have enacted "right to work" laws that either *outlaw or restrict* compulsory union membership arrangements (*e.g.,* Virginia, North Carolina, and Ohio).

b. State Courts Decide Validity

Whether a particular union-shop or agency-shop arrangement is prohibited by state "right to work" provisions is a matter of substantive law to be determined by state courts. [**Retail Clerks International Association, Local 1625 v. Schermerhorn,** 373 U.S. 746 (1963)]

c. Jurisdictional Limitation

However, state "right to work" laws *cannot impinge upon the area of exclusive NLRB jurisdiction.* For example, picketing to compel an employer to hire only union labor—illegal under a state "right to work" law and also illegal under federal law (*i.e.,* picketing for an unlawful objective)—is not subject to state controls (*e.g.,* injunctive relief). Because such picketing violates federal law, the NLRB has *exclusive* jurisdiction. (*See* discussion of federal preemption doctrine, *supra,* pp. 23 *et seq.*)

d. Permanent Job Situs Is Controlling

Whether state "right to work" laws apply in a given situation depends on whether the employees' *predominant job situs* is within the state.

e.g. **Example:** Sailors were hired in Texas and lived there, but did 80% of their work on the high seas. Texas "right to work" laws were held not to apply. [**Oil, Chemical & Atomic Workers International Union v. Mobil Oil Corp.,** 426 U.S. 407 (1976)—agency-shop agreement enforceable despite Texas law]

F. Discipline of Union Members

1. Limitations Imposed by State Law

Courts and legislatures have tried to balance a union's asserted need for authority over its members with the rights of individual workers (protected by federal law) in fashioning rules to govern union disciplinary power. Typically, there has been a delineation of activities that are clearly within the union's disciplinary powers, others that are not, and still others that depend on the particular circumstances in question.

a. Actions with Adverse Economic Impact

In most states, conduct by individuals that has an economic impact adverse to the union (spying for the employer, working for wages below scale, participating in "wildcat" strikes) is properly punishable by the union, since it conflicts with basic union interests as the exclusive bargaining agent. [**Davis v. International Alliance of Theatrical Stage**

Employees & Moving Picture Machine Operators, 60 Cal. App. 2d 713 (1943)—members expelled for joining rival union]

b. Exercise of Individual's Civic Duties

On the other hand, the exercise of an individual's civic duties (such as testifying before congressional committees or in court, or reporting violations of the law by fellow union members) is *not* punishable by the union. [**Abdon v. Wallace,** 165 N.E. 68 (Ind. 1929)]

c. Political Actions Opposed by Union

Somewhere between these two types of conduct may be *political activity* by union members (a civic duty only in a "moral" sense) that the union as a whole opposes. The following factors usually are weighed to test the propriety of the action taken by the member and the corresponding response by the union:

(i) The *interest of the community and the union member* in his membership rights;

(ii) The right to *freedom of expression;*

(iii) The interest of the union in expelling *"obnoxious" members;*

(iv) The need for *union authority and hegemony;*

(v) Whether or not the member *purports to represent the union;* and

(vi) Most importantly, *the nature of the political activity and the manner in which it is conducted.* Unless the activity is "patently" in conflict with the union's "best interests," a member should not be punished for political advocacy.

[**Mitchell v. International Association of Machinists,** 196 Cal. App. 2d 796 (1961)]

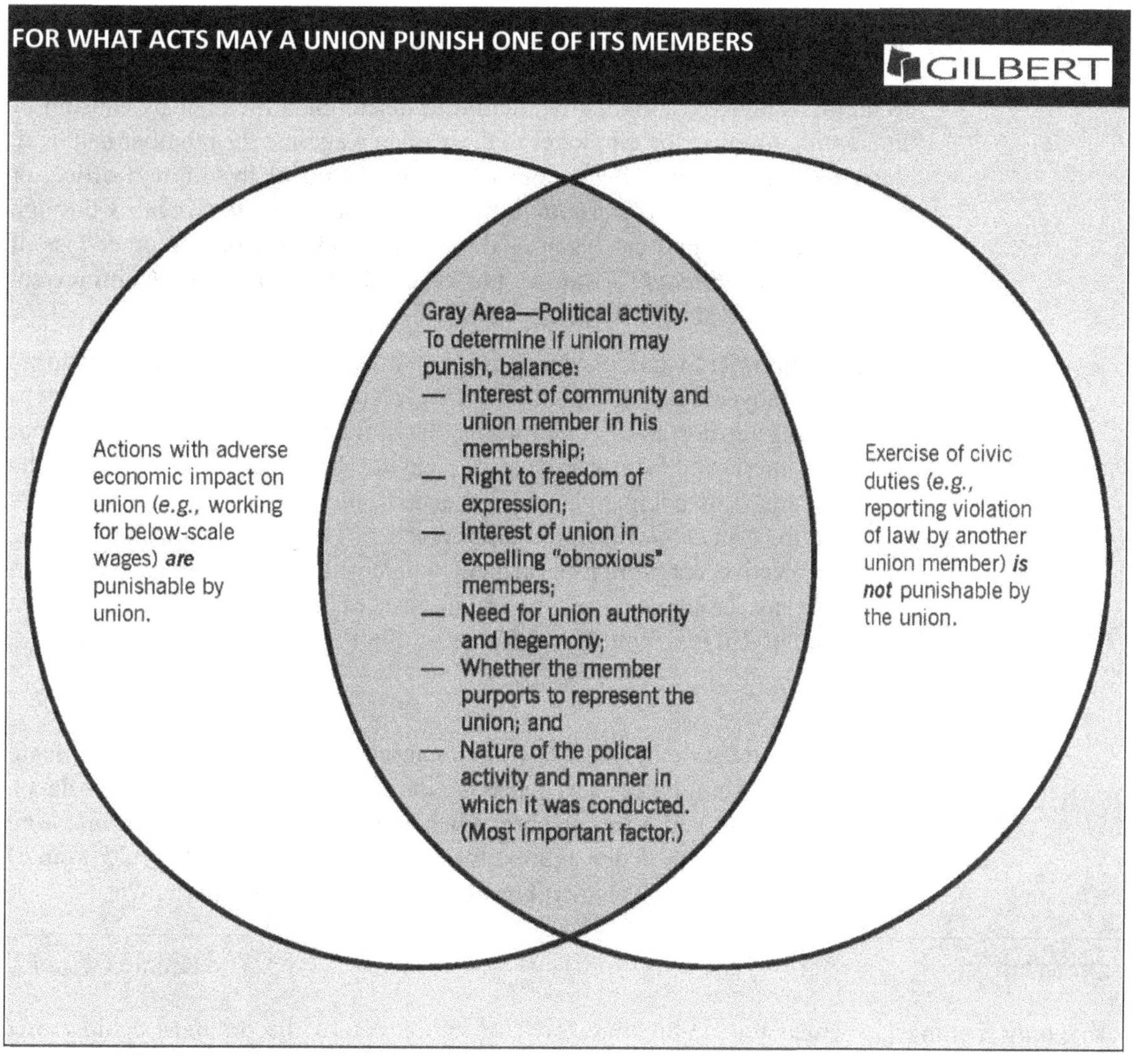

2. Effect of the NLRA

a. Background

The 1947 Taft-Hartley Amendments were designed in part to limit union power to discipline members, and to "insulate" employees' jobs from their union rights and duties.

b. Union Unfair Labor Practices

Taft-Hartley made certain union disciplinary actions unfair labor practices:

(1) Union's Coercion of Employer to Discriminate in Employment

NLRA section 8(b)(2) prohibits unions from causing (or attempting to cause) an employer to discriminate against any employee (*i.e.,* to "hit back" at an obstreperous member). (*Note:* Such discrimination would also be an employer unfair labor practice under section 8(a)(3).)

(a) Exception

Section 8(b)(2) permits the union to force employer discrimination in one instance only—for nonpayment of union dues or initiation **fees where a *valid union security agreement* is in effect** (*see supra,* pp. 77, 212).

(b) Application

With this single exception, any attempt to discipline a member by causing or attempting to cause the employer to discriminate against the member is illegal. ***Internal enforcement*** of sanctions (*i.e.,* fines, removal from union office, or loss of voting rights) is ***permitted,*** but the use of ***external sanctions*** through pressure on the employer (such as demotion, discharge, or any other loss of status) is ***prohibited.*** [**Radio Officers' Union of the Commercial Telegraphers Union v. NLRB,** *supra,* p. 212]

e.g. **Example:** A union's inducing the employer to deny promotion to an employee who had fallen into disfavor with the union (for returning to work during a strike) was held improper discrimination and a union unfair labor practice (interfering with employee's right to strike or not to strike as she pleases). Also, the company's acquiescence to union pressure in *Bell Aircraft* was held to be an ***employer*** unfair labor practice. The court invalidated a clause in the collective bargaining agreement whereby the employer agreed not to promote any employee "while union charges are pending" against that employee. [**NLRB v. Bell Aircraft Corp.,** 206 F.2d 235 (2d Cir. 1953)]

1) Note

Where the union has unlawfully caused an employer to discriminate against an employee (thus depriving the employee of promotion or salary), the Board is authorized to enter a back ***pay order against the union alone*** (***i.e.,*** **without an order against** the employer). [**Radio Officers' Union of the Commercial Telegraphers Union v. NLRB,** *supra*]

EXAM TIP GILBERT

The ***only*** instance in which the union may force an employer to discriminate against an employee is when the employee ***fails to pay union dues and*** a ***valid union security agreement*** exists. ***All*** other cases of discrimination violate NLRA section 8(b)(2).

(2) Unfair Financial Practices

NLRA section 8(b)(5) prohibits unions that negotiate a union security agreement from charging "excessive or discriminatory initiation fees." [*See* **NLRB v. Television & Radio Broadcasting Studio Employees, Local 804,** 315 F.2d 398 (3d Cir. 1963)—union raised initiation fee from $50 to $500 to discourage new members]

(3) Union Restraint and Coercion of Employee Rights

Section 8(b)(1) prohibits unions from restraining or coercing employees in the exercise of rights guaranteed to them by section 7—namely, the rights (i) to self-organization, (ii) to bargain collectively, (iii) to engage in concerted activities for the purpose of collective bargaining, and (iv) to refrain from any of the above activities.

(a) Power of Union to Adopt and Enforce Internal Rules

Section 8(b)(1) is limited by a proviso granting the union ***the right "to prescribe rules with respect to the acquisition or retention of membership in the union."***

1) **Scope of Proviso**

This proviso has been interpreted as giving unions broad authority to promulgate and enforce rules regulating internal union affairs, even though such rules may "restrain or coerce" union members in the exercise of their section 7 rights. [**NLRB v. Allis Chalmers Manufacturing Co.,** 388 U.S. 175 (1967)—unions could assess and collect fines against members who crossed picket lines and worked during strike called by union]

2) **Application**

Hence, the NLRB, while it has authority under section 8(b)(1)(A) to review the reasonableness of union rules affecting *employment* status, does not have power to test the reasonableness of rules affecting *membership* status (including fines) unless they are otherwise prohibited by the NLRA. [**NLRB v. Boeing Co.,** 412 U.S. 67 (1973)]

(b) **Validity of Union Rules**

The following requirements must be met, however, before a union rule is valid and its mode of enforcement proper:

1) **Legitimate Interest**

The rule must be in the "legitimate interests" of the union and must not impair any "overriding" policy of the federal labor laws. The "legitimacy" of the interests served by a union's internal rules and regulations must be determined on an ad hoc, case-by-case basis. [**Scofield v. NLRB,** 394 U.S. 423 (1969)]

e.g. **Example:** In *Scofield,* the Supreme Court upheld a union rule that imposed fines on members who exceeded specified ceilings under a piecework production system. The Court found a legitimate union interest in the apprehension that piecework pay systems would create pressures to lower the piecework rate, so that employee productivity would increase without corresponding increases in wage levels, and that the competitive pressures generated by the system would endanger workers' health and create other job problems. In light of this interest, the fact that an individual employee's section 7 rights were impaired to some degree was considered immaterial.

2) **Legitimate Enforcement**

The rule must not be enforced through union coercion or employer discrimination.

a) **No Discharge or Discrimination**

The union may not "cause or attempt to cause the member to be discharged or discriminated against in his employment." [NRLA § 8(b)(2), (a)(3)]

b) No Violent Means

Nor may the union employ any violent means of enforcement, since that would violate section 8(b)(1). [*See* **NLRB v. Drivers, Chauffeurs, Helpers, Local 639,** *supra,* p. 63]

c) Expulsion

A frequent method of enforcing union rules is expulsion from the union. However, this device may not be particularly effective: Where the union is weak, for example, expulsion of a few members may affect the union's majority status.

d) Fines

Alternatively, the union may seek to enforce its rules by imposing fines on members who violate them. As noted above, the Supreme Court has held that the reasonableness of union fines cannot be investigated by the NLRB. [**NLRB v. Boeing Co.,** *supra,* p. 217]

1/ Note

Since this issue is outside the scope of NLRB authority, such cases are not preempted, and the reasonableness of union fines can be examined in *state courts.* This generally will involve application of contract law to the union-member relationship.

3) Enforced only Against Union Members

The rule can be enforced only against union members. Employees are free to leave the union or to relinquish full membership in order to escape a union rule, although they must follow any reasonable procedures specified in the union constitution for resigning. [**Scofield v. NLRB,** *supra,* p. 217]

e.g. **Example:** A union violates section 8(b)(1) if it fines an employee who has resigned from the union for working during a strike. [**NLRB v. Granite State Joint Board Textile Workers Union of America, Local 1029,** 409 U.S. 213 (1972)]

a) Note

The proviso in section 8(b)(1) (*supra,* p. 216) was once construed as allowing unions to place reasonable restrictions on the manner and timing of resignations by members. Later, the Supreme Court held that the proviso applies only to admission to or expulsion from membership, and does *not* cover resignations from membership. [**Pattern Makers League of North America v. NLRB,** 473 U.S. 95 (1985)]

1/ NLRB Position

On its part, the NLRB has ruled that an employee's right to refrain from concerted activity (*supra,* p. 192) includes the right to resign from a union at any time, thereby *precluding* restrictions on this right even if embodied in the union constitution. [**Machinists Local Lodge 1414 (Neufeld Porsche-Audi),** 270 N.L.R.B. 1330 (1984)] The Board has even found this right to be interfered with by a rule requiring resigned members to file dues objections (*supra,* p. 211) through the month of April in any given year. [**Polymark Corp.,** 329 N.L.R.B. 9 (1999)]

VALIDITY OF UNION RULES
FOR A RULE TO BE VALID AND ITS MODE OF ENFORCEMENT PROPER, THE RULE MUST BE:
☑ In the ***legitimate interests*** of the union;
☑ Enforced only through ***legitimate means;*** and
☑ Enforced only against ***union members.***

3. Limitations on Enforcement of Union Discipline

a. Background

At common law, and under the original NLRA (1935), unions had sweeping disciplinary powers over their members, which invited abuse in union government. The *Labor-Management Reporting and Disclosure Act* ("LMRDA")—the so-called Landrum-Griffin Act—was passed in 1959 to protect more fully the rights of union members, to curb abuses of union power, and to promote internal union democracy.

b. LMRDA Title I—"Labor's Bill of Rights"

Title I of Landrum-Griffin [29 U.S.C. §§ 411 *et seq.*] was passed to guarantee members certain basic rights considered necessary to insure democracy within unions.

(1) Equal Rights

Section 101(a)(1) gives union members "equal rights and privileges" to nominate candidates, vote on internal matters, and attend and participate in membership meetings, "subject to reasonable rules and regulations in the organization's constitution and bylaws."

(2) Freedom of Speech and Assembly

Union members are guaranteed the basic rights of free speech (the right to "assemble freely" and the right to "express any views, arguments and opinions"). [LMRDA § 101(a)(2)] At the same time, section 101(a)(2) permits unions to adopt and enforce *reasonable* rules covering the responsibility of every member to the union as an institution and toward refraining from conduct that would interfere with performance by the union of its legal or contractual obligations. The courts must apply this broad yardstick in each case to determine where free speech rights end and the union's legitimate interests begin. [**Grand Lodge of International Association of Machinists v. King,** 335 F.2d 340 (9th Cir.), *cert. denied,* 379 U.S. 920 (1964)]

e.g. **Example:** Section 101(a)(1) and (a)(2) have been held not to prohibit "patronage" after a union election, so that incumbent union officers or employees may be ousted by new leaders (as long as the basic union membership rights of the incumbents are preserved). [**Finnegan v. Leu,** 456 U.S. 431 (1982)]

e.g. **Example:** A provision in the union constitution prohibiting any candidate for union office from accepting campaign contributions from nonmembers has been held to be a legitimate means of preventing outsider interference in union affairs, despite any limitations on political freedom resulting therefrom. [**United Steelworkers of America v. Sadlowski,** 457 U.S. 102 (1982)]

(a) Speech During Union Meeting

The union may not, however, remove an elected official who speaks out against a union proposal at a meeting of the membership, since this would have a chilling effect on the members' rights of free speech protected by section 101(a)(2). [**Sheet Metal Workers International Association v. Lyon,** 488 U.S. 347 (1989)—*distinguishing* **Finnegan v. Leu,** *supra*]

(b) No Clear Union Interest

When there is no clear union interest at stake, a union member has the right to express his opinions about union officers and their policies, even if the statements are false and libelous. [**Salzhandler v. Caputo,** 316 F.2d 445 (2d Cir.), *cert. denied,* 375 U.S. 946 (1963)]

(3) Dues, Fees, and Assessments

Section 101(a)(3) establishes certain procedural safeguards that must be met before a union may increase its dues, fees, or assessments.

(a) Local Unions

In a local union, any new financial exaction must be approved by majority vote in either a special membership meeting advertised by "reasonable notice" or in a membership referendum. In each case, the vote must be by secret ballot.

(b) National and International Unions

National or international unions and intermediate bodies may increase their dues, fees, or assessments by:

1) *Majority vote in a regular or special convention* called after a 30-day notice to each local;
2) *Secret ballot referendum* of the membership; *or*
3) *Majority vote of the executive board.*

(c) Excessive or Discriminatory Fees

Note that NLRA section 8(b)(5) makes it an unfair labor practice for a union to charge excessive or discriminatory initiation fees *even if the* above procedural requirements are met.

(4) Protection of Right to Sue

Section 101(a)(4) protects the right of union members to sue and testify against the union or its officers in administrative or judicial proceedings, and to participate in legislative proceedings.

(a) Limitation Against Employer Interference

The employer is *prohibited* from encouraging actions against the union that are otherwise protected by the section.

1) But Note

Precluding a "right to work" group from financing suits against unions because the group is funded by contributions from interested employers has been held an unconstitutional infringement of the group's First Amendment rights. [**International Union, UAW v. National Right to Work Legal Defense & Education Foundation,** 433 F. Supp. 474 (D.D.C. 1977)]

(b) Exhaustion of Internal Remedies Required

Before instituting any judicial or administrative action against the union, a member must exhaust the union's internal hearing procedures, if he can do so within four months. [**McPhetridge v. IBEW, Local Union No. 53,** 578 F.3d 886 (2009); LMRDA § 101(a)(4)]

1) Exceptions

This "exhaustion of remedies" rule, however, is subject to numerous common law exceptions. Thus, actions by union members against the union will *not* be dismissed, even though union internal procedures have not been complied with if (i) *no adequate union remedy* exists, (ii) union procedures or bias among union officials *preclude a fair hearing or appeal,* (iii) the appellate procedures within the union are "*unreasonably burdensome*," or (iv) the injury to the employee is either ***irreparable or difficult to calculate,*** and ***immediate action*** is therefore required. [**Falsetti v. Local Union No. 2026, UMW,** 161 A.2d 882 (Pa. 1960)]

A court should also consider the following in deciding whether to require exhaustion: " 'whether union officials are so hostile to the employee that he could not hope to obtain a fair hearing,' 'whether the internal union appeals procedures would be inadequate' and 'whether exhaustion of internal procedures would unreasonably delay the employee's opportunity to obtain a judicial hearing on the merits of his claim.' " [*McPhetridge, supra* (citation omitted); **Amalgamated Transit Union v. Lovelace,** 109 A.3d 96 (Md. 2015) (citation omitted)]

2) Application

Section 101(a)(4) has been interpreted in some cases to mean only that union members "may" (as opposed to "must") be required to exhaust internal union remedies. [**NLRB v. Industrial Union of Marine & Shipbuilding Workers,** 391 U.S. 418 (1968); **Detroy v. American Guild of Variety Artists,** 286 F.2d 75 (2d Cir.), *cert. denied,* 366 U.S. 929 (1961)]

COMMON LAW EXCEPTIONS TO "EXHAUSTION OF REMEDIES" REQUIREMENT

A UNION MEMBER WILL NOT BE REQUIRED TO EXHAUST INTERNAL UNION PROCEDURES WHEN:

- ☑ The procedures do not provide an ***adequate remedy;***
- ☑ The procedures or the bias among union officials ***preclude a fair hearing or appeal;***
- ☑ The appellate procedures are ***unreasonably burdensome;*** or
- ☑ The injury to the union member is either ***irreparable or difficult to calculate,*** and ***immediate action*** is therefore required.

(5) Due Process Safeguards Against Improper Disciplinary Actions

The Landrum-Griffin Act guarantees union members certain basic rights of due process in union disciplinary hearings. *Except for nonpayment of dues,* no member of any labor organization may be fined, suspended, expelled, or otherwise disciplined unless such member has been:

(i) ***Served with specific charges in writing;***

(ii) ***Given a reasonable time to prepare a defense;* and**

(iii) ***Afforded a full and fair hearing.***

[LMRDA § 101(a)(5)]

(6) Statute of Limitations

The Supreme Court has held that the *state law* statute of limitations governs actions under Title I of the Landrum-Griffin Act. [**Reed v. United Transportation Union,** 488 U.S. 319 (1989)]

LABOR'S BILL OF RIGHTS

TITLE I OF LANDRUM-GRIFFIN PROVIDES FOR:

- ☑ ***Equal rights and privileges*** to nominate candidates, vote on internal matters, and attend and participate in membership meetings.
- ☑ ***Freedom of speech and assembly.*** (But unions may adopt and enforce ***reasonable*** rules against such speech and assembly.)
- ☑ ***Procedural safeguards*** that must be met before union ***dues, fees, and assessments may be increased.***
- ☑ ***Right to sue and testify*** against the union or its officers in administrative, judicial, or legislative proceedings.
- ☑ ***Guarantees of due process safeguards*** in union disciplinary hearings.

c. Judicial Review of Union Disciplinary Proceedings

Common law courts did not hesitate to require unions to adhere to the due process provisions of the unions' own constitutions and bylaws, and to require (as a matter of public policy) that such provisions measure up to judicial notions of fairness. The courts have applied the same principles in reviewing union disciplinary procedures under LMRDA section 101(a)(5).

(1) Scope of Judicial Review

Thus, a court may order reinstatement of a union member expelled after a hearing in which it was determined that the member had engaged in "fraudulent activities," where it did not appear that the member had been accorded a "full and fair hearing." [**Vars v. International Brotherhood of Boilermakers,** 320 F.2d 576 (2d Cir. 1963)]

(a) Note

Judicial review of the findings of a union tribunal are *limited,* and the courts will not "re-try" the evidence or substitute their judgment for that of the union tribunal. [**International Brotherhood of Boilermakers v. Hardeman,** 401 U.S. 233 (1971)]

(b) But Note

A "full and fair hearing" requires that there be *some* evidence to support the union determination. To this end, a court may examine the record to insure that the union findings are not totally without basis in the evidence. [**International Brotherhood of Boilermakers v. Hardeman,** *supra*]

(2) Distinction Between Members and Officers—Summary Discipline

The courts have distinguished between union members and union officers in applying section 101(a)(5). The distinction is based on what is considered to be the clear intent of Congress to allow unions to discipline officers suspected of malfeasance in their duties as officers without adhering to the procedural requirements of section 101(a)(5).

(a) But Note

Officers enjoy the same Title I rights (*e.g.,* free speech) as any other union member enjoys. [**Grand Lodge of International Association of Machinists v. King,** *supra,* p. 219]

(3) Civil Enforcement

Any person whose Title I rights have been violated may sue in federal court "for such relief as may be appropriate." [LMRDA § 102; **International Brotherhood of Boilermakers v. Hardeman,** *supra,* p. 223]

(a) "Appropriate" Relief

Relief under section 102 may include damages, reinstatement, and attorneys' fees to be paid out of the union treasury (because the suing employee has vindicated the Title I rights of all union members). [**Hall v. Cole,** 412 U.S. 1 (1973)]

d. Retention of Existing Rights from Other Sources

Landrum-Griffin specifically reserves to union members any rights and remedies existing under state law, "except as explicitly provided to the contrary." This preserves various legislative and common law doctrines that may afford even stronger or more comprehensive protection than the Landrum-Griffin Act (*e.g.,* the right to have a receiver appointed for a union that is fiscally irresponsible). [LMRDA §§ 103, 603(a)]

(1) No Impairment of NLRA or RLA

The Landrum-Griffin Act also disclaims any intention of impairing or superseding the Railway Labor Act, or of conferring any rights upon employers or impairing the rights of any person under the NLRA. [LMRDA § 603(b)]

e. Additional Rights Under the Landrum-Griffin Act

The following additional rights are secured to employees by Landrum-Griffin:

(1) ***The right to exercise the various rights secured by the Landrum-Griffin Act without fear of union discipline*** [LMRDA § 609] and free from violence or the threat thereof [LMRDA § 610];

(2) *The right to inspect union policy and financial statements* [LMRDA § 104];

(3) *The right to sue* (when the union fails to do so) ***in order to recover misappropriated union assets*** [LMRDA § 501(b)] ***and the right to receive a copy of the collective bargaining agreement;***

(4) *The right to sue for violations of the trusteeship provisions* of the Landrum-Griffin Act (Title III of the LMRDA); and

(5) *The* ***right to be informed*** about the provisions of the Landrum-Griffin Act [LMRDA § 105].

G. Election of Union Officers

1. Common Law Background

a. Reluctance of Courts to Review Union Elections

Most courts at common law refused to hear complaints about the election of union officers for several reasons:

(1) ***Unions were considered private, voluntary associations*** whose election procedures were left to private ordering.

(2) ***Former procedures in equity limited actions to the protection of "property rights,"*** and the courts found no property rights in union elections.

(3) ***There was no basis for measuring damage*** to union members.

(4) ***If the complaint was made after an election had been conducted,*** the courts were ***ill-equipped to provide the remedy*** (a new election) because:

(a) ***They lacked pollwatchers, counters, and similar officials*** (although some courts did appoint a "master" to oversee an election, *see* below);

(b) ***A new election involved appointing new election officials*** subject to the same pressures and prejudices as the old union officials; and

(c) *The details of union election procedures* were considered overwhelming.

b. Limited Judicial Review

Some courts did assume jurisdiction of complaints involving union elections. Relief, however, was usually confined to situations where:

(1) The complaint alleged that the ***union had failed to follow its own constitution or bylaws*** in nominating or voting for officials;

(2) Those provisions were ***"contrary to public policy"***; or

(3) ***Judicial intervention could be effective*** (*e.g.,* before the election took place).

2. Landrum-Griffin, Title IV

It became clear that federal legislation was needed to guarantee fair union elections. Federal law had given union officials very broad powers and discretion to negotiate conditions of employment and to process grievances. To insure that such officials would be responsive to their constituents, Congress set out certain minimum requirements for conducting free and democratic union elections.

a. Rights of Union Members Under Title IV

Landrum-Griffin provides the following rules and procedures for nominating and electing union officials:

(1) Voting

All members in good standing are allowed to vote, and each member has the right to one vote. [LMRDA § 401(e)]

(2) Frequency of Elections

Local officers must be elected at least *every three years;* international officers ***every five years.*** [LMRDA § 401(a)]

(3) Secret Ballot

Union officers must be elected by secret ballot.

(a) Note

For the election of national or international officers at a convention, delegates must be chosen by secret ballot. However, the delegates are not required to use secret ballots at the convention. [LMRDA § 5401(a)]

(4) Nomination

Reasonable opportunity must be given for the nomination of candidates. [LMRDA § 401(e)]

(5) Eligibility for Candidacy

Every member in good standing is eligible to be a candidate, subject to "reasonable qualifications uniformly imposed." [LMRDA § 401(e)]

e.g. **Example:** In this regard, union rules requiring a candidate for union office to have attended at least half of all union meetings during the three years preceding the election have been held not to be a "reasonable qualification" under section 401(e), at least where they served to preclude 97% of the union membership from running for office. [**Local 3489, United Steel Workers v. Usery,** 429 U.S. 305 (1977)]

(6) Notice of Election

Members must be notified of the election at least 15 days prior to date of the election. [LMRDA § 401(e)]

(7) Dissemination of Campaign Literature

If campaign literature is distributed by the union, it must be done at the expense of the candidates and without discrimination between or among candidates. [LMRDA § 401(c)]

(8) Membership Lists

A union whose contract requires membership in the union as a condition of employment is required to maintain membership lists and to make such lists available for inspection by bona fide candidates. [LMRDA § 401(c)]

(9) Observers at the Polls

"Adequate safeguards" must be provided for the election itself, including the right of any candidate to have observers at the polls and at the counting of ballots.

(10) Election Expenses

Candidates may not use union funds to finance their campaigns, but the *nondiscriminatory* use of such money (as in nonpartisan statements of issues) is permitted. [LMRDA § 401(g)]

(11) Compliance with Union Constitution and Bylaws

The union must comply with its own constitution and bylaws regarding election requirements, provided the latter are not inconsistent with the provisions of Title IV. [LMRDA § 403]

b. Enforcement Provisions

Title IV of the Landrum-Griffin Act confers upon the Secretary of Labor and the courts the power to protect the rights of union members in connection with union elections.

(1) No Preelection Remedy

The Landrum-Griffin Act provides that the Secretary of Labor has exclusive authority to institute proceedings to enforce the provisions of Title IV, but (as discussed below) this authority commences *after the election has been conducted.* Thus, even though some union rule or act clearly violates the election provisions of the LMRDA, the Secretary of Labor cannot intervene until the election has taken place. [**Calhoon v. Harvey,** 379 U.S. 134 (1964)]

(a) Purpose

The purpose of this provision is to prevent individuals from blocking union elections. Not even a violation of Title IV itself can be used as the basis for suit (under Title I of the LMRDA) to obtain preelection judicial review.

Example: In *Calhoon, supra,* p. 226, union members claimed that certain provisions of the union constitution, which limited their right to nominate and elect union officers, violated their rights under both Title I [LMRDA § 101(a)(2)] and Title IV [LMRDA § 401(e)]. The members argued that since Title I violations are actionable "at any time" (*supra,* pp. 219 *et seq.*), the court could act before the election to grant appropriate relief against the union (*i.e.,* enjoin the election). However, the Supreme Court held that there was no violation under Title I, since the rule in question was imposed and applied uniformly to all members (*supra,* p. 219). Thus the only basis for attacking the rule was under Title IV, which is limited to post-election challenges. *Rationale:* The court reasoned that Congress had limited Title IV remedies to post-election challenges *to prevent individuals from blocking union elections* (thus possibly hamstringing the operations of the union) and also to utilize the expertise and discretion of the Secretary of Labor (*see* below).

(b) Criticism

Denying preelection relief often frustrates the members' rights as provided in Title I. Post-election review is also very time-consuming.

(c) Distinguish—State Law

Some state courts are willing to intervene before elections, under the common law or state statutes regulating union election procedures. This is permissible, since section 403 specifically preserves to union members whatever preelection "rights and remedies" would otherwise be applicable under state law.

(d) Exception for Candidates for Union Office

One limited preelection remedy is recognized in the LMRDA: A bona fide candidate for union office may sue before an election to assure *equal distribution of campaign literature and access to union membership lists* for purposes of the campaign. [LMRDA § 401(c)]

(2) Authority of Secretary of Labor

Once a union election has been held, Title IV *preempts* state authority. Congress vested in the Secretary of Labor the exclusive authority for enforcing those provisions of Title IV relating to the legality of union elections. Basically, the Secretary is empowered to investigate complaints regarding the legality of the election after it has taken place, to sue to have the election set aside, and to supervise any new election ordered. [LMRDA § 402(a)]

(a) Complaint by Union Member

Although the Secretary may initiate her own investigation for violations of any provisions of the Landrum-Griffin Act except Title I, investigations of elections almost always stem from a complaint filed by a union member. [LMRDA § 601(a)]

1) Limitation—Exhaustion of Internal Remedies

The Secretary cannot act on any complaint unless (i) the complaining member has ***exhausted whatever internal union remedies*** are available, ***or*** (ii) ***three months*** have expired from the time the member instituted such internal procedures, without a final disposition of the complaint. [LMRDA § 402(a)] The complaint must be filed with the Secretary within **"one month"** from either the date of exhaustion of internal union remedies defined as the date the union member receives the union's final decision or the three months have expired from pursuing internal procedures without a final disposition. [**Perez v. Postal Police Officers Ass'n,** 736 F.3d 736 (6th Cir. 2013)]

a) Note

If a union member files a complaint with the Secretary of Labor charging that the election was illegal on one ground and the Secretary (while investigating the complaint) discovers other Title IV violations, the exhaustion doctrine does not apply to the latter violations—at least when the union had a fair opportunity to consider and redress such violations in connection with the member's initial complaint. [**Wirtz v. Local Union No. 125, Laborers' International Union of North America AFL-CIO,** 389 U.S. 477 (1968)]

COMPARISON OF "EXHAUSTION" REQUIREMENTS GILBERT

SITUATION	"EXHAUSTION" REQUIREMENT	APPLICABLE STATUTE
EMPLOYEE HAS GRIEVANCE WITH EMPLOYER	Employee must exhaust remedies of grievance procedure—no "time" exceptions	NLRA § 9(a)
EMPLOYEE HAS GRIEVANCE WITH UNION	Employee must exhaust internal union procedures before instituting legal or administrative action, unless she cannot do so within ***four months***	LMRDA § 101(a)(4)
EMPLOYEE IS CHALLENGING A UNION ELECTION	Employee must have exhausted internal union remedies, or ***three months*** must have passed since employee instituted action under the internal union procedures, before Secretary of Labor may act on the complaint	LMRDA § 402(a)

2) Intervention in Suit by the Secretary of Labor

A union member is also permitted to intervene in an action by the Secretary to set aside the election. [**Trbovich v. UMW,** 404 U.S. 528 (1972)]

a) Attorneys' Fees

Although Title IV of the LMRDA does not specifically authorize attorneys' fees, the award of fees to an individual intervenor has been upheld. [**Brennan v. United Steelworkers,** 554 F.2d 586 (3d Cir. 1977), *cert. denied,* 435 U.S. 977 (1978)]

(b) Finding of "Probable Cause" as Prerequisite to Lawsuit

If, upon investigating the member's complaint, the Secretary finds "probable cause" to believe that the Landrum-Griffin Act has been violated, the Secretary must bring suit in federal court *within 60 days of filing* of the complaint to set aside the election. [LMRDA § 402(b)]

1) Where Secretary Does Not Act

If the Secretary decides not to bring suit to set aside the election, a defeated candidate may seek judicial review of the decision. The Secretary must provide a statement of reasons for not suing, which are subject to review on a "not arbitrary or capricious" standard. [**Dunlop v. Bachowski,** 421 U.S. 560 (1975)]

(c) New Elections

The federal court will determine whether the Landrum-Griffin Act has been violated (*see* below), and if it finds a violation, it will order that a new election be held. The Secretary of Labor is empowered to supervise the new election and to certify the names of the winners to the court. [LMRDA § 402(b)]

(3) Judicial Power to Invalidate Elections—"Nexus" Requirement

In any suit filed by the Secretary of Labor to set aside a union election, the federal court may declare the election void and order a new election only if there is a finding based on "a preponderance of the evidence" that (i) ***some provision of section 401 has been violated,*** and (ii) that the violation ***"may have affected the outcome of the election."*** [LMRDA 5402(c)(1), (2)]

(a) Effect

It is not enough merely to show irregularity or illegality in the election. There must also be some showing of a *proximate relationship or "nexus"* between the irregularity and the outcome.

(b) Burden of Proof

Proximate cause may be difficult to establish since any contentions as to what did or did not affect the outcome of an election are necessarily speculative. Recognizing this, the Supreme Court has held that the Secretary of Labor need establish only a "***reasonable** possibility*" that the violation affected the outcome of the election. This is sufficient to demonstrate a prima facie case under Title IV, and the burden of going forward with the evidence then shifts to the union, which must establish that the illegal act or conduct did not affect the outcome. [**Wirtz v. Hotel, Motel & Club Employees Union, Local 6,** 391 U.S. 492 (1968)]

e.g. **Example:** In *Hotel, Motel & Club Employees,* the Supreme Court held that a union rule that imposed unreasonable requirements on members' rights to run for or hold office violated section 401(e) (*supra,* p. 225), and that the very nature of the rule—which excluded most members from qualifying as candidates—was sufficient to establish a prima facie case that the violation "may have affected" the outcome within the meaning of section 402(c).

(4) **Status of Elected Officers Pending Judicial Review**

Once elected, union officers continue to hold office unless and until a new election is ordered by the court, the election is held, and the results are certified by the Secretary of Labor.

(a) **No New Election Ordered**

If the court refuses to order a new election, the challenged election is ***presumed valid*** during any subsequent appeals. [LMRDA § 402(a)]

(b) **New Election Ordered**

If the court orders a new election, the election must be held; *i.e.,* a ***new election cannot be stayed*** pending an appeal. [LMRDA § 402(d)]

(5) **"Mootness" Objection**

The fact that subsequent elections have been held pending appeal, the results of which were not challenged, does not in itself render the challenge moot. [**Wirtz v. Local 153, Glass Bottle Blowers Association,** 389 U.S. 463 (1968)]

e.g. **Example:** In *Glass Bottle Blowers,* the Secretary of Labor challenged a 1963 election because of a union rule restricting candidates, but lost in the district court. The Secretary appealed, and by the time the appeal was heard, another election had taken place (subject to the same rule), the results of which were not challenged. Even so, the Supreme Court held that the intervening election did not render the Secretary's suit "moot"—basing its holding on the literal wording of section 401(c) ("the court shall declare the election void") and also upon the theory that the purpose of Title IV would be frustrated if improper union practices were not declared illegal and redressed.

H. Corruption in Unions—Landrum-Griffin Titles II, III, and V

1. Title II—Reporting and Disclosure Provisions

Title II of the LMRDA is based on the assumption that the availability of information on union activities, when coupled with democratic procedures within the union (Titles I and IV, *supra*), will be an effective means of controlling corruption. The significant provisions of Title II [29 U.S.C. §§ 431–441] are as follows:

a. Basic Union Information

Section 201(a), (b), and (c) require disclosure by the union of certain basic information (names of officers, various procedures, and fiscal condition) and require that all such information be available to members. Section 201(a) mandates the creation of an organizational constitution and by-laws identifying requirements for membership, regular meetings, censure and removal of union officers, and provisions for how the organization's funds may be spent. This information must be disclosed to the Department of Labor's Office of Labor Management Standards (OLMS) along with completing certain forms including the Labor Organization Information Report, Labor Form LM-1. 29 C.F.R. § 402.2. Section 201(b) requires that a union file an annual report disclosing receipts and disbursements to the OLMS and submit a form, either an LM-2, LM-3, or LM-4, depending upon the overall annual receipts of the union. Section 201(c) provides that all the information in the annual report must be also provided to all the members of the labor organization and any member may file a lawsuit in state or federal court "for just cause to examine any books, records, and accounts necessary to verify such report." The court, at its discretion, may also award costs and attorney's fees to the member who brings the court challenge.

(1) Note

In the case of smaller unions, the Secretary of Labor is authorized to reduce and simplify the amount of paperwork required by the LMRDA.

b. Financial Transactions by Officials

Union officers and union employees must disclose financial transactions with the employer or any associated business. Section 202(a) provides that union officers and union employees must disclose their financial interests annually, including those of their family (spouses or minor children), that may present a conflict of interest, Labor Organization Officer and Employee Report, Form LM-30. 29 C.F.R. § 404.3. [LMRDA § 202(a)]

c. Reporting by Employers

Employers must report certain expenditures to, or agreements with, union officials, union employees, or managerial employees. [LMRDA § 203] Section 206 requires the retention of records related to all the other forms and required submissions. 29 U.S.C. § 436. LM-1, LM-2, LM-3, and LM-4 forms may be found on the Department of Labor website. [LMRDA § 206] https://www.dol.gov/agencies/olms/reports/forms/lm-1-lm-2-lm-3-lm-4.

d. Criminal Penalties and Civil Remedies

Willful violation of the reporting provisions of Title II is punishable by a fine of up to $10,000 or imprisonment for not more than one year. [LMRDA § 209] Section 210 authorizes the Secretary of Labor to initiate civil actions, and section 601 gives the Secretary the right to inspect union records and to question such persons deemed necessary in order to determine whether possible Title II violations have occurred.

2. Title V—Limitations on Union Officials

Title V, "Safeguards for Labor Organizations," is intended to aid union members in ridding their organizations of corrupt union officials. It does so, in conformity with common law practice, by placing union officers, agents, shop stewards, and other union representatives and employees in a trustee relationship vis-a-vis the union and its members, *i.e.,* by imposing *fiduciary duties* on union officers. Title V does not spell out such duties in detail, leaving the task of formulating substantive law to the courts. The significant provisions of Title V are as follows:

a. Misappropriation of Union Funds

Union officials are prohibited from using union funds or acquiring financial or other interests for purposes that conflict with the interest of the labor organization. This prohibition applies even where the union constitution, bylaws, or resolutions purport to authorize such activity or include a general "exculpatory" provision absolving the activity. [LMRDA § 501(a)]

e.g. **Example:** Agreements by the union to pay for trial expenses incurred by union officials charged with misappropriating union funds have been held illegal and contrary to the intent and purpose of the LMRDA. [**Highway Truck Drivers & Helpers, Local 107 v. Cohen,** 334 F.2d 378 (3d Cir. 1964)]

cf. **Compare:** The union may, however, reimburse the official for his trial expenses if he is exonerated. [**Highway Truck Drivers & Helpers,** *supra*]

b. Individual Lawsuits

Section 501(b) permits individual union members to sue union officials for damages, an accounting, or other appropriate relief if the union itself fails or refuses to do so.

(1) Limitation

To prevent harassment of union officials and frivolous lawsuits, there is a requirement that the individual member show "good cause" at a *preliminary hearing* before the court will permit the action to proceed.

c. Criminal Penalties

Union officials who are found to have embezzled, stolen, or otherwise willfully misappropriated union funds may be fined up to $10,000 and imprisoned for up to five years. [LMRDA § 501(c)]

d. Other Provisions

The Landrum-Griffin Act makes it illegal for unions to loan funds in excess of $2,000 to union officials [LMRDA § 503(c)] and prohibits persons convicted of certain crimes from holding union office or other positions of responsibility in the union. [LMRDA § 504(a)]

(1) But Note

A provision banning *Communists* from such positions is unconstitutional. [**United States v. Brown,** 381 U.S. 437 (1965); *see* Constitutional Law Summary]

3. Title III—"Trusteeships"

The term "trusteeship," as used in the Landrum-Griffin Act, is defined as "a method of supervision or control whereby a labor organization suspends the autonomy otherwise available to a subordinate body under its constitution or bylaws."

a. Background

Prior to the passage of Landrum-Griffin in 1959, trusteeships had been praised as an effective means of preserving the integrity and stability of labor organizations by empowering officers of the international union to govern local unions in which serious misconduct was found. However, trusteeships frequently were used by union officials as a means of plundering the treasuries of local unions, perpetuating their own power, and preserving the power of international officers by removing "unfriendly" people at the local level and controlling the selection of delegates to international conventions. Congress therefore enacted Title III of the Landrum-Griffin Act to regulate such trusteeships.

b. Requirements for Trusteeships

Section 302 of Title III provides that trusteeships may be established and administered only in accordance with the constitution and bylaws of the labor organization imposing the trusteeship, and then only if the aim is:

(1) *To correct corruption*;

(2) *To prevent misappropriation of assets*;

(3) *To assure performance of the union's contractual and bargaining representative duties*;

(4) *To restore democratic procedures*; and/or

(5) *To carry out "the legitimate objects of [the] labor organization."*

c. Restrictions on Trusteeships

The votes of a local union operating under a trusteeship may not be counted in a convention for the election of national officers unless the convention delegates were chosen by secret ballot among all local members in good standing. Also, in order to prevent trusteeships for the purpose of looting local treasuries, the transfer of local union funds in excess of normal assessments levied upon other locals is prohibited. [LMRDA § 303]

d. Reports by Trusteeships—Enforcement

Within 30 days after a trusteeship is imposed, and thereafter on a semi-annual basis, a report must be filed with the Secretary of Labor supplying all information necessary to assure compliance with the LMRDA. [LMRDA § 301] Lawsuits by local union members to enforce the rights granted by sections 302 and 303 are authorized by section 304.

Review Questions and Answers

Review Questions

FILL IN
ANSWER

1. Determine whether the following statements are true or false:

    a. One basic tenet of early AFL philosophy was the establishment of a strong trade-union political party. __________

    b. The AFL differed from the Knights of Labor in not attempting to organize unskilled or semi-skilled workers. __________

    c. Unlike the criminal conspiracy doctrine, the "objectives" test was frequently applied by the courts to uphold union activities. __________

    d. The Pullman Strike prompted federal legislation favorable to labor. __________

    e. Sections 6 and 20 of the Clayton Act were initially ineffective in permitting union organization and concerted activities. __________

2. The basic problem between the CIO and the AFL during the early 1930s lay in personality differences between the two organizations. True or false? __________

3. When the AFL and CIO were reunited in the 1950s, national union autonomy was largely preserved, but exclusive jurisdiction remained a problem. True or false? __________

4. The Norris-LaGuardia Act stated a federal policy requiring employers to negotiate with labor unions. True or false? __________

5. Norris-LaGuardia made it possible to overturn restrictive judicial interpretations of the Clayton Act handed down in the 1920s. True or false? __________

6. The National Labor Relations Act of 1935 ("NLRA") could not be considered a complete labor code because it imposed bargaining obligations only on the employer. True or false? __________

7. The basic purpose of the Taft-Hartley Act was to impose further limitations on employer conduct during union organizing and collective bargaining. True or false? __________

8. The Landrum-Griffin Act of 1959 was aimed almost exclusively at union tactics and internal union affairs. True or false? __________

9. Industrial peace and stability are the primary goals of national labor policy, and collective bargaining is the basic means for achieving same. True or false? __________

10. Union pickets Employer during a strike at Employer's plant. Several minor altercations occur when suppliers attempt to cross Union's picket line. Can the Employer seek an injunction in state court against the picketing? ______________

11. During the strike, Employer sends a letter to all employees in which he states, "Your wonderful union president has been using union dues to finance his own retirement." The union president wants to sue Employer for defamation in state court. May he do so? ______________

12. The Railway Labor Act covers employees of air carriers as well as railroads. True or false? ______________

13. For an employer to be covered by the National Labor Relations Act, her business activities must be in the flow of interstate commerce. True or false? ______________

14. Rocky is hired by Balboa Co. to collect overdue accounts, for which Rocky is paid an agreed sum plus a percentage of each account collected. Is Rocky an employee under the NLRA? ______________

15. In carrying out its two major functions, the NLRB exercises its authority somewhat more formally in the case of unfair labor practices than in representation matters. True or false? ______________

16. In reviewing NLRB findings regarding unfair labor practices, the court of appeals makes an independent evaluation of the record and is not bound by the Board's decision. True or false? ______________

17. An NLRB finding of unlawful employer discrimination on the basis of union activity will be upheld if it is found to be supported by the evidence in the record. True or false? ______________

18. The International Brotherhood of Unattached Facilities Workers contacts numerous employees of Outhouse, Inc. in an effort to organize the plant. The general manager of Outhouse subsequently asks each individual employee about the union's organizing efforts and inquires whether the employee wants "outside representation." Has Outhouse committed an unfair labor practice? ______________

19. Various employees of Outhouse, Inc. seek to solicit support for the union among their fellow workers. Outhouse announces that it will not permit such solicitation during work hours or in work areas. Is the restriction proper? ______________

a. Would the result be different if the employees wished to distribute union literature, rather than solicit verbally? ______________

20. Suppose that the International Brotherhood of Unattached Facilities Workers sends its own representatives to the plant to solicit employee support. May Outhouse, Inc. properly prevent such representatives from soliciting *anywhere* on company property? ______________

21. Employer is subjected to a long organizing campaign by Union. Employer posts a newsletter to employees on the company bulletin board, in which she states, "The economic consequences of your representation by Union are simply that I will be forced to close the plant and declare bankruptcy." Does this statement constitute improper coercion? ______________

a. If the foregoing statement is not considered coercive, can it nevertheless be used as evidence of *other* unfair labor practices by Employer? ______________

b. Would the propriety of Employer's statement be affected if she refused to allow Union to respond to the prediction? ______________

c. Can Employer lawfully grant a wage increase to her employees shortly before the representation election? ______________

22. The limitations on union influencing of employee rights to self-organization under section 8(b) are somewhat less comprehensive than those imposed on employers by section 8(a). True or false? ______________

23. The free speech guarantees and restrictions applicable to employer statements in the course of an organizing campaign also apply to unions. True or false? ______________

24. Union conducts an organizing campaign in a nonunion plant, and promises to waive the usual initiation fee for all employees signing authorization cards within a 30-day period. Does the promise violate section 8(b)? ______________

a. Would the result be different if the union offered to reimburse employees for wages lost in attending an organization meeting? ______________

b. One night during the organizing campaign, several windows at the plant are broken. The employer discovers that one of those responsible for the incident is a union organizer. Can an unfair labor practice complaint be brought against Union? ______________

c. Would the result be different if the employer sought an injunction against Union as a result of the window-breaking? ______________

25. The Two-Dimensional Actors' Guild and the International Brotherhood of Cartoon Characters ("IBCC") each seek to represent the employees of Cartoon Co. Cartoon Co. believes that the IBCC is a more responsible organization, and accordingly instructs its supervisors to allow employees and union representatives to actively solicit membership in that union. Does this violate section 8(a)? ______________

a. Would the result be different if Cartoon Co. refused to allow representatives of the Guild to solicit or distribute literature on company premises? ______________

26. Carbon Paper Co. lays off 100 employees, claiming a lack of orders and decreased production. Nearly all of those affected were involved in an unsuccessful union organizing campaign the previous year. Has Carbon Paper Co. violated section 8(a)? ____________

a. Could Carbon Paper Co. move the plant to a new location if this has the effect of thwarting further attempts at unionization? ____________

b. Can Carbon Paper Co. discontinue operations in the face of renewed union attempts to organize employees? ____________

27. The Federation of Typesetters, Proofreaders, and Editors is the bargaining representative for the employees of Eastco. Paul, an employee, refuses to pay normal union dues or membership fees to the Federation. Can the Federation compel Eastco to discharge Paul? ____________

a. If there is a valid compulsory union contract in effect, can the Federation seek Paul's discharge for failure to attend union meetings? ____________

28. The NLRB can order affirmative action to offset the effects of unfair labor practices involving union organization. True or false? ____________

29. Under present NLRB procedure, the Regional Directors take charge of the preliminary matters involved with a representation election, but the Board itself conducts all hearings and certification of representatives. True or false? ____________

30. Where certain employees could be considered a separate bargaining unit or be merged into an existing unit, the NLRB always permits such employees to choose between the two alternatives. True or false? ____________

31. As a general rule, only those persons employed during the payroll period immediately preceding the date of a representation election are eligible to vote therein. True or false? ____________

32. Economic strikers who have been replaced by the employer may still be eligible to vote in a representation election, but only permanent replacements can vote. True or false? ____________

33. An employer may file a petition for decertification of the union. True or false? ____________

34. A union petitions the NLRB for a representation election and obtains an "Excelsior" list. The union then *disclaims* its interest in the election (causing the petition to be withdrawn), but continues its organizing activities with the use of the employee list. Is this permissible? ____________

35. In determining the appropriate bargaining unit, the NLRB has sole discretion as long as its decision is not arbitrary or capricious. True or false? ____________

36. Before an election will be ordered, any union involved must produce evidence of support by at least 30% of the employees within the unit. True or false? ____________

37. Union petitions the NLRB for a representation election. Employer immediately files an unfair labor practice charge against the union, alleging that Union has intimidated employees into signing authorization cards. Will the Board proceed with the election? __________

a. Would the result be different if Employer's charge alleged that Union had traditionally afforded better representation for male than for female employees (who constituted a minority of all employees)? __________

38. Union A and Acme, Inc. sign a collective bargaining agreement covering a four-year period. After two years, Union B claims majority support among Acme's employees and seeks an election. Will an election be ordered? __________

a. Would it matter whether Union B had presented majority authorization cards to Acme three years before, but Acme had nevertheless recognized and contracted with Union A? __________

b. Suppose instead that the A-Acme contract was signed following certification of Union A, and that the contract period is two years. Forty-five days before expiration of the agreement, Union B petitions for an election. Twenty days later, Union A and Acme sign a new two-year contract. Is the new contract a bar to Union B's petition? __________

39. If the NLRB refuses to hear unfair labor practice charges with respect to an election, the aggrieved party is foreclosed as a practical matter from a judicial ruling on the propriety of the election. True or false? __________

40. Union wins a representation election and is certified as the representative for employees in the bargaining unit. Six months later, and prior to any agreement, the majority of employees disavow the union. May the employer properly refuse to bargain with the union at this point? __________

a. Would the result be different if the employees approached the employer 18 months after certification? __________

41. Once a union is selected and certified as the bargaining representative, all individual contracts with employees in the bargaining unit are superseded. True or false? __________

42. An employer may properly discipline employees who engage in concerted activity not sanctioned by the authorized bargaining representative. True or false? __________

43. Union and Acme, Inc. commence negotiations on a collective bargaining agreement. Acme indicates that it can pay no more than a 5% general wage increase, and refuses to budge from this position. Is Acme guilty of failing to bargain in good faith? __________

a. Would the result be different if Acme also asked the union to withdraw unfair labor practice charges against Acme in return for concessions in the contract? __________

b. Suppose the union accuses Acme of discriminating against female employees in work assignments. Acme agrees to negotiate a nondiscrimination clause for the contract but delays any discussion of current work assignments. Has Acme failed to bargain in good faith? ______________

44. Is a successor employer bound by the arbitration terms of a collective agreement entered into by her predecessor? ______________

45. Whether or not a successor employer is bound by an existing agreement, he must always bargain in good faith with the existing union representative and must remedy any existing unfair labor practices or Title VII violations by his predecessor. True or false? ______________

46. The United Mudworkers' Union conducts organizing activities at the plant of Ness Co., after which it presents Ness Co. with authorization cards signed by 75% of the plant employees and demands recognition and the right to bargain. On these facts, is Ness Co. required to negotiate with the union? ______________

a. Would the result be different if Ness Co. had interrogated employees about their union activities and sympathies during the organizing campaign? ______________

47. If the NLRB finds an employer guilty of refusing to bargain in good faith, it may order whatever relief it deems appropriate, including compensation. True or false? ______________

48. Retirement health benefits are a compulsory bargaining subject, regardless of the status of the employee affected. True or false? ______________

49. In negotiating a contract with Employer, Union complains about slippery walkways in the plant and seeks to compel Employer to install new flooring. Must Employer bargain with the union on this issue? ______________

a. Suppose Union complains about the walkways during the term of the contract. If the contract contains a "management rights" clause applicable to working conditions, can Employer be forced to remedy the situation? ______________

50. Only subjects that cannot lawfully be included in the contract are classified as illegal subjects of bargaining. True or false? ______________

51. The NLRB and the courts of appeal take somewhat different views on the duty of employers to bargain over managerial decisions such as subcontracting. True or false? ______________

52. A union can waive its bargaining rights on a mandatory subject if the contract is silent thereon. True or false? ______________

53. The United Shoemakers' Union and Spats International negotiate for several weeks on a wage increase but cannot reach agreement. May Spats International temporarily lock out workers as a result of the impasse? ______________

a. Suppose instead that the union calls a strike when the impasse is reached. Must Spats International continue to bargain with the union? ______________

54. The principal difference between mediation and arbitration is that the former is not a decisionmaking process. True or false? ______________

55. Where an arbitration clause covers disputes over "interpretation" or "application" of the agreement, *all* disputes except those expressly withdrawn from arbitration by the contract itself are covered. True or false? ______________

56. Union files a section 301 lawsuit, alleging that Clinton Co. breached the collective bargaining agreement in promoting an employee outside the seniority system. Will the court hear the complaint? ______________

a. Suppose the aggrieved employee presents his complaint to the union, but the union declines to process the grievance against Clinton Co. Must the employee exhaust any grievance procedure directly with Clinton Co. before suing under section 301? ______________

b. Assume instead that Monica, a female employee, alleges that she was not promoted because of sex discrimination by Clinton Co. The union represents Monica in arbitration proceedings, but the arbitrator finds that Clinton Co.'s action was not discriminatory. May Monica then sue Clinton Co. under Title VII of the Civil Rights Act? ______________

57. State courts have concurrent jurisdiction to hear section 301 cases, even where the dispute involves activities arguably protected under the NLRA. True or false? ______________

58. Courtney submits a grievance to arbitration. Widgets, Inc. refuses to arbitrate, claiming that the grievance is not within the arbitration clause of the agreement. If Courtney seeks judicial enforcement of arbitration, will the court rule in her favor? ______________

a. Suppose that Widgets proceeds to arbitration, and the arbitrator orders that back pay be awarded to Courtney. Widgets refuses to pay, claiming that the award is "totally unjustified by the facts presented." Can Courtney enforce the award? ______________

59. Arbitrability of an issue is generally a question for the arbitrator, unless the contract provides otherwise. True or false? ______________

60. Union protests reassignment of overtime by Employer, who refuses to change the assignments. Is Union permitted to schedule a work stoppage over Employer's refusal, rather than seek arbitration? ______________

a. If Union does order a work stoppage, can Employer terminate the collective bargaining agreement? ______________

61. Unlike picketing, the right to strike has never been given express constitutional protection by the Supreme Court. True or false? ______________

62. Picketing enjoys the same constitutional safeguards as other First Amendment activities. True or false? ______________

63. Employees on an oil derrick leave the job because of inadequate fire protection by the employer. If there is a no-strike clause in their collective agreement with the employer, is the workers' action protected? ______________

64. Primary concerted activity is generally permitted, whereas almost all secondary activity is unlawful. True or false? ______________

65. United Buggy Workers ("UBW") wishes to restructure the seniority provisions in its contract with Fjord Wagon Co., but Fjord does not accept the union's proposals when presented with them shortly before the agreement terminates. Can UBW strike Fjord's plant upon termination of the existing contract? ______________

a. Would the result be different if UBW were striking over alleged discrimination in job assignments by Fjord? ______________

b. Suppose that UBW seeks an agreement from Fjord to retain certain employees as "oilers," even though their regular jobs have been eliminated and the new position would require them to perform only a few actual services. Fjord refuses to enter such an agreement, and UBW calls a strike. Has the union committed an unfair labor practice? ______________

66. A union strike to compel recognition despite certification of another representative is illegal if directed against a secondary employer, but is permissible primary activity. True or false? ______________

a. Would the above result be different if the objective of the strike was to obtain recognition as to only a portion of employees in the bargaining unit? ______________

b. Assume instead that the International Brotherhood of Brewmasters ("IBB") already is the certified representative for certain employees at Duff's plant in Springfield, and that the Federation of Beer Tasters represents other employees at the plant. If Duff assigns certain new jobs to members of the IBB, may the other union properly strike the plant to compel assignment of at least some jobs to its members? ______________

67. The Chemical Workers' Union and Un-ionized Particals, Inc. commence negotiations on a wage increase for employees and, when Un-ionized Particals refuses to agree to the increase requested by the union, the union calls a strike. Un-ionized Particals subsequently replaces most of the strikers with permanent employees. Is Un-ionized Particals guilty of an unfair labor practice if it fails to rehire the replaced strikers after a settlement has been reached? ______________

a. Would the result be different if Un-ionized Particals failed to keep the strikers' applications for reinstatement on file, assuming no openings exist when the applications are made? ______________

b. Suppose instead that the union calls a strike against Un-ionized Particals for alleged discrimination on the basis of union membership. Un-ionized Particals hires replacements for the strikers. Must Un-ionized Particals reinstate the striking employees if there are no openings available after the strike? ______________

c. Would the result be the same if the union had engaged in a partial strike because of the alleged discrimination by Un-ionized Particals? ______________

68. Union rents space on a billboard outside Employer's plant and posts a large notice that Employer is nonunion. Does this constitute picketing? ______________

69. An uncertified union may engage in informational picketing even without petitioning for a representation election, provided no other union is lawfully recognized and no secondary work stoppage results. True or false? ______________

70. Where a union engages in unlawful organizational picketing, the NLRB has wide discretion in seeking an injunction against the picketing. True or false? ______________

71. Union wishes to represent employees of Good Day Tires and to that end pickets Fjord Motors (a customer of Good Day Tires). Is the picketing unlawful? ______________

72. NLRA section 8(b)(4) has been enforced by the courts to prevent any pressures on secondary employers. True or false? ______________

73. As a general rule, picketing in common-situs situations is allowed only with respect to the owner of the site. True or false? ______________

74. Union represents carpenters employed by subcontractor Cullen's Carpentry in constructing a large housing project. The general contractor, General Construction Co., also hires a nonunion subcontractor to perform electrical work on the project. Can the union properly picket the job site over this situation? ______________

a. Would the result be different if the union picketed only at the separate gate for the electrical employees? ______________

75. To be actionable under section 8(b)(4), the union's activity must seek concerted action by employees of the secondary employer. True or false? ______________

76. Union has a labor dispute with Widgets, Inc. May the union peacefully picket the retail store owned by Big Mart, which sells, among other things, the products of Widgets, Inc.? ______________

a. Would the result be different if Widgets, Inc. was the supplier of raw materials from which another manufacturer made the widgets? ______________

77. Employer is subjected to an illegal strike by Union, in violation of no-strike provisions in their collective agreement. Employer notifies Union that he regards the entire contract terminated as a result of Union's breach. May Employer also recover damages resulting from the strike? ______________

a. May Employer's customer sue the union for damages resulting from the strike? _______________

78. Labor unions are generally exempt from the antitrust laws unless they combine with nonlabor groups to restrain trade or commerce. True or false? _______________

79. Union negotiates a collective bargaining agreement with Employer. Subsequently, a group of employees in the bargaining unit alleges that Union prejudiced their employment status in the agreement. Is Union guilty of an unfair labor practice if the employees' status has in fact been prejudiced? _______________

80. Employer discrimination on the basis of race is likely to be held an unfair labor practice under section 8(a)(1). True or false? _______________

81. An employee whose claim is covered by grievance and arbitration procedures under the collective agreement must elect whether to seek arbitration or Title VII remedies for his dispute. True or false? _______________

82. Before an employee can sue her employer to enforce an arbitration clause under the contract, she must attempt to exhaust remedies through union representation of her claim. True or false? _______________

83. Union and Rowland Welding Co. have a lawful compulsory union membership agreement. Travis, an employee of Rowland Welding Co., has failed to become a full union member in good standing. May the union properly request Rowland Welding Co. to discharge Travis? _______________

84. Conduct violating state "right to work" laws is subject to preemption by the NLRA. True or false? _______________

85. Under Landrum-Griffin section 101(a)(4), an employer may properly assist employees in a lawsuit against the union or union officers. True or false? _______________

86. Landrum-Griffin preempts state law rights and remedies concerning improper union discipline. True or false? _______________

87. The Secretary of Labor is authorized to seek an injunction against the holding of a union election where there is substantial evidence of union impropriety in the conduct thereof. True or false? _______________

88. Upon suit to set aside an election, the union must prove that its unlawful conduct did not affect the outcome once the Secretary establishes a "reasonable possibility" of such effect. True or false? _______________

89. The duties of union officers as trustees vis-a-vis the union and its members are set forth in some detail by the Landrum-Griffin Act. True or false? _______________

Answers to Review Questions

1.a.	**FALSE**	The AFL advocated political action (such as lobbying) for economic advancement, but rejected the idea of unions as political parties. [p. 3]
b.	**TRUE**	While the Knights admitted any "working man," including farmers, capitalists, unskilled laborers, etc., the AFL concentrated on *skilled* workers. [pp. 2, 4]
c.	**FALSE**	Although the "objectives" test was somewhat less restrictive on its face than the criminal conspiracy doctrine (which held that the union itself was an unlawful combination), it was applied very narrowly to *enjoin* most union activity. [p. 5]
d.	**TRUE**	Even though the Erdman Act (passed in response to the strike) applied only to interstate train operations and was ultimately held unconstitutional, it marked a significant step forward for organized labor. [p. 6]
e.	**TRUE**	Despite the apparent congressional purpose to this effect, the courts read the statute so narrowly when applied to labor that there was no meaningful exemption from the antitrust laws for such activity. [pp. 8–9]
2.	**FALSE**	Personalities may have helped to aggravate the situation, but the basic problems stemmed from the CIO's rejection of skilled craft unionism and exclusive jurisdiction and its strong organizing drives in mass production industries. [p. 11]
3.	**TRUE**	The problem arose from the fact that both craft (AFL) and industrial (CIO) unions had been approved during the prior two decades and from the difficulty of determining "organizing jurisdictions." [pp. 12–13]
4.	**FALSE**	Norris-LaGuardia merely forbade injunctions *against* concerted activity (except under very limited circumstances). [p. 15]
5.	**TRUE**	In *United States v. Hutcheson,* the Supreme Court held that Congress (by passing Norris-LaGuardia) had demonstrated a policy favoring union activity and refused to apply the Clayton Act where labor was acting in its own interests and using lawful means. [p. 16]
6.	**TRUE**	The NLRA was mainly concerned with protecting union organization and imposed duties only on the employer. [p. 17]

7.	**FALSE**	Taft-Hartley was designed to impose obligations on *unions* (as well as employers), to curb certain union abuses, and to permit government intervention (directly and through the courts) into certain types of labor disputes. [pp. 19–20]
8.	**TRUE**	The LMRDA stemmed from aroused public sentiment following publicity on corruption and lack of democratic procedures in a number of unions. [p. 22]
9.	**TRUE**	The remainder of federal labor law is aimed at creating a setting conducive to the proper functioning of the bargaining system and to employee self-organization. [pp. 22–23]
10.	**YES**	When violence or threats thereof occur in a labor dispute, state courts have jurisdiction to enjoin such activity or award damages—even if the conduct is also an unfair labor practice. [p. 26]
11.	**DEPENDS**	To fall outside the preemption doctrine, the union's president must show that the defamation was "malicious" under the rule of *New York Times Co. v. Sullivan* (*i.e.,* uttered with deliberate or reckless disregard for the truth). [p. 27]
12.	**TRUE**	The National Mediation Board determines which airlines are subject to the RLA. [p. 35]
13.	**FALSE**	Such activities do fall within the NLRA (section 2(6)); but an employer whose activities ***affect*** commerce (within the broad meaning of the Commerce Clause) is also covered (under section 2(7)). [pp. 35–36]
14.	**DEPENDS**	Rocky could be either an independent contractor or an employee; the issue probably turns on whether Balboa Co. has the ***right to direct and control*** the manner in which the accounts are collected. [p. 41]
15.	**TRUE**	Field personnel typically handle much of the work in representation matters, whereas the Board follows more formal procedures in the case of unfair labor practices. [p. 44]
16.	**FALSE**	The court of appeals will set aside the Board's finding ***only*** if the decision is not supported by substantial evidence or if the Board has made errors of law. [p. 44]
17.	**FALSE**	Taft-Hartley section 10(c) requires that such a finding be based upon a ***preponderance*** of the evidence. [p. 44]

18.	**PROBABLY**	An employer is allowed to interrogate employees about union activities ***only*** to ascertain the validity of a union claim to majority representation—and then only in a noncoercive atmosphere. Since Outhouse has not made its purposes clear, the questioning is probably unlawful under section 8(a)(1). [pp. 49–50]
19.	**PROBABLY NOT**	While confining such solicitation to free time may be proper, preventing discussions in a work area (on free time) probably is not. [pp. 52–53]
a.	**YES**	Distribution of literature ***can*** be limited to nonwork areas as well as to nonworking time. [p. 53]
20.	**PROBABLY**	Such prohibitions are proper if the union has alternative means of reaching employees, and the trend of authority is to find that such means are available. [p. 54]
21.	**DEPENDS**	Under the rule in *NLRB v. Gissel Packing Co.,* Employer is permitted to make such a statement ***only if*** it is reasonably based on objective facts outside her own control. [pp. 57–58]
a.	**NO**	The Taft-Hartley Act specifically prohibits such use of statements that are noncoercive (and hence privileged). [p. 59]
b.	**NO**	Employer can communicate with employees on company time and property without giving the union "equal time"—unless the union has no reasonable alternative means of responding (in which case Employer may be required to provide such opportunity). In either case, however, the nature of Employer's statement would not be affected. [p. 59]
c.	**DEPENDS**	Employer must conduct "business as usual." If the wage increase was traditional, then it is proper; but no special benefits can be conferred (even if they are not conditional on no union representation—indeed, failure to ***grant*** a customary wage increase may be as actionable as the conferral of special benefits). [p. 62]
22.	**TRUE**	Among other things, section 8(a) refers to "interference" as a type of activity prohibited to employers, while section 8(b) does not use that term. [p. 63]
23.	**TRUE**	Thus, for example, statements that are ***impliedly*** coercive may also constitute a union unfair labor practice. [p. 64]
24.	**YES**	Just as special benefits by the employer constitute economic coercion, so do union offers to waive initiation fees. [p. 65]
a.	**PROBABLY**	The NLRB has held that reimbursement of wages in this situation does not impair employees' free choice of a bargaining representative. [p. 65]

b.	**PROBABLY**	Destruction of company property is at least an implied threat of physical coercion against employees. And the apparent authority may be inferred from the organizer's position, etc. [pp. 64–65, 66–67]
c.	**POSSIBLY**	The scope of union liability for the acts of its "agents" is more limited under Norris-LaGuardia than under the Taft-Hartley Act. [p. 67]
25.	**DEPENDS**	If the "instructions" are followed by means of express endorsements of the IBCC by the supervisors, this could be attributed to Cartoon Co. and could constitute solicitation. However, merely permitting employees to solicit is probably permissible. [pp. 67–68]
a.	**YES**	Allowing access to one union, while denying it to another, is unlawful support violating section 8(a)(2). [p. 68]
26.	**POSSIBLY**	Even if Carbon Paper Co. presents evidence of a legitimate business reason for the layoff, a discriminatory motive could be ***inferred*** from circumstantial evidence. [p. 71]
a.	**DEPENDS**	If the move can be supported by sound economic considerations, it is permissible despite the adverse impact on union organizing. Otherwise, it may be an unfair labor practice. [pp. 72, 74]
b.	**DEPENDS**	Carbon Paper Co. may terminate its ***entire*** business for any reason whatever. However, if the discontinuance is only partial or if it is bogus (*e.g.,* a temporary shutdown), Carbon Paper Co. violates section 8(a) if the purpose and foreseeable effect is to discourage unionization. [p. 74]
27.	**DEPENDS**	If there is a valid compulsory union contract, the Federation ***can*** seek Paul's discharge. Otherwise, the Federation's efforts would constitute an unfair labor practice under section 8(b)(2). [pp. 76–77]
a.	**NO**	The only permissible basis for seeking a discharge in this situation is refusal to pay reasonable (and nondiscriminatory) union fees or dues. [p. 77]
28.	**TRUE**	The type of relief granted will vary with the nature of the violation involved. [pp. 77, 78]
29.	**FALSE**	***All*** of these powers have been delegated to the Regional Directors (although the latter can always transfer cases to the Board, and the parties can seek Board review). [p. 81]
30.	**FALSE**	While the Board often permits a "Globe" election under these circumstances, it may choose not to do so if there is a ***pattern or history*** indicating the appropriate unit. [p. 82]

31.	**TRUE**	This payroll period is usually determinative (though vacations, temporary layoffs, seasonal work, etc., are taken into consideration). [p. 84]
32.	**TRUE**	An economic striker is presumed eligible to vote unless it is shown that he has "abandoned interest" in the job. But while permanent replacements can vote, temporary workers cannot. [pp. 84–85]
33.	**FALSE**	Only employees or employee organizations are permitted to file decertification petitions. [p. 85]
34.	**PROBABLY**	Assuming the union does not continue to press for recognition by the employer, this tactic is allowed and can be effective for the union. [p. 86]
35.	**FALSE**	In addition to this general standard, the Board's discretion is ***also*** limited in certain areas by section 9(b) (*e.g.*, as to plant guards, professionals, etc.). [pp. 87–88]
36.	**FALSE**	While this requirement would apply where one union is petitioning for an election, it does not apply to an intervening union (which needs a showing of only 5% support) or to an ***employer*** petition for certification. [p. 90]
37.	**PROBABLY NOT**	An unremedied unfair labor practice relating to organizing activities is generally sufficient to prevent an election. [p. 90]
a.	**PROBABLY**	The Board would probably proceed with an election where a charge of union discrimination is filed, provided the charge did not relate to the union's organizing activities. [p. 91]
38.	**DEPENDS**	Ordinarily, the "contract bar rule" would prevent an election after two years. However, the existing contract would ***not*** bar an election if, for example, there were illegal discrimination or closed-shop provisions in the contract, a schism in the bargaining unit, or substantial "changes in circumstances" justifying a new election. [pp. 92–95]
a.	**YES**	Here, Acme's recognition is probably not based on a substantial claim, and the subsequent contract does not serve as a bar for any period. [p. 93]
b.	**YES**	Subject to the usual qualifications (illegal clauses, etc.), the new contract is a bar since (i) Union B did not petition "no more than 90 nor less than 61 days" before the expiration date, and (ii) Union A and Acme signed the new agreement prior to termination of the old contract. [p. 94]

39. **FALSE** There can be no judicial ***review*** of the Board's action in this situation; however, the aggrieved party can still obtain ***equitable relief*** from a federal district court (*e.g.*, enjoining an election) if the NLRB action was contrary to the NLRA and may cause irreparable injury or deprivation of a right. [pp. 95–96]

40. **NO** The employer must recognize the union for a reasonable period, which means at least one year from the date of certification. [pp. 98–99]

a. **DEPENDS** Where the employer refuses to bargain in good faith, the one-year period is extended to one year of ***actual bargaining.*** (Moreover, the ***preferred*** course for the employer in this situation is not to refuse to bargain but to petition for an election.) [p. 99]

41. **FALSE** Individual contracts are still permissible as to matters not covered by, and/or not inconsistent with, the collective agreement. However, such contracts ***are*** superseded in all other cases. [pp. 99–100]

42. **TRUE** At least where the employees are being fairly represented by the union, concerted activities by individuals without union approval are not protected by section 7. (Of course, the employee can challenge the discipline imposed in a Title VII proceeding, if appropriate.) [pp. 100–101]

43. **NOT NECESSARILY** "Good faith" does not require a party to make any concessions. However, a complete "take it or leave it" attitude on ***all*** bargaining issues probably would be an unfair labor practice. Acme's ***total course of conduct*** must be examined to determine whether he has bargained in good faith. [pp. 101–103]

a. **PROBABLY** Demands that a party drop pending charges, as a precondition to negotiation, generally evidence a failure to bargain in good faith. [p. 103]

b. **PROBABLY** Refusal to bargain meaningfully about ***existing*** discrimination evidences bad faith—even where the party agrees to discuss a nondiscrimination clause. [p. 103]

44. **NOT NECESSARILY** Whether the successor is bound depends on whether there is substantial continuity in the work force and/or a contractual or statutory obligation to arbitrate. [pp. 106–111]

45. **TRUE** All of these duties are imposed on a successor employer regardless of enforceability of the existing contract. [p. 108]

46. **NO** The employer need not recognize or bargain with a union on the basis of nonelection evidence of majority support. [pp. 112–115]

a. **PROBABLY** Such interrogation may well be an unfair labor practice impairing the electoral process, and if so, the company ***would*** be required to bargain with the union—provided the cards "clearly state their purpose on the face" and another fair election probably cannot be obtained. [p. 112]

47. **FALSE** Compensatory relief is appropriate only where the refusal to bargain is "clear and flagrant." And under ***no*** circumstances can the Board order the employer to accept a ***specific provision*** on which the parties could not independently agree. [pp. 115–116]

48. **FALSE** The manner in which benefits are paid to ***retired*** employees is not a compulsory subject, because it does not vitally affect active employees. [p. 118]

49. **YES** Safety and health conditions are mandatory bargaining subjects. [pp. 119–120]

a. **PROBABLY** Employer cannot be compelled to bargain over the issue, since the subject is already covered in the existing contract. However, Union can use the OSHA procedures to remedy any violation of industry safety standards. [p. 120]

50. **FALSE** Certain fundamental subjects ***must*** be included in the contract, and the employer is not permitted to bargain over them. [p. 121]

51. **FALSE** The Board formerly gave a wide scope to the duty (finding it wherever employee security would be impaired by the decision), while the courts imposed a much narrower standard. Since 1971, however, the NLRB has acquiesced in the narrower judicial standard, and the Supreme Court has formulated a "balancing test" for such cases. [pp. 122–124]

52. **FALSE** No waiver of bargaining rights will be implied by mere silence in the contract. [pp. 124–125]

53. **PROBABLY** The "lockout" is permissible, but only if Spats International has bargained in good faith and is not intending to injure the union thereby. [p. 125]

a. **PROBABLY** Unless the strike breaches an existing contract between the company and the union, or is otherwise illegal or in bad faith, the duty of the company to bargain continues. [p. 126]

54. **TRUE** Mediation attempts to persuade the parties to reach an ***independent*** agreement; no decisions are made by the mediator. [p. 129]

55.	**TRUE**	The Supreme Court has given this extremely broad interpretation to arbitration clauses. (The only exception might be in cases affecting public safety.) [p. 130]
56.	**DEPENDS**	If there is a mandatory arbitration provision in the contract between Clinton Co. and the union, the court would ***not*** hear the claim but would defer to the arbitration process. [p. 135]
a.	**NO**	In this situation, the employee is relieved of any duty to exhaust remedies under the contract and may proceed directly under section 301. [p. 135]
b.	**YES**	An employee's Title VII and contract rights are independent, so that an employee unsuccessful in arbitration may obtain a trial de novo under Title VII. [p. 136]
57.	**TRUE**	The preemption doctrine does not apply where the parties have covered the subject in a collective agreement (and hence made a section 301 lawsuit possible). [p. 139]
58.	**DEPENDS**	If the grievance ***on its face*** falls within the scope of the arbitration clause, Widgets, Inc. will be ordered to arbitrate, and doubts are resolved in favor of arbitration. [pp. 139–140]
a.	**PROBABLY**	In theory, judicial review of arbitration awards is limited to whether the award was within the arbitrator's authority, and if so, it is to be enforced without regard to its support in the evidence. However, the court may nevertheless scrutinize the arbitrator's award to see if there is ***some*** justification for it. [pp. 140–142]
59.	**FALSE**	Substantive arbitrability is a question of law for the courts, unless the agreement otherwise provides. [pp. 140–143]
60.	**NO**	If Employer has signed an agreement to arbitrate, Union ***cannot*** strike (or schedule work stoppages or slowdowns) rather than submit the matter to arbitration—whether or not an express no-strike clause has been incorporated in the agreement. Should Union proceed with the stoppage, Employer may be entitled to injunctive relief. [pp. 144–146]
a.	**PROBABLY**	However, Employer must do so clearly and must abrogate the entire agreement; in so doing he forfeits any claim for damages against Union as a result of the stoppage. [p. 147]
61.	**TRUE**	The Court has discussed criteria that would show that a strike was ***not*** protected, but has not discussed the parameters for constitutionally protected strikes. [p. 151]
62.	**FALSE**	Protection for picketing is more limited: It must be done in a peaceful manner for a lawful objective; and it can still be prohibited if the entire setting is not peaceful. [pp. 151 *et seq.*]

63.	**PROBABLY**	The statutory right to strike (under NLRA sections 7 and 13) can be ***waived*** by a no-strike clause, but leaving the job in good faith because of abnormally dangerous working conditions is ***not*** considered a strike. [p. 155]
64.	**TRUE**	And, where primary activity is designed to accomplish an illegal secondary objective, it is likewise unlawful. [pp. 155–156]
65.	**DEPENDS**	If the Union has not given Fjord 60 days' notice and offered to negotiate on the proposed changes, the strike is illegal. [p. 157]
a.	**YES**	The 60-day cooling-off period does not apply to unfair labor practice strikes. [p. 157]
b.	**PROBABLY NOT**	The definition of "featherbedding" in section 8(b)(6) is narrow, and the courts have generally held that no featherbedding (and hence no illegal strike) is involved where ***some*** actual services are performed. [p. 158]
66.	**FALSE**	Strikes in this situation are illegal whether directed against secondary ***or*** primary employers. [p. 160]
a.	**NO**	The objective is still one prohibited under section 8(b)(4)(C), since another representative has already been certified. [p. 161]
b.	**NO**	Such a strike is an unfair labor practice under section 8(b)(4)(D)—although generally disposed of in a special preliminary hearing by the NLRB. [p. 162]
67.	**NOT NECESSARILY**	If there are no openings available, the company need not "make room" for the strikers. [pp. 164–166]
a.	**YES**	The company's failure to consider the applications when openings do arise is discriminatory and presumptively an unfair labor practice. [p. 165]
b.	**YES**	Since an unfair labor practice (rather than an economic) strike is involved, the company ***must*** reinstate the strikers (even if replacements must be discharged in order to do so). [p. 166]
c.	**NO**	Partial strikes are ***illegal***, and thus afford no protection to the employees involved. [p. 168]
68.	**PROBABLY NOT**	There must be some ***confrontation*** between the pickets and other persons that does not exist if the union merely erects a sign. [p. 169]
69.	**TRUE**	Such picketing is an exception to the general ban on recognition picketing by an uncertified union in section 8(b)(7)(C). [p. 173]

70.	**FALSE**	If the Board has reasonable cause to believe the employer's section 8(b)(7) charge is true, it ***must*** seek an injunction unless a union 8(a)(2) charge (with similar "reasonable basis") is also pending (in which case no injunction is sought). [p. 174]
71.	**DEPENDS**	If Union has no dispute with Fjord Motors, the picketing is unlawful secondary activity. If there is a primary dispute, however, the picketing is lawful even though secondary pressures on Good Day Tires are also intended. [p. 175]
72.	**FALSE**	Such an interpretation would prohibit almost all strike activity. Instead, the courts have read the statute as protecting innocent secondary employers from activity in their own plants. [pp. 176–177]
73.	**FALSE**	Ownership of the job site is ***not*** determinative. However, the picketing must still meet several criteria under the *Moore Drydock* rules (relocation, employer's business at site, etc.). [pp. 177–178]
74.	**NO**	The purpose of the union's picketing is to force secondary employer General Construction Co. to cease dealing with a subcontractor, and hence is illegal. [p. 179]
a.	**NO**	The picketing is still for a prohibited purpose and hence is illegal. [pp. 179–180]
75.	**FALSE**	Under the Landrum-Griffin Amendments, inducing a ***single*** employee ("individual") to refuse to work for his secondary neutral employer is sufficient. [pp. 181–182]
76.	**DEPENDS**	If the union's picketing is designed to produce only a ***partial*** consumer boycott (*i.e.,* of Widgets, Inc.'s products), it is probably permissible. If the union seeks a boycott of ***all*** Big Mart's goods, however, the picketing would be illegal. [pp. 184–185]
a.	**PROBABLY NOT**	"Informational" publicity can be directed toward anyone who enhances the economic value of the product (*i.e.,* anyone in the marketing chain). However, this could present difficult problems in cases like that posed; the situation has not been squarely resolved by the courts. [pp. 182–183]
77.	**NO**	An employer who elects to terminate the contract for breach of a no-strike clause cannot also recover damages resulting from the strike. [p. 188]
a.	**YES**	Section 303 suits for damages can be maintained by any person suffering a direct economic loss as a result of the illegal union activity (provided his relationship with the activity is not too remote). [p. 188]

78.	**TRUE**	However, the Supreme Court may now be scrutinizing union activity in this area more closely. [p. 188]
79.	**NOT NECESSARILY**	A union does not breach its duty of fair representation for all employees simply because a particular employee (or group) is prejudiced by the agreement. However, any invidious or arbitrary discrimination—based on union membership, race, etc.—would violate section 8(b)(1)(A). [pp. 199–200]
80.	**FALSE**	The NLRB has rejected this view (which has been advanced by only one court opinion to date). [p. 202]
81.	**FALSE**	Title VII remedies are ***independent*** of remedies under the contract; the aggrieved employee may pursue both. [p. 203]
82.	**TRUE**	However, if the union arbitrarily refuses to press the grievance through the channels provided, the employee may sue as a third-party beneficiary to enforce the contract against the employer. [pp. 206–207] And, the ***union*** could ***also*** be sued for breach of its duty of fair representation in a private damages action under section 301. [p. 207]
83.	**NO**	Travis could be discharged ***only*** if he failed to tender dues and initiation fees. [pp. 209, 212]
84.	**TRUE**	If certain conduct violates ***both*** the state law and the NLRA, the NLRB has ***exclusive*** jurisdiction of the matter. [p. 213]
85.	**FALSE**	The employer is ***prohibited*** from encouraging actions against the union under section 101(a)(4). [pp. 220–221]
86.	**FALSE**	Landrum-Griffin expressly ***reserves*** all state rights and remedies for employees, unless specifically provided otherwise. [p. 224]
87.	**FALSE**	While the Secretary has exclusive authority to enforce the election provisions of Landrum-Griffin (Title IV), this does not arise until ***after*** the election. There is no pre-election remedy. [p. 226]
88.	**TRUE**	Demonstrating a "reasonable possibility" that the unlawful conduct affected the election results is sufficient to state a prima facie case, thereby shifting the burden of proof to the defendant union. [p. 229]
89.	**FALSE**	While the general fiduciary obligation of a trustee is imposed by the LMRDA, specific duties thereunder have been left for judicial formulation. [p. 231]

Exam Questions and Answers

Question I

For 10 years prior to unionization, Widget Company paid its employees a $30 "turkey money" bonus at Thanksgiving. After a successful organizing campaign, Widget signed its first contract with the union, effective March 1st.

At the negotiations that preceded the signing of the contract, no specific mention was made of the "turkey money" bonus, nor does the contract refer to this benefit. The agreement contains standard grievance and arbitration provisions, although there is no pledge by the employees not to strike. There is also a "zipper" or wrap-up clause in the contract, which reads:

> It is acknowledged that during the negotiations that resulted in this agreement, the Union had the unlimited right and opportunity to make demands and proposals with respect to all proper subjects of collective bargaining. Therefore, for the life of this agreement, the Union agrees that the Company shall not be obligated to bargain collectively with respect to any subject or matter not specifically referred to or covered in this agreement.

The following Thanksgiving, Widget refuses to pay its employees a bonus and advises the union that, since it is not provided for in the contract, such "turkey money" will no longer be paid.

1. In response to Widget's actions, the union files unfair labor practice charges against the company. How is the NLRB likely to dispose of the charges?

2. Suppose that instead of the union filing unfair labor practice charges against Widget, the employees walk off the job in protest over the bonus issue. Can Widget force the employees to return to work? Alternatively, could Widget discharge the employees and hire permanent replacements for them?

3. Assume that instead of filing unfair labor practice charges (or an employee walkout), the union files a grievance on the bonus issue under the contract procedures. Widget agrees to arbitration, and the union claim is denied by the arbitrator. The arbitrator rules that, as a matter of contract interpretation, there is no basis for requiring Widget to pay the bonus. The arbitrator notes the "zipper" clause and points out that there is no reference to the bonus in the agreement, even though other employee benefits (such as health insurance) are clearly spelled out. After learning of the award, the union president asks you whether the union now can file unfair labor practice charges against Widget for refusing to pay the bonus. What advice should you give the union?

Question II

Archer Industries, Inc., owned by the Archer family, operated a sporting goods store in Denver, Colorado. None of its employees were union members until three years ago, when a successful organizing campaign unionized the 16 nonsupervisory employees and a collective bargaining contract was signed. In the owner's viewpoint, things went downhill from that point forward: The previous friendly, "home-like" atmosphere disappeared from the operation; labor costs rose substantially; and such increases, on top of other rising costs, eventually made the business unprofitable. After looking for a buyer, the Archers recently sold the store to Dart Bros., a leading Denver sporting goods firm. Dart Bros, is not unionized, and an express condition of the sales contract was that Dart would not assume the existing collective bargaining agreement at the store. After the sale, the Archer family retired from business.

Dart Bros, management then met with the 16 store employees, indicating that the store would become one of many Dart outlets in the Denver area. The employees were told that they all were welcome to stay on at the store, but that they would have to accept the same terms and conditions as other employees in the Dart system. In addition to some minor changes from the Archer operation, this would involve a 50-cents-per-hour reduction in pay, required periodic overtime work (at time and one-half), and a change to the Dart group health insurance plan (with slightly better coverage than the Archer plan).

Eight of the 16 employees elected to stay on the job at the store. The other eight, believing that their rights had been violated, filed unfair labor practice charges under sections 8(a)(1), 8(a)(3), and 8(a)(5) against both Archer and Dart. After an investigation, the NLRB issues a complaint on all three charges.

Assume you are the administrative law judge assigned to hear the case. What recommendations would you make on the charges?

Question III

The Wagon Workers' Union begins a campaign at Buggy International, seeking to organize its 40 nonsupervisory employees. On a regular payday during the organizing campaign, the employees go to a small assembly room in Buggy's plant to receive their paychecks. From each paycheck, a deduction of $50 has been taken. Buggy's superintendent then reads to the employees from a prepared text, stating that the $50 represents the amount of union dues that each employee would have owed for the five months during which the organizing campaign has been in progress, that the purpose of the deduction is to illustrate that the union is after their money, and that the employees should protect themselves by voting "no" in the upcoming election. The employees are then told that they can pick up the deducted $50 in cash the following day at the cashier's office. Some of the employees are quite upset at this "game," but all of them follow the suggested procedure and receive their $50 payments.

Prior to the paycheck episode, the campaign was relatively civil, but afterwards matters heat up. Several employees begin wearing bright orange buttons, four inches in diameter, which read, "Let's grab Buggy's money—vote 'YES'!" The employees are told to remove the buttons, and when they refuse, they are suspended from work for one week. In the subsequent election conducted by the NLRB, the union loses by a vote of 19 to 16.

The union consults you after the election about what relief it could obtain from the NLRB as to both the election and the suspension of employees. What advice would you give the union?

Answers to Question I

1. Unfair Labor Practice Charge

NLRA section 8(d) requires the employer and the union to bargain collectively over any compulsory subject for bargaining. Unilateral action by Widget on such a subject thus would be an unfair labor practice, unless the union waived the right to bargain over it. [pp. 117, 124] In the present situation, then, there are three basic issues: (i) As a jurisdictional matter, would the NLRB hear the charges, or would it defer to arbitration of the complaint? (ii) Assuming jurisdiction were accepted, is the "turkey money" bonus a compulsory subject for bargaining? (iii) If the subject is compulsory, did the union waive its right to bargain over the matter?

NLRB's jurisdiction: Since the charges have not been submitted to arbitration (or an award entered), the Board's initial decision to accept jurisdiction or defer to arbitration would be based on the *Collyer* standard. Under *Collyer,* deferral is appropriate if (i) the contract calls for final and binding arbitration, and (ii) the dispute is contractual in nature. The first requirement clearly is met in the present case. It can be argued that the second requirement is met only if the "zipper" clause in the agreement is construed as waiving the union's right to bargain over the bonus, and, as discussed below, such a waiver probably would not be found. However, the case does involve the collective rights of employees, and may be deemed sufficiently contractual in nature that the NLRB ***would*** defer to arbitration (especially in light of the Board's strong policy of deferral in refusal-to-bargain cases). [pp. 133–134]

Compulsory subject: Assuming the NLRB ***accepts jurisdiction*** (and this decision is discretionary), whether the bonus is a compulsory subject for bargaining depends on whether it falls within "wages, hours or other terms and conditions of employment" under section 8(d). One might argue that the "turkey money" was merely seasonal gift-giving—too trivial to be covered by the NLRA. However, the Supreme Court has held that a change in in-plant food service prices can be a compulsory bargaining subject where supported by industry practice. In this case, two factors would support a finding that the bonus issue was a mandatory subject. First, there is a long-standing (10-year) pattern, and the value of the bonus to an individual employee probably is not trivial. Second, the fact that the benefit was a fixed sum in cash over a long period tends to establish it as a part of "wages" (rather than the vaguer "conditions of employment" area). Together, these factors probably establish that the "turkey money" is a matter over which bargaining is required. [pp. 117–120]

Union waiver: The final issue is whether the union has waived collective bargaining over "turkey money" in this case. The bonus is not specifically mentioned in the contract, and the "zipper" clause on its face appears to eliminate any obligation of Widget to bargain about it. Even so, the NLRB tends not to give full effect to such blanket waivers, but looks to see if bargaining over a particular area was clearly and expressly waived. In this case, the Board might well view the "zipper" clause as waiving the right to bargain over completely ***new*** subjects, but not necessarily subjects (like the bonus) that were not new and not expressly covered or waived in the contract. Hence, there is a good chance the NLRB might find that Widget violated section 8(a)(5) and (a)(1) by unilaterally discontinuing the Thanksgiving bonus. [pp. 124–125]

2. Employee Walkout

Injunction: If Widget agrees to arbitrate its right to discontinue the "turkey money" bonus under the contract procedures, it could then seek an injunction under *Boys Markets* to force the employees back to work. While there is no express no-strike pledge in the agreement, such an obligation would be ***implied*** from the grievance and arbitration procedures (under *Lucas Flour*) unless the facts show that Widget tried and failed to get such a clause into the contract. The present dispute is arbitrable; if Widget can show a likelihood of irreparable harm greater than any harm to the union from being enjoined, an injunction likely would be granted. [pp. 144–146]

Permanent replacements: Whether Widget could instead discharge the employees and hire permanent replacements depends on whether the walkout is deemed to be an unfair labor practice strike or an economic strike. The prior discussion in answer to part 1 of this question (above) would apply here. ***If*** Widget committed ***serious*** unfair labor practices in unilaterally discontinuing the bonus, it cannot permanently replace its employees. But if no serious unfair labor practice is found (and this may well be the case, given the nature of the dispute), the employees are economic strikers who ***can*** be permanently replaced. Note, however, that the employees must still be retained on Widget hiring lists and given nondiscriminatory consideration for future job openings (unless they have engaged in violence or other flagrant misconduct). [pp. 164–167]

3. **Post-Award Unfair Labor Practice Charge**

The ability of the union to have the NLRB hear unfair labor practice charges at this stage depends upon the *Spielberg* and *United Parcel Services* post-award deferral doctrine. Since the grievance procedure in the contract is a standard one, the proceedings presumably were fair and regular on their face; the parties clearly acquiesced in the procedure; and the arbitrator heard and determined the factual issues underlying the unfair labor practice charges. As the fourth and final criterion in *Spielberg,* the NLRB has held that an arbitration award is not "repugnant to the purposes and policies of the Taft-Hartley Act" unless it is "palpably wrong." This is not likely to be the case here, since—as discussed in answer to part 1 (above)—the unfair labor practice charge is a close one at best. (The issue is also within the arbitrator's competence to decide and the reasons for the decision are set forth, to the extent that these additional factors are considered germane.) Under the circumstances, therefore, the NLRB most probably would decline to hear the union's complaint. The best advice to the union would be to abide by the award and seek to bargain about the bonus during the next contract negotiation.

Answers to Question II

The two basic issues in this case are: (i) Did Archer discriminate on the basis of union membership, and thereby violate section 8(a)(3), in selling its business to Dart? (ii) Did Dart breach a duty to bargain with the Archer employees, thereby violating sections 8(a)(5) and 8(a)(1)?

Section 8(a)(3) charge: The Archers clearly attributed the adverse changes in their company's profitability and general character to unionization, and one might therefore argue that in selling the business on the buyer's express disclaimer of the bargaining contract, Archer had "discriminated" against its employees on the basis of union membership. However, such an argument overlooks the fact that an employer may terminate its entire business for ***any*** reason, including antiunion sentiments, without violating the NLRA. Since the Archers retired after the sale, the transfer to Dart certainly can be viewed as a termination of their business even though the store continued to operate under new ownership. Moreover, since the store had ceased to be profitable to Archer, the owners had sound ***economic*** reasons for the sale, and the movement of business operations under such circumstances is permitted even if it has the effect of thwarting unionization. To the extent that Archer had a "mixed motive" in selling the business, the unprofitability of their operation underscores the economic factor as the motivating force behind the sale. And although it is not specified in the facts, the disclaimer in the contract presumably was a condition imposed by the buyer rather than by Archer. Consequently, there is no real basis for finding a violation on the part of Archer. [pp. 72, 74]

Section 8(a)(5) and 8(a)(1) charges: Whether Dart Bros. had a duty to bargain with the Archer employees, despite the disclaimer in its purchase contract, turns on the successorship doctrine, and more specifically, on the application of the *Howard Johnson* decision to this case. *Howard Johnson* requires the carryover of a majority of employees from seller to buyer as a precondition to any duty to bargain with the union representing the seller's employees. Here, only eight of the 16 employees currently work for Dart. However, ***all*** were invited to remain, and those who left did so because of the alleged unfair labor practices of Dart and/or Archer in changing the terms and conditions of their employment. Thus, one can find the necessary "continuity in work force" to require that Dart recognize and bargain with the union, despite the disclaimer, and its failure to do so would be an unfair labor practice. It should be noted, however, that Dart is not required to honor the entire ***contract*** previously negotiated between the union and Archer (although it may have a duty to arbitrate grievances under that contract). [pp. 106 *et seq.*]

Answers to Question III

In assessing possible relief for the union in this case, there are two main inquiries: (i) Did Buggy commit any unfair labor practices by its paycheck "deduction" and/or by suspending the employees? (ii) Even if there were no unfair labor practices, could the union still obtain a new election?

Paycheck "deduction" and employee suspensions: There is nothing wrong per se with Buggy raising the size of union-dues payments by employees as an issue in the organizing campaign, since employers also have a right of free speech and may state their opposition to unionization. [pp. 47–49] The question is whether the ***method*** of conveying that message was proper—specifically, whether the deduction procedure and accompanying statements interfered with the employees' section 7 rights, thereby violating section 8(a)(1), or discriminated against them because of their union activities, thus violating section 8(a)(3). Since all of the employees were treated alike in the deduction process, no 8(a)(3) violation is apparent. [pp. 70–73] However, the employees were deprived of $50 in pay for one day, solely because of the union campaign; and this seems sufficient to constitute an interference with their section 7 right to choose whether or not to join the union. Accordingly, the union should be able to establish an unfair labor practice against Buggy under 8(a)(1) for this tactic.

With respect to the suspension issue, the wearing of union buttons by the employees was clearly concerted activity under section 7. Whether it was ***protected*** activity, however, depends on its ***propriety*** under the circumstances, and additional facts would be needed to make this determination. For example, if the employees' jobs put them in contact with the public or Buggy's customers, the NLRB might well hold such blunt, conspicuous campaigning unprotected (thereby justifying the suspensions). The same result might be reached if the buttons were disruptive to Buggy's operations (which would also supply a legitimate business reason for the suspensions and negate any section 8(a)(3) discrimination claim on this issue). [pp. 192 *et seq.*]

New election: Whatever the outcome on unfair labor practice charges by the union, it can probably get the election set aside on the grounds that Buggy's actions upset the laboratory conditions necessary for such an election. The Board's rules in this area have changed frequently, but given the closeness of the vote in this case, a new election would probably be ordered. [pp. 56–61]

It is not likely, however, that the union could obtain an order under *Gissel Packing* that the company bargain with the union ***without*** a new election, since the facts here do not indicate an unfair labor practice so serious as to negate the possibility of a new, fair election.

Table of Cases

Index